Online Searching

Online Searching

A GUIDE TO FINDING QUALITY INFORMATION EFFICIENTLY AND EFFECTIVELY

Karen Markey

ROWMAN & LITTLEFIELD
Lanham • Boulder • New York • London

Executive Editor: Charles Harmon
Associate Editor: Robert Hayunga
Production Editor: Kellie Hagan
Interior Designer: Susan Ramundo
Cover Designer: Matthew Pirro
Cover Art: Jay Jackson

Credits and acknowledgments of sources for material or information used with permission appear on the appropriate page within the text or in the list of illustrations.

Published by Rowman & Littlefield
A wholly owned subsidiary of The Rowman & Littlefield Publishing Group, Inc.
4501 Forbes Boulevard, Suite 200, Lanham, Maryland 20706
www.rowman.com

Unit A, Whitacre Mews, 26-34 Stannary Street, London SE11 4AB

British Library Cataloguing in Publication Information Available

Library of Congress Cataloging-in-Publication Data
Markey, Karen, author.
   Online searching : a guide to finding quality information efficiently and effectively / Karen Markey.
      pages cm
   Includes bibliographical references and index.
   ISBN 978-1-4422-3884-8 (hardcover : alk. paper) — ISBN 978-1-4422-3885-5 (pbk. : alk. paper) —
ISBN 978-1-4422-3886-2 (ebook)
   1. Electronic information resource searching.   2. Information retrieval.   I. Title.
   ZA4060.M37 2015
   025.0425—dc23   2015015013

∞™ The paper used in this publication meets the minimum requirements of American National Standard for Information Sciences—Permanence of Paper for Printed Library Materials, ANSI/NISO Z39.48-1992.

Printed in the United States of America

For my brother, Kevin
Mother was right about people coming and going in life,
but you remain ever firm, forthright, and faithful

Contents

List of Illustrations, Tables, Textboxes, and Videos   xi

Preface   xix

Acknowledgments   xxiii

1 Online Searching in the Age of the Information Explosion   1

Searching for Information Before Computers, the Internet, and the World Wide Web   1

The Era of the Internet and the World Wide Web Begins   3

The Erosion of Editorial Oversight in the Era of the World Wide Web   5

High-Quality Information Is Your Library's Specialty   10

Summary   10

Bibliography   11

Suggested Readings   13

2 Accessing Scholarly, Professional, and Educational Information   15

Big-Time Information Industry Players Supplying Search Systems and Databases   15

The Library's Database Hub   16

Accessing the Library's Web-Scale Discovery System   20

Questions   23

Summary   24

Bibliography   24

Suggested Readings   24

Answers   24

3 The Reference Interview for In-Depth Queries   27

Models of the Information Seeking Process   27

The Nature of the Reference Interview   32

Phases of the Reference Interview   33

Knowing When to Stop Searching for Information   43

Some Important Definitions   44

Questions   44

Summary   45

Bibliography   45

Suggested Readings   46

Answers   46

4 Selecting a Relevant Database   **49**
  A Classification of Databases   49
  Surrogate and Source Databases   51
  Genres Contained in Surrogate and Source Databases   51
  Research Databases   57
  Reference Databases   64
  Questions   72
  Summary   72
  Bibliography   73
  Suggested Readings   74
  Answers   74

5 Pre-Search Preparation   **75**
  Conducting the Facet Analysis   75
  Conducting the Logical Combination of Facets   77
  Expressing Relationship Facets   78
  More Facet Analysis and Logical Combination   78
  Typecasting Negotiated Queries   82
  Questions   83
  Summary   83
  Answers   84

6 Controlled Vocabulary for Precision in Subject Searches   **85**
  Overriding Search System Defaults   85
  Database Fields Governed by Controlled Vocabularies   86
  The Structure of Controlled Vocabularies   88
  Conducting Controlled Vocabulary Searches for Focused Queries   89
  The Building Block Search Strategy's Buffet Edition   98
  Conducting Controlled Vocabulary Searches for Unfocused Queries   100
  Benefits of Controlled Vocabulary Searching   103
  Controlled Vocabulary Searching Caveats   104
  Comparing Controlled Vocabulary Functionality Across Search Systems
    and Databases   104
  Questions   107
  Summary   108
  Bibliography   108
  Suggested Readings   109
  Answers   109

7 Free Text Searching for Recall in Subject Searches   **113**
  Overriding Search System Defaults Revisited   113
  Free Text Searching Tools   114
  Conducting Free Text Searches of Surrogate Records   118
  Conducting Free Text Searches of Full-Texts   120

Searching Extended-Boolean Search Systems   125
The Building Block Search Strategy's À la Carte Edition   127
Relevance Feedback for Furthering Searches   128
Benefits of Free Text Searching and Extended-Boolean Searching   133
Comparing Free Text Functionality Across Search Systems and Databases   133
Questions   133
Summary   136
Bibliography   137
Suggested Readings   137
Answers   137

8 Known-Item Searching   **141**
Title Searches   141
Author Searches   145
Citation Verification and Full-Text Fulfillment Searches   151
Database Detective Work   153
The Journal Run   158
Questions   163
Summary   164
Bibliography   165
Answers   165

9 Databases for Assessing Research Impact   **167**
Bibliometrics   167
Journal-Level Metrics   174
Using Article-Level Metrics to Compare Two Authors' Publication Records   176
Altmetrics   177
Social Media Websites for Academic Researchers   178
Questions   178
Summary   179
Bibliography   180
Suggested Readings   180
Answers   181

10 Search Strategies   **183**
Building Block Search Strategy   183
Can't Live Without This Facet First Search Strategy   184
Citation Pearl Growing Search Strategy   187
Shot in the Dark Search Strategy   190
Getting a Little Help from Your Friends Search Strategy   193
Choosing a Search Strategy   196
Questions   198
Summary   198
Bibliography   198
Answers   199

**11 Displaying and Assessing Retrievals and Responding Tactically
to the Search System**   **201**
   Displaying Retrievals   202
   Assessing Retrievals   204
   Search Tactics   206
   Questions   211
   Summary   212
   Bibliography   212
   Suggested Readings   213
   Answers   214

12 Performing a Technical Reading of a Database and Its Search System **217**
   The Ten Questions   217
   Responding to the Ubiquitous Nature of Search   228
   Database Poster Project   229
   Summary   230
   Bibliography   230

13 Interacting with Library Users   **231**
   Retrievals for the Long Haul   231
   Teaching Users during the Reference Interview   238
   Sustained Teaching Events   238
   Teaching Tips   248
   Questions   249
   Summary   250
   Bibliography   251
   Suggested Reading   252
   Answers   252

14 Online Searching Now and in the Future   **255**
   Current Trends and Issues   255
   Future Functionality Wish List   262
   Handing You the Baton   265
   Bibliography   265

Glossary   267
Index   283
About the Author   297

Illustrations, Tables, Textboxes, and Videos

Figures

Figure 1.1.   Scholarly Publishing Cycle.   8

Figure 2.1.   U-M Library's Homepage with "Search Tools" and "Find More Databases"
Links. Screenshots made available under the Creative Commons
Attribution license by the University of Michigan Library.   17

Figure 2.2.   U-M Library's Database Hub Called Search Tools. Screenshots made
available under the Creative Commons Attribution license by the
University of Michigan Library.   17

Figure 2.3.   U-M Library's Full Search Tools Interface. Screenshots made available
under the Creative Commons Attribution license by the University of
Michigan Library.   18

Figure 2.4.   Article Index Databases in the Social Sciences in the U-M Library's Search
Tools Database Hub. Screenshots made available under the Creative
Commons Attribution license by the University of Michigan Library.   19

Figure 2.5.   Entering a Query into the U-M Library's ArticlesPlus WSD System.
Screenshots made available under the Creative Commons Attribution
license by the University of Michigan Library.   22

Figure 2.6.   Search Results in the ArticlesPlus WSD System. Screenshots made
available under the Creative Commons Attribution license by the
University of Michigan Library.   23

Figure 3.1.   Classic Model of Communication. Adapted from Shannon and Weaver
(1949).   28

Figure 3.2.   Berrypicking Model. Adapted from Bates (1989, 410). Created using
symbols from the Noun Project (http://thenounproject.com): "Book"
symbol by Simple Icons; "Music Note" symbol by Parker Foote; "Internet"
symbol by Jaclyne Ooi; "Clapperboard" symbol by Adrien Griveau;
"Document" symbol by Claudiu Sergiu Danaila; "Audio" symbol by
iconsmind.com; "Newspaper" symbol by Quan Do.   31

Figure 3.3.   The Feelings People Experience When Searching for Information.
Adapted from Kuhlthau (2003).   32

Figure 3.4.   Phases of the Reference Interview.   33

Figure 4.1.   A Classification of Databases.   50

Figure 4.2.   Surrogate Record and Downloaded Full-Text from the America: History
and Life Database on EBSCOhost. Thanks to EBSCO Information Services
for granting permission for this and the many screenshots of EBSCO
databases that follow.   52

Figure 4.3.   Surrogate from the AP Image Database. Courtesy of the Associated Press.   53

Figure 4.4.   Clicking on a Retrieved Title in the Filmmakers Library Online Database
Displays Surrogate and Transcript and Streams the Film to Your PC.
Courtesy of Alexander Street Press, LLC.   53

Figure 4.5.   Finding Statistics on Commuting to Work on Foot or on Bicycle in ProQuest's
Statistical Insight Database. The screenshots and their contents are
published with permission of ProQuest LLC. Further reproduction is
prohibited without permission. Inquiries may be made to: ProQuest LLC,
789 E. Eisenhower Pkwy, Ann Arbor, MI 48106-1346 USA. Telephone (734)
761–4700; Email: info@proquest.com; Web page: http://www.proquest.com.   54

Figure 4.6.   Mapping the Percent of Possible Sunshine in the SimplyMap Database.
© 2013–2015 Geographic Research, Inc.   55

Figure 4.7.   Oxford Islamic Studies Online Database's Timeline Page with Advanced
Searching Options Revealed. Courtesy of Oxford University Press.   56

Figure 4.8.   Index Record from the Avery Index of Architectural Periodicals on ProQuest.
The screenshots and their contents are published with permission of
ProQuest LLC. Further reproduction is prohibited without permission.
Inquiries may be made to: ProQuest LLC, 789 E. Eisenhower Pkwy, Ann Arbor,
MI 48106-1346 USA. Telephone (734) 761–4700; Email: info@proquest.com;
Web page: http://www.proquest.com.   60

Figure 4.9.   Citations to Book Reviews in the Book Review Index Database from Gale
Cengage Learning. Courtesy of Gale Cengage Learning.   61

Figure 4.10.   A&I Record from the NTIS Database on ProQuest. The screenshots and their
contents are published with permission of ProQuest LLC. Further reproduction
is prohibited without permission. Inquiries may be made to: ProQuest LLC,
789 E. Eisenhower Pkwy, Ann Arbor, MI 48106-1346 USA. Telephone (734)
761–4700; Email: info@proquest.com; Web page: http://www.proquest.com.   62

Figure 4.11.   Marquis Who's Who Entry for Robert A. F. Thurman. Courtesy of Marquis
Who's Who LLC and Robert A. F. Thurman.   66

Figure 4.12.   Porgy's Entry in the Dictionary of Opera Characters Database in Oxford
Reference. Courtesy of Oxford University Press.   67

Figure 4.13.   Entry in the Associations Unlimited Database from Gale Cengage Learning.
Courtesy of Gale Cengage Learning.   69

Figure 4.14.   Online Entry for the Kirtland's Warbler from the Birds of North America
Online, http://bna.birds.cornell.edu/bna, maintained by the Cornell Lab
of Ornithology.   70

Figure 5.1.   Venn Diagram Demonstrating the Boolean AND Operator.   77

Figure 5.2.   Venn Diagram Demonstrating the Boolean AND and OR Operators.   79

Figure 5.3.   Venn Diagram Demonstrating the Boolean AND and NOT Operators.   81

Figure 6.1.   Entering a Term into the Online PsycINFO Thesaurus in EBSCOhost.   90

Figure 6.2.   Index Terms and Entry Vocabulary Bearing the Searcher's Entered Term
in the PsycINFO Thesaurus on EBSCOhost.   91

Figure 6.3.   Authority Record for "Major Depression" in the Online PsycINFO Thesaurus
on EBSCOhost.   92

Figure 6.4.   Selected Index Terms in the Authority Record for "Depression (Emotion)" in the Online PsycINFO Thesaurus on EBSCOhost.   92

Figure 6.5.   EBSCOhost's Searching Language for Selected PsycINFO Thesaurus Terms.   93

Figure 6.6.   Combining Sets 1, 2, and 3 in a Boolean AND Operation in EBSCOhost's PsycINFO.   93

Figure 6.7.   CV Search Results in EBSCOhost's PsycINFO Database.   94

Figure 6.8.   Direct Entry of Index Term Words in a Search of EBSCOhost's PsycINFO Database.   97

Figure 6.9.   Building Block Search Strategy.   98

Figure 6.10.   Buffet Edition of the Building Block Strategy. Created using symbols from the Noun Project (http://thenounproject.com): "Toast" symbol by Jacob Halton; "Salad" symbol by Peter Chlebak; "Tomato" symbol by Marco Olgio; "Cheese" symbol by Consuelo Elo Graziola; "Salt-Shaker" symbol by Nathan Thomson; "Food" symbol by Mister Pixel; "Steak" symbol by Anuar Zhumaev; "Egg" symbol by Jacob Halton; "Ham" symbol by jon trillana; "Turkey" symbol by Quan Do; "Fast Food" symbol by Saman Bemel-Benrud; "Ice Cream" symbol by Gustav Salomonsson; "Popsicle" symbol by Kristin McPeak; "Cake" symbol by Maurizio Fusillo; "Milkshake" symbol by Diego Naive; "Cupcake" symbol by Alessandro Suraci; "Grapes" symbol by Thomas Hirter.   99

Figure 6.11.   EBSCOhost's PsycINFO Clusters with the *Subject: Major Heading* Cluster Open.   101

Figure 6.12.   Pop-Up Window Bearing Medium-Posted *Subject: Major Heading* Cluster Values in EBSCOhost's PsycINFO Database.   102

Figure 6.13.   Depression Homepage (Above the Fold) Featuring a Topic Overview and Clusters in the Opposing Viewpoints Database from Gale Cengage Learning. Courtesy of Gale Cengage Learning.   103

Figure 6.14.   PubMed Authority Record for the MeSH "Drive." Courtesy of the National Library of Medicine.   106

Figure 7.1.   Entering a Free Text Search Statement for the Farm Women Facet into EBSCOhost's Women's Studies International (WSI) Database.   118

Figure 7.2.   FT Search Results in EBSCOhost's WSI Database.   121

Figure 7.3.   Clicking on the "Advanced Options" Link and Choosing Parameters for a FT Search of the Full-Text LexisNexis Academic Database. Source: LexisNexis, a registered trademark of Elsevier, B.V., image retrieved on 15 March 2015.   123

Figure 7.4.   Entering a FT Search Statement for All Three Facets into the LexisNexis Academic Database. Source: LexisNexis, a registered trademark of Elsevier, B.V., image retrieved on 15 March 2015.   124

Figure 7.5.   Retrievals and Clusters for a FT Search in the LexisNexis Academic Database. Source: LexisNexis, a registered trademark of Elsevier, B.V., image retrieved on 2015 March 15.   124

Figure 7.6.   À la Carte Edition of the Building Block Strategy. Created using symbols from the Noun Project (http://thenounproject.com): "Salad" symbol by Peter Chlebak; "Turkey" symbol by Quan Do; "Grapes" symbol by Thomas Hirter.   127

Figure 7.7.   Using a Relevant Retrieval in ProQuest's ERIC Database to "See similar docu-
               ments." The screenshots and their contents are published with permission
               of ProQuest LLC. Further reproduction is prohibited without permission.
               Inquiries may be made to: ProQuest LLC, 789 E. Eisenhower Pkwy, Ann Arbor,
               MI 48106-1346 USA. Telephone (734) 761–4700; Email: info@proquest
               .com; Web page: http://www.proquest.com.   129

Figure 7.8.   Conducting a Title Search in the Web of Science Database. Data included
               herein are derived from the Web of Science prepared by Thomson
               Reuters, Inc. (Thomson), Philadelphia, Pennsylvania, USA: Copyright
               Thomson Reuters 2015. All rights reserved.   130

Figure 7.9.   Clicking on the Full Surrogate's "Cited References" Link to Display the
               Source's Bibliography in the Web of Science Database. Data included herein
               are derived from the Web of Science prepared by Thomson Reuters, Inc.
               (Thomson), Philadelphia, Pennsylvania, USA: Copyright Thomson Reuters
               2015. All rights reserved.   131

Figure 7.10.   Clicking on a Surrogate's "Times Cited in This Database" to Display Sources
               Citing It in EBSCOhost's PsycINFO Database.   132

Figure 7.11.   Clicking on a Surrogate's "Cited by" Link to Display Sources Citing It in
               Google Scholar. Google and the Google logo are registered trademarks of
               Google Inc., used with permission.   132

Figure 8.1.   Conducting a Title-Begins-With Search in the Classic Version of the Mirlyn
               OPAC. Screenshots made available under the Creative Commons Attribution
               license by the University of Michigan Library.   144

Figure 8.2.   LCNAF'S Labeled Display of a Name Authority Record. Courtesy of the
               Library of Congress.   146

Figure 8.3.   Browsing the Alphabetical Author Index in the Classic Version of the
               Mirlyn OPAC. Screenshots made available under the Creative Commons
               Attribution license by the University of Michigan Library.   149

Figure 8.4.   Conducting an Author Search for Dan Brown in the VuFind Version of Mirlyn
               with Relevance Ranked Retrievals. Screenshots made available under the
               Creative Commons Attribution license by the University of Michigan Library. 150

Figure 8.5.   Scrutinizing High-Posted Descriptors in ProQuest ERIC's *Subjects* Cluster
               for Clues about the Future of Television Violence Research. The screenshots
               and their contents are published with permission of ProQuest LLC. Further
               reproduction is prohibited without permission. Inquiries may be made to:
               ProQuest LLC, 789 E. Eisenhower Pkwy, Ann Arbor, MI 48106-1346 USA.
               Telephone (734) 761–4700; Email: info@proquest.com; Web page: http://
               www.proquest.com.   154

Figure 8.6.   Retrievals and Clusters for a Free Text Search of the Television Violence
               Query in the Scopus Database. Source: Scopus, a registered trademark of
               Elsevier, B.V., image retrieved 16 March 2015.   155

Figure 8.7.   Limiting Retrievals to Literature Reviews Using the *Document Type* Cluster in
               the Scopus Database. Source: Scopus, a registered trademark of Elsevier, B.V.,
               image retrieved 16 March 2015.   156

Figure 8.8.   Pie Chart Summarizing the Subject Areas of Television Violence Retrievals
               in the Scopus Database. Source: Scopus, a registered trademark of Elsevier,
               B.V., image retrieved 16 March 2015.   157

Figure 8.9.   Links to an Alphabetical List of the U-M Library's Online Journals through
               Search Tools. Screenshots made available under the Creative Commons
               Attribution license by the University of Michigan Library.   159

Figure 8.10.   A Journal Holdings Record in Search Tools Revealing Suppliers of Full-Texts.
               Screenshots made available under the Creative Commons Attribution license
               by the University of Michigan Library.   159

Figure 8.11.   Displaying a Journal's Years, Volumes, and Issues in the ProQuest Research
               Library Database. The screenshots and their contents are published with
               permission of ProQuest LLC. Further reproduction is prohibited without
               permission. Inquiries may be made to: ProQuest LLC, 789 E. Eisenhower Pkwy,
               Ann Arbor, MI 48106-1346 USA. Telephone (734) 761-4700; Email: info@
               proquest.com; Web page: http://www.proquest.com.   160

Figure 8.12.   Browsing a Journal Issue's Contents in the ProQuest Research Library
               Database. The screenshots and their contents are published with permission
               of ProQuest LLC. Further reproduction is prohibited without permission.
               Inquiries may be made to: ProQuest LLC, 789 E. Eisenhower Pkwy, Ann Arbor,
               MI 48106-1346 USA. Telephone (734) 761-4700; Email: info@proquest.com;
               Web page: http://www.proquest.com.   161

Figure 8.13.   Searching for a Journal Title in the VuFind Version of the Mirlyn OPAC.
               Screenshots made available under the Creative Commons Attribution license
               by the University of Michigan Library.   162

Figure 8.14.   A Journal Holdings Record in the VuFind Version of Mirlyn Revealing
               Suppliers of Full-Texts. Screenshots made available under the Creative
               Commons Attribution license by the University of Michigan Library.   163

Figure 9.1.   Choosing the Cited Reference Search in the Basic Search Interface of the Web
               of Science (WoS) Database. Data included herein are derived from the Web
               of Science prepared by Thomson Reuters, Inc. (Thomson), Philadelphia,
               Pennsylvania, USA: Copyright Thomson Reuters 2015. All rights reserved.   168

Figure 9.2.   Choosing the Cited Author Index in the Web of Science Database. Data
               included herein are derived from the Web of Science prepared by Thomson
               Reuters, Inc. (Thomson), Philadelphia, Pennsylvania, USA: Copyright
               Thomson Reuters 2015. All rights reserved.   169

Figure 9.3.   Entering an Author's Surname and First Initial into the Web of Science's
               Cited Author Index. Data included herein are derived from the Web of
               Science prepared by Thomson Reuters, Inc. (Thomson), Philadelphia,
               Pennsylvania, USA: Copyright Thomson Reuters 2015. All rights reserved.   169

Figure 9.4.   Selecting Alphabetized Names from the Cited Author Index in the Web of
               Science Database. Data included herein are derived from the Web of Science
               prepared by Thomson Reuters, Inc. (Thomson), Philadelphia, Pennsylvania,
               USA: Copyright Thomson Reuters 2015. All rights reserved.   170

Figure 9.5.   Cleaning Up Entries in Your Selected Author's Cited Reference Index Table in
               the Web of Science Database. Data included herein are derived from the Web
               of Science prepared by Thomson Reuters, Inc. (Thomson), Philadelphia,
               Pennsylvania, USA: Copyright Thomson Reuters 2015. All rights reserved.   170

Figure 9.6.   Your Selected Author's Citation Count with Accompanying Clusters in the
               Web of Science Database. Data included herein are derived from the Web of

Science prepared by Thomson Reuters, Inc. (Thomson), Philadelphia, Pennsylvania, USA: Copyright Thomson Reuters 2015. All rights reserved.   171

Figure 9.7.   Entering an Author's Name to Initiate a Citation Count Search in the Scopus Database. Source: Scopus, a registered trademark of Elsevier, B.V., image retrieved 17 March 2015.   172

Figure 9.8.   An Author's Citation Count and Related Information in the Scopus Database. Source: Scopus, a registered trademark of Elsevier, B.V., image retrieved 17 March 2015.   173

Figure 9.9.   An Author's User Profile in Google Scholar Bearing His Citation Count and Related Information. Google and the Google logo are registered trademarks of Google Inc., used with permission.   174

Figure 9.10.   Journal Entry Featuring the Impact Factor in the Journal Citation Reports Database. Data included herein are derived from the Journal Citation Reports prepared by Thomson Reuters, Inc. (Thomson), Philadelphia, Pennsylvania, USA: Copyright Thomson Reuters 2015. All rights reserved.   175

Figure 9.11.   Altmetric Report for a Very Recently Published Source in the Scopus Database. Source: Scopus, a registered trademark of Elsevier, B.V., image retrieved 17 March 2015.   178

Figure 10.1.   Can't Live Without This Facet First Search Strategy.   185

Figure 10.2.   Citation Pearl Growing Search Strategy.   187

Figure 10.3.   Follow-Up Controlled Vocabulary Search in EBSCOhost's PsycINFO Database Using Index Terms Culled from the Retrievals of a Citation Pearl Growing Search.   189

Figure 10.4.   Shot in the Dark Search Strategy.   191

Figure 10.5.   Getting a Little Help from Your Friends Search Strategy. Friends symbol by Moriah Rich from the Noun Project (http://thenounproject.com).   193

Figure 10.6.   Topic Finder and Retrievals for a Selected Cluster Term in the Academic OneFile Database from Gale Cengage Learning. Courtesy of Gale Cengage Learning.   195

Figure 10.7.   Search Strategy Selection Flow Chart.   197

Figure 12.1.   Default Interface for Conducting Boolean Searches in the Compendex Database on Engineering Village. Source: Engineering Village, a registered trademark of Elsevier, B.V., image retrieved on 18 March 2015.   219

Figure 12.2.   Default (or Basic) Interface for Conducting Searches in the Index Islamicus on EBSCOhost.   219

Figure 12.3.   A Retrieved Surrogate from a Known-Item Search in the Compendex Database on Engineering Village. Source: Engineering Village, a registered trademark of Elsevier, B.V., image retrieved on 18 March 2015.   223

Figure 12.4.   Post-Search Clusters in the Compendex Database on Engineering Village. Source: Engineering Village, a registered trademark of Elsevier, B.V., image retrieved on 18 March 2015.   227

Figure 13.1.   Copying a Retrieval's Permalink in an EBSCOhost Database for Pasting and Sending It to a User in an Email Message.   232

Figure 13.2. A User's Saved Sources in the JStor Database. Reprinted courtesy of JSTOR. JSTOR © 2013. All rights reserved. 233

Figure 13.3. Completing EBSCOhost's Search Alerts Form. 234

Figure 13.4. Zotero's Three-Paned Workspace. Courtesy of the Roy Rosenzweig Center for History and New Media. 235

Figure 13.5. Zotero's Workspace Updated with a Newly Added Source. Courtesy of the Roy Rosenzweig Center for History and New Media. 236

Figure 13.6. Entering Search Terms into Separate Search Boxes Combined by the Boolean AND Operator into the ProQuest Research Library Database. The screenshots and their contents are published with permission of ProQuest LLC. Further reproduction is prohibited without permission. Inquiries may be made to: ProQuest LLC, 789 E. Eisenhower Pkwy, Ann Arbor, MI 48106-1346 USA. Telephone (734) 761–4700; Email: info@proquest.com; Web page: http://www.proquest.com. 244

Figure 14.1. Characterizing a Reference Interview in Gimlet. Courtesy of Sidecar Publications. 257

Tables

Table 2.1. Open Web Databases Suitable for Library Database Hubs 21

Table 3.1. Reasons Why People Don't Reveal Their Real Information Needs, Adapted from Ross, Nilsen, and Radford (2009, 18) 36

Table 3.2. Open-Ended Questions That Give Rise to Negotiated Queries 39

Table 3.3. More Negotiation for In-Depth Queries 41

Table 3.4. Seven Steps of the Search Process 42

Table 4.1. Forms of Research Databases 57

Table 4.2. Catalog Record from an OPAC 59

Table 4.3. Classifying Licensed and Open Web Research Databases 64

Table 4.4. Reference Database Genres 65

Table 4.5. Classifying Licensed and Open Web Reference Databases 71

Table 5.1. Relationship Types 78

Table 6.1. Typical Fields in Surrogate Records 86

Table 6.2. Browsing the Online Thesaurus in Several Search Systems 105

Table 6.3. Direct Entry of Index Terms and Index Term Words in Several Search Systems 107

Table 7.1. Comparing Free Text Searching Functionality 134

Table 9.1. Comparing Two Academics' Publication Records Using Article-Level Metrics 176

Table 10.1. PsycINFO Index Terms Extracted from Retrievals Using the Citation Pearl Growing Search Strategy 188

Table 11.1. Search Tactics, Adapted from Bates (1979; 1987) 207

Table 12.1. Subject and Known-Item Searches 221

Table 12.2. Subject and Known-Item Searches in the Compendex Database on Engineering Village 222

Table 12.3.   Engineering Village's Free Text Searching Language   225
Table 13.1.   Course Design and Deployment Documentation   239
Table 13.2.   Using Prompts to Elicit Queries from Users   242
Table 13.3.   Inviting Users to Dissect Their Queries into Big Ideas   242
Table 13.4.   Advising Users to Break Up or Restate Wordy Big Ideas   243

Textboxes

Textbox 3.1. Helping Users Transition from Q2 (Conscious) to Q3 (Formal Need)
             Questions   30
Textbox 4.1. The Utility of Surrogates in Full-Text Databases   63
Textbox 6.1. The Changes Searchers Make to Ongoing Searches   96
Textbox 7.1. Sources of Free Text Search Terms   115
Textbox 7.2. The Wide Range of Truncation Functionality in the ProQuest
             Search System   117
Textbox 7.3. Precedence of Operators   119

Videos

The following videos accompany chapters 3–10 and 13. They are embedded in the ebook and referenced in the Summary sections of the printed book.

Chapter 3.   The Reference Interview: http://www.onlinesearching.org/p/3-interview.html
Chapter 4.   Selecting a Relevant Database: http://www.onlinesearching.org/p/4-database.html
Chapter 5.   Pre-Search Preparation: http://www.onlinesearching.org/p/5-preparation.html
Chapter 6.   Controlled Vocabulary Searching: http://www.onlinesearching.org/p/6-controlled.html
Chapter 7.   Free Text Searching: http://www.onlinesearching.org/p/7-free.html
Chapter 8.   Known-Item Searching: http://www.onlinesearching.org/p/8-known.html
Chapter 9.   Assessing Research Impact: http://www.onlinesearching.org/p/9-impact.html
Chapter 10. Search Strategies: http://www.onlinesearching.org/p/10-strategies.html
Chapter 13. Interacting with Library Users: http://www.onlinesearching.org/p/13-interacting.html

Preface

For everyday people, searching for information usually means Googling and searching the World Wide Web. Web searches are satisfactory for providing information that gives people a working knowledge of unfamiliar, long-forgotten, or difficult topics. Unfortunately, searching the open Web for useful information gets people just so far. That anyone can publish information on the Web makes it risky for people to make decisions about their health, well-being, and livelihood using the information that they find there. People need to access trusted sources of information where authors, editors, and contributors have the proper credentials to write about topics; they document their facts; and what they have to say is objective, accurate, and reliable. Additionally, people pursue lifelong interests in academic fields, disciplines, and professions, they become gainfully employed, and some even achieve world-class expert status in their chosen domain. Becoming a domain expert means developing disciplinary knowledge. For the time being, trusted sources of information and disciplinary scholarship reside in the licensed Web, largely inaccessible to Google and other Web search engines.

Your job as a librarian will involve uniting library users with trusted sources of information to answer their questions and satisfy their information needs. This means learning how to become an expert intermediary searcher who is in full command of the wide range of functionality that is characteristic of the search systems that access licensed databases and quality information on the open Web. Not only do you want to put *relevant* information in your users' hands but information that is *credible* and supports their decision-making and intellectual growth so that they can pursue their personal, educational, and professional goals.

Librarians are especially biased toward searching the licensed Web. Their portal to the licensed Web is their library's database hub—the centerpiece of the library's virtual services where self-service access to scholarly, professional, and educational information resides, providing access to not only surrogate records but the actual sources themselves in the form of digital full-texts, media, or spatial and numeric data.

Quality information is expensive to produce, and database publishers expect payment from users for publishing, organizing, and making this information available online. Librarians would like to populate their library's database hub with just about every available quality database known to mankind, but they cannot due to the tremendous expense of negotiating licenses with database publishers and aggregators and subscribing to their licensed databases, so they scrutinize the wide range of available licensed databases, choosing ones that support the interests, preferences, and domain expertise of their library's user base. Increasingly, quality content is becoming available on the open Web as a result of the open access movement and the nature of the World Wide Web itself as a low-cost distribution technology.

Underlining the distinctions between librarians and everyday people seeking information is Roy Tennant's oft-cited quip "Only librarians like to search, everyone else likes to find" (Tennant 2004). I believe that Roy was right about librarians liking to search. Librarians memorize the searching languages of the databases and search systems they use repeatedly on the job and rely on their favorite language as a springboard to understanding a new database's searching language. Unfortunately, their efforts to teach end users how to become expert searchers have always failed (Bates, Wilde, and Siegfried 1995); in fact, studies demonstrate that hardly anyone except for librarians use searching languages (Jansen, Spink, and Saracevic 2000; Vakkari, Pennanen, and Serola 2003; Jansen and Spink 2006).

I believe that Roy got the second part wrong—people don't want to find, they want to *know*. In fact, they want to know immediately—right there on the spot and without a moment's hesitation—so they can put the information to work, completing the task that prompted them to pause and search for information in the first place. Before people approach librarians, they search many other sources—friends, family members, their personal libraries, Google, Wikipedia, and the Web—for answers to their questions (Fast and Campbell 2004; Head 2007; Kolowich 2011). Some give up along the way, and others persevere. When they ask you—the librarian—to help them, they are approaching you almost as a last resort. Their focus won't be on how you answer their questions, it will be on the *answers you find* to their questions. A few people might want to know how you found the answers but they won't necessarily attend to online searching details in ways that will enable them to become better searchers. As an expert intermediary searcher, you will walk a curious tightrope, interacting with people who want you to find answers to their questions but restrained about just how much detail you should reveal to them about how you found the answers and whether you should offer to show them right then and there online searching basics that would help to make them better online searchers.

The purpose of *Online Searching* is to teach you how to become an expert intermediary searcher who finds quality information online efficiently and effectively so that you can help library users satisfy their information needs.

Chapter 1 sets the stage, describing how and why scholarly information is split between the open Web and licensed Web. Chapter 2 introduces you to the library's database hub where end users access scholarly, educational, and professional information online. The next nine chapters (3 to 11) are organized according to the seven steps of the online searching process:

1. Conducting the reference interview where you determine what the user really wants (i.e., the negotiated query) (chapter 3)
2. Selecting a relevant database (chapter 4)
3. Conducting a facet analysis and logical combination of the negotiated query (chapter 5)
4. Typecasting the negotiated query as a subject or known item (chapter 5)
5. Representing the negotiated query as input to the search system (chapters 6 to 9)
6. Entering the search and responding strategically (chapter 10)
7. Displaying retrievals, assessing them, and responding tactically (chapter 11)

There are so many databases, search systems, and search engines that you cannot be an expert at searching every single one of them. To quickly come up to snuff, chapter 12 gives you a methodology called conducting a technical reading of a database for quickly and efficiently familiarizing yourself with a database and the system you'll use to search it.

Chapter 13 brings your reference-interview interaction with library users back into focus where you enlist *their* assistance, making sure the search is on track and retrieving relevant information to satisfy their queries. Use this occasion to teach users something about information seeking so that they can put what they learn to work for themselves in the future. What and how much you teach them will require deliberation on your part, taking into consideration your mode of interaction, the nature of their inquiry, and your assessment of their motivation to learn something about information seeking in addition to answers to their questions. Chapter 14 discusses current online searching trends and issues, and it concludes with a wish list of improvements to today's search systems and databases.

Be on the lookout for links to explanatory videos in the summary section of selected chapters. In less than three minutes, each video distills the most important ideas about online searching that you should remember for as long as there are search systems, databases, and library users with information needs. This book's contents will interest:

- *Students* in library and information studies (LIS) programs who are learning how to help library users satisfy their information needs.
- *LIS faculty* who teach the school's online searching course—*this* is your textbook for the course.
- *End users* who frequently seek information for serious pursuits and want to know expert searchers' secrets for finding information (you may be college seniors researching senior theses, graduate students researching master's theses and doctoral dissertations, faculty at colleges and universities, or professional-amateurs who are passionate about your avocations).
- *Practicing librarians* who want to upgrade their searching skills and knowledge.

Online searching resides in the crosshairs of technology where the pace of change is rapid, sudden, and sometimes only a heartbeat away. Be prepared for changes to database interfaces, contents, and search system functionality. Such changes are always likely, and they will affect this book's screenshots of a database or its descriptions of a particular system's features. Such changes also mean that you will find yourself running in place—struggling to keep up with changes to databases and search systems and reflecting them in the instruction you provide to your library's users. What won't change about online searching is the really hard stuff—conducting a successful reference interview in which you gain an understanding of the gap in another person's knowledge that is the impetus for his asking you for help, transforming this into search statements that retrieve relevant information, advising the person about their ongoing search so that he isn't overwhelmed with too much information. You must also sense how far afield you can go in terms of leaving each and every user with at least one information literacy-oriented tip above and beyond the information that answers their questions so they can apply what they learn to further the search in hand and improve their future searches.

Welcome to online searching! As an expert intermediary searcher, you will be the linchpin in between library users with information needs and useful information that satisfies them. This will be a challenging task but one you will be ready to take on as a result of reading this book, searching online to find answers to its many end-of-chapter questions, comparing what you did with its answers, and sharing what you learn about online searching with your instructor and fellow classmates in class discussions. Let's get started!

Bibliography

Bates, Marcia J., Deborah N. Wilde, and Susan Siegfried. 1995. "Research Practices of Humanities Scholars in an Online Environment: The Getty Online Searching Project Report No. 3." *Library and Information Science Research* 17 (Winter): 5–40.

Fast, Karl V., and D. Grant Campbell. 2004. "'I Still Like Google': University Student Perceptions of Searching OPACs and the Web." *Proceedings of the ASIS Annual Meeting* 2004 41: 138–46.

Head, Alison J. 2007. "How Do Students Conduct Academic Research?" *First Monday* 12, no. 8. http://firstmonday.org/issues/issue12_8/head/index.

Jansen, Bernard J., and Amanda Spink. 2006. "How Are We Searching the World Wide Web? A Comparison of Nine Search Engine Transaction Logs." *Information Processing and Management* 42, no. 1: 248–63.

Jansen, Bernard J., Amanda Spink, and Tefko Saracevic. 2000. "Real Life, Real Users, and Real Needs: A Study and Analysis of User Queries on the Web." *Information Processing and Management* 36, no. 2: 207–27.

Kolowich, Steve. 2011. "What Students Don't Know." *Inside Higher Education.* http://www.inside highered.com/news/2011/08//22.

Tennant, Roy. 2004. "Five Easy Pieces." *Library Journal* 129, no. 19 (Nov. 15): 25.

Vakkari, Pertti, Mikko Pennanen, and Sami Serola. 2003. "Changes of Search Terms and Tactics While Writing a Research Proposal: A Longitudinal Case Study." *Information Processing and Management* 39, no. 3: 445–63.

Acknowledgments

Despite the passing of almost forty years, I recall the first time that I saw online searching in action. At the time, research was a tedious, time-consuming, and manual process to which researchers dedicated whole days, pawing manually through print indexes, reading hundreds of titles listed under a subject heading in the hope of finding something related to their interests. I worked at the Milton S. Eisenhower Library of the Johns Hopkins University where our science librarian, the late Edward Terry, was in charge of the Library's new online searching services. Ed sat at a computer terminal that was the size of a small desk and showed me how to conduct a facet analysis and combine facets with Boolean operators. Then he put these to work, demonstrating an online search and accomplishing in fifteen minutes what it took a researcher fifteen hours to do. It was nothing short of a miracle! Earning my master's degree in library science at Syracuse University two years later, my teacher, Professor Pauline Cochrane, was one of the first to offer a course in online searching. Students learned how to search the Dialog and Orbit search systems. Pauline gave me a password to test drive the new BRS search system, and our class visited the Law Library where a librarian demonstrated the brand-new Lexis search system on a dedicated terminal with special key caps that executed system commands. I am indebted to both Ed and Pauline for getting me started in online searching, an area that has always been at the core of my research and teaching.

Over the years, various book editors have asked me to write a textbook on online searching. As much as I've wanted to write it, I've declined due to the various research projects on my plate. Executive Editor Charles Harmon at Rowman & Littlefield was particularly persistent, but he was also patient and deliberate, approaching me minus the pressure and urgency that I felt from other editors. Finally, I decided the time was right for me to put *Online Searching* on my plate. Throughout the writing project, Charles was immediate and frank in his responses to my inquiries, his words of encouragement came at the right time, and his suggestions for breaching an impasse were always spot-on. What a pleasure it has been to work with Charles! Also at Rowman & Littlefield, thanks to Robert Hayunga and Kellie Hagan, who assisted in the final editing and production work. My gratitude also goes to Penny Duke, who shouldered the lion's share of the proofing burden so that I could focus on indexing and last-minute substantive issues.

I am especially grateful to my University of Michigan (U-M) Library colleagues. So many times I have consulted Librarian Kathleen M. Folger, the U-M Library's Chief Electronic Resources Officer, about a wide range of issues, ideas, and facts pertaining to databases and search systems. Her assistance has also been crucial for putting my screenshot-permission requests into the right hands of this and that database publisher and search system supplier. Associate Librarian Angie Oehrli read an early full draft, responding with many suggestions for improvements and additions. Associate Librarian Shevon Desai, Librarian Karen E. Downing, and Librarian Charles G. Ransom sent me ideas for search topics. Senior Associate Librarian Marci Brandenburg has been a rich source of information about PubMed. Worth its weight in gold has been the University of Michigan's Ask-a-Librarian service with its many nameless, faceless librarians available at the touch of a keystroke via email and chat who have answered my particularly vexing questions about this and that database.

Thanks to my colleagues in the U-M's School of Information, Clinical Assistant Professor Kristin Fontichiaro and Associate Professor Soo Young Rieh, who read selected chapters, giving me useful and thoughtful comments that I put to work at improving the book's content. Kristin's colleague, Debbie Abilock, consultant and co-founder of NoodleTools, and Kathleen Folger at the U-M Library also read selected chapters and sent me their input. I salute Christopher Hebblethwaite, Coordinator of Reference Services at SUNY Oswego, who shared search topics and chat transcripts. I am grateful to Professor June Abbas, University of Oklahoma, for her insightful comments on my original proposal. Serving as a sounding board have been my students in SI 665, Online Searching and Databases, who gave me their reactions to various ideas with Emily Brock and Kristen Hansen taking notes for me during class so that I could revisit student input later on. On the U-M home front has been Administrative Assistant Sherry Smith to whom I handed truckloads of clerical tasks so I could stay focused on writing.

Thanks to Cliff Lampe, Associate Professor at the University of Michigan, and Darren Gergle, Associate Professor at Northwestern University, for being good sports about the comparison of their publication records in Google Scholar, Scopus, and Web of Science. That I was able to showcase research impact metrics in a real-life example makes these metrics more salient and vivid to aspiring expert searchers whose superiors will soon task them with comparable analyses.

Chock full of screenshots from a wide range of search systems and databases, *Online Searching* both shows and tells how to search online effectively and efficiently. I am grateful to the many publisher, database, and search system representatives who gave me permission to make screenshots of their online products and services. At EBSCO Information Services, Joel Pratt gave me carte blanche to showcase EBSCOhost and served as an intermediary, helping me obtain permissions for databases and search systems that are connected with the U-M Library's EBSCO license. Heidi Prior at Gale Cengage Learning and Erin Mittendorf at ITHAKA (JStor's administrator) were also very flexible about my using screenshots to showcase their search systems and databases. Truly, I have been heartened by the positive reception that my screenshot-permission inquiries received and want to convey my gratitude to many more representatives: Fiona Carr at Alexander Street Press; Barry Berumudez at the Cornell Lab of Ornithology; Elizabeth Dyas, Antonio Gull, David Neal, and Sarah Tyrchniewicz at Elsevier B.V.; Steven Swartz at Geographic Research; Eric Larson and Nate Vack at Gimlet; Ann Della Porta at the Library of Congress; Dana Slocum at Marquis Who's Who; Kathleen Cravedi at the National Library of Medicine; Robert Repino and others at Oxford University Press; Mary Ann Vass at Pearson Education; Kim Bastian, Corye Bradbury, and Paul Webb at ProQuest; Sean Takats at the Roy Rosenzweig Center for History and New Media (Zotero's administrator); Timothy Otto and Jeffrey Clovis at Thomson Reuters; and Lynne Raughley at the University of Michigan Library.

Bolstering *Online Searching*'s graphical presentation of online searching is its many figures that TattleTail Design executed with care, precision, and attention to detail. Thanks to the Noun Project's (http://thenounproject.com) library of symbols that streamlined TattleTail's production.

Especially compelling is *Online Searching's* series of explanatory videos. Created by Studio Librarian Emily Thompson at the University of Tennessee at Chattanooga, the videos capture the essence of the reference interview, controlled vocabulary, free text searching, and other important online searching concepts and distill them into short videos. A graduate of the U-M's School of Information, Emily has built on what she learned in my Online Searching class a half decade ago, drawing on her experience as a reference librarian and applying her creative abilities in a masterful way to tell stories about difficult technical concepts in visual terms so that they are easy for aspiring expert searchers to understand.

1

Online Searching in the Age of the Information Explosion

For most everyday people, online searching means searching Google and the World Wide Web for information. This scenario is actually comparatively new, evolving over the last fifteen to twenty years in response to the rapid growth of web-based information. Online searching has an almost fifty-year history, stretching back to the Cold War, when Eastern and Western Blocs invested heavily in education, science, and technology to keep pace with each other and to keep each other at bay militarily. In the West, the investment gave birth to an information explosion. Scientists and scholars churned out new publications at a record pace, overwhelming librarians whose nineteenth-century technologies—card files, book indexes, printed loose-leaf services— bogged down under the sheer numbers of new publications issued by science, technology, and scholarly publishers.

This first chapter looks backward at these and other factors that gave rise to online searching to harness the information explosion and forward to advances in new technology that have steered online searching onto its present course. On the surface, online searching seems as simple as one-stop searching in a Web search engine, but it is actually more complicated due to a whole host of factors that collided, resulting in two parallel streams of online searching development and fracturing access to information along quality lines ranging from scholarship that undergoes rigorous peer review and editorial scrutiny to popular culture tidbits, unsubstantiated hearsay, anonymous postings, speculation, and rumor. How the people you help will put the information you find for them to work will impact your decision about which stream of information you should dip into for answers to their questions.

Searching for Information Before Computers, the Internet, and the World Wide Web

During the 1960s, the phrase "information explosion" became commonplace for describing the rapid increase in the amount of information available to people from all walks of life (Emrich 1970). Back then, the Cold War was the impetus for the rapid increase in information (Hayes 2010). The heavy investments that Eastern and Western Blocs made in education, science, and technology were first and foremost meant to channel new discoveries into the arms and space races; however, the payoffs were more varied and far-reaching in the West where investments led to increased student enrollment in colleges and universities, the development of new private-sector industries and new disciplines at the academy, the availability of new jobs for highly qualified graduates, and, eventually, more discoveries made by scientists and scholars in industry and the academy. Fueling the cycle of discovery and the information explosion generally was the free flow of information in which scientists and scholars disseminated details about their discoveries in not-so-free scholarly publications.

Searching for Information Before Computers

While the production of new knowledge was at an all-time high before computers, keeping abreast of the latest discoveries and finding information generally was tedious, boring, and tremendously time consuming. Let's flashback to the mid-1960s to find out what it *was* like. Your topic is "escape systems from earth-orbital vehicles in emergency situations." You visit the university library; plunk yourself down in a chair at a desk lined with rows and rows of print indexes, usually one volume for a year's worth of scholarly publishing on a subject; reach for the volume for 1966, the most recent year; open it to the E's. Thankfully, "Escape Systems" is an index term. Next, you scan titles listed under this term to determine whether they discuss your topic. Finding no promising titles in the 1966 volume, you grab the 1965, 1964, 1963, and as many volumes as you need until you find enough sources with promising titles. By the way, finding these titles is just the beginning. You have to *write down* (there were no personal computers back in the 1960s!) each title's citation, search the library catalog to see if the library subscribes to the journal, then fetch the right volume from the library bookshelves for the article. If the journal volumes you want are in circulation, you have to start all over again or wait until the borrower returns them.

The Birth of Online Searching

Funding research and development for a more efficient way to search for information was the U.S. Department of Defense's Advanced Research Projects Agency (ARPA) that issued a request for proposal (RFP) for the development of computer-based online search systems. Receiving ARPA funding was the Lockheed Missiles and Space Company that gave birth to Dialog, one of the first online search systems. Lockheed implemented Dialog on NASA computers where it searched a database of surrogate records on foreign technology, defense, and space research topics (Bourne 1980; Summit 2002). (Surrogate records are just that—surrogates for full-texts, typically limited to titles, citations, and a few index terms that describe the content of full-texts.)

By the early 1970s, Lockheed was exploring the commercial potential of its Dialog search system. The key to its success was government service contracts from the U.S. Office of Education, National Technical Information Service, National Agricultural Library, and National Library of Medicine that supported the development of the ERIC, NTIS, Agricola, and Medline databases, respectively (Bourne 1980). Minus a database, search systems have nothing to search. Over time, the number of databases grew through the efforts of for-profit companies and learned and professional societies that converted their card catalogs, book indexes, and loose-leaf services to databases and licensed them to Lockheed and its competitors. Database publishers either specialized in the published literature of a discipline such as chemistry, education, or psychology or a particular genre such as journal articles, dissertations, or newspapers.

Online Searching: Initially the Domain of Expert Intermediary Searchers

By the end of the 1970s, Lockheed, System Development Company (SDC), and Bibliographic Retrieval Services (BRS) had become database aggregators, hosting databases from a variety of database publishers and marketing online searching of these databases through their Dialog, Orbit, and BRS search systems, respectively, to libraries and information centers (Björner and Ardito 2003). Only librarians who were expert intermediary searchers with special training from search system representatives or faculty and students in schools of library and information science (LIS) were authorized to use these search systems for several reasons:

- Special training was necessary because each search system had its own searching language that operated within a terse command-line interface
- Online searching was a high-cost enterprise that involved the purchase and maintenance of computer equipment and supplies that few people could afford
- Search systems billed librarians for every search they conducted, and to pay for these services, librarians had to pass much of the cost of the enterprise on to people who used the services

Online searching eliminated the most tedious, boring, and time-consuming elements of the task—consulting year after year of book indexes and writing down citations. It also increased the efficiency and accuracy of the results. Manual searches had been limited to checking one index term at a time (e.g., "Escape Systems"), but computers could now search for surrogates bearing multiple index terms (i.e., "Escape Systems," "Earth-Orbital Vehicles," and "Emergencies") in one fell swoop. This was an almost *immeasurable improvement* of online searching over manual searching!

The First Online Search Systems for Everyday People

It wasn't until the early to mid-1980s that everyday people could perform their own searches, first through the library's online public access catalog (OPAC) that accessed its book collection (Markey 1984), and later through the library's CD-ROM search systems that accessed many of the same databases that expert intermediary searchers accessed through the Dialog, Orbit, and BRS search systems (Mischo and Lee 1987).

Back then, search systems had terse, command-line interfaces (Hildreth 1983). They were difficult to search, but it didn't matter to end users. They lined up to search these systems, and even if their searches were not as sophisticated or their results as precise as expert searchers' searches for the same queries, *end users* wanted to conduct online searches *on their own* (Mischo and Lee 1987).

The Era of the Internet and the World Wide Web Begins

The Cold War was also the impetus for the Internet. In the 1960s, scientists and military strategists worried that a Soviet attack could wipe out the nation's telephone system. In 1962, computer scientist J.C.R. Licklider proposed a solution in the form of an "intergalactic network of computers" that would continue working even if attacks on one or more computers succeeded (Hafner and Lyon 1996, 38). ARPA, the same U.S. agency that funded the development of the earliest search systems, funded the building of such a network and named it ARPANET. From the 1970s through the 1990s, scientists in the United States (U.S.) and around the world routinely used ARPANET and its successor NSFNET to send messages, share files, and conduct their research on the network's supercomputers.

In the late 1980s, computer scientist Tim Berners-Lee envisioned an online information space where information stored across the vast network of interlinked computers (i.e., the Internet) could be shared with anyone anywhere (Berners-Lee 1999). By the early 1990s, he had prototyped a suite of tools that transformed his vision into reality—HyperText Markup Language (HTML)—for encoding a new document type called hypertext, the Hypertext Transfer Protocol

(HTTP) language that computers used to display hypertext documents, the Universal Resource Identifier (URI) scheme that gave hypertext documents addresses on the Internet, Web server software that stored hypertext documents on a computer, and a prototype Web browser that retrieved and displayed hypertext documents from the Internet. Ensuring the success of Berners-Lee's new invention that he called the World Wide Web were computer enthusiasts who set up Web servers, populated them with hypertext documents, and developed free Web browsers that people could use to surf the Web.

Technology Spawns New Communication Paradigms

For everyday people, the Web and the Internet generally gave birth to a *revolution* in human communication. Before their invention, everyday people interacted with one another via the *one-to-one* communication paradigm—writing letters, making phone calls, sending telegrams, or conversing face-to-face. The *one-to-many* communication paradigm was off-limits to everyday people because of the tremendous expense involved with this paradigm. It was the domain of powerful, deep-pocketed gatekeepers—book, journal, and newspaper publishers, local and national radio and television broadcasters, and film and game production studios—who decided the content the "many" would read, watch, listen to, and play based on their careful assessments of the content's marketability.

The invention of the World Wide Web changed everything, making it possible for *anyone* to publish directly to the Web and communicate almost instantaneously with potentially hundreds, thousands, and even millions of people. It also spawned entirely new modes of *many-to-many* communication such as blogs, file sharing, tagging, and wikis. With so many new and compelling ways for both individuals and groups to express themselves and interact with others, the Web grew at an astonishing rate over its twenty-year existence, and it is now the dominant communications medium on the planet.

Searching for Information on the World Wide Web

Initially, finding websites of interest meant clicking on a series of links until you found something of interest. Some people published their saved links, and the popularity of their websites encouraged teams of editors to browse the Web in search of quality websites, solicit website recommendations from Web users, and share their recommendations in the form of Web directories. Although such directories continue to the present day (pages 194–95), they were quickly overshadowed by Web search engines that indexed Web content automatically, dispatching Web spiders (also called Web crawlers) to navigate the links between Web pages, finding and indexing new Web content. Their search interfaces consisted of a search box into which people entered words and phrases that described their interests, and they retrieved Web pages bearing these words and phrases.

In the Web's first decade of existence, no one particular search engine was favored by a majority of Web users for longer than a year or two. That all changed in the new millennium when the Google Web search engine rose to prominence, topping the most-popular list where it still stands today. Google's initial success at achieving better search results was a result of its PageRank innovation that ranked retrieved Web pages based on the number of and quality of Web pages that linked to them (Battelle 2005).

The Library's Response to the Web's Popularity

Everyday people searched the Web right from the start. The reason why was that the Web began a full decade after the PC (personal computer) revolution. People were familiar with PCs as a result of using them at school or on the job, and by the time the Web got started in the early 1990s, PCs were being marketed as an affordable household consumer electronics device. Replacing the PC's command-line interfaces were graphical user interfaces (GUIs) that increased their overall usability.

Noticing that the number of Web queries far surpassed the number of OPAC queries, librarians reluctantly admitted that the Web search engine and the Web had become the search system and database of choice, respectively, for many everyday people seeking information, supplanting the library's long-time role in this regard (Fast and Campbell 2004; Yu and Young 2004; Donlan and Carlin 2007). To win users back, librarians gutted their OPAC's command-line interface in favor of Web browser technology and put pressure on database publishers to phase out CD-ROMs in favor of web-based search systems. It didn't take long for academic and public libraries to transform themselves into places that users could visit physically or virtually and where the centerpiece of the library's virtual services was a database hub where scholarly, professional, and educational information resides, not only access to surrogate records but access to the actual sources themselves in the form of digital full-texts, media, or spatial and numeric data.

Especially in academic libraries, users have found the sheer number of search systems and databases daunting (King 2008). An alternative to the database hub is the web-scale discovery (WSD) system, one-stop shopping for academic information. Into a Google-like search box users enter their search statement, and the WSD system searches a humongous index bearing content from a wide variety of quality databases. WSD systems are a cutting-edge development for libraries—the new Google for academic content (Vaughan 2011).

The Erosion of Editorial Oversight in the Era of the World Wide Web

In summer 1993, not long after the Web's inception, *The New Yorker* published a cartoon showing two dogs, one dog sitting on the floor looking up at the second dog seated at a PC saying, "On the Internet, nobody knows you're a dog" (Wikipedia contributors 2015). Although several interpretations are possible, I have always felt that this cartoon underlines the danger of blindly accepting anything you read on the Web at face value because *anyone* can publish there. That anyone can publish on the Web with a modest investment in the right technology is both a blessing and a curse. With regard to the former, people who want to broadcast messages are able to have their say and reach anyone who cares to read, listen, watch, or play. With regard to the latter, it means that the recipients of web-based communications have to judge for themselves whether the information is trustworthy because there is no guarantee that gatekeepers such as editors, publishers, peer reviewers, broadcasters, or producers are involved in the publication process, making sure authors have the right credentials to communicate their messages and reviewing what they say for accuracy and reliability.

Despite warnings from instructors, librarians, and even the mainstream news media about the need to evaluate web-based information, most people pay lip service to evaluation, telling anyone who asks that they recognize its importance. In practice, if they evaluate sources at all, they do so in a cursory manner (Metzger 2007; Julien and Barker 2009; Walraven, Brand-Gruwel, and Boshuizen 2009). Since librarians know that people often sidestep evaluation, they have created safe havens—their library's OPAC, its WSD system, and its database hub—where evaluation is less of a concern because librarians themselves have evaluated these resources in advance for their users. Librarians evaluate these resources because access to them isn't free; in fact, according to Kathleen M. Folger, Electronic Resources Officer, at the University of Michigan (U-M) Library, the largest libraries may pay tens of millions of dollars for safe-haven resources. Thus, librarians want to make sure that what they select and pay for is a good match with their library users' needs and interests.

Librarians negotiate licenses with publishers and aggregators that require them to put authentication procedures in place to allow access to search systems and databases only for their library's cardholders. Thus, when you link from your library's database hub to one or more specific databases, your hub asks you to authenticate yourself as a library cardholder by entering your username and password. *Online Searching* refers to hub-based databases as "licensed databases," and it refers to the online space in which they reside as the "licensed Web."

If it seems like the publishers of licensed databases are overly concerned about unauthenticated uses of their databases, *they are* and with good reason. Databases are costly to produce, update, and maintain, and the search systems that access these databases are costly to build, improve, maintain, and support 365 days a year. Thus, in the absence of license fees, they would go out of business.

Not all scholarly, professional, and educational databases require authentication through your library's database hub. Some are available free of charge on the open Web to anyone with a Web browser and Internet connection. Publishers realize that access to information has the potential to push back the frontiers of knowledge and improve the quality of life for all so they make their databases freely available to anyone on the Web. Ultimately, someone has to pay the bills, and thus most open Web databases are funded by governments, foundations, and for- and non-profit organizations. Librarians add links from their database hubs to many open Web databases, but before they do, they evaluate these databases to make sure they provide quality information.

By the mid-noughties, both Google and Microsoft had applied their search engines to scholarly, professional, and educational information through their Google Scholar and Microsoft Academic Search databases, respectively. Searching and displaying retrieved surrogates is free. The moment you click to display a full-text, you have entered the licensed Web where the database publisher's system pops up, asking you to enter your credit card to purchase the source outright or rent it for a limited period of time. Had you searched your library's database hub or its WSD system and retrieved these sources, their full-texts would be free. Of course, the full-texts really *aren't* free. The licenses your library has negotiated with publishers gives you and other library cardholders unrestricted access to scholarly, professional, and educational information. The bottom line is that libraries *subsidize access to quality information* for their institution's users. When you use your library's database hub or its WSD system, you authenticate yourself and access to whatever you retrieve appears to be free.

Why Scholarship Isn't Free

When students progress from high school to college and beyond, they learn how to become domain experts in a discipline, profession, or trade. Initially they learn from textbooks and assigned readings that verse them on the foundations of their chosen domain; from instructors who help them understand, interpret, and apply what they read and transition them to increasingly more difficult and challenging material; and from labs, practicums, and internships where they experience for themselves what it is like to be a domain expert. When students complete assignments, they might search online for information that gives them ideas, supports their arguments, or increases the depth of their understanding of a topic. Becoming a domain expert means developing disciplinary knowledge and, for the time being, much disciplinary scholarship resides in the licensed Web, largely inaccessible to Google and Web search engines generally. Your job as librarian is to transition students from their reliance on Google, Wikipedia, and the Web to scholarly, professional, and educational information, much of which resides in the licensed Web.

Scholarship (also known as scholarly communication) is the process of sharing new discoveries, theories, ideas, information, and data. Its origins trace back five hundred years to the

European Renaissance when scholasticism gave way to science, technology, and humanism. Scholars wanted to meet like-minded scholars, share their ideas, and build on each others' knowledge. They formed scholarly societies and published their research in society-sponsored journals that were issued periodically and distributed to society members. Thus, scholarly societies were exclusive, limiting the dissemination of new knowledge to their own members.

For a long time, scholarship was a closed circle of scholarly creators and consumers who were one and the same. Loosening up scholarship's exclusivity in the U.S. was a series of events, beginning with the Morrill Land-Grants Acts. Passed by the U.S. Congress in 1862 and 1880, the Acts funded universities, required university faculties to conduct research that benefited society, and fueled a surge in the establishment of new publishing venues by both public and private sectors. When the Second World War ended in 1945, veterans cashed in their G.I. Bill benefits and swamped college campuses where faculty shortages led universities to embrace tenure to attract faculty and to establish formal promotion and tenure review processes to select the best faculty. Faculty cashed in too, competing for federal grants that funded their research and included tuition and living support for the doctoral students who worked on their research teams.

Pressured by the insatiable demands of promotion and tenure committees, faculty publications surged, feeding the demand for new publication venues and swamping editorial offices with journal manuscripts. Commercial publishers realized the opportunity to make a profit, launching new journals and negotiating with university presses and scholarly societies to conduct the business of their scholarly publications. Eventually, commercial publishers gained control of the academic marketplace and increased the cost of journal subscriptions many times over the cost of inflation (Lynch 1992; Cummings et al. 1992; Guédon 2001). Librarians dubbed this a "crisis in scholarly communications" and responded by cutting journal subscriptions and complaining to anyone who would listen that the academy pays several times over for scholarship that emanates from the very place where it is born (Guédon 2001; Edwards and Shulenberger 2003; Bosch 2005). Let's examine the scholarly publishing cycle to see what motivates their complaints.

At the academy, faculty pursue their research agendas, reading the latest research from sources at the library's database hub which helps them generate ideas for research proposals. The academy pays faculty salaries. Some larger grants pay a percentage of the faculty members' work effort, and most grants pay doctoral student tuition and living support. Faculty seek the most prestigious journals in which to report their research findings because promotion and tenure committees give greater weight to such communication venues.

Faculty submit their manuscripts via a journal management system (JMS) to an unpaid journal editor who is usually a full-time faculty member at a college or university and whose recompense for serving as editor is the full or partial fulfillment of their institution's service or research commitment. The journal editor uses the JMS to send manuscripts to unpaid peer reviewers who are also full-time faculty members at a college or university and whose recompense for serving as reviewers partially fulfills their institution's service commitment. Based on one or more reviews for a submitted manuscript, journal editors make decisions about whether to accept or reject the manuscript, including acceptance that is contingent upon the author making reviewer-suggested revisions. Accepted manuscripts are already in digital form, so all that remains is for the journal publisher's production assistant to format the article, inserting figures and tables supplied by authors and converting the manuscript into the style that is characteristic of the particular journal. Journal publishers release new full-text issues of journals bearing faculty-authored articles to database publishers who append full-texts with surrogates bearing citations, index terms, and abstracts. Database publishers license database aggregators to offer online searching of their databases to libraries, or the database publishers themselves offer online searching of their database(s) directly to libraries. Libraries negotiate licenses with database publishers and aggregators so library users can search online databases.

Our discussion of the scholarly publishing cycle has now come full circle, returning to the starting point where faculty pursue their research agendas, reading the latest research at the library's database hub, which helps them generate ideas for new research proposals (figure 1.1). Indeed, the academy pays *four times* for scholarship—it pays the salaries of faculty who write the manuscripts, edit the journals, and review new manuscripts, and it pays publishers for full-texts that are the scholarship their faculty produce.

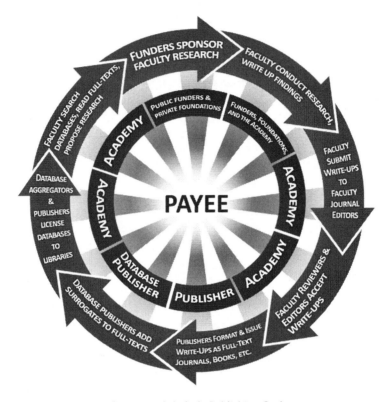

Figure 1.1. Scholarly Publishing Cycle.

The Open Access Movement: Unrestricted Access to Scholarship

It has not been lost on librarians that the academy has been paying multiple times for its own scholarship. For a time, librarians put their hopes into technology, thinking that it would lessen scholarly publishing costs for publishers, and that publishers would pass the savings on to libraries. Contrary to expectations, publishers have continued to increase prices. Librarians have had little recourse except to cut more journal subscriptions and licensed databases. Enraged by these cuts, scholars, scientists, and researchers joined librarians in the search for solutions to the crisis, giving birth to the open access movement with the goal of unrestricted online access to scholarship.

The open access movement has spawned new publishing models that has thrust the academy into the scholarly publishing enterprise (Willinsky 2006; Borgman 2007). One such model involves the establishment of an institutional repository (IR), a combined search system and online database that a learning institution such as a college, university, or laboratory supports where institution members (e.g., faculty, students, researchers) archive digital materials that are the products of their teaching, research, learning, and/or service activities (Lynch 2003). IRs are now commonplace in academic institutions, and people can search them individually or collectively using the OAIster database (http://oaister.worldcat.org) or via Web search engines.

Another model involves the establishment of discipline-specific databases where experts in a discipline, subject, or field of study archive digital materials that are the products of teaching, research, and service activities. Especially successful in this regard has been the arXiv database (http://arXiv.org) where domain experts in physics have contributed scholarship for almost a quarter century. To defray the costs of hosting arXiv, Cornell University Library receives funding from the Simons Foundation and solicits membership fees from academic and research institutions around the world (arXiv 2015).

Dedicated to the open access movement, librarians have been proactive about encouraging faculty to negotiate with publishers, retaining some or all of their legal rights to distribute and use their published scholarship that includes posting their published works on their professional website and/or in their institution's IR. Enterprising individuals, faculties, and entire research communities have established open access journals (OAJs). OAJs that do not receive financial sponsorship from colleges, universities, scholarly societies, laboratories, etc., levy fees on authors of accepted manuscripts to defray the costs associated with open access (e.g., Web servers, journal identification numbers such as ISSNs and DOIs, and production assistance).

Deciding Whether to Publish on the Licensed Web or the Open Web

Since the first OAJs were established, researchers have studied whether scientists and scholars consult them and whether their contents are more likely to be cited than articles from traditional publishers. On both fronts, results are positive and encouraging (Xia 2010; Mischo and Schlembach 2011; Fowler 2011). With respect to prestige, traditional journals still hold sway, and it may take a decade or more for OAJs to equal or surpass them. Until the balance shifts from traditional to OAJs, scientists and scholars are inclined to publish in the former, believing that their peers read and cite articles in their field's most prestigious journals and that promotion and tenure committees weigh prestige over other factors pertaining to published scholarship. About the only event that could suddenly change the status quo would be legislative policies that mandate publication of research findings that are the result of government funding in open access venues.

Faculty, researchers, and professional practitioners want to publish their scholarship in the most prestigious journals and conference proceedings (Lynch 1993). For the time being, these sources reside behind pay-walls where publishers profit from the direct sale of articles to individuals and on the licensed Web where libraries subsidize access for their cardholders. Searching the licensed Web is accomplished through your library's database hub and WSD system. Whether you are a librarian at an academic institution where students are studying to become experts in a field, subject, or discipline or at a public library where people's reasons for searching for information not only involves academics such as helping children with homework, homeschooling their children, or completing their own homework but also includes the serious personal business of handling their own or a family member's health and well-being, making decisions connected with their jobs, finding employment, and so on, you will want to solve their information needs by retrieving the best and most credible and accurate information for them. Thus, your starting point should be licensed Web resources. This does not mean you should ignore Google, Wikipedia, and the open Web entirely. They are great places for people to develop a working knowledge of a topic, and they use them as such (Head and Eisenberg 2010; Porter 2011; Colón-Aguirre and Fleming-May 2012). Additionally, Google Scholar and Microsoft Academic Search regularly index scholarship published in open access vehicles such as IRs, discipline-specific databases, and OAJs; thus, people who have no access to the licensed Web aren't entirely locked out of scholarly, professional, and educational information.

High-Quality Information Is Your Library's Specialty

People prefer to conduct their own online searches, and when they reach an impasse, they are much more likely to ask a friend, a colleague, their instructor, or a family member for help than a librarian (Emrich 1970; Head and Eisenberg 2010; Markey, Leeder, and Rieh 2014). In fact, the librarian is usually the *last* person whom library users consult about their information needs (Head and Eisenberg 2009; Head 2013). Some people even experience library anxiety, "an uncomfortable feeling or emotional disposition experienced in a library setting" (Onwuegbuzie, Jiao, and Bostick 2004, 25), that prevents them from approaching librarians for help. When library users ask librarians for help, they have probably exhausted the people they usually consult and searched Google, Wikipedia, and the open Web. Thus, librarians must be prepared to answer the most difficult questions people have.

People search Google, Wikipedia, and the Web because they are easy, quick, and convenient (Fast and Campbell 2004; OCLC 2010; Connaway, Dickey, and Radford 2011). They complain about how difficult it is to search the library's search systems and databases—they can't find the right keywords, are stymied by their complex and bloated interfaces, overwhelmed with too many irrelevant retrievals, and stumped about how to narrow their topics (Armstrong 2009; Head and Eisenberg 2010; Colón-Aguirre and Fleming-May 2012; Head 2013). Yet, people sense that the sources they find through the library's search systems are more credible, accurate, and reliable than open Web sources (Fast and Campbell 2004; Colón-Aguirre and Fleming-May 2012; Markey, Leeder, and Rieh 2014).

People want searching the library to resemble Google, consolidating multiple search systems and databases into a single interface, correcting their spelling, and responding with relevance-ranked retrievals to their natural language queries (Fister, Gilbert, and Fry 2008; Brophy and Bawden 2005). Libraries have responded by doing just that—deploying WSD systems that make the experience of searching licensed Web content resemble Google searching (Vaughan 2011).

For the foreseeable future, most high-quality information will reside in the licensed Web. High-quality information *is* your library's specialty. Familiarize yourself with your library's search systems and databases so that whenever you interact with library users, you know instantaneously what high-quality sources have the most potential for satisfying their information needs.

Summary

This first chapter has a historical bent to it, looking backward at the factors that have given rise to online searching to harness the information explosion and forward to advances in new technology that have steered online searching onto its present course. Online searching was born to harness the information explosion that sparked new discoveries in science and technology to keep the U.S. and its Western Bloc allies ahead of the Soviets militarily during the Cold War. The first online search systems and databases were expensive and difficult to search, so their users were librarians who were trained as expert intermediary searchers to search on behalf of others. It wasn't until the 1980s that everyday people could perform their own searches. Despite the difficulty of querying early search systems, users were delighted to search for information on their own.

The Internet was also a by-product of the Cold War. What made it so usable was Tim Berners-Lee's several inventions that gave birth to the World Wide Web. Infinitely more versatile than the printed page, the Web was an overnight success. Not only could people access information on the Web, but with a nominal investment in a computer, Internet connection, and Web browser, they could become publishers, posting anything they wanted to say to the Web, communicating instantaneously with anyone who cared to read, listen, look, watch, play, share, or like their messages. The Web grew so quickly that online searching was necessary to find what you wanted.

By the early noughties, Google became the Web search engine of choice. The number of Google searches far outnumbered searches of the library's online search systems, prompting librarians to improve their systems, going so far as to reinvent them in the image of Google with the deployment of WSD systems.

What distinguishes library- from web-based information is editorial oversight. Libraries load their database hub, OPAC, and WSD systems with high-quality information that domain experts have written, their peers have reviewed, and scholarly publishers have issued. Editorial oversight is expensive. Despite the progress of the open access movement toward its goal of unrestricted online access to scholarship, most quality information resides behind pay-walls in the licensed Web. Libraries subsidize access to the quality information in the licensed Web for their institution's users. Whether you are helping a youngster find information for a science fair project or a doctoral student conduct a thorough literature search, you will want to solve their information needs by retrieving the best, most credible, and accurate information. Thus, your starting point should be licensed Web resources—your library's gateway to high-quality information.

Bibliography

Armstrong, Annie R. 2009. "Student Perceptions of Federated Searching vs. Single Database Searching." *Reference Services Review* 37, no. 3: 291–303.

arXiv. 2015. "Five-Year Member Pledges." Last modified March 2, 2015, accessed March 25, 2015. https://confluence.cornell.edu/display/culpublic/arXiv+five-year+member+pledges.

Battelle, John. 2005. *The Search: How Google and Its Rivals Rewrote the Rules of Business and Transformed Our Culture.* New York: Portfolio.

Berners-Lee, Tim. 1999. *Weaving the Web: The Original Design and Ultimate Destiny of the World Wide Web.* New York: HarperCollins.

Björner, Susanne, and Stephanie C. Ardito. 2003. "Early Pioneers Tell Their Stories, Part 2: Growth of the Online Industry." *Searcher* 11, no. 7 (Jul./Aug.): 52–61. http://www.infotoday.com/searcher/jul03/ardito_bjorner.shtml.

Borgman, Christine. 2007. *Scholarship in the Digital Age: Information, Infrastructure, and the Internet.* Cambridge, MA: MIT Press.

Bosch, Stephen. 2005. "Buy, Build, or Lease: Managing Serials for Scholarly Communications." *Serials Review* 31, no. 2: 107–15.

Bourne, Charles P. 1980. "On-line Systems: History, Technology, and Economics." *Journal of the American Society for Information Science* 31, no. 3: 155–60.

Brophy, Jan, and David Bawden. 2005. "Is Google Enough? Comparison of an Internet Search Engine with Library Resources." *Aslib Proceedings* 57, no. 6: 498–512.

Colón-Aguirre, Mónica, and Rachel A. Fleming-May. 2012. "You Just Type in What You Are Looking For: Undergraduates' Use of Library Resources vs. Wikipedia." *Journal of Academic Librarianship* 38, no. 6: 391–99.

Connaway, Lynn Sillipigni, Timothy J. Dickey, and Marie L. Radford. 2011. "If It Is Too Inconvenient I'm Not Going After It: Convenience as a Critical Factor in Information-Seeking Behaviors." *Library & Information Science Research* 33, no. 3: 179–90.

Cummings, Anthony, et al. 1992. *University Libraries and Scholarly Communication.* Washington, DC: Association of Research Libraries.

Donlan, Rebecca, and Ana Carlin. 2007. "A Sheep in Wolf's Clothing: Discovery Tools and the OPAC." *Reference Librarian* 48, no. 2: 67–71.

Edwards, Richard, and David Shulenburger. 2003. "The High Cost of Scholarly Journals (And What to Do About It)." *Change* 35, no. 6 (Nov./Dec.): 10–19. http://kuscholarworks.ku.edu/bitstream/handle/1808/12546/Highe Cost of Scholarly - Change.pdf?sequence=1.

Emrich, Barry R. 1970. *Scientific and Technical Information Explosion.* Dayton, Ohio: Air Force Materials Laboratory, Wright-Patterson Air Force Base.

Fast, Karl V., and D. Grant Campbell. 2004. "'I Still Like Google': University Student Perceptions of Searching OPACs and the Web." *Proceedings of the ASIS Annual Meeting 2004* 41: 138–46.

Fister, Barbara, Julie Gilbert, and Amy Ray Fry. 2008. "Aggregated Interdisciplinary Databases and the Needs of Undergraduate Researchers." *portal: Libraries and the Academy* 8, no. 3: 273–92.

Fowler, Kristine K. 2011. "Mathematicians' Views on Current Publishing Issues: A Survey of Researchers." *Issues in Science & Technology Librarianship* no. 67 (Fall). http://www.istl.org/11-fall/refereed4.html.

Guédon, Claude. 2001. *In Oldenburg's Long Shadow: Librarians, Research Scientists, Publishers and the Control of Scientific Publishing.* Washington, DC: Association of Research Libraries. Accessed March 25, 2015. http://www.arl.org/storage/documents/publications/in-oldenburgs-long-shadow.pdf.

Hafner, Katie, and Matthew Lyon. 1996. *Where Wizards Stay Up Late: The Origins of the Internet.* New York: Touchstone.

Hayes, Robert M. 2010. "Library Automation: History." In *Encyclopedia of Library and Information Sciences.* 3rd ed. Volume 11, pp. 3326–37. Boca Raton, FL: CRC Press.

Head, Alison J. 2013. *How Freshmen Conduct Course Research Once They Enter College.* Accessed March 25, 2015. http://ssrn.com/abstract=2364080.

Head, Alison J., and Michael B. Eisenberg. 2010. "How Today's College Students Use Wikipedia for Course-Related Research." *First Monday* 15, no. 3. http://firstmonday.org/htbin/cgiwrap/bin/ojs/index.php/fm/article/view/2830/2476.

Head, Alison J., and Michael B. Eisenberg. 2009. "How College Students Seek Information in the Digital Age." Accessed March 25, 2015. http://www.educause.edu/library/resources/how-college-students-seek-information-digital-age.

Hildreth, Charles R. 1983. *Online Public Access Catalogs: The User Interface.* Dublin, Ohio: OCLC.

Julien, Heidi, and Susan Barker. 2009. "How High-School Students Find and Evaluate Scientific Information: A Basis for Information Literacy Skills Development." *Library and Information Science Research* 31, no. 1: 12–17.

King, Douglas. 2008. "Many Libraries Have Gone to Federated Searching to Win Users Back from Google. Is It Working?" *Journal of Electronic Resources and Librarianship* 20, no. 4: 213–27.

Lynch, Clifford. 1992. "Reaction, Response, and Realization: From the Crisis in Scholarly Communication to the Age of Networked Information." *Serials Review* 18, nos. 1/2 (Spring/Summer): 107–12.

Lynch, Clifford. 1993. "The Transformation of Scholarly Communication and the Role of the Library in the Age of Networked Information." *Serials Review* 23, nos. 3/4: 5–20.

Lynch, Clifford. 2003. "Institutional Repositories: Essential Infrastructure for Scholarship in the Digital Age." *portal: Libraries and the Academy* 3, no. 2: 327–36.

Markey, Karen. 1984. *Subject Searching in Library Catalogs.* Dublin, Ohio: OCLC.

Markey, Karen, Chris Leeder, and Soo Young Rieh. 2014. *Designing Online Information Literacy Games Students Want to Play.* Lanham, MD: Rowman & Littlefield.

Metzger, Miriam. J. 2007. "Making Sense of Credibility on the Web: Models for Evaluating Online Information and Recommendations for Future Research." *Journal of the American Society for Information Science and Technology* 58, no. 13: 2078–91.

Mischo, William H., and Jounghyoun Lee. 1987. "End-User Searching of Bibliographic Databases." *Annual Review of Information Science & Technology* 22: 227–63.

Mischo, William H., and Mary C. Schlembach. 2011. "Open Access Issues and Engineering Faculty Attitudes and Practices." *Journal of Library Administration* 51, nos. 5/6: 432–54.

OCLC. 2010. *Perceptions of Libraries, 2010: Context and Community.* Dublin, Ohio: OCLC. Accessed March 25, 2015. http://oclc.org/reports/2010perceptions.en.html.

Onwuegbuzie, Anthony J., Qun G. Jiao, and Sharon L. Bostick. 2004. *Library Anxiety: Theory, Research, and Applications.* Lanham, MD: Scarecrow Press.

Porter, Brandi. 2011. "Millennial Undergraduate Research Strategies in Web and Library Information Retrieval Systems." *Journal of Web Librarianship* 5, no. 4: 267–85.

Summit, Roger. 2002. "Reflections of the Beginnings of Dialog: The Birth of Online Information Access." *Chronolog* (June): 1–2, 10.

Vaughan, Jason. 2011. "Web Scale Discovery Services." *Library Technology Reports* 47, no. 1: 5–59.

Walraven, Amber, Saskia Brand-Gruwel, and Henry P. A. Boshuizen. 2009. "How Students Evaluate Information and Sources When Searching the World Wide Web for Information." *Computers & Education* 52, no. 1: 234–46.

Wikipedia contributors. "On the Internet, Nobody Knows You're a Dog," in *Wikipedia, The Free Encyclopedia.* Accessed March 25, 2015. http://en.wikipedia.org/wiki/On_the_Internet,_nobody_knows_you%27re_a_dog.

Willinsky, John. 2006. *The Access Principle: The Case for Open Access to Research and Scholarship.* Cambridge, MA: MIT Press.

Xia, Jingfeng. 2010. "A Longitudinal Study of Scholars' Attitudes and Behaviors toward Open-Access Journal Publishing." *Journal of the American Society for Information Science & Technology* 61, no. 3: 615–24.

Yu, Holly, and Margo Young. 2004. "The Impact of Web Search Engines on Subject Searching in OPAC." *Information Technology and Libraries* 23, no. 4 (Dec.): 168–80.

Suggested Readings

Badke, William. 2013. "The Path of Least Resistance." *Online Searcher* 37, no. 1 (Jan./Feb.): 65–67. The skinny on how most college students conduct library research.

Bourne, Charles P., and Trudi Bellardo Hahn. 2003. *A History of Online Information Services, 1963–1976.* London: MIT Press. A history of the first search systems, beginning with the experimental and demonstration systems of the 1960s and ending with the successful deployment of commercial search systems in libraries where expert intermediary searchers searched them.

Gillies, James, and Robert Cailliau. 2000. *How the Web Was Born: The Story of the World Wide Web.* Oxford: Oxford University Press. A history of the World Wide Web from its Cold War origins to the new millennium, just as Google began to rise in popularity.

2

Accessing Scholarly, Professional, and Educational Information

Not limited to brick-and-mortar buildings anymore, libraries have an online presence in the form of a homepage where they extend library services to users whether they are or aren't physically located in the library building, at any time of the day or night, and every day of the year. An important homepage service is the database hub where users access licensed and open Web databases.

Chapter 2 orients you to the library's database hub beginning with journal publishers, database publishers, database aggregators, and journal aggregators. These are big-time players in the information industry that supply the search systems and databases that librarians plug into the hub. You can rest assured that librarians have evaluated each and every database they've added to their hub, making sure the database's content is in sync with the interests of their library's users and provides access to quality information. Despite the availability of database selection tools at the hub, users rail about database selection. They want the library's search system to resemble Google where they search everything in one fell swoop. How have librarians responded? Read on!

Big-Time Information Industry Players Supplying Search Systems and Databases

Publishers of licensed and open Web databases come from the government, for-profit, and not-for-profit sectors. Especially important are professional societies that have assumed the publisher role, producing databases that serve their membership specifically and entire professions generally. Social media has also given rise to databases, making everyday people database publishers when they contribute citations, media, and/or tags to websites such as CiteULike, Flickr, and YouTube.

Database publishers employ professional staff to select content and organize it into databases. For example, database publishers may index all of the articles in a journal or index the journal selectively. For each selected article, they generate a citation, add index terms from a controlled vocabulary that describe its big ideas, and an abstract that summarizes its contents. Full-texts come from journal publishers or from journal aggregators that journal publishers license to distribute their digital content. Full-texts that are HTML files or PDFs look like a printed page in a journal. A few databases deliver full-texts in the form of text files that open in the user's preferred word processing program. Database publishers either offer online searching to their databases via their own search system or they license access to their databases to one or more database aggregators. The database aggregator indexes the database and makes it (along with many other publishers' databases) accessible to users via its proprietary search system. Because database aggregators provide access to so many databases, they are sometimes referred to as database supermarkets. Some database aggregators are also database publishers, adding their own databases to their supermarket-like search services.

The Library's Database Hub

Adding a database to a library's hub is a lengthy six-step process that begins with both librarians and prospective database users evaluating the database. Examples of the many factors dominating the evaluation are the database's contents, the range of its functionality, the usability of the database's interface, its potential user base, and its overall value (Powers 2006). Licensed databases that pass the evaluation proceed to the license negotiation and purchasing steps. The final three steps pertain to both licensed and open Web databases—profiling the database at the library's database hub, marketing it to prospective users, and maintaining it at the hub. Be prepared to evaluate new databases and shoulder responsibilities for profiling, marketing, and maintaining some of your hub's databases. At the largest libraries, one librarian may serve as the library's chief electronic resources officer, managing all of the business connected with databases, their evaluation, selection, licensing, renewal, or deselection (Weir 2012).

Accessing the Library's Database Hub

To familiarize you with a library's database hub, *Online Searching* features Search Tools, the database hub of the University of Michigan (U-M) Library, where its author is authorized to access licensed databases. Search Tools is the U-M Library's brand for its database hub. While you read about Search Tools, open your Web browser to your library's homepage and navigate to its database hub. On this homepage, look for a link named "Databases," "Research," "Articles," "Resources," "Articles and Databases," "Article Resources," or "Online Journals and Databases." Clicking on it should launch your library's database hub. Compare how Search Tools and your library's hub organize databases.

On the U-M Library's homepage (figure 2.1), the searcher clicks on the "Search Tools" link on the top right or on the "Find More Databases" link on the bottom left to navigate to the U-M Library's database hub (figure 2.2). By the way, just about everything connected with databases and search systems changes periodically, so don't be surprised if you use a database or search system and it looks different from those depicted in *Online Searching*.

According to Kathleen M. Folger, the U-M Library's chief electronic resources officer, the U-M Library provides access to over 1,200 databases. That's a lot of databases! Search Tools lends a helping hand, giving U-M Library users five ways to find relevant databases: (1) searching for a database by entering its name, subject, format, or publisher into a search box, (2) listing databases alphabetically by name from A to Z, (3) listing databases by subject from A to Z, (4) limiting databases by subject (e.g., arts, business, engineering), (5) limiting databases by resource type (e.g., article index, dictionary, images, newspapers), and (6) limiting databases by access restrictions (e.g., authorized users, on campus only, open access for all). Figure 2.3 circles and numbers these ways 1 to 6 on the full Search Tools interface.

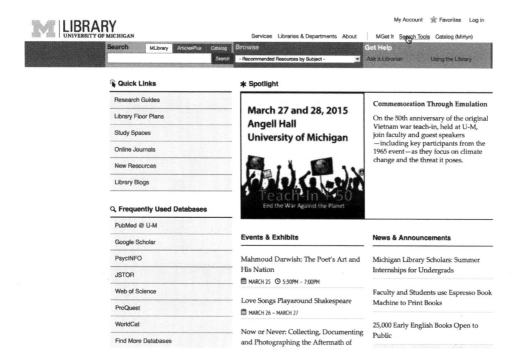

Figure 2.1. U-M Library's Homepage with "Search Tools" and "Find More Databases" Links. Screenshots made available under the Creative Commons Attribution license by the University of Michigan Library.

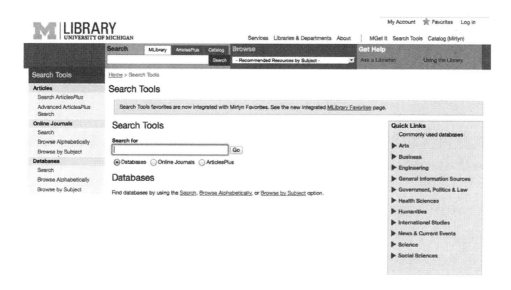

Figure 2.2. U-M Library's Database Hub Called Search Tools. Screenshots made available under the Creative Commons Attribution license by the University of Michigan Library.

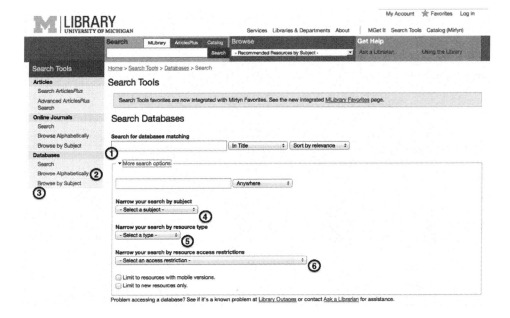

Figure 2.3. U-M Library's Full Search Tools Interface. Screenshots made available under the Creative Commons Attribution license by the University of Michigan Library.

Figure 2.4 shows that the searcher has left the search box empty, limited to the Social Sciences subject and the Article Index type to which Search Tools responds with a list of 152 databases matching these selections.

The moment the searcher clicks on a licensed Search Tools database (figure 2.4), Search Tools prompts the searcher to enter her U-M username and password. You should be able to use any library's database hub, but the moment you click on a licensed database's link, the hub will prompt you to authenticate.

Because I am a resident of the city of Ann Arbor and the State of Michigan, I can also access the database hubs of the Ann Arbor District Library (AADL at http://www.aadl.org/research) and the Michigan eLibrary (MeL at http://mel.org/Databases), authorizing with my AADL library card number or State of Michigan driver's license number, respectively.

The licenses that libraries negotiate with publishers for access to online databases are very specific about who is and who is not an authorized user. Libraries also negotiate with publishers to offer guest access to anyone who walks into the library to search licensed Web databases from their computer workstations. The U-M Library's chief electronic resources officer asserts that costs can exceed $2.5 million annually for licensed access to the most expensive databases. Personally, I couldn't afford to write *Online Searching* without the U-M Library's subsidy. Thank you, U-M Library!

Not all databases listed at a library's database hub are licensed. Librarians add links to open Web databases when they think access will benefit their library's users. Databases published by national governments, professional associations, and cultural heritage institutions such as libraries, museums, colleges, and universities are typical of the open Web databases that librarians add to their database hubs.

Whether your library has 12, 120, or 1,200 databases available to its users, finding just the right database to answer a user's query is a difficult task but one that will become increasingly easier as you gain experience using databases and answering user queries.

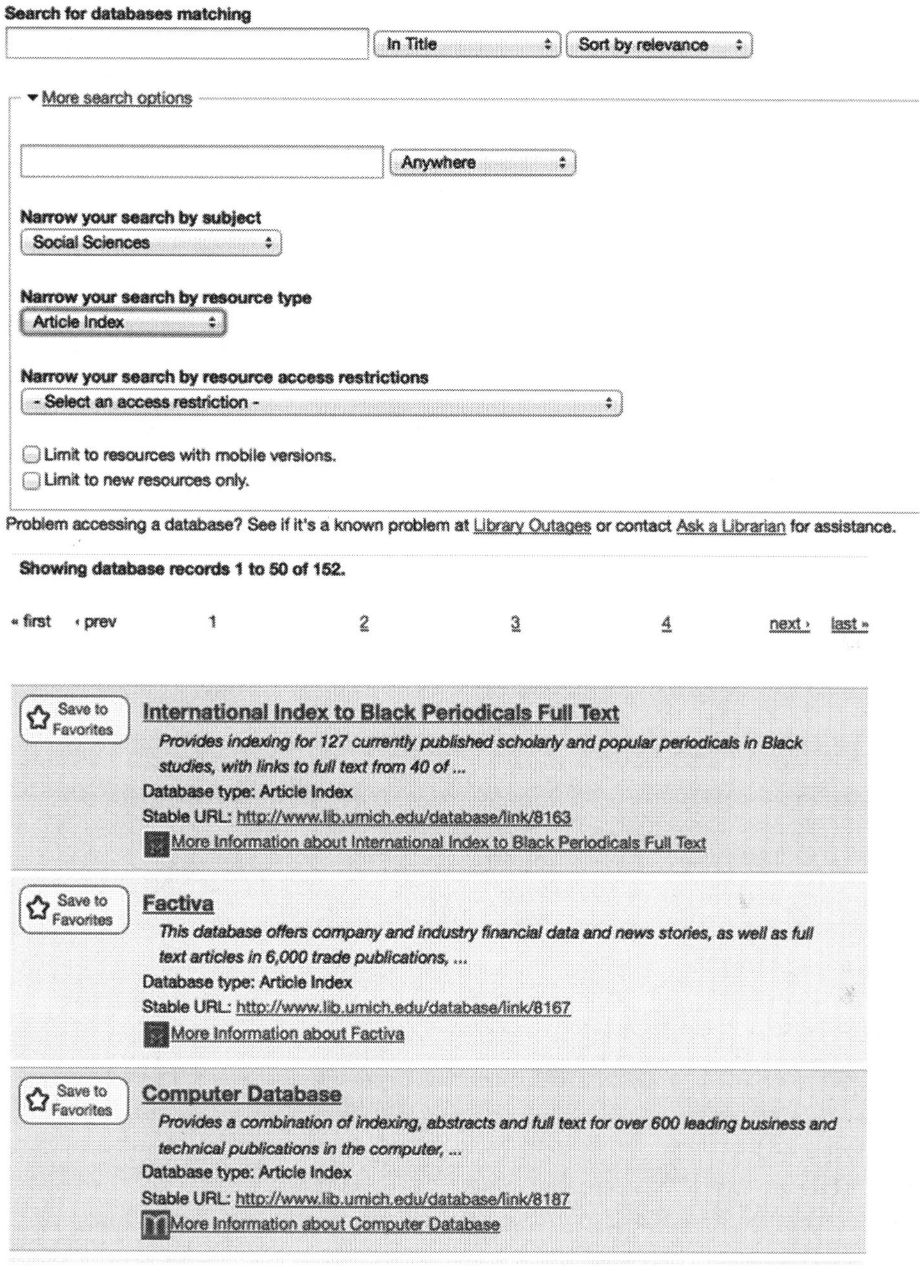

Search for databases matching

| | In Title ⇕ | Sort by relevance ⇕ |

▼ More search options

| | Anywhere ⇕ |

Narrow your search by subject
| Social Sciences ⇕ |

Narrow your search by resource type
| Article Index ⇕ |

Narrow your search by resource access restrictions
| - Select an access restriction - ⇕ |

☐ Limit to resources with mobile versions.
☐ Limit to new resources only.

Problem accessing a database? See if it's a known problem at Library Outages or contact Ask a Librarian for assistance.

Showing database records 1 to 50 of 152.

« first ‹ prev   1   2   3   4   next ›   last »

☆ Save to Favorites   **International Index to Black Periodicals Full Text**
Provides indexing for 127 currently published scholarly and popular periodicals in Black studies, with links to full text from 40 of ...
Database type: Article Index
Stable URL: http://www.lib.umich.edu/database/link/8163
More Information about International Index to Black Periodicals Full Text

☆ Save to Favorites   **Factiva**
This database offers company and industry financial data and news stories, as well as full text articles in 6,000 trade publications, ...
Database type: Article Index
Stable URL: http://www.lib.umich.edu/database/link/8167
More Information about Factiva

☆ Save to Favorites   **Computer Database**
Provides a combination of indexing, abstracts and full text for over 600 leading business and technical publications in the computer, ...
Database type: Article Index
Stable URL: http://www.lib.umich.edu/database/link/8187
More Information about Computer Database

Figure 2.4. Article Index Databases in the Social Sciences in the U-M Library's Search Tools Database Hub. Screenshots made available under the Creative Commons Attribution license by the University of Michigan Library.

Including Open Web Databases in the Hub

Everyone searches Google and Web search engines generally because doing so is quick, easy, and convenient, and they are very good at retrieving relevant information (page 5). Evaluating web-based information has become less of an issue since Google partitioned scholarly Web sources into Google Scholar. Searching Google Scholar, searchers benefit from the same search and retrieval capabilities that have made Google the go-to search engine for millions of people around the world. Google has applied these same capabilities to Google Scholar and optimized them so that Google Scholar searches give higher weights to high-cited scholarly sources than to no- or low-cited sources, ranking the high-cited sources atop Google Scholar retrieval lists.

To populate Google Scholar with scholarly content, Google scours the Web for as much free scholarly content as it can find and negotiates with database publishers for access to their content. By the way, these are the same database publishers that license their content to libraries for their database hubs and to vendors of web-scale discovery (WSD) systems for indexing in their massive indexes. Google Scholar searches retrieve scholarly sources from both the open and licensed Webs. The moment that searchers click on a full-text link from the latter, Google Scholar refers them to the full-text fulfillment websites of database publishers and journal aggregators where searchers have to enter their credit card number to download full-texts. To make such publisher pay-walls transparent to their users, libraries have enhanced Google Scholar with resolver links so that users who launch Google Scholar at the library's database hub are automatically authorized to retrieve the library's licensed content.

Table 2.1 lists several open Web databases for scholarly, professional, and educational information.

If an academic institution excels in a particular subject or field of study or hosts a special collection, check its database hub in case it sponsors an open Web database that may be of interest to your library's users and warrants entry into your library's database hub. For example, Cornell University's world-renowned Lab of Ornithology publishes the All About Birds database on the open Web, a database that would be especially appropriate for public library database hubs and for academic libraries in educational institutions where ornithology is taught because of the Lab's leadership in bird study, appreciation, and conservation (Cornell Lab of Ornithology 2015).

Accessing the Library's Web-Scale Discovery System

An alternative to choosing a database at the hub is searching the library's web-scale discovery (WSD) system. The WSD system is a new innovation, available since 2007, and one that is particularly attractive to academic libraries because it enables users to search a large portion of the library's digital holdings in one fell swoop—just like they search Google. Libraries have a choice of four WSD systems: (1) Discovery Service from EBSCO, (2) Primo from Ex Libris, (3) Summon from ProQuest, and (4) WorldCat Local from OCLC. The U-M Library's WSD is ProQuest's Summon but the Library brands it as "ArticlesPlus" (figure 2.1). Authorized U-M users click on the ArticlesPlus tab and enter a query that the ArticlesPlus WSD system searches across massive indexes that represent a large portion of the U-M Library's digital content. Like Google, ArticlesPlus responds with relevance-ranked results.

Check your library's homepage for its WSD system, looking for a single search box and a tab or link named:

- "Everything"
- The brand name of the WSD system such as "Primo" or "Summon"

Table 2.1. Open Web Databases Suitable for Library Database Hubs

Database Name	Contents	Database Publisher	URL
arXiv	Full-text research articles in physics and related scientific disciplines	Cornell University	http://arxiv.org/
CORSAIR	Full-color images from the library's collection of medieval manuscripts	The Pierpont Morgan Library	http://corsair.morganlibrary.org/
ERIC	Surrogate records and selected full-text journal articles and gray literature in education and library and information science	(U.S.) Institute of Education Sciences	http://eric.ed.gov/
Making of America	Full-text primary sources on American social history	University of Michigan and Cornell University and funded by the Mellon Foundation	http://quod.lib.umich.edu/m/moa/
OAIster	Digital artifacts that are the by-product of academic research initiatives	OCLC Online Computer Library Center	http://oaister.worldcat.org/
Perseus Digital Library	Full-text primary and secondary sources for the study of ancient Greece and Rome	Tufts University	http://www.perseus.tufts.edu/hopper/

- A list of library resources such as "Search articles, journals, books, media, and more," "Find articles, journals, books, videos, and more," or "Articles and books"
- The library's brand name such "ArticlesPlus," "CatSearch," "ChinookPlus," "Esearch," "Herdsearch," "Powersearch," "Smart Search," and "UDiscover"

Figure 2.5 simulates how a college student would search a WSD system—the searcher enters his natural language query "effect of sleep on academic performance" directly into the ArticlesPlus search box. If your library has a WSD system, choose it on your library's homepage and enter the same search statement to experience a WSD system firsthand.

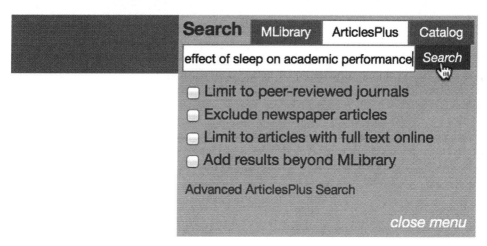

Figure 2.5. Entering a Query into the U-M Library's ArticlesPlus WSD System. Screenshots made available under the Creative Commons Attribution license by the University of Michigan Library.

In figure 2.6, ArticlesPlus responds with a report of about a quarter-million results and lists the first twenty retrievals. Accompanying retrievals are the U-M Library's branded MGetIt buttons. These buttons are resolver links—click on one and it goes to work, passing the retrieval's citation data to a link resolver that checks to see whether the library holds or owns full-text or media in another database, and when it does, retrieves and displays the actual source to the user. ArticlesPlus also clusters search results, using *Publication Date, Format, Subject*, and *Language* to characterize the search's quarter-million results alongside the left side of the page. The *Subjects* cluster is especially helpful, enabling users to browse co-occurring subtopics and click on ones that pique their interest or express something they had in mind but failed to express in their query. In figure 2.6, the first two listed sources seem particularly relevant. The searcher could click on the "more . . ." link to read these sources' abstracts, click on accompanying MGetIt buttons to retrieve full-texts, or explore the clusters listed on the left side of the page.

For WSD-system vendors to develop and maintain a comprehensive database, they must cultivate a relationship with just about every publisher on the planet, securing their digital content, preferably *both* surrogates and full-text sources, for their WSD systems to index, retrieve, and display. Establishing successful relationships with database publishers may seem simple for WSD-system vendors to do, but such relationships are actually very complicated because the content that database publishers license to libraries for their database hubs is the same as the content WSD-system vendors want to add to their systems. Database publishers know that the WSD system will compete with libraries' database hubs, and they are quick to do the math—counting four WSD-system vendors versus thousands of libraries hosting database hubs.

When it comes to securing digital content from database publishers, WSD-system vendors fight an uphill battle. They might secure citations only from database publishers because database publishers want to be exclusive, marketing their databases of citations *enhanced* with index

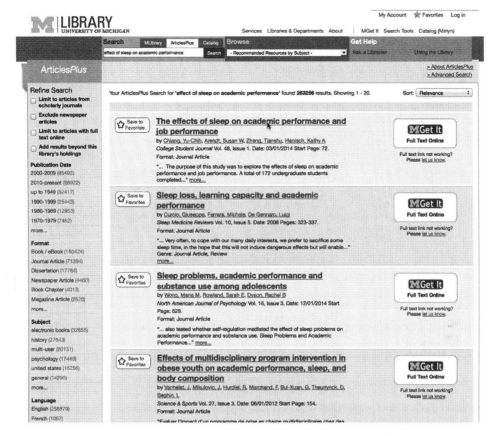

Figure 2.6. Search Results in the ArticlesPlus WSD System. Screenshots made available under the Creative Commons Attribution license by the University of Michigan Library.

terms, abstracts, author-supplied keywords, and even cited references to libraries for their database hubs. Ultimately, WSD-system vendors are likely to negotiate "some kind of reciprocal arrangement of other incentives" to win over database publishers (Breeding 2014, 13–14).

Questions

Here are questions to give you hands-on experience using your library's database hub, WSD system, online public access catalog (OPAC), and institutional repository (IR). Answers conclude the chapter.

1. Launch your library's homepage. On what link(s) do you click to navigate to your library's database hub? What is the name of the link that launches the hub? How far can you drill down into the hub before you must authenticate as a library cardholder? What tools does the hub give to you to find relevant databases?
2. Revisit your library's homepage. On what link(s) do you click to navigate to your library's WSD system? What is the name of the link that launches the system? How far can you drill down into the system before you must authenticate as a library cardholder?
3. Repeat question #2, replacing your library's WSD system for its OPAC.
4. Repeat question #2, replacing your library's WSD system for its IR.

Summary

Chapter 2 orients you to the library's database hub where librarians plug in licensed and open Web databases that they have evaluated and deemed useful for their clientele. Some licensed databases come with a hefty price tag, the most expensive ones costing the library in the millions of dollars annually. To access databases, users authenticate themselves as library cardholders at the database hub so that they can download content to read, see, watch, or hear. Typical database selection tools that hubs feature to help users find promising databases are direct searches for databases by name and alphabetical lists of databases by subject, name, or format.

Some users of academic libraries circumvent the database hub, searching the library's web-scale discovery (WSD) system that features a simple Google-like interface to the library's quality content with its single search box and relevance-ranked retrievals accompanied by resolver links. Users who search Google Scholar directly encounter publisher pay-walls that request credit card payment every time they want to download retrieved full-texts or media. Avoid these links by launching Google Scholar through your library's database hub.

Bibliography

Breeding, Marshall. 2014. "Library Resource Discovery Products: Context, Library Perspectives, and Vendor Positions." *Library Technology Reports* 50, no. 1.

Cornell Lab of Ornithology. 2015. "The Birds of North America Online." http://bna.birds.cornell .edu/bna/.

Powers, Audrey. 2006. "Evaluating Databases for Acquisitions and Collection Development." In *Handbook of Electronic and Digital Acquisitions*, edited by Thomas W. Leonhardt, 41–60. Binghamton, NY: Haworth Press.

Weir, Ryan O. 2012. (See Suggested Readings below.)

Suggested Readings

Breeding, Marshall. 2012. "Looking Forward to the New Generation of Discovery Services." *Computers in Libraries* 32, no. 2: 28–31. A very brief overview of the functionality of state-of-the-art WSD systems and how they will evolve in the years to come. For an in-depth analysis, consult this author's *Library Technology Reports* in this chapter's bibliography above.

Mischo, William H. 2001. "Library Portals, Simultaneous Search, and Full-Text Linking Technologies." *Science & Technology Libraries* 20, nos. 2/3: 133–47. Sensing that users will prefer one-stop shopping over the database hub, Mischo builds and deploys Search Aid, a federated (also called metasearch) engine at the University of Illinois' Grainger Library, that submits the user's query to multiple databases in one fell swoop. Federated search is the precursor to today's WSD systems.

Weir, Ryan O. 2012. *Managing Electronic Resources.* Chicago: ALA Techsource. Learn about the job responsibilities of the electronic resources officer who manages much of the library's business connected with electronic resources.

Answers

1. *Database hub.* On your library's homepage, look for a link named "Databases," "Research," "Articles," "Resources," "Articles and Databases," "Article Resources," or "Online Journals and Databases." Most likely your hub requires you to authenticate when you click on a link that opens a licensed database where you enter a search statement. Here are ten selection

approaches, and your research may reveal even more: (1–5) searching by database name, keyword, database publisher, database aggregator, or ISSN, (6–9) browsing lists of databases organized by subject, by database names A–Z, by most commonly used databases, or by genre, or (10) consulting the library's LibGuides especially for specific disciplines or fields of study.

2. *WSD system.* Not all libraries have a WSD system. On your library's homepage, look for a single search box, possibly accompanied by a label such as "Find articles, journals, and more." Most likely your WSD system requires you to authenticate when you click on a resolver link that downloads a full-text or media.

3. *OPAC.* All libraries have an OPAC. On your library's homepage, look for a link bearing the word "catalog" or "books" or given a name with local significance such as Mirlyn, Consort, or Magic. Authentication shouldn't be necessary unless you aren't a library cardholder and visit the library, fetching materials from its bookshelves with the intent of borrowing them.

4. *IRs.* IRs are typical of academic libraries, but not all such libraries have an IR. The link to your library's IR might not be obvious because the phrase "institutional repository" isn't likely to be understandable to end users. Your IR might be a name with local significance such as Deep Blue, Knowledge Bank, and IDEALS, or a "Services" link might display a secondary page where the IR is listed. Open access is fundamental to the IR's mission so authentication won't be necessary. Accompanying surrogate records will be direct links to the actual sources themselves.

3

The Reference Interview for In-Depth Queries

Ultimately, you are learning about online databases, search systems, and searching tools so that you can apply your knowledge to help library users satisfy their information needs. Your interaction with users in which they express these needs is called the reference interview. "Without doubt, the negotiation of reference questions is one of the most complex acts of human communication. During this process, one person tries to describe for another person not something he knows, but rather something he does not know" (Taylor 1968, 180).

Online Searching's treatment of the reference interview probes interviews that elicit in-depth queries from users and require thorough database searches. These are searches that produce multiple retrievals, none of which answers the user's question entirely. To generate answers, users must extract useful information from retrievals and synthesize what they learn to answer their queries.

Now that reference collections in particular have gone almost entirely digital, you may respond to most user queries with online searches. Initially, it may be difficult to distinguish queries that require in-depth searches from all the rest of the queries that come your way. Eventually, you will sense the open-ended nature of in-depth queries, and instead of searching for hard-and-fast answers for them, you will respond with in-depth searches and engage users in the process of identifying relevant retrievals so you can use them to find more information or take the search in new directions.

Because this chapter's focus is on reference interviews that give rise to in-depth queries, you should round out your understanding by consulting books that focus exclusively on the reference interview (Ross, Nilsen, and Radford 2009; Harmeyer 2014) or the briefer one-chapter treatments of the reference interview in the major textbooks on reference services (Bopp and Smith 2011; Cassell and Hiremath 2011). The reference interview is core to librarianship, so prepare yourself to the nines.

Models of the Information Seeking Process

This chapter's examination of the reference interview begins with information seeking models. Models are used to shrink real-world situations, processes, and systems down to their essential components. They help us understand complex phenomena and make them easier to study. Here are five models of the information seeking process to help you bridge the gap between understanding this process and being a key participant in it.

Classic Model of Communication

The classic model of communication is represented as a one-way street involving a sender, message, transmission, noise, channel, reception, and receiver (Shannon and Weaver 1949, 5). Although this model has been criticized for its one-sided nature, you merely have to turn it on its head to represent communication that is a conversation between two people or an interaction between a user and a search system.

Consider how the typical reference interview unfolds. The sender is an undergraduate student, the message is his query, the transmission is human speech, the noise is one or more factors affecting one or more elements in the chain, the channel is the English language, the reception is hearing, and the receiver is you—the reference librarian. Consider the noise that might affect each element in the chain (figure 3.1). Sender noise may be the student's low-level understanding of the topic he seeks. Message noise may be the student's partial expression of what he wants. Transmission noise may be the student's English-language description of his information needs, trying to put into words something he doesn't know. Reception noise may be actual noise—the hustle and bustle of classes changing that increases the noise level in the library making it hard for the librarian to hear what the student is saying. Receiver noise may be you, the reference librarian, tired as a result of heavy partying the night before. When the classic model is applied to the reference interview, a host of factors may impinge on the user's query so that its initial expression in the sender's mind will be quantitatively and qualitatively different from its eventual representation in the mind of the receiver. This is especially important when one considers that our scenario's receiver is the reference librarian who will eventually assume much of the burden of resolving the sender's message by searching for information online.

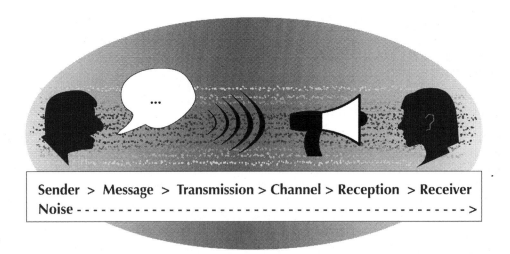

Sender > Message > Transmission > Channel > Reception > Receiver
Noise ->

Figure 3.1. Classic Model of Communication. Adapted from Shannon and Weaver (1949).

Levels of Question Formation

Putting the queries that users pose to librarians under the microscope is Robert S. Taylor's levels of question formation model. In an oft-cited article, Taylor (1968, 182) defines four question types, Q1 to Q4:

Q1 Actual but unexpressed need for information (*visceral* need). A conscious or unconscious need that changes in form, quality, and concreteness as the user encounters everyday life.

Q2 Conscious, within-brain description of an ill-defined area of indecision (*conscious* need). This may be a rambling statement, and it is at this stage that the user may talk to someone to sharpen his focus or initiate a search.

Q3 Formal need statement (*formalized* need). The user is able to form a qualified and rational statement in concrete terms. The user may or may not be thinking of the context or constraints of the system from which he wants information.

Q4 Question as presented to the information system (*compromised* need). This is the representation of the user's information need within the constraints of the search system and database.

Taylor's model demonstrates that queries do not pop up instantaneously without some forethought and deliberation on the part of the user. Users experiencing Q1 might not even be aware that they have an information need. They encounter life, various phenomena garnering their attention momentarily and passing away. Their Q2 expressions may range from a patchwork of words and phrases that they can barely put into a sentence to rambling statements that have little focus or substance. When librarians encounter users with Q2 needs, they may find it difficult to understand them and embark on a plan of action, but they should be prepared for this eventuality. Textbox 3.1 describes a role-playing exercise in which you may be able to experience Q2 questions from the perspective of the end user or reference librarian or both.

The Q3 question is a qualified and rational statement of the end user's desires in concrete terms. While negotiation that enables the librarian to develop a full understanding of the user's query might be necessary, it is less protracted than in Q2 questions and transitions in a timely manner to related concerns such as how much information is needed, how technical or scholarly the information should be, deadlines connected with the project, and so on. Q4 questions are the actual search statements that users or librarians enter into search systems. Taylor's name for Q4 questions—the compromised need—is especially appropriate because it acknowledges that user queries and the search statements that librarians helping them enter into search systems are not one and the same.

Search Strategy Process Model

The Search Strategy Process (SSP) Model uses genre to rank order reference sources so that users' exposure to sources ranked early in the process primes them intellectually for the more complex, technical, and advanced reference sources ranked later in the process (Kirk 1974). Encyclopedias and dictionaries come first because their entries are basic and foundational, intended for readers whose knowledge of a discipline and its topics is elementary. Next, the SSP Model recommends users consult cited sources in encyclopedia and dictionary entries because such sources are usually seminal, enabling users to gradually build up their knowledge of a topic. The SSP Model recommends the library catalog next, then abstracting and indexing (A&I) sources, and, finally, citation indexes, because increasingly greater sophistication and domain knowledge are needed to understand the sources that these three genres serve up.

Textbox 3.1. Helping Users Transition from Q2 (Conscious) to Q3 (Formal Need) Questions

To perform this role-playing exercise, work with a partner from your Online Searching class. One person plays the role of the end user and the second person plays the role of the reference librarian. You could even switch roles at some point.

Before getting started, the person playing the end user role should think about a topic that interests him or her and hasn't had time to pursue in terms of conducting research online. It could be a topic of personal interest or a topic that she or he must write about for another class but hasn't yet started to research. Don't give this much thought and *don't* spend time searching online in advance.

Here is your role-playing assignment. The end user approaches the librarian and expresses his or her query. The librarian reacts, getting the end user started. Both end user and librarian need to decide what "started" means within the context of the role-playing episode and when to stop. The episode should include these events:

- The end user describing his or her information needs to the librarian
- The librarian listening to the end user and negotiating with the user to arrive at a full understanding of the user's query
- Getting the user started on his or her search for information that might include user and librarian working together online to find relevant information.

When you are done, take a few minutes to answer these questions:

1. (For both) Do you think that the end user's initial expression of his or her query was comparable to the Q2 question that Taylor had in mind? Why or why not? Was it a Q3 question instead? Why do you think it was a Q3 question?
2. (For the librarian) Do you think that you understood the user's query? Why or why not? What strategies did you use to facilitate your understanding? What worked, what didn't work, and why?
3. (For the end user) Do you think the librarian understood your query? Why or why not? How do you think she or he could have done a better job developing such an understanding?
4. (For both) As a result of the negotiation that went on between the two of you, what does the user really want? Are you both in agreement as to what the negotiated query is? (The negotiated query is the librarian's understanding of what the user wants as a result of conducting a reference interview with the user.) Do you detect differences between the initial query and negotiated query, and if you do, what are they?
5. (For both) Did you go online to find relevant information? If yes, did the two of you contribute equally to the finding process or did one person contribute more than the other? What were your respective contributions during the finding process?

If you role play in class, be prepared to share your answers to questions in a class discussion.

Berrypicking Model

Accounting for searches that aren't one-time events is the Berrypicking Model (Bates 1989). This model acknowledges that people search for information repeatedly on the same or similar topics, that they apply the sources that they've found to the situation at hand, and in the course of doing so, their knowledge increases (figure 3.2). As a result, the next time they search, their follow-up query has changed, which effects changes in the questions they ask librarians, the search statements they enter into search systems, and their relevance assessments of the new sources that their follow-up searches retrieve. This sequence of events may continue for many years, especially in the case of domain experts—scholars, scientists, and veteran researchers—who build on the results of current research initiatives when proposing new research and advising and teaching students.

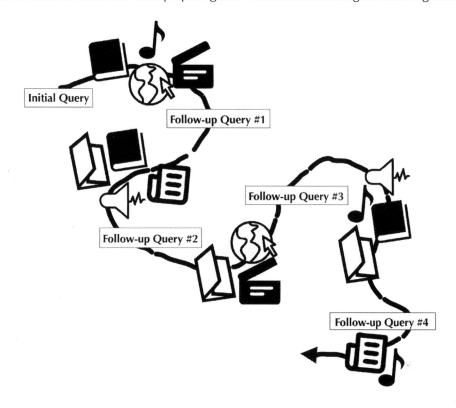

Figure 3.2. Berrypicking Model. Adapted from Bates (1989, 410). Created using symbols from the Noun Project (http://thenounproject.com): "Book" symbol by Simple Icons; "Music Note" symbol by Parker Foote; "Internet" symbol by Jaclyne Ooi; "Clapperboard" symbol by Adrien Griveau; "Document" symbol by Claudiu Sergiu Danaila; "Audio" symbol by iconsmind.com; "Newspaper" symbol by Quan Do.

Information Search Process (ISP) Model

The Information Search Process (ISP) Model describes the user's information seeking experience as an evolving process that involves specific thoughts, feelings, and actions (Kuhlthau 2003). Dividing information seeking into six stages, Kuhlthau (2013) names and describes each stage along with the feelings users experience:

1. Initiation, when a person first becomes aware of a lack of knowledge or understanding. Feelings of uncertainty and apprehension are common.
2. Selection, when the person identifies a general area, topic, or problem, and his or her initial uncertainty often gives way to a brief sense of optimism and a readiness to begin the search.

3. Exploration, when inconsistent, incompatible information is encountered and uncertainty, confusion, and doubt frequently increase and people find themselves "in the dip" of confidence.
4. Formulation, when a focused perspective is formed and uncertainty diminishes as confidence begins to increase.
5. Collection, when information pertinent to the focused perspective is gathered and uncertainty subsides as interest and involvement deepen.
6. Presentation, when the search is completed with a new understanding enabling the person to explain his or her learning to others or in some way put the learning to use. Accompanied by feelings of relief with a sense of satisfaction for a search gone well or disappointment if it has not.

Figure 3.3 lists these stages from left to right along with the feelings people experience at each stage. In between is the "feeling" space with the middle, top, and bottom areas representing neutral, comfortable, and uncomfortable feelings, respectively. Flowing from left to right through this space is a purposeful line that represents how information seekers feel at each stage in the process. Notice how this line has several possible ending points depending upon whether people are satisfied, relieved, or disappointed with their search.

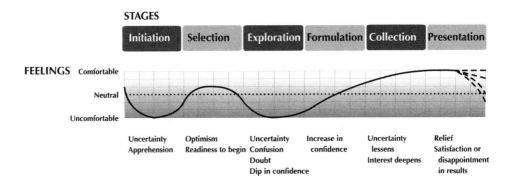

Figure 3.3. The Feelings People Experience When Searching for Information. Adapted from Kuhlthau (2003).

No one likes feeling uncomfortable, but the ISP Model tells us that such feelings are inevitable and experienced more than once in between spates of neutral or comfortable feelings (Kuhlthau 2003; Kracker and Wang 2002). Because information seeking is an emotional roller coaster, it may be worthwhile for librarians to tell information seekers to expect ups and downs so that they know what to expect, are less likely to procrastinate, and don't give up when they feel bad.

The Nature of the Reference Interview

The reference interview is a conversational exchange between a librarian and a library user in which the user is likely to describe something she doesn't know, and thus, requires negotiation so that the librarian is able to determine what the user really wants. The interview usually but not necessarily includes the librarian's search of the library collection for what he believes is relevant information that he passes on to the user with the expectation that it has the potential to completely or partially resolve the user's unknowable state. The crux of the exchange is the negotiation between user and reference librarian in which the librarian queries the user to find out what she wants so that he can search library resources for answers. Some reference interviews are brief because the user expresses what she wants right from the get-go, and others are protracted due to the negotiation that is needed for the librarian to develop an understanding of what the user wants and the complexity of using certain library resources to generate usable answers.

Researchers who have studied the reference interview observe that certain behavioral attributes on the part of the reference librarian are likely to leave library users with positive perceptions of the librarian's performance and of libraries generally. In response, the Reference & User Services Association (RUSA), the division of the American Library Association that specializes in reference services, has published guidelines for the behavioral performance of reference interview providers that advise them to be approachable, interested, a good communicator, an effective searcher, and capable of conducting follow-up to the original interaction (RUSA 2015).

Make a mental note of the guidelines you know you will accomplish with ease and capitalize on them initially. As your confidence increases, identify guidelines you know are not your forte, observe how your more experienced librarian colleagues handle themselves, and model their behavior. Consider complimenting them on their performance and asking if they had difficulties initially, what they were, and how they have been able to overcome them.

Phases of the Reference Interview

Underlying the RUSA guidelines is a seven-phased reference interview process. Figure 3.4 shows this process along with iterative loops back to earlier phases for reference interviews that fail or get off track.

Initially, researchers evaluated the reference interview based on the accuracy of the answers the librarian gave to users (Hernon and McClure 1986; 1987). Subsequent research has demonstrated that library users rate the success of the reference interview less on whether the provided information is useful and on-target and more on the quality of their interaction with the librarian, especially whether they would consult the librarian in the future; conversely, librarians rate success based on the quality of the information they provide to users (Durrance 1989; Radford 1999; Saxton and Richardson 2002).

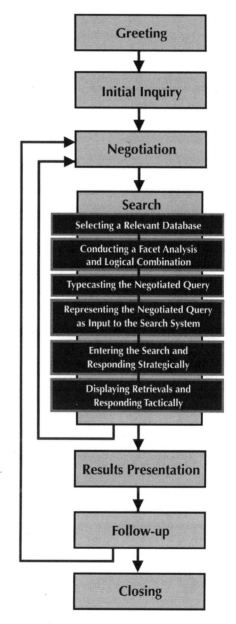

Figure 3.4. Phases of the Reference Interview.

Greeting Phase

The in-person reference interview begins with a greeting such as "Hi, may I help you?" The librarian's smile, relaxed demeanor, eye contact, and open body stance all contribute to putting the user at ease and establishing rapport so that the user feels comfortable and the interview begins on a positive note.

Personally, I do not like the greeting "Hi, how may I help you?" because it might suggest to the user that she must know *how* the librarian can help her, and thus, predispose her to phrase her initial question in a way that anticipates what the librarian should do with the query, for example, what database the librarian should choose or what search statements he should enter to produce useful retrievals. Use instead a greeting that encourages users to say what is on their mind, to "spill the beans," so to speak, so that you can gain an understanding of what they want and use it to initiate the search.

First impressions go a long way toward setting the tone of the interaction yet to come, and thus, your overall demeanor should convey the message to everyone around you that you are approachable, friendly, and eager and willing to help. If you are working on an unrelated task while you are on duty at the reference desk, make sure it isn't a task that will totally consume your attention and every inch of the desk in front of you because users may be hesitant to approach and interrupt you, especially those who have the slightest inkling of reluctance to ask for help. Because one insignificant sign of non-approachability could send them scurrying in the opposite direction, it is important to send a message that you are ready, prepared, and pleased to help everyone, and it is your job to do so.

If you are helping one user and notice more users approaching, smile and make eye contact so they know they have been seen. You may be uncomfortable interrupting the on-going reference interview to verbally acknowledge them with a comment such as "I'll be with you shortly," so a non-verbal signal such as a nod of the head while you smile and make eye contact may be a good substitute.

Library reference staff may have an agreed-upon greeting for answering the phone at the reference desk that includes the name of the library and varies depending upon how busy the staff member is. If you smile while you answer the phone, your voice is likely to convey the smile, sending a signal to the inquirer that you are pleased they have called and ready and willing to help them. If you can't manage a smile, answer the phone with an upbeat and enthusiastic tone of voice so that the interaction starts on a positive note.

Email reference service usually requires users to complete a web-administered form that asks them about themselves and their query so you'll be able to jumpstart your interaction with them. Users contacting you via your library's chat/instant messaging service might test the waters, asking if there's anyone there, or blurt out what's on their mind.

Initial Inquiry Phase

The interview transitions to the initial inquiry when users make a statement that describes what they want. Librarians agree that users' initial inquiries rarely describes what they really want, and there is a mountain of research that confirms their suspicions (Dewdney and Michell 1997; Ross 2003; Radford et al. 2011). Consider this reference interview:

Librarian: Hi, can I help you?

User: I need some books on alcoholism.

Librarian: Okay. [Types the subject heading "Alcoholism" into the library catalog.] We have lots of books on alcoholism. It looks like most of them have the call number 362.29. I'll write that down for you. Take a look at the books there and you'll probably find what you're looking for.

User: Thanks. [Leaves for the bookshelves.]

No negotiation between the librarian and the user takes place. The librarian takes this user's query at face value, checks the library catalog for the right call number, and dispatches the user to the bookshelves where she can browse books on alcoholism. Let's see what happens when the librarian negotiates the user's initial query:

Librarian: Hi, can I help you?

User: I need some books on alcoholism.

Librarian: We have lots of books on alcoholism. Tell me what it is about alcoholism that interests you. [Navigates to the library catalog just in case.]

User: Like I'm interested in recovery and meetings and stuff.

Librarian: Okay. We can look for books that talk about what happens at meetings . . . how meetings help with recovery.

User: Yes, meetings. Are there meetings around here?

Librarian: Well, let's check a local events calendar for campus and then for Ann Arbor . . .

This reference interview has a different outcome because the librarian probes the user's interest in alcoholism by saying "Tell me what it is about alcoholism that interests you," to which the user volunteers more information, first "recovery and meetings" and then "meetings around here." These cue the librarian to what the user really wants—a list of the closest Alcoholics Anonymous meetings to campus, their exact locations, and meeting times. Consider this reference interview:

Librarian: Hi, can I help you?

User: Do you have a map of the UP?

Stop right there and ponder the librarian's next step. He could take this initial query at face value, referring the user to the library's map room where atlases and maps are stored or to map websites on the open Web. Instead, he probes the user's initial interest in maps:

Librarian: Sure, but is there something in particular about the Upper Peninsula that interests you?

User: Yeah. The UP's parks and wilderness areas.

Librarian: Okay. So you are interested in the parks and wilderness areas up north. Anything else?

User: I'm going birding.

Librarian: Okay. Is there a particular type of forest or wilderness area that is best for birding in the UP?

User: I want to see a Connecticut Warbler—that's where they nest, up in the UP— and see a few other northern species while I'm there.

Librarian: Okay. So you are interested in finding Connecticut Warblers and other birds in the UP.

User: Yeah.

Librarian: Let's search the eBird database where birdwatchers record the species they've seen. Maybe they've reported the bird you want to see plus its location in the UP . . .

This second reference interview starts with the user pursuing a map of Michigan's Upper Peninsula (UP) and ends with the librarian and the user searching the eBird database on the open Web for reports of the species that interests the user. The librarian may work with the user for a while, both of them figuring out how to search eBird for a particular species in the geographical location that interests the user. When they do, the librarian is likely to pass the searching task on to the user so she can search all the species that interest her and triangulate an area where she'll see most of the birds that interest her.

Both chats above capture interactions with users who don't immediately disclose their interests to the librarian. Table 3.1 tells why people aren't forthcoming about their interests.

Of these reasons, the user seeking "some books on alcoholism" is probably concerned about self-disclosure, and the user seeking "a map of the UP" probably doesn't think the librarian knows enough about her subject to be able to help her. These are just guesses. You'll never know, and knowing the reason doesn't help you answer the question. The bottom line is that users' initial inquiry rarely describes what they really want, and as a consequence, you have to negotiate all your interactions with users to find out what they really want.

Table 3.1. Reasons Why People Don't Reveal Their Real Information Needs, Adapted from Ross, Nilsen, and Radford (2009, 18)

Overall Reasons	Specific Reasons
The nature of the reference interview	Users' initial inquiries are their way of starting up and getting involved in the interaction.
	Users think they are being helpful by expressing their queries in ways that anticipate the systems that librarians will search to produce relevant retrievals or the genres that will characterize relevant retrievals.
The difficulty of developing a searchable topic	Users express their queries in broader terms than their specific topics, thinking that if the library has information on the former, they will be able to find information on the latter.
	Users don't know the "enormous extent of information" that is available in the library.
	"Users are just beginning to explore" their topics and are sampling what's available in the library.
	Users don't know whether there is anything to be found on their topic.
	Users asking an imposed query are unsure what the original requestor wants.

(continued)

Table 3.1. Reasons Why People Don't Reveal Their Real Information Needs, Adapted from Ross, Nilsen, and Radford (2009, 18) *continued*

Overall Reasons	Specific Reasons
The difficulty of expressing one's information needs to someone else	Users don't know what they want, and it is difficult for them to express what they don't know in the course of asking someone else to help them find it.
	Users think that they have to express their queries in ways that anticipate what librarians will do to find useful information for them.
	Users don't realize that even simple requests such as "I'd like information on football" are bereft of the context that they have in mind. To successfully communicate their needs, they have to add context to their queries, for example, "football in the United States . . . the college game . . . injuries . . . particularly to the head."
The erroneous assumptions users have about libraries and their resources	Users think libraries are information supermarkets where they are on their own except to ask for directions when they can't find something.
	Users think libraries and their systems are simple and they can figure them out if only they had a few clues as to how things work.
	Users don't "volunteer information that they do not perceive as relevant, and they don't understand the relevance because they don't know how the system works."
	Users don't know that the library's mission includes a commitment to service and helping people like themselves find information.
The erroneous assumptions users have about librarians	Users don't know that librarians are there to help them satisfy their information needs.
	Users don't think librarians know enough about their specific topics to be able to help them.
	Users don't want to bother librarians who they think have more important things to do.
Users who want to be seen as competent, secure, and knowledgeable	Users avoid self-disclosure, especially if their queries reveal financial, health, or legal issues they are dealing with or sensitive personal matters that they feel expose something about them or makes them feel vulnerable.
	Users think that the librarian will consider them to be incompetent, dumb, or worse because they have to ask for help.
	Users think that the librarian will think they are cheating when they ask for homework help.

Negotiation Phase

The negotiation phase is the crux of the reference interview when the librarian determines what the user really wants. Getting it wrong means that whatever you do or advise the user to do may be for naught because both you and the user are on the wrong path toward an answer. As a result, the user might regret her interaction with you, making her less likely to consult you or librarians generally in the future. Even when the user appears confident, assertive, and totally knowledgeable of the topic, you should probe by asking open-ended questions such as "what kind of information are you looking for?," "what specifically are you looking for relating to the [topic]?," or "tell me more about your [topic]?," just in case the user has something in mind that she is not revealing. Consider this chat between user and librarian:

User:	Hi, I'm looking for something on the Vietnam War.
Librarian:	Welcome to Ask a Librarian. What specifically are you looking for relating to the Vietnam War?
User:	Well, I'm interested in the response to the war that old veterans are having.
Librarian:	Okay, so how veterans of the Vietnam War are looking back at it in a more current time?
User:	More like the old veterans who are going back to Vietnam. Some just visit and others actually stay and do good things. I want to know the reasons why they go back, okay?
Librarian:	Okay, please hold while I look . . .

The user begins the interaction, telling the librarian she is interested in the Vietnam War. Do not expect the interaction to proceed immediately from initial query to the negotiated query just because you used one open-ended question. It may take several back-and-forth interactions for you to understand what exactly the user wants. Be prepared for reference interviews that leave you hanging, wondering whether you truly understood what the user wanted. In some of these interviews, the user won't know what she wants—she is testing the waters, determining whether there is any information available to warrant her further investment in the topic and seeing what interests her.

Vietnam War Vets is an example of an in-depth subject query that may take time to set up and conduct, so you might ask the user whether she is in the library or at home, and in the case of the former, invite her to meet you at the reference desk or your office where you can involve her in the search more directly, negotiating her interests, gathering search terms, getting her immediate feedback on retrievals' relevance, and so on.

Distinguishing features of in-depth queries are their open-endedness—the impossibility of finding one rock-solid answer to the question. Instead, users must gather as much information as possible, study it, and generate an answer or course of action based on their knowledge and understanding of everything they have read. Especially in academic settings, users typically report the results of their analysis in written form—an essay, journal article, or book; however, they could just as well put the results to work—arriving at a decision, making a diagnosis, or building something.

OPEN-ENDED QUESTIONS

Open-ended questions are your secret weapon for getting users to open up about their real interests because they are meant to elicit anything *but* the user's yes or no response. Interspersed between several queries in Table 3.2 are the librarian's open-ended questions that were instrumental in eliciting the user's negotiated query.

Table 3.2. Open-Ended Questions That Give Rise to Negotiated Queries

User's Initial Query	Librarian's Open-Ended Questions	Negotiated Query
The war in the Middle East	That's a big topic. What specifically interests you about the war?	The book *Three Cups of Tea* by Greg Mortensen and David Oliver Relin
Conversions	When you say "conversions," what do you mean?	A biography of Thomas Merton
School lunches	Tell me more about your interest in school lunches.	Do kids ever outgrow peanut allergies?
The library's history books	We have lots of history books. What time period in history interests you?	Sherman's March to the Sea
jackass tails	I'm not sure I know what you mean. Tell me more.	Jataka tales
Walmart	What would you like to know about Walmart?	Statistics on the rise of methamphetamine labs in rural America

Open-ended questions encourage users to open up about their topics and explain them in their own words. They elicit user responses that reveal the context of their queries. For example, the Conversions query brings to mind metric conversions, religious conversions, monetary conversions, and scoring points in football. The only way to find out which type of conversion interests the user is to ask her in a way that doesn't predispose or bias her to answer one way or another. The librarian's open-ended question does just that, revealing the user's interest in the religious conversion pertaining to Thomas Merton.

The initial queries for School Lunches, History, and the Middle East are broader representations of users' negotiated queries. Such representations are typical of initial queries. The reasons why users express their queries in broad terms may be due to their way of summing up their interests at the start of the reference interview, their limited knowledge of the subject, their desire to sample what the library has on a topic before committing to something specific, their knee-jerk reaction to a topic imposed by a college instructor or a boss, and so on. The imposed query comes from someone else, typically a teacher, family member, boss, neighbor, friend, colleague, et al. Whether users who approach you with imposed queries have negotiated them with the original inquirer, identifying the impetus for the query or what the inquirer really wants, is doubtful so you will have to do the best you can with the information they are able to provide. Imposed queries are the norm at public, academic, and school libraries, accounting for one-quarter to one-half of the queries posed to reference librarians (Gross 2001; Gross and Saxton 2001). Find out whether the user you are interviewing is dealing with an imposed query, and if he is, the "trick . . . is to get him to talk about what he *does* know, not what he doesn't" (Ross, Nilsen, and Radford 2009, 139–40).

On occasion, you won't understand what a user means. For example, the librarian hears the user say "jackass tails" and maybe that's what she actually said. Rather than repeat what the user says, the librarian tells the user he isn't sure what she means and asks for more clarification. Eventually the user provides enough information so that the librarian understands what he is saying and responds accordingly.

As a reference librarian, you will encounter just about every topic under the sun. You cannot be an expert on everything, but you can be an expert on how to find information for just about any topic including information on topics that is geared for domain novices, experts, and people somewhere in between. Getting in the habit of responding to users' initial questions with open-ended questions—your key to unlocking what users know about their topics so you can find relevant information for them.

BEING PRESENT

In the context of the reference interview, "being present" means actively listening to the user, being interested in the task of answering the user's question, and enlisting both verbal and non-verbal cues to reassure the user that you truly are present and engaged in their particular problem.

Active listening is a communications skill that requires the librarian to listen to what the user says and repeat it back, paraphrasing it in his own words so that he can confirm his understanding of the message with the user. Active listening enables librarians to successfully usher user queries from initial to negotiated status. Unfortunately, active listening is hard to do because the rapid pace and constant interruptions of everyday life make it difficult to settle down. The only way to develop your active listening skills is to practice them, concentrating single-pointedly on the reference interaction to the exclusion of almost everything else.

"Interest" means your interest in the task of answering the user's question, not in the actual question itself. How you demonstrate your interest in the task is conveyed to the user both non-verbally and verbally. Non-verbal cues are your eye contact with the user, smile, head nods in response to the user's replies, and open stance. Resist the temptation to cross your arms, fold your hands, or put your hands in your pockets because these are closed-body gestures that users may interpret as your disinterest, non-approval, or even outright hostility. Avoid nervous gestures such as tapping your fingers, playing with your hair, or fidgeting with an object. While assisting one user, resist the temptation to multitask, working on another user's inquiry or your own work.

In person and on the phone, verbal cues are your explanations of the online sources you are accessing and why you are accessing them, and possibly, sentence fragments that are indicative of what you are reading. Your cues need not be a "play-by-play" account of everything you are experiencing but enough to assure the user that she has your attention and you are working on her problem. Verbal cues are essential when responding to phone calls, chat, and texts because users cannot see you. When the user is talking on the phone, an occasional "uh-huh," "okay," or "I see" substitutes for the head nods that are characteristic of in-person reference interactions. Called encouragers, these utterances function as "noncommittal acknowledgments that you are actively listening to and mentally processing what the user is saying" (Bopp and Smith 2011, 67).

Somewhat comparable are the simple "searching . . ." and "working . . ." messages that you should send to a user every two or three minutes or so when you are trying to answer a reference question during a chat or text-message reference interview. Such messages give you time to think or work during the interview while reassuring the user that you are busy solving their problem.

When you have answered the same question on numerous past occasions or are close to the end of your shift on the reference desk, demonstrating interest may be difficult. Get in the habit of physically and mentally regrouping in between users. Take at least two or three long breaths—not shallow ones—but deep, long belly breaths that feature longer exhalations than inhalations, relax your shoulders, your jaw, and any other part of your body that tenses when you are under pressure. While checking yourself physically, think about your breaths and not on this or that inquiry past, present, or to come. Taking at least twenty seconds to regroup from time to time should refresh you physically and mentally for the next user.

CLOSED-ENDED QUESTIONS

When users have in-depth queries in mind that warrant a comprehensive database search, more negotiation may be necessary to shed more light on user queries and to answer database-specific questions (Table 3.3). Closed-ended questions requiring the user's yes-no or short answers are appropriate for obtaining answers to most of these questions.

Table 3.3. More Negotiation for In-Depth Queries

What You Want to Know	How to Ask
What discipline or field of study underlies the user's query	Are you looking for answers from a particular perspective or discipline? What is it?
What is the user's level of sophistication with both the topic and discipline	Do you want advanced material or something basic and easy to understand?
What kind of information does the user want	What instructions did your instructor give you about the types of information he or she wants you to use?
	What kind of information do you want? [Statistics, news stories, lesson plans, scholarly journal articles, etc.]
What research has the user already done	What have you done so far?
	If you've found something you really like, could you show it to me so we can use it to find more like it?
Whether the search should produce high recall or high precision results	Do you want to find everything written about this topic or do you want a few useful articles?
How the user intends to use the information he or she finds	It would help me to answer your question if you could tell me a little about how you will use the information we find.
	We have lots of information on [topic]. I could help you better if I knew what you are trying to do.
When the user needs the info	When do you need this information?
	What's your deadline?

Knowing the user's discipline or field of study, the kind of information she wants, her level of sophistication with the topic and discipline, and what research she has already done helps the librarian make database selection decisions.

Of all the questions listed in Table 3.3, asking users how they intend to use the information may be the most sensitive. Asking this in an academic library might not be problematic because so many uses pertain to coursework and publicly funded research; however, special library and public library users might balk at a direct question that asks how they will use the information they find. The rule of thumb is to ask indirectly, explaining to users that knowing how they intend to use the information will help you answer their question. Users who respond with "I'm not sure yet" or "I'm helping a friend" are probably not ready to share their intended uses with you, so back off and do the best you can with the information they *are* willing to share with you.

Resist the temptation to make assumptions about users. If you find yourself sizing them up based on personal appearance cues such as dress, hairstyle, age, and accessories, you run the risk of voicing your assumptions during the interaction or letting your personal reactions to them affect your assistance to them. The well-known adage—you can't judge a book by its cover—applies here. A user who looks homeless or poor might have interrupted yard work to run errands that includes stopping at the library. A user who looks like an ex-con with body piercings and tattoos may be a highly paid digital artist seeking background information and inspiration for a new project he just took on. Do your best to help each user, treat everyone with respect, respect their privacy, and let them be in control of what they are willing to share about their information needs.

Search Phase

The next phase is the librarian's search for information. Some reference interviews don't involve searches, for example, referrals, directional questions, or explanations about the most appropriate database for a broad-based subject or discipline. Depending on the circumstances, the librarian may conduct the search himself or guide the user through the searching process while explaining the ongoing search using language that is relatively jargon-free and understandable to the user.

Table 3.4 lists the seven steps that make up the search process. Included are each step's objective and the numbers of chapters that cover each step in-depth. In fact, these seven steps of the search process are the framework for *Online Searching*'s chapters 3 through 11.

Table 3.4. Seven Steps of the Search Process

Step	Objective	Chapters
1. Conducting the reference interview	To determine what the user really wants	3
2. Selecting a relevant database	To produce useful information that is in sync with the user's knowledge of her topic	4
3. Conducting a facet analysis and logical combination	To plan for search statements that address the big ideas, concepts, or themes that make up the negotiated query	5
4. Typecasting the negotiated query as a subject or known-item	To reveal clues about formulating search statements	5
5. Representing the negotiated query as input to the search system	To formulate search statements that produce relevant retrievals	6 to 9
6. Entering the search and responding strategically	To conceptualize the search overall so that its execution is efficient and effective	10
7. Displaying retrievals, assessing them, and responding tactically	To ensure that the execution of important aspects of the search are done efficiently and effectively	11

The seven steps of the search process function as a road map to tell you where you have been, where you are, where you are going, and what you can expect to accomplish along the way. Iteration and looping might occur during steps 6 and 7 when searchers enter their searches, display retrievals, and assess the relevance of retrieved sources. Should the search fail, you might loop back to step 2 to choose another database, then continue forward. As a last resort, you might loop back to step 1, consulting the user for additional clarification and direction so that you can put subsequent searches on track.

Results Presentation Phase

The interview's results presentation phase could involve a simple fact, the answer conveyed verbally, on the spot, along with the source of the answer. For in-depth queries regardless of their being in-person, phone, or virtual reference interviews, this phase will probably involve an email message from you or from the system you searched bearing links to the ongoing search, search results, and/or attached full-texts. Your email message should invite the user to contact you or your colleagues with additional questions about the search results or anything else and close the interview on a positive note.

Follow-Up Phase

Users who have additional questions set the follow-up phase into motion. Some users might ask you to explain the search results, the terminology you used to conduct the search, or the databases you searched. Other users might tell you that the search results are not relevant, making the follow-up phase loop back to the negotiation and searching phases so that you can further develop your understanding of the user's query and respond with additional searches and relevant retrievals. (Refer back to figure 3.4 on page 33.)

Closing Phase

The final phase of the reference interview is the closing in which you verify that the information satisfies the user's query. Your closing should make users feel good that they sought your assistance and assure them that they can ask follow-up questions on this particular project or on something else. Examples are the simple "Glad to help; come back and see us anytime" or the somewhat longer "Glad I could help; come back if you need help on this or anything else you are working on, and if I'm not here, one of my colleagues will be happy to help."

Knowing When to Stop Searching for Information

Knowing when to stop searching for information may be easy for referrals, directional questions, and fact-finding queries. It's not as easy for in-depth queries because there's always more information available in licensed databases and on the open Web, and you are the expert intermediary searcher who knows it's there and how to retrieve it. Users will usually tell you when they have enough information. They will also give non-verbal cues that they are saturated—a deep breath, eyes wide open, head tilted backward, crossed arms. Let them get started with what you found initially. In your closing, tell users that you know that you can find more information and they are welcome to contact you in the event they need it. Then back off.

Consider the implications of the Berrypicking Model (pages 30–31). Your initial assistance produces information for users. They process what you have found and in the course of doing so, not only does their original query evolve but they may generate new and different queries altogether. Their subsequent searches (with or without your assistance) may yield retrievals that they deem more useful than the original ones or build on what they learned from the originals. If users revisit you for additional information, don't be surprised if they express new and entirely different queries due to their exposure to information you helped them find earlier.

When users aim to be comprehensive in their search for information, finding the same sources repeatedly or failing to find sources that say something new and different is an indication that the search is achieving high recall. Yet, there are so many ways to search for information (chapters 6 to 9), different strategies (chapter 10), and tactics (chapter 11) that conducting a comprehensive search for information that retrieves all the relevant information on a topic may be well-nigh impossible.

Some Important Definitions

That the end user initiates a reference interview thrusts the librarian on the stage, bifurcating the information seeking process into what the user does and what the two of them accomplish together. *Online Searching* acknowledges this bifurcation, using separate terms and definitions for concepts that could be considered equivalent but really aren't. Listed below are a handful of such terms and their definitions. Acquaint yourself with the differences between them so that you can choose the right terms to communicate with your instructor, classmates, and future librarian colleagues.

- Information need. The user's recognition that what she knows is inadequate or incomplete to satisfy an overarching goal.
- Query. The user's immediate expression of her information need.
- Negotiated query. The librarian's understanding of what the user wants as a result of conducting a reference interview with him or her.
- Keywords. The words and phrases that end users enter into search systems to express their queries.
- Search statement. An expression of the negotiated query that the expert intermediary searcher formulates with reference to the search system's searching language and the database's controlled and free text vocabularies and enters into the search system with the expectation that on its own or in conjunction with other search statements, it will produce relevant retrievals.

Questions

Is negotiation *always* necessary? Scrutinize each of the five initial queries below, deciding which ones you should negotiate and which ones you should take at face value. When you've made your decision, jot down the characteristics of initial queries that fit into your "negotiate" and "don't negotiate" categories. Answers are given at the end of the chapter.

1. Good morning! Where would I be able to find really good information on fashion? I tried women's studies but didn't get much.
2. Do you have a current travel guidebook to France?
3. Hi. I need something on etiquette.
4. I'm having trouble using PubMed.
5. Hi. I know about Bob Hope, the comedian who entertained the troops, but how did all that entertaining the troops stuff get started in the first place?

Summary

Enter http://www.onlinesearching.org/p/3-interview.html into your Web browser for a video on the reference interview.

This chapter begins with an examination of several models of the information seeking process to help you, the reference librarian, bridge the gap between your understanding of this process and being a key participant in it. These models anticipate incongruity between what users say they want and what they really want, placing the burden on you to resolve the incongruity during the reference interview, gaining a complete and thorough understanding of what the user wants. Make users feel comfortable and at ease during the interview so that they are forthcoming about their information needs and positively inclined to consult you or your colleagues to help them with their information needs in the future. Eventually, you'll put your knowledge of the user's information needs to work, conducting online searches that produce relevant information.

This chapter spotlights the reference interview, dividing it into seven steps and describing each in more depth: greeting the user, eliciting the user's initial query, negotiating the query, searching for relevant information online, presenting search results, following up, and closing the interview in a positive manner that encourages the user to seek the assistance of reference staff in the future.

Bibliography

Bates, Marcia J. 1989. "The Design of Browsing and Berrypicking Techniques for the Online Search Interface." *Online Review* 13, no. 5: 407–24.

Bopp, Richard E., and Linda C. Smith. 2011. (See Suggested Readings below.)

Cassell, Kay Ann, and Uma Hiremath. 2011. (See Suggested Readings below.)

Dewdney, Patricia, and Gillian Michell. 1997. "Asking 'Why' Questions in the Reference Interview: A Theoretical Justification." *Library Quarterly* 67 (Jan.): 50–71.

Durrance, Joan C. 1989. "Reference Success: Does the 55 Percent Rule Tell the Whole Story?" *Library Journal* 114, no. 7: 31–36.

Gross, Melissa. 2001. "Imposed Information Seeking in Public Libraries and School Library Media Centers: A Common Behaviour?" *Information Research* 6, no 2. http://www.informationr.net/ir/6-2/paper100.html.

Gross, Melissa, and Matthew L. Saxton. 2001. "Who Wants to Know? Imposed Queries in the Public Library." *Public Libraries* 40: 170–76.

Harmeyer, Dave. 2014. (See Suggested Readings below.)

Hernon, Peter, and Charles R. McClure. 1986. "Unobtrusive Reference Testing: The 55 Percent Rule." *Library Quarterly* 111, no. 7: 37–41.

Hernon, Peter, and Charles R. McClure. 1987. *Unobtrusive Testing and Library Reference Services.* Norwood, NJ: Ablex Publishing Corporation.

Kirk, Thomas. 1974. "Problems in Library Instruction in Four-Year Colleges." In *Educating the Library User,* edited by John Lubans Jr., 83–103. New York: R. R. Bowker.

Kracker, Jacqueline, and Peiling Wang. 2002. "Research Anxiety and Students' Perceptions of Research: An Experiment. Part II. Content Analysis of Their Writings on Two Experiences." *Journal of the American Society for Information Science and Technology* 53, no. 4: 295–307.

Kuhlthau, Carol. 2003. *Seeking Meaning: A Process Approach to Library and Information Services.* 2nd ed. Westport, CT: Libraries Unlimited.

Kuhlthau, Carol. 2013. "Information Search Process." Last modified October 2013, accessed March 25, 2015. http://comminfo.rutgers.edu/~kuhlthau/information_search_process.htm.

Radford, Marie L. 1999. *The Reference Encounter: Interpersonal Communication in the Academic Library*. Chicago: American Library Association.

Radford, Marie L., Lynn Sillipigni Connaway, Patrick A. Confer, Susanna Sabolcsi, and Hannah Kwon. 2011. "'Are We Getting Warmer?' Query Clarification in Live Chat Virtual Reference." *Reference & User Services Quarterly* 50, no. 3: 259–79.

Ross, Catherine Sheldrick. 2003. "The Reference Interview: Why It Needs to Be Used in Every (Well, Almost Every) Reference Transaction." *Reference & User Services Quarterly* 43, no. 1: 38–43.

Ross, Catherine Sheldrick, Kirsti Nilsen, and Marie L. Radford. 2009. (See Suggested Readings below.)

RUSA (Reference & User Services Division). 2015. "Guidelines for Behavioral Performance of Reference and Information Services Providers." Accessed March 25, 2015. http://www.ala .org/rusa/resources/guidelines/guidelinesbehavioral.

Saxton, Matthew L., and John V. Richardson, Jr. 2002. *Understanding Reference Transactions: Transforming an Art into a Science*. Amsterdam, NY: Academic Press.

Shannon, Claude E., and Warren Weaver. 1949. *The Mathematical Model of Communication*. Urbana, IL: University of Illinois Press.

Taylor, Robert S. 1968. "Question-Negotiation and Information Seeking in Libraries." *College & Research Libraries* 29, no. 3 (May): 178–94.

Suggested Readings

Bopp, Richard E., and Linda C. Smith. 2011. *Reference and Information Services: An Introduction*. 4th ed. Santa Barbara, CA: Libraries Unlimited. This text's third chapter focuses on the reference interview.

Cassell, Kay Ann, and Uma Hiremath. 2011. *Reference and Information Services in the 21st Century*. New York: Neal-Schuman. This text's second chapter focuses on the reference interview.

Harmeyer, Dave. 2014. *The Reference Interview Today: Negotiating and Answering Questions Face to Face, on the Phone, and Virtually*. Lanham, MD: Rowman & Littlefield. See for yourself how librarians are effective at solving the most vexing reference questions.

Ross, Catherine Sheldrick, Kirsti Nilsen, and Marie L. Radford. 2009. *Conducting the Reference Interview: A How-To-Do-It Manual for Librarians*. New York: Neal-Schuman. Drawing on research findings for its practical guidelines and exercises, this book is the go-to source for everything you always wanted to know about the reference interview.

Answers

Of the five initial queries, only two describe exactly what the user wants—the Travel Guidebook and Entertaining the Troops. As a result of negotiation, the three remaining queries on Fashion, Etiquette, and Difficulty using PubMed become these negotiated queries:

- Successful entrepreneurs in the fashion industry
- Whether it's ever appropriate or acceptable to cry in the workplace
- Antiretroviral therapy for treating HIV

There's nothing special, unique, or distinctive about the former or latter queries that identifies them up front as candidates for negotiation. Sometimes one-faceted queries such as Fashion or Etiquette mean that users are stating their interests broadly to get the interview started. Other times, users really are interested in their one-faceted queries. They just need to shop around for ideas to limit their topics, possibly using the clusters that accompany search results in some databases.

The bottom line on negotiation is to negotiate each and every query. "If it turns out to have been unnecessary then no harm is done" (Ross, Nilsen, and Radford 2009, 5).

4

Selecting a Relevant Database

As a result of the negotiation phase in the reference interview, you should have an understanding of what the user wants in the form of a negotiated query. You should also have a sense of whether consulting a particular reference source will answer the negotiated query or whether you are dealing with an in-depth query for which you will have to conduct an online search that produces several sources, each contributing a modicum of information that the user must synthesize into an answer. You have now arrived at the second step of the online searching process—database selection.

A Classification of Databases

There are thousands of databases. Even if your library provides access to a small percentage of them, remembering each database's specifics is difficult to do except for the databases you use on a daily basis. To help you conceptualize the universe of databases, figure 4.1 classifies databases based on form and genre. Form is defined as the structure of the database. Genre is defined as the nature of the source or sources contained in the database—what the source *is* such as text, media, or numeric and spatial data.

Your library's database hub will have tools to help you with database selection, at the very least, classifying databases as encyclopedic or specific to a particular subject, discipline, or field of study (pages 16–19). Whether a database is a source or surrogate database takes place along two dimensions—what document representation the database searches to produce retrievals and whether its retrievals are actual sources themselves or surrogates for sources that reside in another database or in the library's physical collection. Considered broadly, sources are *texts*, *media*, or *numeric and spatial data*, or a combination of these called a *digital library*. Scrutinize the database's sources to determine whether you'd check them for reference, helping users find facts and answer simple questions, or for research, helping users satisfy their in-depth queries. For the former, prefer a *reference* database, and for the latter, a *research* database.

It is difficult to present a perfect classification of databases. Give this classification a chance, because knowing database forms and genres will facilitate the task of database selection, enabling you to pinpoint the one particular database from among the dozens, hundreds, or thousands available at your library's database hub and on the open Web that has the most promise for satisfying a user's query.

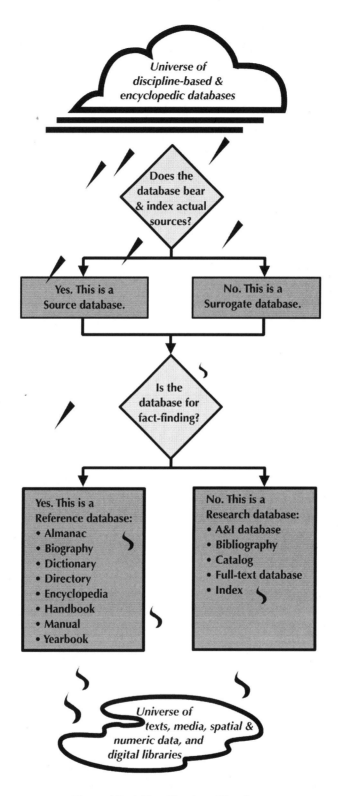

Figure 4.1. A Classification of Databases.

Surrogate and Source Databases

Whether a database is a *source* database or a *surrogate* database must be determined along two dimensions.

The first dimension addresses whether your search statements *search* the actual sources themselves. When they search an abbreviated form of the actual source such as an abstract or summary, it is a *surrogate* database. When they search the actual sources themselves, it is a *source* database. This implies that media cannot be source databases because media are experienced with one's senses such as hearing, seeing, and touching; however, when text-rich media such as plays, screenplays, broadsides, and video are transcribed into words and become the representation that queries search, then they are *source* databases.

The second dimension addresses whether the database produces retrievals that are the actual sources themselves or retrievals that are descriptions of actual sources such as a citation or summary. The former is a *source* database and the latter a *surrogate* database. Most surrogate databases at the library's hub bear resolver links that query other databases for desired sources and when they find them, display them to users along with the option to download them to their personal computers. Rarely is it apparent to end users that another database other than the one they are searching supplies their desired sources. To be honest, most users don't care who supplies actual sources as long as obtaining them is straightforward and effortless; however, one could argue that a database that relies on resolver links for a sizable share of its actual sources isn't a source database on its own.

Genres Contained in Surrogate and Source Databases

Three types of sources are contained in databases—texts, media, and numeric and spatial data. Digital library databases usually excel at two or all three genres.

Texts

Texts are written documents. The most common text-based genres contained in online databases are the products of *academic scholarship* such as journal articles, conference papers, dissertations, theses, research reports, books, and book reviews, and the products of *news reporting* such as newspaper articles, newswire stories, magazine articles, and blogs. In surrogate databases, search systems index and search the texts of surrogates, usually citations, index terms, and abstracts. In source databases, search systems index and search the texts of both full-texts and their accompanying surrogates. Whether searching a surrogate or source database, systems usually give searchers the option to search one particular field (e.g., author, title, journal name, number of pages), a combination of fields, or all fields.

Figure 4.2 shows a surrogate record topped by a downloaded full-text from the America: History and Life (AH&L) with Full Text database on EBSCOhost. AH&L is a surrogate database that searches surrogates and relies mostly on the library's resolver links to supply the actual sources themselves from journal aggregator databases.

Media

Source databases that specialize in media have become more commonplace as a result of the development of media encoding formats that are able to compress media and avoid compromising on quality. Because most media document what people experience via their visual, auditory, or tactile senses, they do not search the media per se; instead, they search surrogates that describe

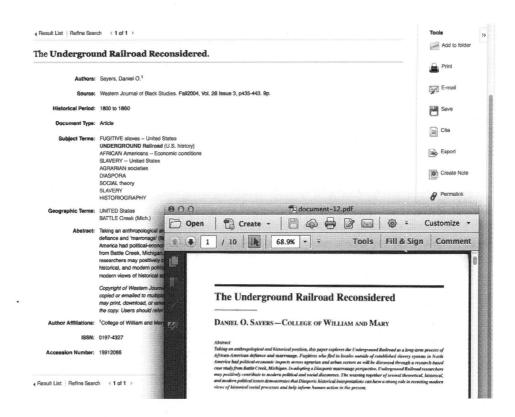

Figure 4.2. Surrogate Record and Downloaded Full-Text from the America: History and Life Database on EBSCOhost. Thanks to EBSCO Information Services for granting permission for this and the many screenshots of EBSCO databases that follow.

in words what they see or hear. For example, the AP Images database bears millions of photographs. You don't search the actual photographs themselves; you search their accompanying surrogate records bearing fields for image caption, event, location, creation date, subject, and much more. Figure 4.3 shows one of several retrievals that AP Images produces in response to the search statement **baby panda**. Providing context for the accompanying photo (not shown in figure 4.3) are this surrogate's fields for caption, location, event, and creation dates.

Retrievals in the Filmmakers Library Online database are streaming documentary films on anthropology, education, health, history, gender studies, and psychology topics (Alexander Street Press 2014). Figure 4.4 shows the film *Dancing Through Death* that the search system retrieves for the search statement `assimilation cambodians`. It displays streaming video on the left and matching terms in the film's transcript and accompanying surrogate on the right.

Google Images is one of the few available media databases that users can search using images. In response to an image that the user submits to Google Images, the system probably (because how Google actually performs image retrieval is a trade secret) performs content-based image retrieval using features such as colors, textures, and shapes in the submitted image to find images with similar features in its image database. Try it! Go to http://images.google.com and click on the camera icon.

BABY PANDA #00012602819

Jump to: Caption, Photo, Summary **« Prev Next »** Select

Download Print Preview Quick Save

Hua Mei, the female giant panda cub, balances on a branch Wednesday, Jan. 26, 2000, in the outside exhibit area of the Pacific Bell Foundation Giant Panda Research Station at the San Diego Zoo in San Diego. Hua Mei, is scheduled for her public debut in mid-February, is acclimating well to the new terrain. (AP Photo/San Diego Zoo)

Location	SAN DIEGO, CALIFORNIA, UNITED STATES
Event	**BABY PANDA**
Creation Date	Wednesday, January 26, 2000
Submit Date	Wednesday, January 26, 2000 7:56 PM
Transmission Reference	WXS113
Image ID	00012602819
Image Resolution*	1450 x 1992 - 502.27 KB
Byline Title	HO
Credit	ASSOCIATED PRESS
Archive Signature	4270289
Category	Domestic News

Figure 4.3. Surrogate from the AP Image Database. Courtesy of the Associated Press.

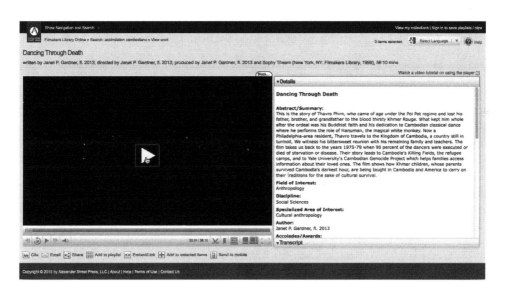

Figure 4.4. Clicking on a Retrieved Title in the Filmmakers Library Online Database Displays Surrogate and Transcript and Streams the Film to Your PC. Courtesy of Alexander Street Press, LLC.

Numeric and Spatial Data

Numeric data are data expressed in numbers. They reside in a numeric database's tables, graphs, maps, charts, and figures. You don't necessarily query the numbers per se; instead, you query surrogates that describe in words what the numbers mean or the words that accompany the numbers in actual tables, graphs, maps, charts, and figures.

ProQuest's Statistical Insight database indexes publications bearing statistics issued by U.S. federal agencies, state governments, private organizations, intergovernmental organizations, and selected international sources (ProQuest 2013). It might be a productive source for the query "I need statistics on how much Americans walk and bike to work." In fact, a search of Statistical Insight for the search statement (walk* or bicycl*) and commut* produces over one hundred retrievals topped by a U.S. Census Bureau report entitled *Modes Less Traveled: Bicycling and Walking to Work in the U.S., 2008–12.* Figure 4.5 displays the report's A&I record enumerating table captions describing exactly what the user wants.

Entirely new are databases of numeric and spatial data with built-in datasets and searchable parameters that users choose to find answers to their queries and, in the process, are able to generate their own unique graphs, maps, charts, and/or tables. Choose the SimplyMap database

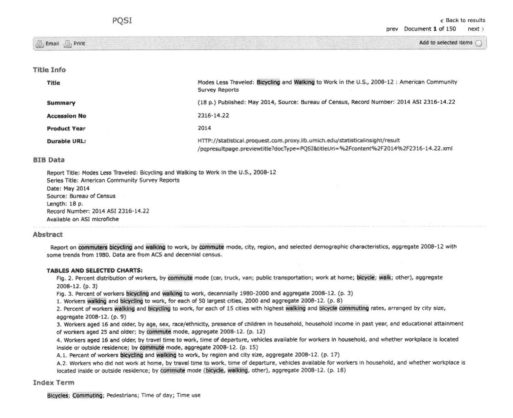

Figure 4.5. Finding Statistics on Commuting to Work on Foot or on Bicycle in ProQuest's Statistical Insight Database. The screenshots and their contents are published with permission of ProQuest LLC. Further reproduction is prohibited without permission. Inquiries may be made to: ProQuest LLC, 789 E. Eisenhower Pkwy, Ann Arbor, MI 48106-1346 USA. Telephone (734) 761-4700; Email: info@proquest.com; Web page: http://www.proquest.com.

to draw on its business, demographic, and marketing data for creating custom maps (Geographic Research 2015). Get started by mousing down on the database's "I want to . . ." link and mousing up on its "Make a map" option. SimplyMap then ushers you through a multistep map-making process. For example, to create the sample map in figure 4.6 showing the percent of possible sunshine, these steps are:

1. Choosing a variable> Quality of Life
2. Choosing a dataset> 2010 Data
3. Choosing a specific variable> Percent of Possible Sunshine
4. Choosing a location> States
5. Choosing an exact location> Michigan

Voilà! SimplyMap creates figure 4.6's sunshine map, outlining Michigan and adding a zoom bar that you can manipulate to see how much sunshine all fifty states, a particular region, state, or municipality got in 2014.

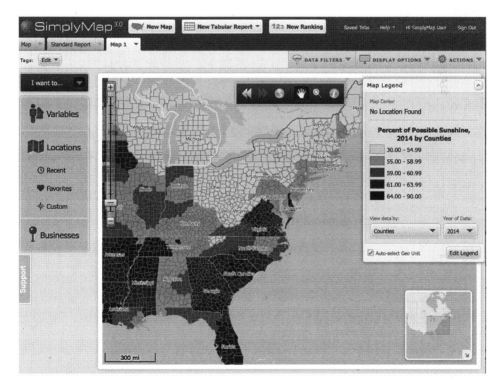

Figure 4.6. Mapping the Percent of Possible Sunshine in the SimplyMap Database. © 2013–2015 Geographic Research, Inc.

SimplyMap users can export high-resolution images of their custom-made maps into written reports, slide-show presentations, and websites, and accompany their maps with tables bearing the exact data points that their maps represent graphically. In addition to maps, users can use SimplyMap to generate custom reports using data from one or more variables that interest them or export SimplyMap data into Excel, CSV, or DBF files for follow-up financial and statistical analyses in a software application of their choice.

Digital Libraries

Digital library databases are libraries in and of themselves. They are focused collections of digital artifacts on a particular subject, practice, or genre. The database's digital artifacts may run the gamut from text and media to numeric and spatial data or specialize in one or two of these. Some digital libraries strive to be one-stop service centers, satisfying users' information needs entirely, while others are more like bus stops, being one of several databases that users search during the course of their research.

Into the one-stop shopping category is the Oxford Islamic Studies Online (OISO) database from Oxford University Press (2015b). Get started by reading the introductory essay entitled "What Everyone Needs to Know about Islam." To achieve more depth, explore the database's wide array of content:

- Thousands of topical entries from Oxford publications
- Primary source documents with accompanying commentary
- Learning resources such as bibliographies, glossaries, lesson plans, and thematic guides
- Images and maps
- Timelines for Islamic history and world events
- Two translations of the Qur'an
- A concordance of the Qur'an

Figure 4.7 shows OISO's timeline page where the user has moused down on the Advanced Search link and is poised to choose the Biography search, limiting his search to people. The user could also search the Qur'an, its concordance, images, maps, primary sources, or OISO content generally.

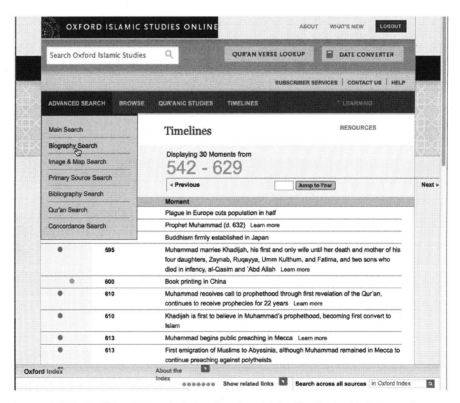

Figure 4.7. Oxford Islamic Studies Online Database's Timeline Page with Advanced Searching Options Revealed. Courtesy of Oxford University Press.

Research Databases

When reference librarians and users search research databases, they are typically (but not always) engaged in seeking answers to in-depth queries that require exhaustive database searches through the system's subject searching functionality and produce multiple retrievals, none of which answers the user's question entirely. To answer their questions, users must synthesize the useful information they extract from retrievals and exercise their judgment, weighing the evidence and taking into account their particular situation and circumstances.

Bibliographies are the simplest of all research databases. They are surrogate databases limited to citations with only titles to convey sources' subject content. Indexes and catalogs build on bibliographies, adding index terms to surrogate records describing subjects and genres to describe what the source is about and what it is, respectively. A&I databases build on indexes and catalogs, adding summaries to surrogate records to describe in greater detail what the source is about. Full-text databases build on A&I databases, providing users with on-the-spot access to full-texts so that they don't have to fetch the full-text's physical manifestation from the library's bookshelves, and possibly, adding these full-texts to subject indexes for subject searching.

When choosing a research database, expert searchers take form into consideration—bibliographies, catalogs, and indexes providing fewer approaches to subject searching and A&I and full-text databases providing more approaches. Table 4.1 defines the five forms of research databases, classifying them as surrogate or source databases and ordering them from their simplest to most complex forms.

Table 4.1. Forms of Research Databases

Form	Definition	Surrogate or Source
Bibliography	A systematic listing of citations, usually organized alphabetically by author name, and restricted in coverage by one or more features such as subject, publisher, place of publication, or genre.	Surrogate
Index	A systematic organization of values (e.g., words, phrases, codes, or numbers) contained in a database's surrogate records along with the pointers, references, or addresses that the search system uses to retrieve the surrogates in which the values occur.	Surrogate
Catalog	A special type of index bearing surrogate records that describe sources contained in a collection, library, or group of libraries and that are organized according to a formal scheme or plan.	Surrogate
A&I database	A special type of index enhanced with abstracts (also called summaries) that describe sources' contents.	Surrogate
Full-text database	A systematic organization of values (e.g., words, phrases, codes, or numbers) contained in a source database's full-text sources along with the pointers, references, or addresses that the search system uses to retrieve the full-texts in which the values occur.	Source

Bibliographies and Indexes

A bibliography is a systematic listing of citations, usually organized alphabetically by author name, and restricted in coverage by one or more features such as subject, publisher, place of publication, or genre. An example of an entry in a bibliography is:

Thurman, Robert A. F. 1999. *Inner Revolution: Life, Liberty, and the Pursuit of Real Happiness.* 1st Riverhead trade paperback ed. New York: Riverhead Books. 322 p.

The entry bears just enough identificatory information so that the user can find the actual source in a source database or physical collection. Converting a bibliography into an index is easy. An editor parses citation data into separate fields:

Title	Inner Revolution: Life, Liberty, and the Pursuit of Real Happiness
Author	Thurman, Robert A. F.
Edition	1st Riverhead Trade paperback
Place of publication	New York
Publisher	Riverhead Books
Date	1999
Pages	322

Add the fielded entry into a search system, and the system's indexing program processes field values (words, phrases, codes, or numbers) into separate indexes, one for each field type and into one big combined index. When you search multiple fielded entries like the one above, the bibliography has become an index.

Users want more than just citations, so over the years, publishers of bibliographies have enhanced them with index terms, summaries, even full-texts, and in the process, bibliographies have become indexes, catalogs, A&I databases, and even full-text databases.

If a database's title bears the word "bibliography," chances are that it has transitioned or it is in the process of transitioning into a different form of research database. Examples are ARTbibliographies Modern, Bibliography of the History of Art, and MLA International Bibliography. The same applies to national bibliographies that contain surrogates for sources written by a country's citizens, published by the country's publishers, in its national language(s), and about the country. Why their publishers have not changed their names to reflect their more-than-a-bibliography status may be due to the many loyal and long-time users of these databases who are so familiar with their names.

Catalogs and Indexes

A catalog is a special type of index. It bears surrogate records that describe sources contained in a collection, library, or group of libraries and that are organized according to a formal scheme or plan. The most familiar catalog is the library's online public access catalog (OPAC). The plans that organize OPACs are subject headings, a library classification, and the main-entry principle. Most libraries in the English-speaking world choose subject headings from the controlled vocabulary called the Library of Congress Subject Headings (LCSH). A subject heading is a subject word or phrase to which all material that the library has on that subject is entered in the catalog. Table 4.2 shows a catalog record from an OPAC bearing index terms from LCSH. In the absence of subject headings, the user would not know what the book is about because the book's title is not descriptive of its subject contents.

Table 4.2. Catalog Record from an OPAC

Field	Surrogate Data
Call number	D811.5 W486
Title	Green Armor
Author	White, Osmar
Edition	1st
Place of publication	New York
Publisher	W. W. Norton & Co.
Date	1945
Physical description	288 p., maps, 22 cm.
Subject headings	World War, 1939-1945—Personal narratives—New Zealand; World War, 1939-1945—New Guinea; World War, 1939-1945—Solomon Islands
Language	English
Bibliographic level	Monograph/Item

Indexes are almost the same as catalogs, but missing from their definition are emphases on collections and organizational schemes. An example is ProQuest's Avery Index to Architectural Periodicals database that indexes journal articles from periodicals in the fields of architecture and architectural design and history (Columbia University 2010). Figure 4.8 shows an Avery index record bearing a citation and index terms that describe the subject matter of the indexed article.

Book Review Index is an index that culls book reviews from journals, newspapers, and general interest publications. Search Book Review Index using names or titles and retrieved are citations to book reviews. For example, a search for book reviews for the book entitled *Scaredy Squirrel Has a Birthday Party* yields three reviews in recent issues of *The Horn Book Guide*, *School Library Journal*, and *Kirkus Reviews* (figure 4.9). Clicking on the accompanying MGetIt resolver links unites U-M users with full-text reviews from a journal aggregator's database or initiates an interlibrary loan request for the desired source.

A&I (Abstracting and Indexing) Databases

A&I databases are indexes that have been enhanced with an abstract (also called summary) of the source's contents. Informative, indicative, and a combination of the two are the types of abstracts you'll encounter in A&I databases. *Informative* abstracts function as a substitute for the source, detailing its quantitative or qualitative substance. *Indicative* abstracts function like tables of contents, describing the source's range and coverage and making general statements about the source. *Indicative-informative* abstracts are part indicative of the source's more significant content and part informative of its less significant content.

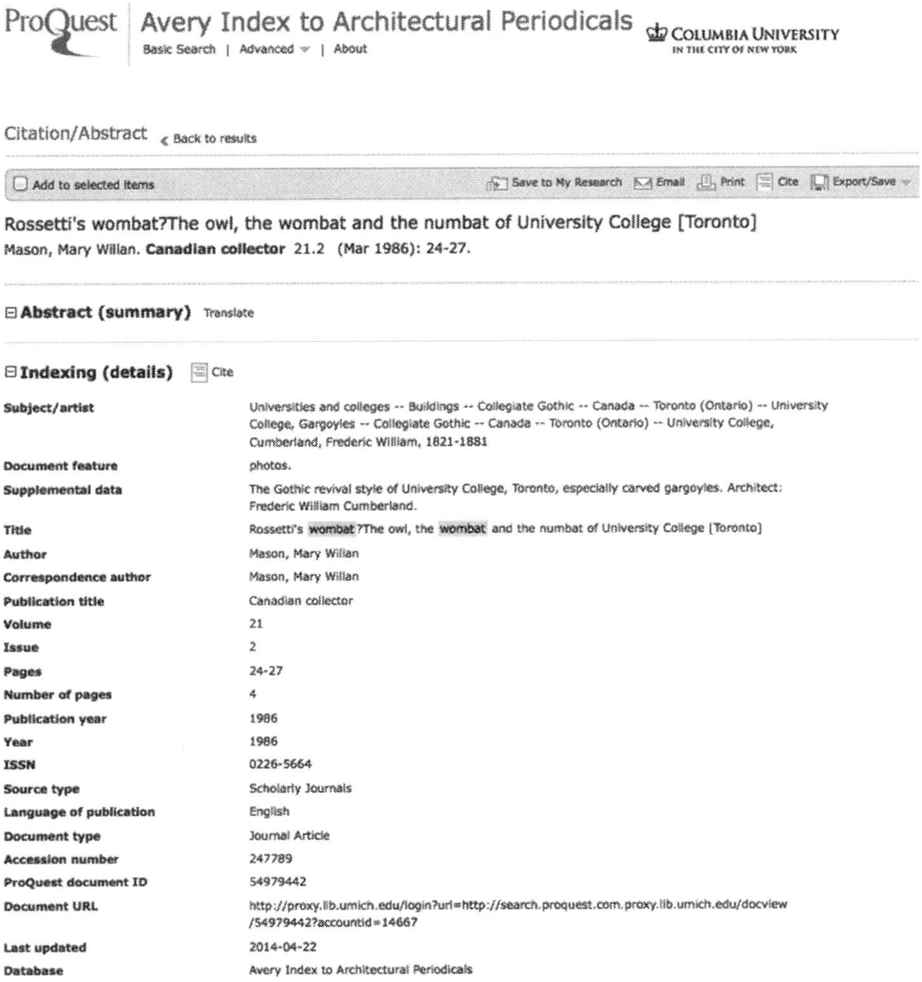

ProQuest | Avery Index to Architectural Periodicals — Columbia University in the City of New York

Basic Search | Advanced | About

Citation/Abstract « Back to results

Add to selected items | Save to My Research | Email | Print | Cite | Export/Save

Rossetti's wombat?The owl, the wombat and the numbat of University College [Toronto]

Mason, Mary Willan. **Canadian collector** 21.2 (Mar 1986): 24-27.

Abstract (summary) Translate

Indexing (details) Cite

Subject/artist	Universities and colleges -- Buildings -- Collegiate Gothic -- Canada -- Toronto (Ontario) -- University College, Gargoyles -- Collegiate Gothic -- Canada -- Toronto (Ontario) -- University College, Cumberland, Frederic William, 1821-1881
Document feature	photos.
Supplemental data	The Gothic revival style of University College, Toronto, especially carved gargoyles. Architect: Frederic William Cumberland.
Title	Rossetti's wombat?The owl, the wombat and the numbat of University College [Toronto]
Author	Mason, Mary Willan
Correspondence author	Mason, Mary Willan
Publication title	Canadian collector
Volume	21
Issue	2
Pages	24-27
Number of pages	4
Publication year	1986
Year	1986
ISSN	0226-5664
Source type	Scholarly Journals
Language of publication	English
Document type	Journal Article
Accession number	247789
ProQuest document ID	54979442
Document URL	http://proxy.lib.umich.edu/login?url=http://search.proquest.com.proxy.lib.umich.edu/docview/54979442?accountid=14667
Last updated	2014-04-22
Database	Avery Index to Architectural Periodicals

Figure 4.8. Index Record from the Avery Index of Architectural Periodicals on ProQuest. The screenshots and their contents are published with permission of ProQuest LLC. Further reproduction is prohibited without permission. Inquiries may be made to: ProQuest LLC, 789 E. Eisenhower Pkwy, Ann Arbor, MI 48106-1346 USA. Telephone (734) 761-4700; Email: info@proquest.com; Web page: http://www.proquest.com.

Many A&I databases began life as indexes and as the technology became more powerful and storage space less costly, their publishers added abstracts, transitioning them to A&I databases. Few pure A&I databases exist today because full-texts may be available via the database itself or via journal publishers and journal aggregators through accompanying resolver links.

One of the few A&I databases that relies entirely on the library's resolver links for full-text fulfillment is NTIS (National Technical Information Services). For sixty years, NTIS has been indexing and abstracting the results of federally sponsored grants that grant recipients issue in the

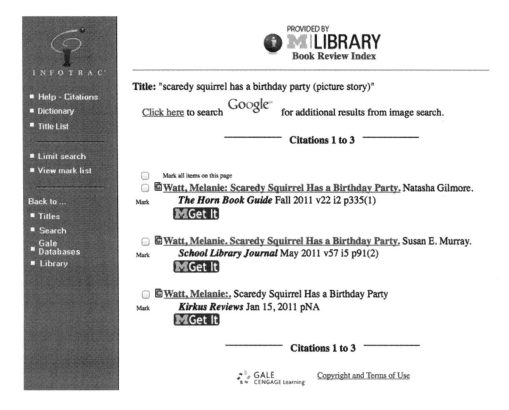

Figure 4.9. Citations to Book Reviews in the Book Review Index Database from Gale Cengage Learning. Courtesy of Gale Cengage Learning.

form of research reports, computer software, videos, audio files, and so on (NTIS 2015). NTIS A&I records are lengthy, so figure 4.10 shows all but the source and database identification fields of ProQuest NTIS A&I records. The result of a search for suicide terrorism, figure 4.10's A&I record bears fields for abstract, subject, classification, identifier, and title fields and an indicative abstract to describe the report's contents.

Full-Text Databases

Search a full-text database and the search system matches your search terms with words in full-texts and surrogates. Finding matches, the system displays elements from surrogates, typically titles, index terms, and snippets from abstracts to help users assess relevance. Full-text databases deliver digital full-texts to users in HTML, PDF, and various media formats or give them a choice of format. When users print digital full-texts and their accompanying tables, figures, diagrams, and photographs, they might look almost exactly like a photocopy of the printed page—even better—like an original snipped from the pages of the print journal! Examples of full-text databases are LexisNexis, ABI/Inform, and JStor on the licensed Web, and arXiv, Google, and YouTube on the open Web. Textbox 4.1 explains in detail the utility of surrogates in full-text databases.

Figure 4.10. A&I Record from the NTIS Database on ProQuest. The screenshots and their contents are published with permission of ProQuest LLC. Further reproduction is prohibited without permission. Inquiries may be made to: ProQuest LLC, 789 E. Eisenhower Pkwy, Ann Arbor, MI 48106-1346 USA. Telephone (734) 761–4700; Email: info@proquest.com; Web page: http://www.proquest.com.

Selecting a Research Database

Table 4.3 classifies examples of research databases as follows:

- The form of their retrievals as surrogates or the actual sources themselves (column 2)
- Whether your search statements search surrogates or the actual sources themselves (column 3)
- The genre of the database's sources as texts, media, numeric data, or digital libraries (column 4)
- Their form as a research database (column 5)

Textbox 4.1. The Utility of Surrogates in Full-Text Databases

Let's take a moment to determine why source databases bear both surrogates and full-texts. You may think that the existence of the latter should contradict the former; that is, surrogates should be superfluous in a full-text database because of the availability of the full-texts. Yet, full-text databases almost always include surrogate records, typically in the form of A&I records bearing citations, index terms, and abstracts. Why do these databases go the extra mile, enhancing full-texts with A&I records?

To answer this question, think about the searches you've conducted in full-text databases. Most likely, they've produced hundreds of retrievals. Retrieving all those sources minus the surrogate records that bear citations and possibly, index terms and abstracts, would be akin to someone plunking down a stack of three hundred books on your desk. How would you respond? After rolling your eyes and sighing deeply, you'd probably scan through the pile, reading their titles, winnowing the list down to the most promising titles, then reading their book jackets, forewords, or introductions to determine whether you should put the effort into reading the whole book. That's exactly how surrogates function. You review surrogate contents, scanning their titles and their index terms, then reading their abstracts, all the while looking for evidence that the source is relevant. Convinced of relevance, you are then ready to invest your time reading the full-texts of the most promising ones.

Marcia Bates (1998) reports on the findings of researchers who have studied "levels of access," counting the number of characters that readers encounter as they proceed from a book's title to its table of contents, back-of-the-book index, and full-text. Summarizing their research, she reports that book readers encounter thirty times more characters at each level along the way. It is the same for journal articles—their titles being one-thirtieth the size of their index terms, their index terms being one-thirtieth the size of their abstracts, and their abstracts being one-thirtieth the size of their full-texts. Because this research was conducted long before the Internet and World Wide Web, there are no data for websites, but I bet that website readers encounter thirty times more characters as they proceed from the website's title to the snippets matching their search terms, to the Web page, and finally to the full website. About these research findings, Marcia Bates (2003, 27) concludes that "the persistence of these ratios suggests that they represent the end result of a shaking down process, in which, through experience, people became most comfortable when access to information is staged in 30:1 ratios."

These findings are intriguing because they appear to confirm how readers familiarize themselves with retrievals before making the commitment to read full-texts from start to finish. Thus, the utilitarian nature of surrogate records alongside full-texts makes perfect sense. Surrogate records enable readers to decide whether to invest their time and effort in reading full-texts.

Subject searching is the hallmark of research databases, and that's how most users will search them. When research databases don't supply sources, users can click on accompanying resolver links to determine if another database at their library's hub can supply them.

Table 4.3. Classifying Licensed and Open Web Research Databases

(1) Database Name	(2) Form of Retrievals	(3) What Is Searched	(4) Genre of the Database's Sources	(5) Form
American Film Scripts Online	Source	Source	Texts: Scripts and screenplays	Full-text
arXiv (http://http://arxiv.org/)	Source	Source	Texts: Journal articles and reprints in physics	Full-text
Catalog of U.S. Government Publications (http://catalog.gpo.gov/F)	Surrogate and source	Surrogate	Texts: Books, pamphlets, reports	Catalog
Google Scholar (http://scholar.google.com)	Source	Surrogate or source	Texts: Journal articles, conference papers, research reports	Varies depending on what publishers provide: Index, A&I, or full-text
Index of Christian Art	Source	Surrogate	Media: Photographic images	A&I
International Medieval Bibliography	Surrogate	Surrogate	Texts: Journal articles, conference papers, festschriften	Index
Internet Movie Database (http://www.imdb.com)	Surrogate	Surrogate	Media: Films, television programs, video games	A&I
Naxos Music Library	Source	Surrogate	Media: Streaming audio	A&I
WorldCat (http://openworldcat.org)	Surrogate	Surrogate	Texts and media: Books, music, maps, sound recordings, films	Catalog
YouTube (http://www.youtube.com)	Source	Surrogate	Media: Videos, television shows, video blogs	Index

Reference Databases

When expert intermediary searchers consult reference databases, they are typically (but not always) engaged in fact-finding and seeking answers to the simple questions users pose such as "What is the average yearly rainfall in the rainiest and driest cities in Texas?" and "What really happened to the two protagonists in the movie *Chariots of Fire*?"

Before reference sources were digitized and their contents configured into databases, they were print-based reference books. No one actually ever read a reference book cover to cover; instead, they consulted its alphabetized entries or special indexes, matched the event, name, phrase, or word that interested them, and read the corresponding entry. This is still true today but the book structure from which digital reference databases emanated is hardly apparent.

Furthermore, that reference sources are now online databases makes it possible for users to search them in many more ways than were possible before digitization.

When indexing programs process digitized reference books, they cut up the text into separate entries and index each entry separately. For example, consider a reference database that is a biographical directory of famous people living in America today. The search system would cut the text up into separate entries, one entry per famous-person biography, and index each biography separately. Thus, a reference database with ten thousand biographical entries has the potential of producing ten thousand retrievals in response to a user's query but it would rarely do so. Most likely, searches for unique names like "Amelia Earhart" and "Theodore Roosevelt" would retrieve one and only one biography, but common names like "John Brown" and "Joseph Smith" would retrieve several biographies and the searcher would have to scan retrievals in search of the particular "John Brown" and "Joseph Smith" that interests him.

Table 4.4 gives definitions of the major reference database genres along with their classification as surrogate or source databases.

Table 4.4. Reference Database Genres

Genre	Definition	Surrogate or Source
Almanac	"A collection of facts, statistics, and lists" (Bopp and Smith 2011, 440).	Source
Biography	Accounts of a person's life, often supplemented with one or more other appropriate genres, e.g., bibliography, catalog, discography, filmography, etc., to report their accomplishments.	Source
Language Dictionary	A collection of entries for acronyms, proper nouns, phrases, or words giving definitions, etymology, foreign language equivalents, grammar, orthography, pronunciations, regionalisms, synonyms, usage, visual imagery, and/or written-out forms.	Source
Discipline-based dictionary	A collection of entries for concepts, events, objects, or overarching topics in a discipline, subject, or field of study along with definitions and short explanations.	Source
Directory	A collection of entries for persons and organizations bearing contact information and other potentially useful information such as age, gender, occupation for persons, and founding date, number of employees, and contact person's name for organizations that bear definitions and explanations.	Source
Encyclopedia	Same as discipline-based dictionary but encyclopedia entries have more depth and detail, giving background information, definitions, explanations, current issues and trends, and bibliographical references to seminal sources.	Source
Handbook	"A handy guide to a particular subject, with all of the critical information that one might need" consolidated into a single source (Bopp and Smith 2011, 443).	Source
Manual	"A convenient guide to a particular procedure, typically with step-by-step instructions" (Bopp and Smith 2011, 444).	Source
Yearbook	A review of trends, issues, and events pertaining to a topic, place, or phenomenon in a particular year.	Source

Biographies

Consult a biography for information about a person's life, anything from their accomplishments to factual data such as their birthdate, birthplace, names of immediate family members, or education. The licensed Marquis Who's Who database is a biography that retrieves entries for well-known modern persons bearing their birth and death dates, family members, education, career history, accomplishments, interests and hobbies, (if still living) contact information, and much more (Marquis Who's Who 2015). Be prepared for differences between fielded entries, for example, the fields that describe an educator (figure 4.11) will be different from the fields that describe an actress because of differences in the nature of the work and accomplishments.

Not only can you enter people's names into Marquis Who's Who and expect to retrieve their biographies, you can search for classes of well-known people, for example, people born in your hometown (or anywhere else for that matter), graduates of your alma mater (or anyone else's), people who work at certain occupations or enjoy certain hobbies. Such searches are possible because Marquis Who's Who indexes and searches every word in biographical entries.

Biographies may cover living persons, dead persons, or both, and they may be national, regional, or international in scope. Encyclopedias and dictionaries are also excellent sources of biographical information. The open Web is a source of biographical information, but be careful about accepting web-based information at face value. Someone who publishes a website about a famous person, living or dead, may be doing so to promote a personal agenda or one that is consistent with

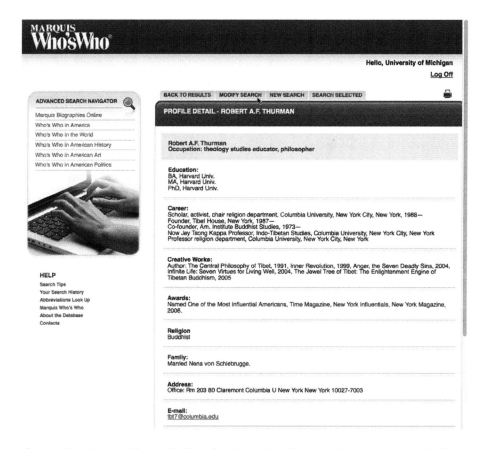

Figure 4.11. Marquis Who's Who Entry for Robert A. F. Thurman. Courtesy of Marquis Who's Who LLC and Robert A. F. Thurman.

an offbeat group. Verify what you find on the Web in other more trusted sources. Social networking sites such as Facebook and LinkedIn may also provide the biographical information you are seeking.

Dictionaries

Most people are familiar with language dictionaries that give definitions, etymology, pronunciations, and usages of words. Less familiar are discipline-based dictionaries that give definitions for and explanations of concepts, events, objects, and overarching topics.

The open web-based Acronym Finder is an encyclopedic language dictionary (http://www.acronymfinder.com/). Enter an acronym and in response, the system lists written-out forms of the acronym. Peruse the list and you are likely to recognize the one that fits your situation. That's all there is to it.

The most comprehensive and authoritative dictionary of the English language is the Oxford English Dictionary database (Oxford University Press 2013). Enter a word to learn its meaning, history, and pronunciation. Alternatively, launch the advanced interface, choose "definition" or "quotation" from the pull-down menu and enter a word or phrase—breaking wind, an empty space, evanescent—to see what meanings and quotes it figures into.

Discipline-based dictionaries run the gamut. Some focus narrowly on a specific topic, and others are encyclopedic or cover whole disciplines. Some bear one-line entries, and others feature signed articles that are comparable to encyclopedia entries and rival scholarly journal articles in length and comprehensiveness. Also, be prepared for discipline-based dictionaries that use the terms "encyclopedia," "companion," and "reference guide," in place of "dictionaries" in their titles.

A Dictionary of Opera Characters focuses narrowly on opera characters and responds to user queries with one-paragraph descriptions of a character's role in an opera (Oxford University Press 2015a). Figure 4.12 shows the database's entry for Porgy from the opera *Porgy and Bess*.

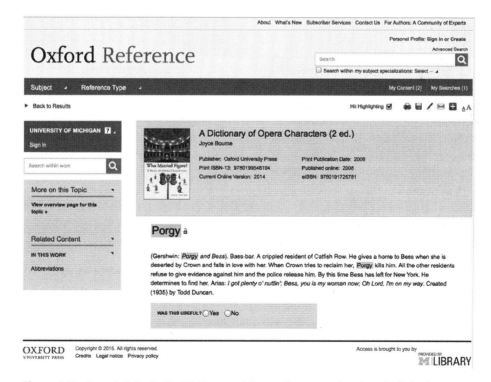

Figure 4.12. Porgy's Entry in the Dictionary of Opera Characters Database in Oxford Reference. Courtesy of Oxford University Press.

Because the Dictionary of Opera Characters is one subfile within the larger, more comprehensive Oxford Reference database, clicking on links may divert you to other Oxford Reference subfiles.

The licensed Gale Virtual Reference Library is organized much like Oxford Reference. You can restrict your searches to one particular Gale reference subfile such as the Encyclopedia of Sustainability, The 9/11 Encyclopedia, or Eating Disorders Sourcebook. Alternatively, you can conduct a brute-force search of all one hundred or so Gale digital reference sources that represent every reference genre including various combinations of genres.

Directories

Consult a directory for contact information for persons and organizations. Online directories are so much more versatile than their print counterparts. Perhaps you remember the print-based white pages and yellow pages telephone directories where you were totally limited to browsing their alphabetical lists of names of persons and organizations for the one(s) you wanted. Now you can search telephone directory entries on the open Web, the white pages at http://www.whitepages.com and yellow pages at http://www.yellowpages.com, entering names, categories, phone numbers, addresses, or combinations of these. Reference USA is the licensed database equivalent of the print-based white pages and yellow pages.

The licensed Associations Unlimited database covers non-profit associations and professional societies from around the world. Entries for each association include contact information (e.g., name, street and email addresses, phone number, website URL), contact name, and a brief description of the association's purpose, services, and/or activities (Gale Cengage Learning 2008). Association Unlimited's custom search form lets users target their searches to one or more fields or search the entire entry. Figure 4.13 displays an entry for the Women's Professional Rodeo Association bearing contact information, description, founding date, publications, membership dues, and much more.

Becoming familiar with the directories available at your library's database hub will help you answer a host of queries posed by certain classes of people. For example, job seekers researching potential employers and business intelligence specialists researching products, inventions, and competitors benefit from business directories such as Ward's Business Directory of Public and Private Companies, Standard and Poor's NetAdvantage, and Mergent Online. Scholars searching for grants, publishing venues, like-minded scholars, and research centers benefit from the Foundations Directory, Europa World of Learning, Cabell's Directory of Publishing Opportunities, American Men and Women of Science, and Scholar Universe.

Encyclopedias

An encyclopedia is a collection of entries for concepts, events, objects, or overarching topics in a discipline or subject that give background information, definitions, detailed explanations, and current issues and trends and include bibliographical references to seminal sources. Consulting encyclopedias for information enables users to develop a working knowledge of the topics that interest them and direct them to relevant sources for more information. Encyclopedias are also satisfactory for finding facts about phenomena to answer simple reference questions such as "Why isn't Pluto considered a planet anymore?" and "In what years did the Hekla volcano erupt?"

Published by the Cornell Lab of Ornithology (2015), the licensed Birds of North America (BNA) Online is an encyclopedia bearing illustrated and comprehensive life histories for the more

Document 1 of 1

Women's Professional Rodeo Association (WPRA)

431 S Cascade Ave.
Colorado Springs, CO 80903 USA

Phone:(719) 447-4627
Fax: (719) 447-4631
URL: http://www.wpra.com
This URL was provided by the association; Gale is not responsible for its content. To return to GaleNet after viewing the website, use the BACK button on your browser.

Primary Contact: Carolynn Vietor, President

Founded: 1948. **Members:** 2000. **Membership Dues:** permit, $300 annual; gold card competing, $125 annual; roping division, $190 annual. **Staff:** 3. NATIONAL. **Description:** Produces and competes in All Professional Girl Rodeos and Barrel Races in rodeos sanctioned by the Professional Rodeo Cowboys Association. Conducts seminars and clinics on fundamentals of horsemanship and rodeo events. Operates National Cowgirl Hall of Fame. **Formerly:** (1980) Professional Women's Rodeo Association; (1981) Girls Rodeo Association.

Publications: Women's Pro Rodeo News, monthly. Newsletter. **Price:** $45 /year. **Circulation:** 3,900. **Advertising:** accepted. • WPRA Rule Book, annual. Book.

SIC: 8699 - Membership Organizations Nec; 7999 - Amusement and Recreation Nec
Subject Descriptor(s): Rodeo
Subject Category: Athletic and Sports Organizations

GALE
CENGAGE Learning™   Copyright and Terms of Use

Figure 4.13. Entry in the Associations Unlimited Database from Gale Cengage Learning. Courtesy of Gale Cengage Learning.

than seven hundred birds on the North American continent. All entries are signed and include range maps, video, audio and photo galleries, and bibliographies. Figure 4.14 displays the beginning of the lengthy introduction to the Kirtland's warbler's entry—click on the "Multimedia" tab to hear this warbler's lusty song. If your library doesn't have access to BNA, explore the Cornell Lab's All About Birds database on the open Web bearing basic information about birds including range maps, songs and calls, and photographs of bird species.

Encyclopedias are available for important topics within disciplines, entire disciplines, and for knowledge generally. That Wikipedia (http://wikipedia.com/), a web-based encyclopedia for knowledge generally, is one of the most visited sites on the open Web attests to the popularity of encyclopedias for getting started on a topic, answering simple questions about it, and developing a working knowledge of the topic.

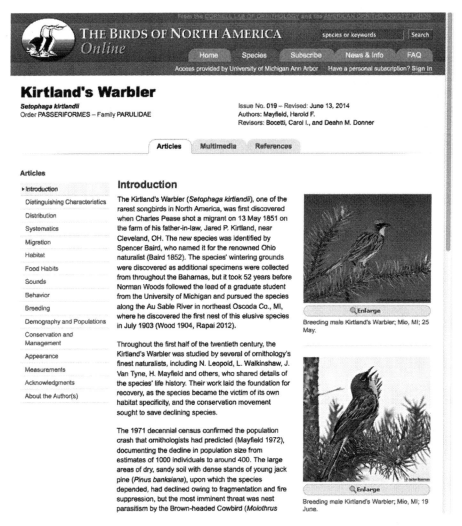

From the CORNELL LAB OF ORNITHOLOGY and the AMERICAN ORNITHOLOGISTS UNION

THE BIRDS OF NORTH AMERICA
Online

species or keywords   Search

Home   Species   Subscribe   News & Info   FAQ

Access provided by University of Michigan Ann Arbor   Have a personal subscription? Sign In

Kirtland's Warbler

Setophaga kirtlandii
Order PASSERIFORMES – Family PARULIDAE

Issue No. 019 – Revised: June 13, 2014
Authors: Mayfield, Harold F.
Revisors: Bocetti, Carol I., and Deahn M. Donner

Articles   Multimedia   References

Articles

- ▶ Introduction
- Distinguishing Characteristics
- Distribution
- Systematics
- Migration
- Habitat
- Food Habits
- Sounds
- Behavior
- Breeding
- Demography and Populations
- Conservation and Management
- Appearance
- Measurements
- Acknowledgments
- About the Author(s)

Introduction

The Kirtland's Warbler (*Setophaga kirtlandii*), one of the rarest songbirds in North America, was first discovered when Charles Pease shot a migrant on 13 May 1851 on the farm of his father-in-law, Jared P. Kirtland, near Cleveland, OH. The new species was identified by Spencer Baird, who named it for the renowned Ohio naturalist (Baird 1852). The species' wintering grounds were discovered as additional specimens were collected from throughout the Bahamas, but it took 52 years before Norman Woods followed the lead of a graduate student from the University of Michigan and pursued the species along the Au Sable River in northeast Oscoda Co., MI, where he discovered the first nest of this elusive species in July 1903 (Wood 1904, Rapai 2012).

Throughout the first half of the twentieth century, the Kirtland's Warbler was studied by several of ornithology's finest naturalists, including N. Leopold, L. Walkinshaw, J. Van Tyne, H. Mayfield and others, who shared details of the species' life history. Their work laid the foundation for recovery, as the species became the victim of its own habitat specificity, and the conservation movement sought to save declining species.

The 1971 decennial census confirmed the population crash that ornithologists had predicted (Mayfield 1972), documenting the decline in population size from estimates of 1000 individuals to around 400. The large areas of dry, sandy soil with dense stands of young jack pine (*Pinus banksiana*), upon which the species depended, had declined owing to fragmentation and fire suppression, but the most imminent threat was nest parasitism by the Brown-headed Cowbird (*Molothrus*

Enlarge

Breeding male Kirtland's Warbler; Mio, MI; 25 May.

Enlarge

Breeding male Kirtland's Warbler; Mio, MI; 19 June.

Figure 4.14. Online Entry for the Kirtland's Warbler from the Birds of North America Online, http://bna.birds.cornell.edu/bna, maintained by the Cornell Lab of Ornithology.

Almanacs, Handbooks, Manuals, and Yearbooks

This final group of reference sources is a potpourri that yields facts to answer typical reference questions. Much of the information published in almanacs, handbooks, manuals, and yearbooks is available elsewhere, but a number of factors have conspired to give rise to these genres. When a user asks a reference question to which a factual answer is possible, librarians keep these handy reference sources in mind.

Consult almanacs for facts, statistics, and lists (Bopp and Smith 2011). An example is the Information Please Almanac (http://www.infoplease.com/almanacs.html) on the open Web that can answer questions such as "What was the cost of a first-class stamp in 1965?" and "What religions have current and former U.S. Supreme Court justices practiced?"

Yearbooks review trends, issues, and events pertaining to a topic, place, or phenomenon in a particular year. Part almanac and part yearbook is the licensed CQ Almanac that "organizes, dis- tills, and cross-indexes for permanent reference the full year in Congress and in national politics" (CQ Press 2015).

Handbooks "serve as a handy guide to a particular subject, with all of the critical information that one might need" consolidated into a single source (Bopp and Smith 2011, 443). Manuals do much the same but they cover procedures. A prime example of a handbook is the Diagnostic and Statistical Manual of Mental Disorders (DSM) that health professionals consult to diagnose mental disorders (American Psychiatric Association 2014).

Selecting a Reference Database

Initially you may find it difficult to characterize the genre of reference sources that have potential for answering users' reference questions. Compounding this difficulty is the nature of these genres themselves, in a state of flux due to their migration from print to online sources, new functionality that is transforming their online versions into a different or entirely new genre that defies classification into one of the traditional reference genres, and their publishers' reluctance to update their names with terminology that reflects their different or new form. When you use a reference source successfully to answer a user's question, think about its genre and how the characteristics of the genre teamed up to make it possible for you to answer the question, so that the next time a user asks a comparable question, you will be prepared to seek out this particular reference source or others of the same genre to answer it. Table 4.5 classifies a handful of reference databases as follows:

- The form of their retrievals as surrogates or the actual sources themselves (column 2)
- Whether your search statements search surrogates or the actual sources themselves (column 3)
- The genre of the database's source as texts, media, numeric data, or digital libraries (column 4)
- Their reference database genre (column 5)

Table 4.5. Classifying Licensed and Open Web Reference Databases

(1) Database Name	(2) Form of Retrievals	(3) What Is Searched	(4) Genre of the Database's Sources	(5) Reference Genre
CRC Handbook of Chemistry and Physics	Source	Source (full-text)	Texts: Explanations, facts, tables, data, and statistics in Chemistry	Handbook
Europa World of Learning	Source	Source (full-text)	Texts: Contact info for cultural, educational, and scientific organizations	Directory
Merriam-Webster Online (http://www.merriam-webster.com/)	Source	Source (full-text for the licensed version only)	Texts: Definitions of words, etymology, grammar, orthography, pronunciation, regionalisms, synonyms, visual imagery	Language dictionary
Stanford Encyclopedia of Philosophy (http://plato.stanford.edu)	Source	Source (full-text)	Texts: Essays and biographies including bibliographical references	Encyclopedia and biography
Wikipedia (http://www.wikipedia.org)	Source	Source (full-text)	Texts: Essays and biographies including bibliographical references	Encyclopedia and biography

Questions

The table below lists several open Web databases. The first-listed database has been classified according to the four parameters below. Classify the rest of them, adding this information:

- The form of their retrievals as surrogates or the actual sources themselves (column 2)
- Whether your search statements search surrogates or the actual sources themselves (column 3)
- The genre of the database's sources as texts, media, numeric data, or digital libraries (column 4)
- Their form as a research database or their genre as a reference database (column 5)

(1) Database Name	(2) Form of Retrievals	(3) What Is Searched	(4) Genre of the Database's Sources	(5) Research Form or Reference Genre
WordReference (http://www.wordreference.com)	Source	Source	Texts: Definitions and translations of words	Language dictionary
Air University Library's Index to Military Periodicals (AULIMP) (http://www.dtic.mil/dtic/aulimp/)				
Kelley Blue Book (http://www.kbb.com/)				
Puerto Rico Encyclopedia (http://www.enciclopediapr.org/)				
WorldImages (http://worldimages.sjsu.edu/)				
U.S. Board on Geographic Names (http:// http://geonames.usgs.gov/)				
First World War Poetry Digital Collection (http://www.oucs.ox.ac.uk/ww1lit/)				

Summary

Enter http://www.onlinesearching.org/p/4-database.html into your Web browser for a video on databases.

Having gained an understanding of the user's query during the reference interview, you arrive at the second step of the online searching process—choosing a database. The sheer number of databases at your library's database hub may make database selection a daunting task, so most hubs organize databases by subject, discipline, or field of study. This chapter classifies databases according to their form and genre, defining form as the structure of the database and genre as the nature of the source or sources contained in the database.

This chapter's database classification is depicted visually in figure 4.1. Whether a database is a *source* database or *surrogate* database must be considered along two dimensions. The first dimension addresses whether your search statements search the actual sources themselves. When they search an abbreviated form of the actual sources such as an abstract or summary, it is a *surrogate* database. When they search the actual sources themselves, it is a *source* database. The second dimension addresses whether the database produces retrievals that are the actual sources themselves or retrievals that are descriptions of actual sources such as citations. The former is a *source* database and the latter a *surrogate* database.

Considered broadly, sources are *texts*, *media*, or *numeric and spatial data*. Databases that specialize in a combination of these are *digital libraries*.

Databases suited to fact-finding and answering simple questions are *reference* databases, and of the several reference database genres, biographies, dictionaries, and encyclopedias should be able to answer many of the questions users pose to you. *Research* databases are systematically organized collections of data or information that people search, producing multiple retrievals from which they must synthesize answers to their questions. The five types of research databases vary in form, the simplest being a bibliography and the most complex being a full-text database.

Bibliography

Alexander Street Press. 2014. "Filmmakers Library Online Series." Last modified March 26, 2014, accessed March 25, 2015. http://alexanderstreet.com/sites/default/files/products/FLON Series Brochure Reader 3.27.14_0.pdf.

American Psychiatric Association. 2014. "About DSM-5: Frequently Asked Questions." Accessed March 25, 2015. http://www.dsm5.org/about/pages/faq.aspx.

Bates, Marcia J. 1998. "Indexing and Access for Digital Libraries and the Internet: Human, Database, and Domain Factors." *Journal of the American Society for Information Science* 49 (Nov. 8): 1185–1205.

Bates, Marcia J. 2003. "Task Force Recommendation 2.3 Research and Design Review: Improving User Access to Library Catalog and Portal Information; Final Report (Version 3). June 1." Accessed March 25, 2015. http://www.loc.gov/catdir/bibcontrol/2.3BatesReport6-03.doc.pdf.

Bopp, Richard E., and Linda C. Smith. 2011. *Reference and Information Services: An Introduction.* 4th ed. Santa Barbara, CA: Libraries Unlimited.

Columbia University. 2010. "Avery Architectural & Fine Arts Library." Last modified 2010, accessed March 25, 2015. http://library.columbia.edu/locations/avery/avery-index.html.

Cornell Lab of Ornithology. 2015. "The Birds of North America Online." http://bna.birds.cornell.edu/bna/.

CQ Press. 2015. "About CQ Almanac Online Edition." Accessed March 25, 2015. https://library.cqpress.com/cqalmanac/static.php?page=about&type=public.

Gale Cengage Learning. 2008. "Associations Unlimited Navigation Guide." Accessed March 25, 2015. http://www.gale.cengage.com/pdf/navguide/assun_nvg.pdf.

Geographic Research. 2015. "SimplyMap: Powerful Data, Professional Results." Accessed March 25, 2015. http://geographicresearch.com/simplymap/.

Marquis Who's Who. 2015. "Our History." Accessed March 25, 2015. http://www.marquiswhoswho.com/about-us.

NTIS (National Technical Information Service). 2015. "About NTIS." Accessed March 25, 2015. http://www.ntis.gov/about/.

Oxford University Press. 2013. "OED Oxford English Dictionary: About." Accessed March 25, 2015. http://public.oed.com/about/.

Oxford University Press. 2015a. "A Dictionary of Opera Characters 2d ed." Accessed March 25, 2015. http://www.oxfordreference.com/view/10.1093/acref/9780199548194.001.0001/acref-9780199548194.

Oxford University Press. 2015b. "About 'Oxford Islamic Studies Online.'" Accessed March 25, 2015. http://www.oxfordislamicstudies.com/Public/about.html.

ProQuest. 2013. "Statistical Collections: Comprehensive Coverage of Business and Social Sciences Data." Accessed March 25, 2015. http://cisupa.proquest.com/ksc_assets/statistical/stat collections.pdf.

Suggested Readings

Munson, Doris M. 2006. "Link Resolvers: An Overview for Reference Librarians." *Internet Reference Services Quarterly* 11, no. 1: 17–28. Find out how clicking the resolver links accompanying retrievals automatically delivers the desired full-texts straight to your desktop.

Answers

(1) Database Name	(2) Form of Retrievals	(3) What Is Searched	(4) Genre of the Database's Sources	(5) Research Form or Reference Genre
AULIMP	Surrogate	Surrogate	Texts: Surrogates for journal articles, interviews, book reviews, speeches in military science	Catalog
Kelley Blue Book	Source	Source	Texts and numeric data: Product specifications for motor vehicles	Directory
Puerto Rico Encyclopedia	Source	Source	Texts: Essays and biographies on Puerto Rico	Encyclopedia and biography
WorldImages	Source	Surrogate	Media: Photographs of the natural and built environment	Encyclopedia
U.S. Board on Geographic Names	Source	Source	Texts and numeric and spatial data: Geographical names of places, natural features, and manmade structures	Directory
First World War Poetry Digital Collection	Source	Surrogate	Texts and media: Poetry and history	Digital library

5

Pre-Search Preparation

Search systems have had plenty of time to evolve over their fifty-year history. Their developers have listened to both expert searchers and end users, responding to their needs by implementing a wide range of tools in their systems. Yet, successful searches don't start with great system functionality. They start with the expert intermediary searcher developing a clear understanding of the user's query and restating this query in the language of the search system so that the system produces relevant retrievals. Chapter 5 covers the pre-search preparation that enables you to bridge the gap between your understanding of the user's query and your transformation of it into the system's searching language.

Conducting the Facet Analysis

Online searching starts with a user entering his keywords into a search system or asking you, the reference librarian, for assistance, an event that initiates a series of activities that may culminate with you conducting the search for the user or helping him conduct his own search. When you understand what the user wants and believe that searching online has potential for providing an answer, your next task is to conduct a facet analysis of the user's query, expressing it in no more than a handful of big ideas, major concepts, or facets that should or should not be present in retrievals. A facet is a word or very short phrase that describes a single concept or idea.

Despite the passing of nearly forty years since I conducted my first facet analysis, I remember the sample query that the late Ed Terry, expert intermediary searcher at the Johns Hopkins University's Milton S. Eisenhower Library, posed to me. It was "Does smoking cause lung cancer?" Take a few moments to think about this query's facets. If you are stumped, restate the query:

- "Is there a relationship between lung cancer and smoking?"
- "If I smoke, am I gonna get lung cancer?"
- "Lung cancer may be due to smoking."

Your facet analysis should produce these two facets:

    A. **Smoking**
    B. **Lung Cancer**

If it did, then you detected two facets, one facet expressed as the one-word noun, cancer, and the second facet expressed as the two-word adjectival phrase, lung cancer. Perhaps you analyzed this differently arriving at these three facets:

A. **Smoking**
B. **Lungs**
C. **Cancer**

If you did, then you divided the facet **Lung Cancer** into two separate and broader facets, **Lungs** and **Cancer**. To determine whether your division is right, wrong, or somewhere in between, a discussion of adjectival phrases is in order. Adjectival phrases are common in the English language. On their own, these phrases convey ideas that are both specific and complex. Examples are:

- College athletes
- Home schooling
- Role playing
- Health care reform
- Academic achievement

Torn apart, the individual pieces **Colleges** and **Athletes**, **Roles** and **Playing**, or **Academics** and **Achievement** convey ideas that are broader and simpler than their original forms, **College Athletes**, **Role Playing**, or **Academic Achievement**. The English language uses adjectival phrases to express many specific, complex ideas. Accustomed to the English language, you understand an adjectival phrase as a specific, complex idea but understand it as a single, unitary, and indivisible idea. In fact, if your doctor gave you *lung cancer* as his diagnosis for the symptoms that you are experiencing, you wouldn't break this adjectival phrase into two separate parts, **lungs** and **cancer**; you'd be blown away by his diagnosis, thinking to yourself, "Oh my! I've got *lung cancer*!" You have conceptualized the combination of the two words into an adjectival phrase as a single, unitary, and indivisible concept. Using adjectival phrases frequently in everyday speech, English-language speakers have come to think of them as one concept, not two or three concepts or however many words make up the phrase. In library and information science, this phenomenon is called *precoordination*, the combination of individual concepts into complex subjects *before* conducting a search for them.

So that you can distinguish facets from other online searching conventions, *Online Searching* represents facets in bold type and capitalizes the first letter of facet words. Examples are **Lung Cancer** and **Smoking**.

Let's revisit the facet analysis for Ed's query "Does smoking cause lung cancer?" Now, knowing about precoordination, which facet analysis is right—the two facets **Smoking** and **Lung Cancer** or the three facets **Smoking**, **Lungs**, and **Cancer**?

For the time being, both facet analyses are tentative. You won't know for sure which is correct until you choose a database and represent these facet names with the search terms that the database uses to express these facets; however, the two-facet formulation is probably more correct than the three-facet formulation because of precoordination. Most likely, databases bearing relevant retrievals for this query will use an index term in the form of the precoordinated phrase "Lung Cancer" for the facet **Lung Cancer** and not break the facet up into the two broader facets **Lungs** and **Cancer**, using the index term "Lungs" for the former and the index term "Cancer" or "Neoplasms" for the latter. Discussing here how databases represent these facets in index terms and searchers represent these facets in search terms delves into complicated stuff that can wait until chapters 6, 7, and beyond.

Conducting the Logical Combination of Facets

Your next step is to indicate to the search system how it should combine the query's facets in an online search. Boolean-based search systems use Boolean operators for combining facets. (These operators are named for George Boole, a famous nineteenth-century English mathematician, who invented Boolean logic.) The most well-known Boolean operators are:

- AND. Inserted in between two facets, this operator tells the search system to find sources bearing both facets.
- OR. Inserted in between two facets, this operator tells the search system to find sources bearing either facet.
- NOT. Inserted in between two facets A and B, this operator tells the search system to exclude sources bearing the second facet B but not the first facet A.

Online Searching represents Boolean operators in capital letters so you can distinguish the Boolean operators AND and OR from the English-language conjunctions "and" and "or" and the Boolean operator NOT from the English-language adverb "not." Whether you would capitalize Boolean operators when you enter a search is dependent upon the particular search system you are using—complicated stuff that can wait until chapters 6, 7, and beyond. For this query, you want the search system to find sources bearing both facets, and thus, you insert the Boolean AND operator in between them:

Smoking AND **Lung Cancer**

Venn diagrams are helpful visual representations of Boolean combinations. In figure 5.1, the rectangle represents all the sources in the database. The light gray circle on the left represents all sources in the database that discuss the **Smoking** facet. The light gray circle on the right represents all sources in the database that discuss the **Lung Cancer** facet. Where the two circles overlap reside sources that discuss both concepts, smoking and lung cancer. This is the area of the database that the search system retrieves as the result of a Boolean search for **Smoking** AND **Lung Cancer**. You don't want the search system to retrieve the areas where there is no overlap because those areas discuss only **Smoking** or only **Lung Cancer**, not both facets at a time. Presumably, sources that discuss both facets **Smoking** and **Lung Cancer** talk about the cause-and-effect relationship between the two, that is, whether smoking causes lung cancer. (By the way, Venn diagrams like the one in figure 5.1 were named for the English logician John Venn who popularized their usage over one hundred years ago.)

Figure 5.1. Venn Diagram Demonstrating the Boolean AND Operator.

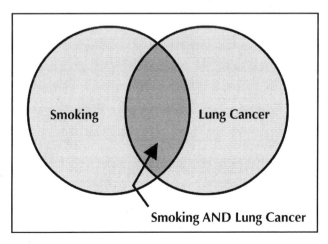

Expressing Relationship Facets

Some user queries are expressed in ways that anticipate a *relationship* between one, two, or more conditions A and B that tempt the searcher to express a third facet C describing a type of relationship between the conditions. The query "Does smoking cause cancer?" is definitely a candidate in this regard, inviting the searcher to identify a relationship or a causality facet.

For the time being, omit the relationship facet from your facet analysis. Sometimes you can convince yourself that the relationship facet isn't needed by restating the query. In fact, when you restate this query as "If I smoke, am I gonna get lung cancer?," causality disappears—a clue that the causality facet isn't needed in this query's facet analysis and logical combination.

Table 5.1 describes other relationship types that predispose the searcher to establish a relationship facet and add it to the facet analysis and logical combination.

Table 5.1. Relationship Types

Relationship Type	Query Example	Description
Effect	I am doing a project on how steroid use affects voting into the Baseball Hall of Fame.	Do one, two, or more conditions A, B, etc., affect C?
Impact	What was the impact of the alleged connection between vaccines and autism?	Do one, two, or more conditions A, B, etc., impact C?
Influence	How does religion influence non-marital sexuality?	Do one, two, or more conditions A, B, etc., influence C?

Queries like these scream at you to establish an effect, impact, or influence facet. Convince yourself such a facet isn't necessary by restating the query and noticing that these facets disappear. Let the Boolean operator AND establish the relationship for you. Conduct the search minus the relationship facet and invite the user to *read retrieved sources* to find out what their authors have to say in this regard.

There will be occasions when you will add a relationship facet to your facet analysis and logical combination. Those occasions coincide with your decisions about database selection, controlled vocabulary, and searching full-texts—complicated stuff covered in chapters 6, 7, and beyond. When *Online Searching* discusses these topics, it will revisit this discussion about the need for relationship facets. For the time being, omit relationship facets from your facet analysis and logical combination.

More Facet Analysis and Logical Combination

Let's work together on a second facet analysis and logical combination. The query is "I really need to know whether switching to flextime or flexible work schedules will improve my employees' morale and motivation."

Take a few moments to think about this query's facets. If you are stumped, restate the same query in different ways:

- Is there a relationship between flextime and employees' morale and motivation?"
- "Does flextime matter when it comes to the morale and motivation of employees?"
- "What is the impact of flextime on employees' morale and motivation?"

The facet analysis for this query yields four facets:

A. **Flextime**
B. **Employees**
C. **Morale**
D. **Motivation**

Your next step is to indicate to the search system how it should combine these four facets in an online search. You want the search system to find sources bearing the **Flextime** and **Employees** facets, and thus, insert the Boolean AND operator in between them. Then things get tricky. The user is interested in her employees' morale, and she's also interested in her employees' motivation. She probably doesn't care whether retrieved sources discuss both; as long as they discuss one or the other in the context of flextime and employees, she would be satisfied. Thus, insert the Boolean OR operator in between the **Motivation** and **Morale** facets. The logical combination for this query is:

Morale OR **Motivation** AND **Flextime** AND **Employees**

Use a Venn diagram to represent the logical combination of this query's facets. In figure 5.2, the rectangle represents all the sources in the database. Drawn are four circles, one each around the sources in the database that discuss the concepts **Flextime**, **Employees**, **Morale**, and **Motivation**. Medium and dark gray splotches mark the area of the database that you want to retrieve. Notice that you retrieve one area where all four facets intersect and two areas where three of the four facets intersect.

Figure 5.2. Venn Diagram Demonstrating the Boolean AND and OR Operators.

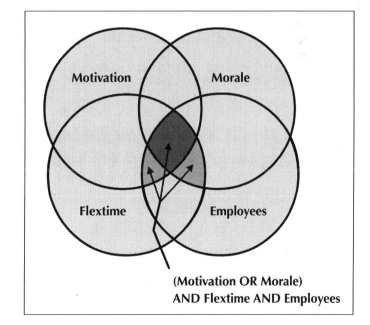

(Motivation OR Morale)
AND Flextime AND Employees

Your logical combination for this query bears a combination of Boolean operators: one OR and two AND operators. Each search system has its own rules for processing queries. Some process them left to right, and others right to left. Some systems have a rule called the *precedence of operators*; for example, they process ANDs first, then ORs, or vice versa. Memorizing precedence of operator rules for thousands of search systems is a waste of your time and energy. Instead, insert parentheses into your logical combinations to force the system to perform Boolean operations correctly. The use of parentheses is called nested Boolean logic, and it works the same way as the parentheses you used in algebra, e.g., (5 x 5) + 3 = 28 or 5 x (5 + 3) = 40. That is, the search system *first* performs the Boolean operation(s) *nested in parentheses*, then moves on to operations not in parentheses. When nested Boolean logic is added to the logical combination, the query becomes:

(**Morale** OR **Motivation**) AND **Flextime** AND **Employees**

The discussion of the Flextime query purposely uses the conjunction "and" in between the **Motivation** and **Morale** facets to demonstrate that Boolean operators (i.e., AND, OR, NOT) and English-language parts of speech (i.e., the conjunctions "and" and "or" and the adverb "not") are *not* one and the same. When users discuss their queries with you, they will use *English-language parts of speech*. Disregard the parts of speech they use when conducting the facet analysis and logical combination. If you are unsure whether the user would agree with your logical combination, ask her, for example, "Would you be satisfied with sources that discuss whether flextime improves employee morale but fail to mention motivation? Would you also be satisfied with sources that discuss whether flextime improves employee motivation but fail to mention morale, or are you only interested in sources that discuss all four ideas?" How she responds determines your search's logical combination:

(**Morale** OR **Motivation**) AND **Flextime** AND **Employees**
or
Morale AND **Motivation** AND **Flextime** AND **Employees**

Let's conduct a third facet analysis and logical combination together. The user's query is "I am researching the use of humor to treat people who are depressed but not with bipolar disorder." Take a few moments to think about this query's facets. If you are stumped, restate the query in your own words. The facet analysis for this query yields four facets:

A. **Humor**
B. **Depression**
C. **Treatment**
D. **Bipolar Disorder**

Your next step is to indicate to the search system how it should combine these four facets in an online search. You want the search system to find sources bearing the three facets **Humor**, **Depression**, and **Treatment**, so you insert the Boolean AND operator in between them:

Humor AND **Depression** AND **Treatment**

The user isn't interested in people with bipolar disorder so you can add this facet to the logical combination with the Boolean NOT operator. Because you are mixing two types of Boolean operators, you need to add nested Boolean logic (the parentheses) to tell the search system how to process the statement logically. Nesting the facets combined with AND tells the system to process this combination first, then subtract from it retrievals that bear the concept **Bipolar Disorder**.

(**Humor** AND **Depression** AND **Treatment**) NOT **Bipolar Disorder**

Use a Venn diagram to represent the logical combination of this query's facets visually. In figure 5.3, the rectangle represents all the sources in the database. Drawn are four circles, one each around the sources in the database that discuss the concepts humor, depression, treatment, and bipolar disorder. The white area represents all **Bipolar Disorder** retrievals that are excluded by the NOT operator. The dark gray area marks the area of the database that the searcher wants to retrieve—the intersection of **Humor**, **Depression**, and **Treatment** facets minus the **Bipolar Disorder** facet.

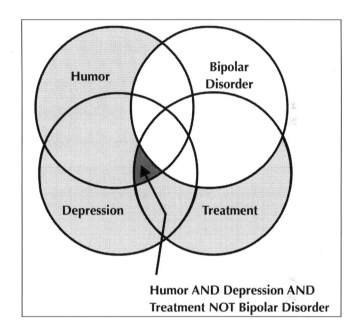

Figure 5.3. Venn Diagram Demonstrating the Boolean AND and NOT Operators.

There's almost always a hitch when using the NOT operator; that is, this operator is likely to eliminate relevant retrievals. For example, envision a perfectly relevant source that is an experiment comparing the use of humor to treat people who are depressed and who have bipolar disorder with the use of humor to treat people who are depressed but who aren't bipolar. The experiment's results show that humor relieves depression for people generally, whether or not they are bipolar. Such a relevant source would not be retrieved in a search that enlists the Boolean NOT operator. When you build logical combinations bearing the NOT operator, think about the relevant retrievals that the logical combination eliminates. For this query, a logical combination bearing the three ANDed facets should suffice:

Humor AND **Depression** AND **Treatment**

Eventually you may conduct a search for this topic. If the concept bipolar disorder predominates retrievals, then add a **Bipolar Disorder** facet to the search using the NOT operator.

Successful searches start with pre-search preparation that involves a facet analysis and logical combination. The facet analysis and logical combination are abstract activities that take place at a conceptual level. You are working with concepts and logical relationships between concepts. You are not getting your hands dirty, so to speak, choosing databases and entering search statements into them. If you are thinking about keywords and quotation marks when you conduct the facet analysis and logical combination, you are working ahead. Resist the temptation to do so, and think instead about identifying the concepts or big ideas that make up user queries, establishing them as facets, naming them, and formalizing relationships between facets using the Boolean AND, OR, and NOT operators.

When you select a database, you might have to adjust your facets based on the index terms that the database uses to express big ideas and concepts. The adjustments you make might affect facets and their logical combination, but that shouldn't stop you from performing an initial facet analysis and logical combination.

Typecasting Negotiated Queries

One of the reference interview's milestones is the negotiated query—your understanding of what the user really wants. Examples of negotiated queries are:

1. The use of humor to treat people who are depressed but not with bipolar disorder.
2. What is the highest temperature ever recorded in Miami, Florida?
3. The user wants to read more novels by the author of *The Lovely Bones*.
4. The impact of screen time on children.
5. Get the complete citation for a source with the title "Trends in Extreme Apparent Temperatures over the United States, 1949–2010" by Andrew Grundstein and John Dowd.
6. How did President Johnson convince conservative lawmakers to pass his War on Poverty legislation?
7. Eating disorders, possibly with an emphasis on women.

Also during the reference interview, you deliberate about database selection, facet analysis and logical combination, and whether a known-item or a subject search is likely to produce the desired information. A known-item is a request for a specific source that you know exists (e.g., an encyclopedia article, a journal article, a book, a conference paper, an organization, a blog, a magazine or journal, a directory entry, an author, even an advertisement). Subject searches are requests for information about a topic, idea, object, phenomenon, person, organization, etc., and they almost always retrieve several sources (e.g., encyclopedia articles, journal articles, books, conference papers, blogs, magazines, journals, directory entries, and combinations of these) from which the user synthesizes an answer.

Take a moment right now and decide whether a subject search or known-item would satisfy each of the negotiated queries above. When you are done, compare your answers with the discussion below.

Queries 1, 4, and 7 are open-ended queries with no rock-solid answers. Users will have to conduct subject searches in research databases, reading relevant retrievals and developing a greater understanding of all their topics. The problem with query 7 is the sheer volume of information about eating disorders generally and about women with eating disorders. This user needs to focus on something more specific. To get her started, conduct a subject search in a reference database such as an encyclopedia that will address the topic broadly and survey the various issues, trends, and ideas that occupy the research community studying this topic. Invite her to revisit you when she has targeted a specific interest so that you can help her find information specific to her topic via subject searches in a research database.

A subject search in a reference database such as an almanac that lists major cities and their high and low temperatures should produce the fact that answers query 2. Queries 3 and 5 are requests for known-items. Search your library's OPAC for the former, conducting a title search to identify the novel's author and following up with an author search to determine the availability of additional titles by this author. The latter appears to be a journal article, so search your library's WSD system, entering as much of the citation as the user has in hand and eliminating one or more citation elements when retrievals fail to include the desired one. Query 6 definitely calls for a subject search. If the user has little knowledge of Johnson and the domestic issues that besieged the nation during his administration, get him started with a subject search for Johnson in a reference database; otherwise, search the OPAC for book-level biographies of Johnson that focus on his domestic politics.

Questions

Perform a facet analysis and logical combination on these queries. If you are stumped, rephrase the queries in your own words and draw Venn diagrams to represent the logical combination visually. Omit relationship facets. Answers conclude the chapter.

1. We need to determine whether the various intervention programs out there are effective at reducing bullying.
2. Are teens from broken homes likely to develop eating disorders?
3. Should college athletes be paid?
4. New technology devices that help ALS patients communicate with family, friends, and caregivers.
5. Testing ice hockey helmets to make sure they are safe.
6. Someone told me that a wandering mind is an unhappy mind. Really? Show me the research!
7. Parents setting limits on their children's use of social networking sites and the Internet generally.

Summary

Enter http://www.onlinesearching.org/p/5-preparation.html into your Web browser for a video on facet analysis and logical combination.

Chapter 5 gives you a pre-search routine that will enable you to bridge the gap between your understanding of the user's query and your transformation of it into the system's searching language. This routine has three steps:

1. Facet analysis: Expressing the essence of the query in no more than a handful of facets that should or should not be present in retrievals.
2. Logical combination of facets: Adding the Boolean operators AND, OR, and NOT in between facets to indicate to the search system how it should combine them during retrieval.
3. Typecasting the user's query: Determining whether a known-item or a subject search is likely to produce the desired information.

There is no set order through these steps, and you'll even find yourself revisiting database selection. With experience and practice, your execution of all pre-search tasks—reference interview, database selection, facet analysis, logical combination, and typecasting—will take place simultaneously.

On occasion, the facet analysis reveals queries that would benefit from a relationship facet. For the time being, restrain yourself from adding such a facet because the Boolean AND operator usually sets it up for you, that is, producing retrievals with full-texts that elaborate on the relationship for users who bother to read them.

Answers

1. **Bullying** AND **Intervention** AND **Program Effectiveness**
2. **Eating Disorders** AND **Broken Homes** AND **Adolescents**
3. **College Athletes** AND **Payment**
4. **ALS (Amyotrophic Lateral Sclerosis)** AND **New Technology Devices** AND **Communication**
5. **Hockey** AND **Helmets** AND **Testing**
6. **Wandering Mind** AND **Unhappiness** (Note: Choosing a database such as PsycINFO makes the **Research** facet implicit because of the database's focus on research.)
7. **Social Networking** AND **Parents** AND **Safety** (Note: Minus the **Safety** facet, retrievals would be about parents doing social networking.)

6

Controlled Vocabulary for Precision in Subject Searches

Four steps of the online searching process are now behind you. You've conducted the reference interview, selected a database, performed a facet analysis and logical combination, and typecast the negotiated query for a subject search. Next you'll represent the search as input to the search system. If your selected database is spot-on, then your subject search should retrieve more than enough information; consequently, it makes sense to search the database's controlled vocabularies (CVs). A CV is a carefully selected list of words, phrases, or codes that human indexers assign to surrogate records to describe a source's intellectual contents and to facilitate online searching. CVs yield high precision results, that is, searches with mostly relevant retrievals.

CVs are characteristic of a wide variety of databases. In Boolean search systems, searchers are deliberate about their use of CV tools to search online. CVs factor into the relevance-ranking algorithms of extended-Boolean search systems such as Web search engines and WSD systems. Because such algorithms are a behind-the-scenes computational process, CVs may be transparent to users of the latter systems but they help to ensure that first-listed retrievals are relevant ones.

Overriding Search System Defaults

In the absence of specific search-language instructions from the user, all search systems default to a particular index that they search to effect matches of user-entered search terms and to a particular Boolean operator that effects a logical combination of multiple search terms. For example, the user enters a search statement in the form of a two-word phrase into the search box and hits the search system's search button. The search system's response is to search its default keyword index bearing words from sources' titles, index terms, abstracts, and full-texts and perform a Boolean AND operation, retrieving surrogates or full-texts that bear both words.

Expert intermediary searchers rarely rely on the system's default. Instead, they formulate search statements that put to work their understanding of how databases are structured and how search systems work. Here's the skinny on how they do this:

- Expert searchers script search statements into the system's searching language to divert the system from its default index to the index they want the system to search,

- They use search terms that they expect the system will find in that index, and
- They combine search terms with Boolean operators to effect the correct search logic and produce relevant retrievals.

Database Fields Governed by Controlled Vocabularies

Databases use fields to designate information about sources. A field is a set of characters in a database which, when treated as a unit, describe a particular kind of data like an author, title, or summary. Fields perform a very useful function—they designate the meaning or semantics of fielded data. When search systems index the values in fields, they keep track of the fields from which the values were extracted. Eventually a user comes along, enters his terms into the search system, and designates them for a title search. This prompts the system to conduct a title search, comparing the user's search terms to values it extracted from title fields and placed in its title index. When there's a match, the system reports the match to the user, and hopefully, the match is exactly the title that the user wants.

Eliminate fields from surrogate and source records and the search system isn't able to identify the meaning of surrogate-record or source-record data. About all the system can do is process all the data into one big index. Searches would be possible but the results would lack precision. For example, a search for paris would retrieve sources published in Paris, about the city, Greek god or celebrity named Paris, written by authors whose first, middle, or last name is Paris, issued by the city government of Paris, and much more.

Table 6.1 lists fields that are typical of surrogate and source records in databases containing scholarly, professional, and educational information, grouping them into broader divisions by function. Italicized functions indicate that databases may use one or more CVs to represent field values.

Table 6.1. Typical Fields in Surrogate Records

Function	Examples of Field Names	Notes about Source Function
Author name	Author, artist, composer, contributor, creator, corporate author, institutional author, investigator, organization, photographer, review author, statement of responsibility	Person or organization who created or contributed to the source
Occupation	Career, occupation, profession, role	Profession of the source's creator and contributors or their creative role pertaining to this source
Affiliation	Affiliation, employer, institution, membership	Organizations with which the creator and contributors are connected
Degrees	Degrees, certification, credentials	Creator and contributor credentials
Title	Document title, parallel title, subtitle, title, translated title, uniform title	Source's title

(continued)

Table 6.1. Typical Fields in Surrogate Records *continued*

Function	Examples of Field Names	Notes about Source Function
Source title	Conference name, publication title, section (of a newspaper), series title, source, source title	Publication in which the source is published
Publication	Volume number, issue number, number of pages, pagination	Additional information about the publication in which the source is published
Publisher	Designer, endorser, publisher, sponsor	Persons or organizations responsible for the design, development, deployment, production, dissemination, or publication of the source
Place	Address, conference location, location, place of birth, place of publication, place of employment, place of residence	Places associated with the source, its creator, contributors, or publisher
Date	Publication date, copyright date, conference date, last updated, revision date, date of birth, date of death, graduation year, entry date (of the record to the database)	Dates pertaining to the source, its creator, contributors, or publisher
Physical description	Dimensions, duration, extent, number of references, pages, size, volumes	Source's physical characteristics
Language	Language	Language(s) of the source or abstract
Audience	Audience, intended audience, target audience	Persons, groups, or organizations for which the source was created
Subject	Abstract, author-supplied keywords, classification, controlled terms, descriptor, event, family names, index terms, geographic terms, historical period, identifier, keywords, organization names, personal names, place, population, school, style, subject, summary, text, uncontrolled terms	What the source is about
Document type	Document type, format, genre, medium, methodology, peer reviewed, publication type	What the source is
Numbers	Accession number, CODEN, grant number, EC/RN number, ISBN, ISSN, LC card number, OCLC number, report number, unique identifier	Unique numbers assigned to the source by the creator, contributors, publishers, issuing bodies, database publishers, search system suppliers, etc.
Availability	Availability, URL, DOI	How to obtain the source

The Structure of Controlled Vocabularies

CVs vary in complexity. Some feature a simple base of authorized subject terms and unused synonyms directing users to authorized terms, and others add subject term relationships, scope notes, and even more to this simple base.

Simple Controlled Vocabularies

A simple CV is an alphabetical list of authorized subject search terms (also called index terms). For example, a CV for a sports database is likely to include the index term "Sneakers" in the list. Checking the CV for index terms for a query's **Athletic footwear** facet, you look under "Athletic Shoes," "Running Shoes," and "Racing Shoes." Finding nothing, you finally look under "Sneakers" and hit pay dirt. "Sneakers" is the simple CV's authorized index term for this phenomenon in your chosen sports database.

Many simple CVs have one added layer of complexity. They enlist "see references" or "use references" for the unused synonyms "Athletic Shoes," "Running Shoes," and "Racing Shoes." You look under "Athletic Shoes," and instead of arriving at a dead end, the CV says "Use Sneakers," directing you to the authorized index term for this phenomenon. Simple CVs are flat, consisting only of authorized index terms or authorized index terms and unused synonyms.

The Thesaurus: A Controlled Vocabulary with Term Relationships

More sophisticated is the CV called a thesaurus, and its sophistication is expressed in relationships between authorized terms. These relationships are editorially established by lexicographers, the people who build and maintain CVs. The broader term-narrower term (BT-NT) relationship between index terms is hierarchical and one of two types:

- Genus : Species | (example) Apparel : Clothes
- Whole : Part | (example) Shoes : Soles

The related term (RT) relationship is associative, designating relationships between index terms that are closely related conceptually but not hierarchically.

Our sports thesaurus designates three authorized index terms in **bold** for "Apparel," "Shoes," and "Sneakers." All three have BTs, NTs, or both; two have RTs. On the printed page here, there's only room for "Racing Shoes," one of the CV's six unused synonyms; its entry means "Racing Shoes, Use Sneakers."

Apparel UF Clothing RT Dress Codes NT Shoes	Racing Shoes Use Sneakers	**Shoes** UF Footwear UF Footgear BT Apparel NT Sneakers	**Sneakers** UF Athletic Shoes UF Racing Shoes UF Running Shoes RT Gymnasiums BT Shoes

The UF (used for) designation traces an authorized index term's unused synonyms. For example, the unused synonym "Racing Shoes" is traced under the index term "Sneakers," and it means "'Sneakers' is Used For Racing Shoes."

Most thesauri are limited to common nouns. Although proper nouns such as Michael Jordan, Nike, and Under Armour may be unacceptable in a thesaurus, indexers might assign them to the personal name, corporate body, and identifier fields of surrogate records. Some databases feature an identifier field where indexers assign proper nouns and new subjects. Lexicographers monitor the latter, promoting them to index terms when there is literary warrant, that is, enough domain experts have written about them.

The thesaurus network of index term relationships—BTs, NTs, RTs, and UFs—is called a syndetic structure. Also added to thesauri may be scope notes, that is, brief statements of the intended usage of an index term or explanations that clarify an ambiguous term or restrict the term's usage; add dates, i.e., the date when the index term was added to the thesaurus; categories, classification captions, or classification codes, that is, a broad category or class that describes this index term.

Searching databases with index terms that come from a thesaurus is easy because the syndetic structure gives you so many ideas for search terms to add to your searches. CVs are especially helpful when you have to search databases in fields of study and disciplines that are unfamiliar to you.

Conducting Controlled Vocabulary Searches for Focused Queries

You are now ready to put your knowledge of facet analysis, Boolean operators, and thesaurus relationships to work at searching Boolean search systems. Each Boolean search system has its own unique searching language. You can expect similarities between languages and rely on your browser's graphical user interface to perform some search operations for which searching language can be used. For the most part, you will want to learn the specifics of the unique searching languages for the Boolean search systems that you use all the time so you can search them quickly, effectively, and efficiently.

Conducting subject searches in databases that have an online thesaurus requires very little knowledge of the search system's searching language. The only new searching language feature that you will encounter is *sets*. Sets are temporary storage bins for search results. You enter a query into the Boolean search system, and the system saves your retrievals in set 1. You enter a second query into the system, and it saves your retrievals in set 2, and so on. You can recall your saved sets later in the search and use Boolean operators to combine sets.

Facet Analysis and Logical Combination

Demonstrated here is a CV search for the query "The use of humor to treat people who are depressed but not with bipolar disorder." The facet analysis for this query results in the three facets **Humor**, **Depression**, and **Treatment**. The **Bipolar Disorder** facet is disregarded because the NOT operator almost always eliminates relevant retrievals (pages 80–82). The logical combination is:

Humor AND **Depression** AND **Treatment**

Database Selection

Facets for **Depression** and **Bipolar Disorder** are big-time hints that a psychology database is best for this query. The go-to psychology database is PsycINFO. Published by the American Psychological Association, PsycINFO began as an abstracting and indexing (A&I) database bearing surrogate records with citations, index terms, and abstracts. Its 3.6 million A&I records describe the scholarly literature of psychology published in journal articles, books, and dissertations back to the field's seventeenth-century origins (American Psychological Association 2015). PsycINFO's CV for subject index terms is the *Thesaurus of Psychological Index Terms*. It is the real deal, featuring authorized index terms, a syndetic structure, unused synonyms, scope notes, and more. PsycINFO indexers assign up to fifteen index terms per surrogate record. They may designate up to five index terms per surrogate record as *major* index terms meaning that the source is really, *really* about the subjects described by its major index terms.

Browsing the Online Thesaurus

Browse PsycINFO's online thesaurus, choosing index terms for each facet. Start with the **Depression** facet. Switch to PsycINFO's advanced search interface and click on the "Thesaurus" link. EBSCOhost's PsycINFO allows you to find authorized index terms in three ways: (1) browsing for index terms beginning with the entered term depression, (2) browsing for index terms bearing the entered term depression, or (3) browsing for index terms based on relevance ranking. Get used to each approach because they are helpful for matching the ideas you have in mind with a database's index terms. Choose "Term Contains" and enter the term depression into the search box and click on the "Browse" button (figure 6.1).

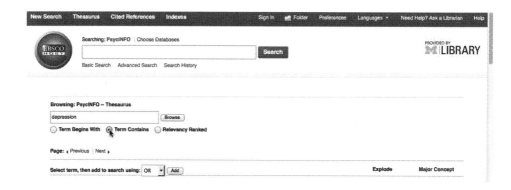

Figure 6.1. Entering a Term into the Online PsycINFO Thesaurus in EBSCOhost.

PsycINFO responds with a list of authorized index terms and entry vocabulary bearing your entered term depression (figure 6.2). No PsycINFO index term is an exact match of this entered term. The closest match is "Major Depression."

In response to selecting the index term "Major Depression," the EBSCOhost search system displays these elements in this index term's authority record (figure 6.3):

- The index term "Major Depression."
- The date this index term was added to the PsycINFO Thesaurus.
- The index term's scope note—an index term's definition and/or explanatory information about the index term's proper usage such as clarifying an ambiguous term or restricting the term's usage.
- The index term's history note—information about the term's representation in the thesaurus such as changes over the years, special instructions for searching this term online, and the range of years an unused term was in use.
- The index term's syndetic structure in the form of BTs, NTs, and RTs.
- The index term's entry vocabulary, that is, its unused synonyms designated as used for (UF) terms in the authority record.

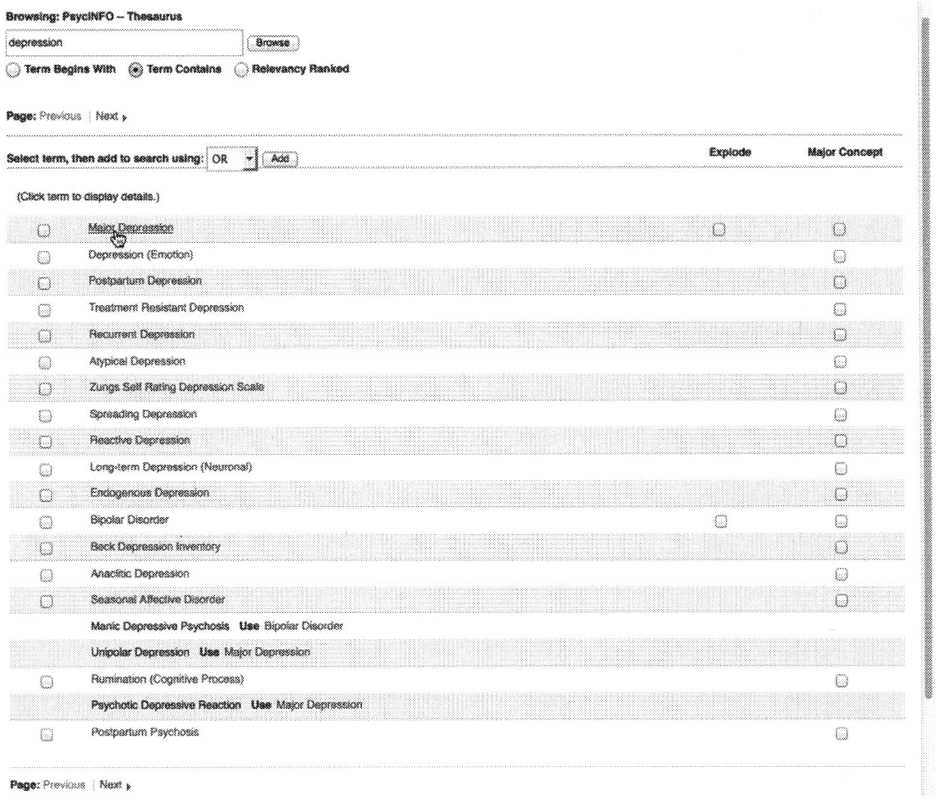

Figure 6.2. Index Terms and Entry Vocabulary Bearing the Searcher's Entered Term in the PsycINFO Thesaurus on EBSCOhost.

Examine the authority record, first reading the index term's scope note to make sure this term is in sync with your interests. This scope note defines "Major Depression" and suggests the index term "Depression (Emotion)" for PsycINFO content on people with nonclinical depression. After finishing up here, you'll check the authority record for "Depression (Emotion)" for additional index terms. "Major Depression" has one BT, and several NTs and RTs. Almost all listed NTs are satisfactory for representing the **Depression** facet. You can check the boxes to the left of these index terms to add them to the search. When you deem all NTs relevant, check the box to the right of the index term in the "Explode" column.

Always be circumspect about checking "Explode" and "Major Concept" columns in authority records. "Explode" automatically selects all listed NTs—make sure this is really what you want because doing so could pollute retrievals with many non-relevant ones and tracking down the source of non-relevant retrievals will be difficult and time consuming. (Whether the system also chooses the NTs of selected NTs is database- and system-dependent.) Checking "Major Concept" limits retrievals to major index terms. Use it sparingly, perhaps to reduce very high posted searches. In figure 6.3, checkmarks indicate the index terms selected by the searcher.

Next, click on "Depression (Emotion)," scan its syndetic structure for relevant index terms and check their selection boxes (figure 6.4).

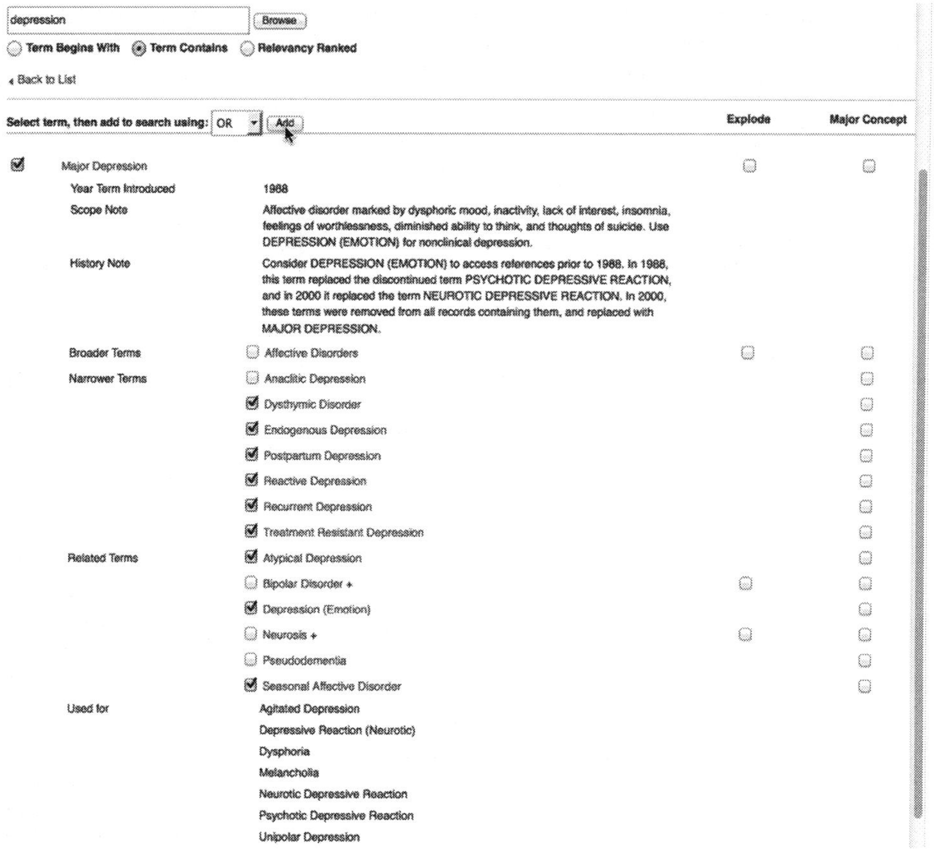

Figure 6.3. Authority Record for "Major Depression" in the Online PsycINFO Thesaurus on EBSCOhost.

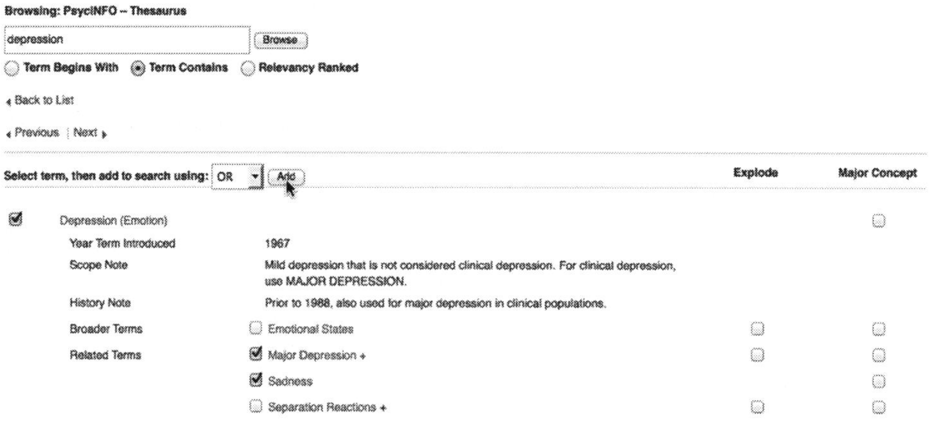

Figure 6.4. Selected Index Terms in the Authority Record for "Depression (Emotion)" in the Online PsycINFO Thesaurus on EBSCOhost.

When you are done selecting index terms from the "Major Depression" and "Depression (Emotion)" entries, click the "Add" button and leave the default Boolean operator set to OR (see where the searcher's cursor is positioned in figure 6.4). In response, EBSCOhost encodes your PsycINFO thesaurus selections in its searching language and places a search statement into the search box (figure 6.5).

Figure 6.5. EBSCOhost's Searching Language for Selected PsycINFO Thesaurus Terms.

Your next step is to click on the "Search" button. EBSCOhost places PsycINFO retrievals into set 1, reports the number of retrievals, and displays the first twenty retrievals.

Search for this query's remaining two facets, **Humor** and **Treatment**, the same way, entering search terms for each facet into the PsycINFO Thesaurus and choosing relevant index terms from authority records. Ultimately, the expert searcher's objective is to gather index terms for each query's facet using the online PsycINFO thesaurus, save the results for each facet in sets, for example, **Depression** index terms in set 1, **Humor** index terms in set 2, and **Treatment** index terms in set 3, then combine these three sets using the Boolean AND operator.

When you are done creating three separate sets for this query's three facets, click on the "Search History" link under the search boxes. EBSCOhost lists your search's sets, presumably one for each facet. Combine retrievals using the Boolean AND operator—checkmarking sets 1, 2, and 3 and clicking the "Search with AND" button (figure 6.6). In response, EBSCOhost combines the three separate sets 1, 2, and 3 in a Boolean AND operation, retrieving surrogate records bearing at least one index term per facet. Alternatively, combine sets directly, entering their set numbers bound by the Boolean AND operator into the search box: s1 AND s2 AND s3

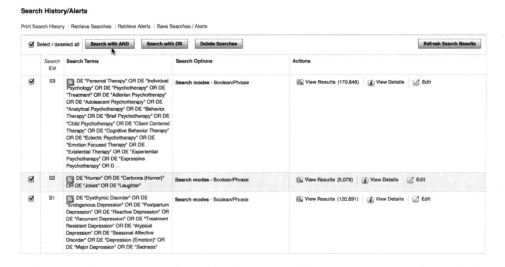

Figure 6.6. Combining Sets 1, 2, and 3 in a Boolean AND Operation in EBSCOhost's PsycINFO.

EBSCOhost's search of the PsycINFO database yields about a dozen retrievals. Figure 6.7 displays these results along with a few surrogate records, listing the most relevant ones first. Considering how few retrievals this search produces, you don't need to add the **Bipolar Disorder** facet to the search because combining it in a Boolean NOT operation with the three other ANDed sets would reduce retrievals even more.

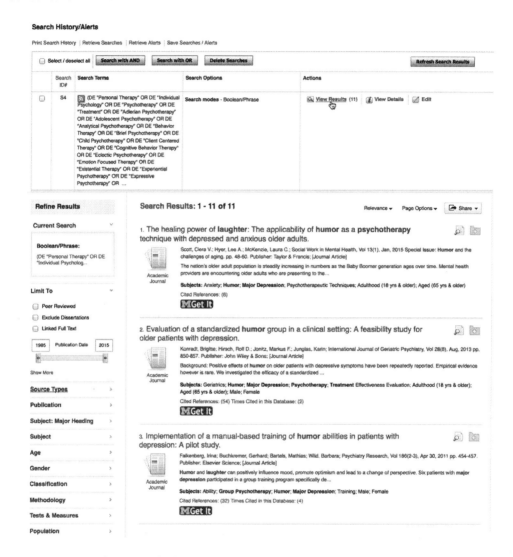

Figure 6.7. CV Search Results in EBSCOhost's PsycINFO Database.

Tips for Controlled Vocabulary Searching

Here are important points to keep in mind about CV searching.

RULE OF SPECIFIC ENTRY

When you check a database's thesaurus for index terms, you may find several relevant index terms to represent one or more of the query's facets. Choose as many relevant index terms as possible per facet so that you retrieve surrogates bearing these index terms. That there are several relevant index terms per facet has to do with the rule of specific entry (also called specificity). This rule governs indexers' assignment of index terms to surrogate records, requiring them to assign the *most specific* index term to the surrogate that describes the subject content of the actual source, not a broader index term that encompasses the specific term. Here are three examples of the rule of specific entry in action:

- If the source is about the use of humor to treat patients diagnosed with recurrent depression in client centered therapy, the PsycINFO indexer will assign the index term "Recurrent Depression," not the broader term "Major Depression."
- If the source is about the use of humor to treat clinically depressed patients in client centered therapy, the PsycINFO indexer will assign the index term "Client Centered Therapy," not the broader term "Psychotherapy."
- If the source is about the use of jokes to treat clinically depressed patients in client centered therapy, the PsycINFO indexer will assign the index term "Jokes," not the broader term "Humor."

When performing CV searches, expert searchers have to accommodate the rule of specific entry, choosing the most specific index terms to represent each facet. Strive to be comprehensive, selecting as many relevant index terms as there are for each facet and avoiding going too far afield.

AUTHOR-KEYWORDS

PsycINFO and many other A&I databases include an author-keyword field in their surrogate records. In this field are words and phrases that journal editors ask authors to add to their manuscripts when they submit them to the journal for review. Don't expect author-keywords to conform to the rule of specific entry because authors add keywords that describe their manuscript's contents; they do not choose them from the CV(s) used in the database(s) where their articles will be indexed, nor are authors aware of or given instructions to formulate keywords that are faithful to the rule of specific entry.

THE SOURCE OF DYNAMIC TERM SUGGESTIONS

Some search systems respond with a list of suggested terms while you enter your terms into the database's online thesaurus or enter your search statements into the system's search box. If you don't know where the system is getting these terms, avoid them like the plague! You want suggestions that are the database's CV but you may get user-entered keywords instead. Keeping track of the source of each system's dynamic term suggestions requires too much memorization or note-taking on your part, so just keep on typing, ignoring the system's suggestions, responding instead to the CV terms you browse and select from the database's online thesaurus.

ENTERING SEARCH STATEMENTS SINGLY OR IN ONE FELL SWOOP

Personally, I prefer entering search statements for facets one at a time, creating separate sets for each facet, then combining sets with set numbers and the Boolean AND operator. In the case of the Humor query, I would create sets 1, 2, and 3 bearing retrievals for the **Humor**, **Depression**, and **Treatment** facets, respectively. Then I would click on "Search History" where EBSCOhost lists my previously created sets and provides me with a search box into which I would enter set numbers combined with the Boolean AND operator, s1 AND s2 AND s3. It is easy to make changes to my search with its separate-sets approach to data entry. The one-fell-swoop approach means reentering the *entire search* to make changes. Featured in Textbox 6.1 are the changes searchers make to ongoing searches.

Textbox 6.1. The Changes Searchers Make to Ongoing Searches

1. Correcting misspelt search terms
2. Fixing logic errors due to missing parentheses or incorrect Boolean operators
3. Tightening up or loosening proximity operators
4. Adding relevant search terms to facets that the searcher culls from relevant retrievals
5. Omitting terms from search statements that have an adverse effect on retrievals
6. Eliminating search statements from the final logical combination to increase retrievals

---

WHETHER NTS HAVE FEWER POSTINGS THAN BTS

Don't be fooled into thinking that NTs have fewer postings than BTs. This is *not true*. For example, the index term "Major Depression" produces a whopping eighty-nine thousand retrievals in comparison to only twelve thousand for its broader term "Affective Disorders."

Direct Entry of Index Terms

Choosing index terms from a database's online thesaurus saves time and effort. To enter them manually into the EBSCOhost search system, the searcher has to search the thesaurus, jot down relevant index terms on a piece of paper or digital sticky note, then clothe them in the system's searching language. In the EBSCOhost search system, this includes:

- Prefacing the search statement with the DE field label
- Capitalizing Boolean operators (OR)
- Putting straight quotes around your entered index terms ("psychotherapy")
- Enclosing your entered index terms in parentheses

Here is a search statement that produces the same results as selecting the relevant index terms "Major Depression" and "Depression (Emotional)," their narrower terms, and the related term "Atypical Depression" from the PsycINFO Thesaurus:

```
DE ("dysthymic disorder" OR "endogenous depression" OR "postpartum depres-
sion" OR "reactive depression" OR "recurrent depression" OR "treatment re-
sistant depression" OR "atypical depression" OR "seasonal affective disorder"
OR "depression (emotion)" OR "major depression" OR "sadness")
```

That's a lot of typing. By the way, the searcher can either preface nested index terms with the DE field label or select "DE subjects [exact]" from the "Select a Field" pull-down menu. Doing so restricts the search system's retrieval of these phrases to index term fields of PsycINFO surrogate records. Search results from the direct entry of index terms are the same as selecting index terms from authority records (figure 6.4). The search system places the results in the next set. The searcher could do the same for the **Humor** and **Treatment** facets, entering each term individually instead of selecting them from the index terms from the BTs, NTs, and RTs displayed in authority records. The searcher's final statement would combine sets for all three facets:

```
s5 AND s6 AND s7
```

The "s" preceding each number refers to the set number. Omit the "s" and EBSCOhost searches for the numbers 5, 6, and 7. Alternatively, searchers can check the box to the left of each set in the "Search History" display, then click the "Search with AND" option atop the "Search History" table.

Direct Entry of Index Term Words

On occasion, there are so many relevant index terms for a facet that entering them directly would not only be time consuming, but it would require much effort, patience, and attention to detail to collect the index terms, spell them correctly, and type them into the advanced search interface. Search systems such as EBSCOhost offer a shortcut, allowing users to search for the words that occur repeatedly in index terms. Take your sample query's **Treatment** facet as an example. The scope note under "Treatment" advises searchers to use more specific index terms. Checking several other index terms' authority records reveals that the number of relevant index terms under "Treatment," "Psychotherapy," "Therapy," and "Counseling" may surpass six dozen or so. Keeping in mind the rule of specific entry, the searcher might want to include all of them to be comprehensive about retrievals. Typing them into the system's advanced search interface or placing checkmarks in the boxes accompanying these terms in authority records could take a long time. You also know that the CV search for this topic results in few retrievals (pages 90–94). Populating your CV search with *all* index terms bearing the words "treatment," "psychotherapy," "therapy," and "counseling" may increase the final result set without sacrificing precision because the search is still based on index terms.

Here are your next steps. Enter the relevant index term words "treatment," "psychotherapy," "therapy," and "counseling" into the advanced search box, nest these terms inside parentheses, and preface them with the SU field label. Here is a search statement for the **Treatment** facet:

```
SU (treatment OR psychotherapy OR therapy OR counseling)
```

By the way, the searcher can either preface nested index terms with the SU field label or select "SU Subjects" from the "Select a Field" pull-down menu (figure 6.8). EBSCOhost's response is to retrieve surrogate records bearing these words in index terms and in author-keyword fields. Putting quotes around each word limits retrieval to the word in quotes, not its plural, singular, and possessive forms. Omitting quotes retrieves the word *and* its plural, singular, and possessive forms.

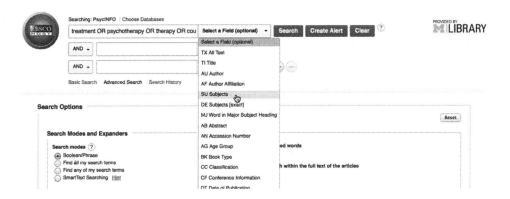

Figure 6.8. Direct Entry of Index Term Words in a Search of EBSCOhost's PsycINFO Database.

Substituting the search statement that retrieves index *words* for the search statement that retrieves full index *terms* for the **Treatment** facet almost doubles the retrievals for this query. Examples of relevant titles are:

- "Effects of Laughter Therapy on Depression, Cognition, and Sleep among the Community-Dwelling Elderly"
- "The Use of Humor in Cognitive-Behavioral Therapy with Outpatient Depressed Male Adolescents"
- "The Empathic Use of Sarcasm: Humor in Psychotherapy from a Self Psychological Perspective"

You can preview the index term words that the search system retrieves by browsing the thesaurus, choosing the "Term contains" option, and entering the index term word you intend to search. If you think that the majority of listed index terms are relevant, then shortcut. If not, select index terms from the display of authority records or search for index terms directly.

The Building Block Search Strategy's Buffet Edition

The execution of the search for the Humor query is planned, deliberate, and systematic—choosing index terms for each facet, combining synonymous index terms for each facet with the Boolean OR operator, creating sets of retrievals for each facet, and combining sets with the Boolean AND operator. The inspiration for search execution is search strategy. Search strategy is defined as "a plan for the whole search" (Bates 1979, 206). The search strategy that you used to conduct the Humor query is called the Building Block Strategy. Its name refers to the searcher's building-block approach to the overall search formulation, developing each facet of the query separately as if it were a subsearch on its own, then making the final logical assembly of the individual subsearches. Figure 6.9 is a diagram depicting the Building Block Search Strategy using three separate blocks, one atop the other, to represent separate sets of retrievals for the individual facets, and arrows protruding from the three blocks' right sides, all meeting on the left side of a single block representing the final set of search retrievals. Building Block is the strategy that all library and information science (LIS) instructors (present company included) use as the basis for teaching their students how to conduct in-depth searches of research databases (Markey and Atherton 1978; Meadow and Cochrane 1981; Hawkins 1982).

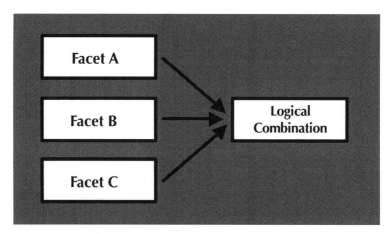

Figure 6.9. Building Block Search Strategy.

Over the years, I have observed certain students struggle with Building Block searches in Boolean search systems. Thinking that this strategy's name and the diagram associated with it fail to capture *how searchers build individual facets*, I have long sought an elaboration of the Building Block Strategy that is more illustrative of what goes on during building block construction. Dubbed the *Buffet Edition* of the Building Block Search Strategy, this elaboration pertains to searching Boolean search systems.

Let's examine this Buffet Edition up close and personal. A user approaches you with a query, and your negotiation results in a three-faceted query. You search the thesaurus, finding several index terms that are satisfactory for describing the first facet, including selecting several of their BTs, NTs, and RTs, then combine everything with the Boolean OR operator. Done with the first facet's construction, you proceed with the second, repeating the process until you have constructed separate search statements for every facet in the search formulation. Your final step is to combine sets for the separate ORed facets using the Boolean AND operator. This is analogous to what happens when you eat from a buffet. You visit separate buffet tables—one each for appetizers, soups and salads, entrees, side dishes, beverages, and desserts. These tables are analogous to your query's facets. You choose several items per buffet table, arrange everything onto your plate, and chow down. Choosing several food items per buffet table is like choosing index terms and their relevant BTs, NTs, and RTs from the database's thesaurus displays to construct ORed search statements for each of the query's facets. Figure 6.10 depicts the Buffet Edition of the Building Block Strategy visually, bearing several selections on your plate from each buffet table.

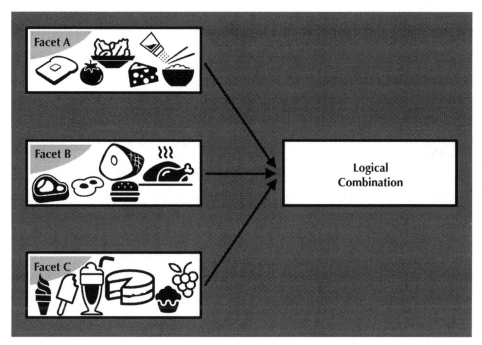

Figure 6.10. Buffet Edition of the Building Block Strategy. Created using symbols from the Noun Project (http://thenounproject.com): "Toast" symbol by Jacob Halton; "Salad" symbol by Peter Chlebak; "Tomato" symbol by Marco Olgio; "Cheese" symbol by Consuelo Elo Graziola; "Salt-Shaker" symbol by Nathan Thomson; "Food" symbol by Mister Pixel; "Steak" symbol by Anuar Zhumaev; "Egg" symbol by Jacob Halton; "Ham" symbol by jon trillana; "Turkey" symbol by Quan Do; "Fast Food" symbol by Saman Bemel-Benrud; "Ice Cream" symbol by Gustav Salomonsson; "Popsicle" symbol by Kristin McPeak; "Cake" symbol by Maurizio Fusillo; "Milkshake" symbol by Diego Naive; "Cupcake" symbol by Alessandro Suraci; "Grapes" symbol by Thomas Hirter.

Conducting Controlled Vocabulary Searches for Unfocused Queries

So far, this discussion of CV searching requires the expert searcher to specify what she wants. Often users aren't sure what they want. They have a vague notion—"Depression interests me," "It has to be something about K–12 students," or "Maybe something about the local food movement but I don't know much about it." Each one of these queries is vague, unfocused, and bears one facet—depression, K–12 students, local food movement. CV searches for these one-facet queries are likely to result in thousands of retrievals.

Databases and search systems are able to help users who have unfocused queries, situating them in a search space that addresses their interests but placing the burden on the database to suggest fruitful avenues that they might explore within the search space. One approach enlists clusters of CV terms that characterize salient aspects of retrievals. Use the "Depression interests me" query as an example. A CV search for this query yields over one hundred thousand retrievals in EBSCOhost's PsycINFO database (refer back to figure 6.6, set 1). On the left side of the window, EBSCOhost invites the searcher to "refine results" with clusters (figure 6.11). By the way, clusters vary depending on the number of retrievals—the more retrievals, the more clusters. In high-posted searches, it is useful to conceive of clusters as occupying two camps: *non-subject clusters* and *subject clusters*. Applying these *non-subject clusters* will reduce retrievals without affecting their overall subject matter:

- *Peer Reviewed*
- *Excluding Dissertations*
- *Linked Full-Texts*
- *Source Types* (e.g., journals, dissertations, books, encyclopedias)
- *Publication* (e.g., *Dissertation Abstracts International*, *Journal of Affective Disorders*, *American Journal of Insanity*)

Applying these *subject clusters* will not only reduce retrievals but, depending on the selected cluster value, change the overall subject matter of retrievals.

- *Age* (adolescence [13–17 yrs], middle age [40–64 years], very old [85 yrs & older])
- *Gender* (female or male)
- *Population* (outpatient, inpatient, male, female, human, or animal)
- *Methodology* (empirical study, interview, clinical case study)
- *Subject: Major Heading* (various PsycINFO index terms such as "Self-esteem," "Social Support," and "Dementia")
- *Subject* (various PsycINFO index terms such as "Drug Therapy," "Risk Factors," "Epidemiology," and "Mothers")
- *Classification* (various PsycINFO classification captions such as "Clinical Psychological Testing," "Military Psychology," and "Childrearing & Child Care")
- *Tests & Measures* (names of specific tests and measurements such as "Hamilton Rating Scale for Depression," "Beck Depression Inventory," and "Mini Mental State Examination")

Clicking on the arrow adjacent to each facet opens the cluster, revealing its details. For example, open in figure 6.11 is the Subject: Major Heading cluster where major subjects (i.e., PsycINFO index terms) are listed, beginning with the highest posted ones.

The highest-posted cluster values aren't very useful because they are PsycINFO index terms you searched for. Clicking on the "Show More" link opens a pop-up window bearing more subjects than can be listed along the left side of the page. Scroll down to the medium-posted subjects and you will see several major subjects that are likely to pique the interests of users researching Depression. Examples are "posttraumatic stress disorder," "aging," and "suicide" (figure 6.12). Selecting one of these subjects reduces this search's retrievals to several hundred.

Not all search systems have a cluster capability. When it is available, put it to work helping users who come to you with ill-defined, diffuse, or unfocused queries. Get the process started for the user by conducting a CV search for the one or two facets that are present in the user's unfocused query, then invite the user to browse a cluster's entries, not just the highest-posted entries but entries farther down the list. Advise them to choose an entry, scan the titles of retrieved sources, read their abstracts, and rethink their topic. Although this process takes time, concentration, and patience, reassure the user that he is making progress all the while, becoming more familiar with the topic generally and sampling fruitful subtopics that he might want to pursue in greater depth.

Another approach to helping users with ill-defined topics is to seek out a digital library database that is narrowly focused on a particular subject, practice, issue, genre, etc. Using the database may start the user at an encyclopedia-like article that briefs him on the subject. Then the database invites the user to explore, using pre-determined clusters to organize sources on the subject.

Opposing Viewpoints is such a digital library database. It is focused on today's hot topics. Clicking on one of its over four hundred "Hot Topics" displays the hot topic's homepage where the hot topic is described in a one-page summary. Opposing Viewpoints invites users to increase their familiarity with the topic, reading featured viewpoint essays, news and magazine stories, and journal articles. A wide range of sources are here including statistics that pertain to the topic, primary sources, images, and investigative news reports. By the way, Opposing Viewpoints has a hot topic homepage on Depression. Opposing Viewpoints organizes content so that users first encounter a basic one-page overview of their chosen hot topic (figure 6.13).

Under the overview is the *Featured Viewpoints* cluster bearing pro-con viewpoint essays. Other clusters are format-based, enabling users to consult easy-to-read and understand sources from *Newspapers, Magazines,* and *Videos,* before tackling more advanced material in the form of *Journal Articles, Primary Sources,* and *Statistics.* Each cluster bears a handful to thousands

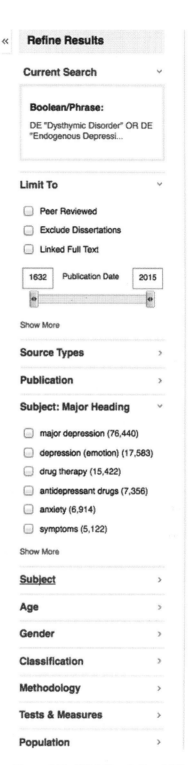

Figure 6.11. EBSCOhost's PsycINFO Clusters with the *Subject: Major Heading* Cluster Open.

Figure 6.12. Pop-Up Window Bearing Medium-Posted *Subject: Major Heading* Cluster Values in EBSCOhost's PsycINFO Database.

of sources and lists three sample titles. Users might not have to supplement their search with sources from other databases, finding everything they need at Opposing Viewpoints to write a paper, prepare for a debate, or create an oral presentation. When a user's topic doesn't map entirely onto an Opposing Viewpoints hot topic, users should explore related topics. For example, the user who is vague about "K–12 students" could explore these hot topics to concretize his interests:

- Bullying
- Charter Schools
- Childhood Obesity
- Homeschooling
- Peer Pressure
- School Violence
- Underage Drinking

Figure 6.13. Depression Homepage (Above the Fold) Featuring a Topic Overview and Clusters in the Opposing Viewpoints Database from Gale Cengage Learning. Courtesy of Gale Cengage Learning.

Benefits of Controlled Vocabulary Searching

When your chosen database has a thesaurus, *use it* to represent the concepts that interest the user. The database publisher has gone to great lengths to develop the thesaurus, establishing each authorized term editorially, deciding which of several synonyms should be the authorized term for a concept, linking term variants and synonyms to the authorized term, and characterizing relationships between authorized terms as broader, narrower, or related. Indexers assign CV terms to surrogate records to represent the concepts, big ideas, and themes that sources discuss. CV searching is nothing more than indexing in reverse. Instead of consulting the thesaurus to choose CV terms to index sources, the searcher consults the thesaurus to choose CV terms to *search* for sources. Matching CV terms that indexers assign to surrogate records should produce mostly relevant retrievals—high precision searches.

Controlled vocabulary is like the utensils you use to eat food—forks, knives, and spoons. When you don't have these utensils, you have to use your fingers or put your head into the bowl to eat. All the food gets mixed together and what you chow down doesn't necessarily come in the proportions that you want. Using eating utensils, you can be precise and on target about choosing exactly what is on your plate to eat and placing it in your mouth. That is exactly how CV searching works, enabling you to conduct high-precision searches bearing mostly relevant retrievals.

Whenever there is good reason to believe that the searcher can do a good job of representing the facets of the patron's query in appropriate CV terms, controlled vocabulary searching is the most effective way to search!

Controlled Vocabulary Searching Caveats

You won't be able to rely entirely on CV searching. First, there are databases that don't have a CV. Second, be on the lookout for database publishers that "fastcat" (fast-catalog) sources into their database. Fastcat databases omit index terms from surrogates for several reasons: (1) they want to put new content into users' hands as fast as possible, (2) they are catching up on back-logs and will add index terms to surrogates in good time, (3) they might have a policy of never adding index terms to certain surrogates, and (4) a combination of these three. When you notice surrogates bereft of index terms, check the database's help, FAQs, and tutorials for its indexing policies and practices. Third, the database's CV doesn't have index terms to express one or more of your query's facets. For all three situations, you'd conduct a free text (FT) search, a topic that chapter 7 covers in depth.

Occasionally, you'll search several databases simultaneously at a database supermarket or successively from different database publishers. When you do, you'll have to be deliberate about selecting index terms from each database's CV because these databases use different CVs. For example, five different databases use a total of three different index terms to describe an **Academic Performance** facet:

- "Academic Achievement" (ERIC, PsycINFO, Sociology Abstracts databases)
- "Performance" (Communications & Mass Media Complete database)
- "Achievement" (PubMed database)

Collecting relevant index terms and representing them in each system's searching language may take more time and effort than expert searchers are able to devote to the search, so they conduct free text searches (FT) instead (see chapter 7), knowing that their FT representations of another database's CV terms are likely to produce retrievals as a result of matching words and phrases in titles, abstracts, and full-texts.

Comparing Controlled Vocabulary Functionality Across Search Systems and Databases

CV searching is not a given across all databases and search systems. You have to scrutinize the database's homepage, advanced search, or expert search pages looking for links or tabs with names like "Thesaurus," "Thesaurus Search," "Browse," "Subjects," or "Subject Guide Search." CV functionality isn't always obvious, so click on various links and tabs to see whether they reveal index terms. Some CVs have thesaurus relationships, that is, BTs, NTs, and RTs. Other CVs are flat, limited to authorized index terms, maybe UFs. One search system may display the scope notes and history notes in a database's thesaurus, and other systems won't.

Tables 6.2 and 6.3 compare CV searching across five search systems. How searchers browse the database's online thesaurus is the focus of table 6.2.

Browsing the online thesauri in selected ProQuest and Engineering Village (EV) databases is quite similar to EBSCOhost. For an entirely different CV searching experience, search PubMed. You'll search two databases, first the Medical Subject Headings (MeSH) database (i.e., PubMed's CV), then the PubMed database bearing twenty-four million A&I records for journal articles in the biomedical sciences. To search for a MeSH heading, choose "MeSH" from PubMed's pull-down "database" menu to the immediate left of the search box. Enter drive, and the MeSH

Table 6.2. Browsing the Online Thesaurus in Several Search Systems

System | Database	Browsing the Thesaurus Online	Displays for Finding Index Terms	Contents of Authority Records	Search Multiple Index Terms	Explode Index Terms
EBSCOhost	Click on "Thesaurus"	Alphabetical, keyword, relevance	Authorized index term, scope note, BTs, NTs, RTs, UFs, year term added, and history note	X	X
ProQuest	Click on "Thesaurus"	Alphabetical, keyword	Two separate displays: (1) authorized index term, BTs, and NTs, (2) RTs, UFs, and scope notes	X	X
Engineering Village	Click on "Thesaurus Search"	Alphabetical, keyword, exact term	Authorized index term, BTs, NTs, RTs, UFs, and subdivisions	X	
PubMed	Mouse down on the database pull-down menu and choose "MeSH"	Keyword	Hierarchical displays of BTs, NTs, and RTs in which the authorized index term resides, scope note, UFs, subdivisions, and year term added	X	X
Gale's Gen. OneFile, Gen. Ref. Ctr. Gold, and Acad. OneFile databases	Click on "Subject Guide Search"	Keyword with dynamic term suggestions	Listed separately from the authorized index term are its BTs, NTs, RTs, UFs, and subdivisions		

database displays "Drive's" authority record (figure 6.14). The record display shows subdivided forms of "Drive" and one or more hierarchies in which "Drive" resides. The hierarchy reveals Drive's BTs (MeSH headings listed above "Drive" and indented to the left) and NTs (MeSH headings listed below "Drive" and indented to the right). To see "Drive's" RTs, click on its most immediate BT, "Motivation," and MeSH displays "Motivation's" authority record in which "Drive's" RTs are listed immediately above and below it. Also included in MeSH authority records are options to limit retrievals to the MeSH as a major index term and to turn off the system's automatic explode capability, limiting retrieval to "Drive" only and not to Drive's three NTs "Craving," "Hunger," and "Thirst" and their NTs. On the top right of the page is the PubMed Search Builder where the system displays both subdivided and unsubdivided forms of your selected MeSH. The Search

Builder's default operator is AND. If you are choosing both unsubdivided and subdivided forms of a MeSH, change the default from AND to OR.

You can enter a single search statement bearing all CV terms and Boolean operators into the Search Builder Box or break things up, limiting your search statements to CV terms for each facet, then combining sets using PubMed's search history capability. To familiarize yourself with the MeSH database's hierarchical structure and the bifurcation of PubMed searching between the MeSH and PubMed databases, take a dozen minutes to watch the MeSH tutorial at http://www.nlm.nih.gov/bsd/disted/video/ (National Library of Medicine 2013). It's time well spent.

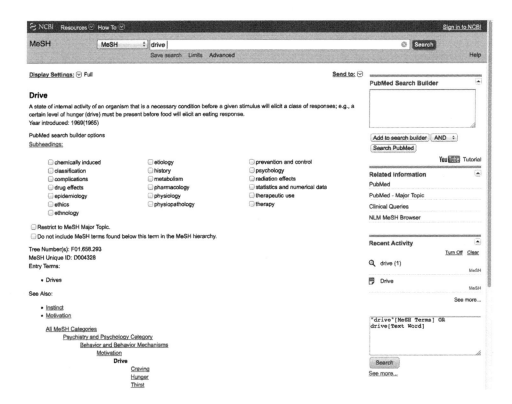

Figure 6.14. PubMed Authority Record for the MeSH "Drive." Courtesy of the National Library of Medicine.

The direct entry of index terms and index term words is table 6.3's focus. Listed in the far left column are five search systems and two databases (for EBSCOhost, Engineering Village, and ProQuest), sample search statements for the direct entry of index terms are in the middle column, and the direct entry of index term words appear in the far left column.

Except in Gale's research databases, searchers must enclose their index terms with punctuation such as double quotes (EBSCOhost, ProQuest, PubMed, Engineering Village) or curly brackets (Engineering Village), and prefix (EBSCOhost, ProQuest) or suffix (Engineering Village, PubMed) their index terms with a field label.

The searching language for the direct entry of index terms or index term words is complicated. Unless you search these search systems and databases every day, you are likely to forget their direct-entry conventions. Use table 6.3 as a template for making your own direct-entry comparison tables for systems and databases you want to remember.

Table 6.3. Direct Entry of Index Terms and Index Term Words in Several Search Systems

System | Database	Direct Entry of Index Terms	Direct Entry of Index Term Words
EBSCOhost | ERIC	DE ("moral values" OR "ethics")	SU ("ethics" OR "values")
EBSCOhost | PsycINFO	DE ("personal values" OR "ethics")	SU ("ethics" OR "values")
ProQuest | ERIC	su.exact ("moral values" or "ethics")	su ("ethics" or "values")
ProQuest | ABI/INFORM	su.exact ("cultural values" or "business ethics" or "ethics")	su ("ethics" or "values")
Engineering Village | Compendex	Choose Expert Search mode: ({ethanol fuels} wn cv) or ({ethanol} wn cv)	Choose Expert Search mode: ethanol wn cv
Engineering Village | Inspec	Choose Expert Search mode: ({web sites} wn cv) or ({portals} wn cv)	Choose Expert Search mode: web wn cv or portals wn cv
PubMed	Enter into the Search Builder Box: "drive"[mesh] OR "drive/drug effects"[mesh]	(Not applicable)
Gale's Gen. OneFile, Gen. Ref. Ctr. Gold, and Acad. OneFile databases	Choose Advanced Search mode, choose "Subject" from the "Index" pull-down menu: stress management	(Not applicable)

When searching a database's CV, browsing is much easier than direct entry because the search system displays an index term's syndetic structure and all you have to do is checkmark the terms you want. On occasion, you will encounter systems that provide display-only CV searching minus checkboxes for selecting index terms. Your only recourse is to jot down index terms on a piece of paper or digital sticky note and enter them directly into the system.

Questions

Conduct online searches for one or more of the queries below. Choose search terms only from the database's CV, selecting them from the database's online thesaurus or entering them directly using the search system's CV searching language. Consult tables 6.2 and 6.3 for CV searching language details. If you don't have access to some databases, the ERIC database produces relevant retrievals for half of the queries so start with it. You can search ERIC on EBSCOhost or ProQuest. ERIC is also available on the open Web at http://eric.ed.gov; however, its online thesaurus selection functionality is limited. Suggested CV search formulations for these queries conclude this chapter.

1. For the ERIC database: We need to determine whether the various intervention programs out there are effective at reducing bullying.
2. For the PsycINFO (or ERIC) database: Are teens from broken homes likely to develop eating disorders?
3. For the Academic OneFile (or ERIC) database: Should college athletes be paid?
4. For the PubMed database: New technology devices that help ALS patients communicate with family, friends, and caregivers.
5. For the COMPENDEX database: Testing ice hockey helmets to make sure they are safe.
6. For the PsycINFO database: Someone told me that a wandering mind is an unhappy mind. Really? Show me the research!
7. For the ERIC database: Parents setting limits on their children's use of social networking sites and the Internet generally.

Summary

Enter http://www.onlinesearching.org/p/6-controlled.html into your Web browser for a video on controlled vocabulary.

Into the index term fields of surrogate records, human indexers assign controlled vocabulary (CV) terms to describe the subject contents of sources indexed in databases. CV terms describe the concepts, big ideas, or themes in these sources, not just topics that they mention in passing. Because CV terms are comparable to the names you give to a query's facets, replacing facet names with relevant CV terms and adding them and their broader, narrower, and related terms to your search statements are the surest ways to retrieve relevant information. Searching a database's online thesaurus, you are able to select index terms and bypass the system's searching language almost entirely. To finish off the search, enter each facet's set number combined with the Boolean AND operator. Searchers can also enter CV terms or words in CV terms directly into a system's search box, but to do so they must learn the system's CV searching language.

Search strategies are helpful for giving searchers an overall plan for conducting the search. CV searches for the Humor query enlist the Building Block Strategy. You could apply this strategy to searches for every *multifaceted* query. Executing this strategy, the searcher develops each facet of the query separately as if it were a subsearch on its own, then makes a final logical assembly of the individual subsearches. Specifically, this is the Buffet Edition of the Building Block Strategy for which the searcher enlists the full range of Boolean search functionality to build individual facets of synonyms then combines them so that retrievals are guaranteed to address every facet of the query.

Bibliography

American Psychological Association. 2015. "PsycINFO." Accessed March 25, 2015. http://www.apa.org/pubs/databases/psycinfo/index.aspx.

Bates, Marcia J. 1979. "Information Search Tactics." *Journal of the American Society for Information Science* 30 (July): 205–14.

Hawkins, Donald T., and Robert Wagers. 1982. "Online Bibliographic Search Strategy Development." *Online* 6, no. 3: 12–19.

Markey, Karen, and Pauline Atherton. 1978. *ONTAP: Online Training and Practice for ERIC Database Searchers.* Syracuse, NY: ERIC Information Resources Clearinghouse. ED160109.

Meadow, Charles T., and Pauline A. Cochrane. 1981. *Basics of Online Searching*. New York: Wiley.
National Library of Medicine. 2013. "Branching Out: The MeSH Vocabulary." Last modified November 15, 2013, accessed March 25, 2015. http://www.nlm.nih.gov/bsd/disted/video/.

Suggested Readings

Bates, Marcia. 1988. "How to Use Controlled Vocabularies More Effectively in Online Searching." *Online* 12, no. 6 (Nov.): 45–56. Surveys the wide range of controlled vocabularies in online search systems: category codes, descriptors, faceted classification, hierarchical classification, post-controlled vocabulary, and subject headings.

Shiri, Ali. 2012. *Powering Search: The Role of Thesauri in New Information Environments*. Medford, NJ: Information Today. A comprehensive treatment of the thesaurus in online search systems.

Answers

The tables that follow are topped with rows bearing index terms that you can select from the search system's online thesaurus or search directly. The remaining rows tell how to combine intermediary sets for each facet into a final results set and list a couple of relevant titles. By the way, there are multiple ways to conduct CV searches for these topics, so don't think that these search formulations are definitive.

1. ERIC: Reducing Bullying . . .

Facets	Choosing Terms for Search Statements (in EBSCOhost)
Bullying	DE "bullying"
Intervention	DE ("intervention" OR "feasibility studies" OR "early intervention" OR "behavior modification" OR "response to intervention")
Program Effectiveness	DE ("program effectiveness" OR "program evaluation" OR "program implementation" OR "comparative analysis" OR "prevention" OR "program development" OR "outcomes of education")
To combine sets:	Choose "Search history." Checkmark set numbers for these three facets and click on the "Search with AND" button.
Retrieved titles:	"The Effects of a Bully Intervention Program on the Relational Aggressive Behaviors of 5th Grade Girls" and "Lessons from a Concurrent Evaluation of Eight Antibullying Programs Used in Sweden"

2. PsycINFO: Eating disorders . . .

Facets	Choosing Terms for Search Statements (in EBSCOhost)
Eating Disorders	Click the "Thesaurus" tab and enter `eating disorders`. Checkmark the "Explode" box under "Eating Disorders" forcing PsycINFO to select all NTs. Choose "Add to search using OR."
Broken Homes	Click the "Thesaurus" tab and enter `divorce`. Select relevant index terms such as "Divorce," "Child Custody," "Divorced Persons," "Marital Separation." Click on these index terms to browse and select their BTs, NTs, and RTs such as "Parental Absence," "Mother Absence," and "Father Absence." Choose "Add to search using OR."
Adolescents	Be prepared to choose a relevant value from the *Age Groups* cluster.
To combine sets:	Choose "Search history." Checkmark set numbers for the first two facets and click on the "Search with AND" button. Then choose "adolescence 13–17 yrs" from the *Age Group* cluster.
Retrieved titles:	"Incidence of Broken Home Family Background in Bulimia" and "Risk Factors for Bulimia Nervosa: A Controlled Study of Parental Psychiatric Illness and Divorce"

3. Gale General OneFile or Academic OneFile: College athletes . . .

Facets	Choosing Terms for Search Statements
College athletes	Choose the Subject Guide Search, enter `college athletes,` and jot down relevant related terms. Choose Advanced Search, choose "Subject" from the fields' pull-down menu, and enter relevant terms into the first search box: `"college athletes" OR "college sports" OR "college baseball" OR "college basketball" OR "college football" OR "college hockey"`
Payment	Same instructions as above, except for entering relevant terms into the second search box: `"pay for performance" OR "wages and salaries" OR "antitrust law"`
To combine sets:	Having filled the first two search boxes with relevant index terms, click the "Search" button.
Retrieved titles:	"Should College Athletes Be Paid?" and "Players 0, Colleges $10,000,000,000: University Sports"

4. PubMed: ALS patients . . .

Facets	Choosing Terms for Search Statements (in PubMed)
ALS	"amyotrophic lateral sclerosis"[Mesh]
New Technology Devices	Select these two unsubdivided MeSH: "Self-Help Devices"[Mesh:NoExp] OR "Communication Aids for Disabled"[Mesh]. Select also these two MeSH bearing these subdivisions: methods, standards, supply and distribution, therapeutic use, trends, utilization.
To combine sets:	Click Advanced Search. Into the Builder, enter set numbers for the two facets combined with the Boolean AND operator: #1 AND #2.
Retrieved titles:	"Technology to Help Persons with Extensive Neuro-Motor Impairment and Lack of Speech with Their Leisure Occupation and Communication" and "Eye Tracking Communication Devices in Amyotrophic Lateral Sclerosis"

5. COMPENDEX: Hockey helmets . . .

Facets	Choosing Terms for Search Statements
Hockey	Choose the "Thesaurus Search" tab and enter sports. Choose "Sports" and "Sports Medicine." (Watch the system fill up the "Search Box" with terms.) Choose "Combine Search with OR."
Helmets	Choose the "Thesaurus Search" tab and enter protective. Choose "Safety Devices" and "Protective Clothing." Choose "Combine Search with OR."
Testing	Choose the "Thesaurus Search" tab and enter testing (exact term). Choose BTs, NTs, RTs, and subdivided terms such as "Acceptance Tests," "Equipment Testing," "Impact Resistance," "Impact Testing," "Inspection," "Low Temperature Testing," "Materials Testing—Impact," "Materials Testing—Low Temperature," "Safety Testing," "Shock Testing," "Standardization," "Standards," "Testing." Choose "Combine Search with OR."
To combine sets:	Choose "Search History." Checkmark set numbers for these three facets. The system automatically inserts the Boolean AND operator in between set numbers in the "Combine Searches" box. Click on the "Search" button.
Retrieved titles:	"Comparison of International Safety Standards for Ice Hockey Helmets" and "Hockey Headgear and the Adequacy of Current Designs and Standards"

6. PsycINFO: Wandering mind . . .

Facets	Choosing Terms for Search Statements (in EBSCOhost)
Wandering Mind	DE ("mind" OR "wandering behavior" OR "daydreaming")
Unhappiness	DE ("happiness" OR "pleasure" OR "sadness" OR "well-being" OR "depression (emotion)" OR "major depression" OR "moodiness" or "emotional states")
Emotions	Choose the "Thesaurus" tab and enter emotional responses. Choose "Emotional Responses," "Emotions," "Affective Valence." Click on the "Add" button adjacent to the instructions "Select term, then add to search using:" and choose the default OR operator.
To combine sets:	Choose "Search history." Checkmark set numbers for these three facets and click on the "Search with AND" button.
Retrieved titles:	"Wandering or Unhappy Mind?" and "Mind-Wandering and Negative Mood: Does One Thing Lead to Another?"

7. ERIC: Parents setting limits . . .

Facets	Choosing Terms for Search Statements (in ProQuest)
Social Networking	su.exact ("internet" OR "social networks" OR "web sites" OR "web 2.0 technologies" OR "computer mediated communication" OR "information networks")
Parent Participation	Choose the "Thesaurus" tab and enter parent participation. From this index term's entry *and* the entries of its RTs, choose "Child Rearing," "Parent Child Relationship," "Parent Role," "Parent Participation," "Parenting Skills," "Parenting Styles," "Parent Influence," "Parents as Teachers."
Safety	Choose the "Thesaurus" tab and enter child safety. Choose "Child Safety," "Computer Security," "Responsibility," "Safety Education," Safety."
To combine sets:	Choose "Search history." Enter set numbers for these three facets into the "Combine searches" box and click on the "Search" button.
Examples of retrieved titles:	"Teenagers' Internet Use and Family Rules" and "Upholding the Convention on the Rights of the Child: A Quandary in Cyberspace"

7

Free Text Searching for Recall in Subject Searches

Free text (FT) searching allows searchers to use any words and phrases in their search statements, not just those that come from the database's controlled vocabulary (CV). Because it extends searching to the entire surrogate record, even to entire full-texts such as journal articles, encyclopedia entries, conference papers, and whole books, it yields high recall results, that is, searches with as many relevant sources as possible. FT searching is an especially fruitful approach for searching queries that explore cutting-edge topics for which there is no consensus about the right terminology to apply to the object, event, or phenomenon. For example, when the AIDS virus became front-page headlines in the late 1970s, the disease was entirely new, the medical community did not know how people contracted it, nor did they have a name for it. Eventually, the U.S. Centers for Disease Control and Prevention (CDC) assigned the name Acquired Immune Deficiency Syndrome (AIDS) to the disease, but if you were researching AIDS back then, FT searching was the *only* way to search for information on AIDS. It still is the only way to search for today's cutting-edge topics.

This chapter presents FT searching of surrogate records and full-texts in Boolean and extended-Boolean systems. Extended-Boolean systems have few FT searching tools because their indexing, searching, and ranking algorithms do automatically what searchers of Boolean systems must do deliberately with FT searching tools.

Overriding Search System Defaults Revisited

FT searching requires you to think about how people would express ideas and concepts in a written text, and it isn't easy because of the many different ways people use language to communicate. Rarely are you able to predict the exact words that a person will say. Even when greeting a long-time friend, what you say varies greatly:

- Hi, how are you?
- How's it going?
- Waz up?
- Yo.
- Hey.

Your friend's responses vary even more, ranging from a positive response such as "Fine thanks and you?" to a negative one that includes a list of his or her latest troubles such as "Not so good. I hate my job, I know my boss is out to get me, I don't get paid enough, and I have a sore throat." Predicting your greeting is probably much easier than your friend's response, but typically, both texts are highly variable. So it is with formal, written text, even text that is highly formalized, compact, and goal-oriented such as a scholarly text's summary or abstract. Despite the difficulty of predicting text, you must do so to conduct FT searches because CVs don't cover every concept under the sun.

Expert searchers wield FT searching tools that give them the power to search some or all database fields. To make decisions about what to search, it is helpful to think about database fields coming in the following flavors:

- *CV fields* bearing editorially established words and phrases that designate the big ideas, important concepts, and ideas discussed in full-texts.
- *Uncontrolled surrogate record fields* bearing summary information (usually in the form of a title and abstract) that describes the intellectual contents of full-texts and media.
- *Citation information* such as journal title, publisher, place, and date of publication that helps people find full-texts or media in libraries, bookstores, and databases and cite them in their written works.
- *Full-text.* The text of the actual source itself.
- *Cited references.* Sources that the source in hand cite.
- *Citing references.* Sources that have cited the source in hand since its publication.
- A combination of two or more of the flavors above.

When expert searchers conduct FT searches, they scrutinize the flavors that databases come in, then choose the best FT tools at hand for producing search results bearing as many relevant retrievals as possible while minimizing the retrieval of non-relevant material.

Free Text Searching Tools

Like CV searching, FT searching begins with a facet analysis and logical combination. When you are certain that you understand what the user wants, represent their query using facets and combine these facets using Boolean operators. Some databases don't have CVs so your searches will be FT exclusively. Other databases will have CVs but there may be no or not enough CV terms to represent one or more of the query's facets, requiring you to conduct FT searches for them. Terminology for FT search terms starts with the user's terminology and snowballs outward (textbox 7.1).

Search systems index each and every word in surrogate records and full-texts (when available) for FT searches. How search systems define a word varies across systems, but basically they define a word to be a string of alphabetical, numeric, or alphanumeric characters separated by spaces, tabs, paragraph breaks, or symbols. To avoid memorizing the three different ways systems can index hyphenated words, searchers who strive for high recall search them as hyphenated phrases (decision-making), phrases ("decision making"), and closed-up phrases (decisionmaking). Failure to do so may result in fewer relevant retrievals than you expected.

Here's a topic for a free text search, "The entrepreneurial activities of women whose livelihoods depend on farming." Your facet analysis and logical combination result in two facets combined by the Boolean AND operator.

Entrepreneurship AND Farm Women

Checking the database's CV, you can't find suitable index terms for the **Farm Women** facet. Thus, your only recourse is to represent this facet using FT terms.

Adjacency, Nearby, and Word Order Matters

Starting with the **Farm Women** facet, you want to retrieve an exact match (ignoring capitali-
zation) of the adjective phrase "farm women" in text. Thus, a retrieval must meet these three
conditions:

1. The word "farm" and the word "women" must reside in the same surrogate or full-text
2. The word "farm" must be adjacent to the word "women"
3. The word "farm" must come before the word "women"

The Boolean AND operator is satisfactory for handling condition #1 only. You need a proximity
operator to make sure the two words are adjacent and word order is preserved. Many Boolean
systems have just such an operator, but be prepared for operator names and syntax to vary from
system to system. EBSCOhost's adjacency-and-word-order-matters proximity operator is w0 and
ProQuest's is pre/0 or p/0. Here are EBSCOhost and ProQuest search statements that retrieve
the phrase "farm women" in text:

    farm w0 women | EBSCOhost
    farm pre/0 women | ProQuest
    farm p/0 women | ProQuest

In both systems, you can substitute quotes for this particular proximity operator:

    "farm women" | EBSCOhost or ProQuest

For the sake of brevity, *Online Searching* refers to the adjacency-and-word-order-matters proximity operator as the *adjacency* operator.

In text, the idea of "farm women" could be expressed in many different ways. For example,
consider these strings of text in which the word "farm" is a few words away from the word
"women," but the string still conveys the idea of farm women:

- ". . . farm and rural women . . ."
- *All We Knew Was to Farm: Rural Women in the Upcountry South, 1914–1941*
- ". . . farm, rural, and country women . . ."
- ". . . farm hardened, agrarian women . . ."

Adjacency operators bear a number that searchers can manipulate to designate the maximum number of intervening words between their search words. For example, replace the 0 in EBSCOhost's **w0** or the 0 in ProQuest's **pre/0** or **p/0** adjacency operator with a number to designate how far apart your search words can be. Here are examples:

> `farm w1 women` | retrieves only the second example above in EBSCOhost
> `farm w5 women` | retrieves all three examples above in EBSCOhost
> `farm pre/4 women` | retrieves all three examples above in ProQuest
> `farm p/1 women` | retrieves only the second example above in ProQuest

The farther apart the two words are, the more likely that intervening words will contribute to the source's non-relevance or steer meaning in one or more undesirable directions. Furthermore, words adjacent or in close proximity to one another do not always express the desired concept. One or more of the above search statements would retrieve non-relevant sources bearing these sentence fragments below:

- ". . . grew up on a farm where women worked hard and moved away . . ."
- ". . . this is not about farm, rural, or country women but about . . ."
- ". . . the historic farmhouse that women architects designed . . ."

Retrieving non-relevant retrievals is the chance searchers take when they conduct FT searches. FT searching enlists *post-coordination* to produce retrievals—the searcher's deliberate combination of words into search statements *after* the search system has extracted words from texts into its searchable indexes. There's no guarantee that FT searches will produce relevant retrievals for the ideas searchers have in mind.

Adjacency, Nearby, and Word Order Does Not Matter

The idea of farm women need not be limited to the word "farm" preceding the word "women." Consider these four phrases in which the words are reversed but still convey the idea of farm women:

- ". . . women who farm . . ."
- ". . . women work hard, full-time on the farm . . ."
- *Characteristics of Women Farm Operators and Their Farms*

Boolean systems enlist the nearby (also called near or neighbor) proximity operator to retrieve search words that are adjacent or close to one another and for which word order does not matter. EBSCOhost's nearby proximity operator is **n0**, and ProQuest's nearby operator is **near/0** or **n/0**. Replace the zero with a positive number to designate how many intervening words can separate your search words. Search statement examples are:

> `farm n0 women` | EBSCOhost retrieves the third example above
> `farm near/1 women` | ProQuest retrieves the first and third examples above
> `farm n3 women` | EBSCOhost retrieves the first and third examples above
> `farm n/6 women` | ProQuest retrieves all three examples above

The nearby proximity operator is handy for FT searches involving names. If you are unsure whether the system indexes names in direct (e.g., Friedman, Thomas) or indirect (e.g., Thomas Friedman) form, use the nearby proximity operator to retrieve multiple forms (`thomas near/1 friedman`).

Truncation

The concept of farm women comes through despite changes to the forms of the words themselves. Consider these texts:

- "... women farmers ..."
- "The woman took over several farms ..."
- "... farming is for both women and men ..."
- "These fields, farmed exclusively by women ..."

Explicit truncation is a FT search tool for retrieving singular and plural forms of words and word variants. It usually involves the insertion of a symbol such as a question mark (?), pound sign (#), exclamation point (!), or asterisk (*) to the beginning or end of a word stem or embedded somewhere in between. When it comes to explicit truncation, few systems are as fully featured as ProQuest (textbox 7.2).

Textbox 7.2. The Wide Range of Truncation Functionality in the ProQuest Search System

ProQuest's truncation functionality demonstrates how extensive and complicated truncation can get.

- *Unlimited left-hand truncation.* Preface the truncated stem with a symbol. For example, *graph retrieves holograph, mimeograph, photograph, serigraph, telegraph, and many more words bearing these five letters.
- *Unlimited right-hand truncation.* Enter the truncated stem appending a symbol onto it. For example, observ* retrieves observe, observer, observes, observing, observant, observation, and many more words beginning with these six letters.
- *Variable truncation.* Enter the truncated stem to retrieve it and as many characters as your truncation symbol specifies. For right-hand variable truncation, enter the truncated stem beginning with a dollar sign and number: $5beat retrieves upbeat, offbeat, heartbeat, and more. For left-hand variable truncation, enter the truncated stem ending with a dollar sign and number: cat$1 retrieves cat, cats, cat's, catv, and cato.
- *Wildcard.* Entering a stem with one or more symbols retrieves the stem bearing as many characters as there are symbols: observ??? retrieves words bearing any three trailing characters such as observing, observers, and observant.
- *Embedded truncation.* Use embedded truncation to retrieve any characters embedded in a word or word stem. ProQuest has several embedded truncation flavors: (1) one embedded character, e.g., wom?n, retrieves woman, women, or womyn, and hypothes?s retrieves hypothesis or hypotheses, (2) variable embedded characters, e.g., cent$2fold, retrieves the exact word fragments cent and fold with any two characters between them such as centerfold or centrefold, and (3) unlimited embedded characters, e.g., c*tion, retrieves caption, caution, computation, contraption, and many more words (up to this system's limit of 125 characters).

In the absence of truncation symbols or quotes around FT terms, most search systems default to retrieving simple singular, plural, and possessive forms of your search terms, e.g., squirrel and squirrels, party and parties, but not necessarily irregular ones, e.g., goose and geese, child and children. Few systems are as comprehensive as ProQuest with respect to explicit truncation, so consult your chosen search system's online help pages under topics such as truncation, wildcards, singular, plural, and possessives, then formulate your search statements accordingly.

Conducting Free Text Searches of Surrogate Records

FT searching tools in most Boolean search systems are proximity operators, truncation, and nested Boolean logic. Not all Boolean systems have these tools and when they do, there may be restrictions on their use, for example, allowing one type of proximity operator per search statement or one truncation operator per search term. Demonstrated here is a FT search in EBSCOhost's Women's Studies International (WSI) database, an A&I database that searches surrogates and delivers full-texts (mostly through resolver links).

A major objective of FT searching is high recall, retrieving as many relevant retrievals as possible. Thus, enter several FT search terms per search statement that are synonymous for representing each facet. For example, FT search terms for the **Farm Women** facet are:

```
farmwom?n
wom?n n5 farm*
female n5 farm*
```

The first- and second-listed terms retrieve one- and two-word variants for the expression "farm women." The second-listed term disregards word order and takes into account phrases bearing the singular and plural variants of the word "women" within five words of the word "farm." The third-listed term replaces the truncated word "women" with the synonym "female." The expert searcher's next step is to script these FT terms into a FT search statement inserting the Boolean OR operator between them:

```
farmwom?n OR (wom?n n5 farm*) OR (female n5 farm*)
```

Figure 7.1 shows the entry of this search statement into the WSI database (minus the statement's initial characters due to the search box's small size). The searcher mouses down on the "Select a Field" pull-down menu. The first-listed choice named "Select a Field (optional)" is the system's default, an unqualified search to which the system responds with searches of author, subject, keyword, title, and abstract fields. The second-listed choice named "TX All Text" searches these same fields plus citation data such as the titles, authors, and publications that authors cite in their bibliographies. Opt for comprehensive results and choose TX. If citation data produce many non-relevant retrievals, re-enter the statement choosing the more restrictive default.

Figure 7.1. Entering a Free Text Search Statement for the **Farm Women** Facet into EBSCOhost's Women's Studies International (WSI) Database.

This initial FT search statement retrieves about 2,200 retrievals. The statement bears nested Boolean logic (the parentheses) around FT terms that are phrases bearing word proximity operators. Added to this statement is nested Boolean logic because two different operators (i.e., two Boolean OR operators and two proximity nN operators) reside in it.

Boolean search systems are governed by a precedence of operators telling them which operator to process first, second, third, and so on. To override a system's precedence of operators, expert searchers use nested Boolean logic. This logic uses parentheses in the same way that algebra uses parentheses—to designate which operations should be done first, second, third, and so on. Textbox 7.3 expands on the precedence of operators.

Textbox 7.3. Precedence of Operators

Search systems process search statements in one of several different ways:

1. From left to right
2. From right to left
3. By a precedence of operators that says process this operator first, then this one, and so on
4. By the logic that nested Boolean operators specify

Consider this search statement: athletes AND college OR professional. A search system governed by approach #1 (left to right) would process it as (athletes AND college) OR professional, that is, retrieving all sources bearing the word "athletes," retrieving all sources bearing the word "college," and combining these results in a Boolean AND operation. The system would then retrieve all sources bearing the word "professional" and combine it in a Boolean OR operation with the ANDed results. Most likely, such results are *not* what the user wants because all occurrences of the word "professional" are retrieved, regardless of whether the word "athlete" is also present.

A search system governed by approach #2 (right to left) would process the search statement as athletes AND (college OR professional), that is, retrieving all sources bearing the word "college," retrieving all sources bearing the word "professional," and combining these results in a Boolean OR operation. The system would then retrieve all sources bearing the word "athletes" and combine it in a Boolean AND operation with the earlier ORed results. Most likely, these are the results that the user wants because they bear sources on college athletes and on professional athletes.

Approach #3 applies to search systems that are governed by a precedence of operators—rules that tell the system which operator to process first, which second, and so on. Because there are no standards for the precedence of operators, expect a lot of variation from system to system. Check the system's help to learn its precedence of operators using words such as precedence, order, or operators.

Approach #4, nested Boolean logic, overrides all these approaches. The searcher applies this logic using parentheses in the same way that algebra uses parentheses—to designate which operations should be done first, second, third, and so on. Almost every search system heeds nested Boolean logic, and it is much simpler applying nested Boolean logic to your search statements than it is to learn each system's precedence of operators (if you can find it in the system's help).

Here is the rule of thumb regarding the presence of two or more different types of Boolean and/or proximity operators in your search statements: Use nested Boolean logic, adding parentheses to instruct the system which operation to do first, second, etc. Thus, your nested Boolean for this search statement bearing ANDs and ORs would be: athletes AND (college OR professional).

Your objective for this search is high recall, so you would also conduct a FT search for the **Entrepreneurship** facet, searching *all* available database fields, not just CV fields. Here is an example of a FT search statement that transforms WSI's index terms, "Entrepreneurship," "Small Business," "Businesspeople," and "Economic Development" into this FT search statement:

```
TX (entrepreneur* OR (small w0 business) OR (business w0 enterprise) OR
businesspeople OR businessm?n OR businessperson OR (economic w0 development))
```

This FT search statement produces over 13,500 retrievals. It truncates the index term "entrepreneur," retrieving its singular and plural forms and the words "entrepreneurship" and "entrepreneurial." Added are irregular singular and plural forms of the index term "businesspeople." Adjacency proximity operators have been inserted into phrase index terms enabling the search system to retrieve these phrases from every database field. Choosing TX (text) instructs EBSCOhost to search all available database fields, even citation data, that is, the titles, authors, and publications that authors cite in their bibliographies.

Your final step is to combine intermediate results for the two FT search statements using the AND operator. Click on the "Search History" link and EBSCOhost lists your search's sets, presumably one for the **Farm Women** facet and a second for the **Entrepreneurship** facet. Combine retrievals using the Boolean AND operator—checkmarking sets 1 and 2 and clicking the "Search with AND" button. In response, EBSCOhost combines the two separate sets 7 and 8 in a Boolean AND operation, retrieving surrogate records bearing at least one search term per facet (figure 7.2). Alternatively, combine sets directly, entering their set numbers bound by the Boolean AND operator into the search box:

```
s7 AND s8
```

Conducting Free Text Searches of Full-Texts

To search full-texts, online searchers use the search system's FT searching capabilities—proximity operators, truncation, and nested Boolean logic. Thus, FT searching tools suffice for searching full-texts. Some systems have added specialized proximity operators for FT searching of full-texts. Examples are proximity operators for retrieving search words in the same or nearby sentences or paragraphs and allowing searchers to prefix proximity operators with the Boolean NOT operator so that they can eliminate certain words and phrases from retrievals. These specialized proximity operators are not unique to FT searching of full-texts. Expert searchers also use the full range of proximity operators routinely for FT searching of surrogate records. Because free text searching and full-text searching are one and the same, *Online Searching* uses the phrase "free text searches of full-texts" or the abbreviated form "FT searches of full-texts." It does not use the term "full-text searching."

The Facet Analysis for Free Text Searches of Full-Texts

When conducting FT searches of full-texts, you must keep in mind that full-texts can be lengthy; for example, books, research reports, some journal articles, and systematic reviews could range from thirty to hundreds of dense, text-filled pages. Searchers cannot depend on Boolean operators to produce relevant retrievals because their search words may be separated by dozens, even hundreds of pages! If your FT search of full-texts isn't producing relevant retrievals, replace its Boolean AND and NOT operators in between facets with the system's nearby, sentence, or paragraph proximity operators.

Figure 7.2. FT Search Results in EBSCOhost's WSI Database.

Conducting FT searches of full-texts involves searching texts such as news stories written by journalists, journal articles and books written by scholars and scientists, blogs written by everyday people, and so on. To generate search terms, put yourself in their shoes, thinking about how they would write about the topics that interest you. A useful exercise might be writing a few sentences that you would like to see in your retrievals. If you retrieve full-texts bearing these sentences, you would expect them to be relevant. Then analyze what you have written, performing a facet analysis and logical combination. Check your sentences, distributing relevant words and phrases into the facets where they belong and doing the same for search terms you find in other sources such as another database's CV, Roget's Thesaurus, or a relevant source that the user has in hand. In fact, make a practice of asking users to show you a relevant full-text or surrogate record that they found on their own. Then cull its relevant search terms, adding them to your search statements.

Free Text Searches of Full-Texts in the LexisNexis Academic Database

The LexisNexis Academic database excels in up-to-date coverage of news, business, and legal matters (LexisNexis 2015). Retrievals are full-text newspapers, magazines, wire services, broadcast media transcripts, newsletters, blogs, and much more.

Like other Boolean retrieval systems, the LexisNexis system features the usual three Boolean operators but uses AND NOT instead of NOT. Of these operators, OR gets the most workout, enabling the searcher to combine synonymous search terms within each facet. Because you are searching full-texts, don't use the Boolean AND and NOT operators. Instead insert this system's nearby w/N proximity operator in between facets, loosely setting the N in w/N between 9 and 15, a range that roughly approximates the length of a sentence in a newspaper or magazine. Still too many retrievals? Tighten the operator with a number from 5 to 8. LexisNexis has many proximity operators:

- Adjacency is pre/N (word order matters) and w/1 (word order doesn't matter)
- Nearby is w/N (word order matters) and w/N (word order doesn't matter)
- In the same sentence is w/s
- In the same paragraph is w/p
- In the same field (LexisNexis calls them segments) is w/seg
- Negative versions of these are not pre/N, not w/N, not w/s, not w/p, and not w/seg

The system's unlimited truncation symbol is an exclamation point (!) and its wildcard symbol is an asterisk(*). Like EBSCOhost, LexisNexis automatically searches for singular, plural, and possessive forms of all but irregular words (i.e., goose and geese, child and children).

Demonstrated is a FT search for the topic "The impact of screen time on children." This query has three facets: (1) **Impact**, (2) **Screen Time**, and (3) **Children**. The logical combination uses proximity instead of Boolean operators to combine facets:

Impact NEARBY **Screen Time** NEARBY **Children**

Under each facet are suggested FT search terms clothed in tight proximity operators:

Impact	Screen Time	Children
impact	screentime	child
effect	screen pre/1 time	children
affect	screen-time	youngster
negative	electronics pre/1 time	kid
positive	technolog! w/3 addict!	boy
consequence		girl

Notice that this query's facet analysis bears an **Impact** facet. Chapter 6 downplays such a facet in CV searches. The reason why is that CV searching is concept searching and the presence of two concepts in a source usually indicates a relationship between them (page 78). FT searches of full-texts isn't concept searching. It is the letter-for-letter matching of words and phrases in search statements with the occurrences of words and phrases in texts. That the system is able to effect matches between the words and phrases in search statements and texts does not necessarily mean that retrieved sources are actually about the matched terms. Thus, searchers who want to establish relationships between one or more conditions and effects should add relationship facets to their facet analysis and logical combination in their FT searches of full-texts just like you are doing in the Screen Time search.

The LexisNexis system does not have sets but it does have an "edit search" capability. The searcher could express the entire search in a single search statement or enter it successively, starting with the first two facets, checking retrievals to see if they are on track, then entering the third facet using the system's edit capability. This single search statement represents the entire search in one fell swoop:

```
(impact or effect or affect or negative** or positive** or consequence) w/10
(screentime or (screen pre/1 time) or screen-time or (electronics pre/1 time)
or (technolog! w/3 addict!)) w/10 (kid or child or youngster or children or
toddler or boy or girl)
```

LexisNexis sports a single interface. Clicking on the "Advanced Options" link (where the cursor resides in figure 7.3) opens a pop-up box where the searcher sets up various parameters for the search she's about to perform, for example, limiting retrievals to certain dates, to a certain publication (like the *New York Times* newspaper or *All Things Considered* news program), or to certain content types. For your search, limit retrievals to "Newspapers" only by placing a checkmark in its box, removing checkmarks from the other "Content Type" boxes, and clicking on the "Apply" button.

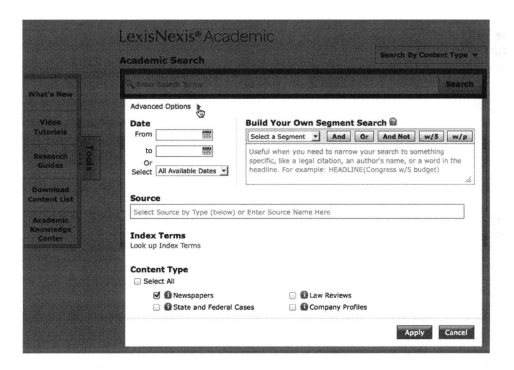

Figure 7.3. Clicking on the "Advanced Options" Link and Choosing Parameters for a FT Search of the Full-Text LexisNexis Academic Database. Source: LexisNexis, a registered trademark of Elsevier, B.V., image retrieved on 15 March 2015.

Your next step is to enter your search statement into the search box by clicking on the "Search" button. Figure 7.4 shows this step. The search statement is longer than the search box so only its trailing portion is visible in this box.

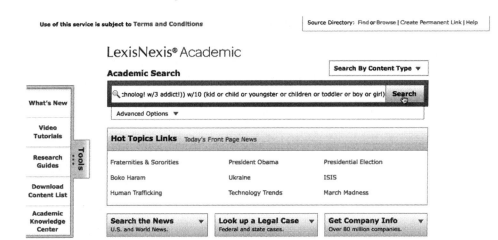

Figure 7.4. Entering a FT Search Statement for All Three Facets into the LexisNexis Academic Database. Source: LexisNexis, a registered trademark of Elsevier, B.V., image retrieved on 15 March 2015.

LexisNexis Academic produces over 350 retrievals, beginning with the most relevant ones and displaying their title, date, number of words, byline, and publication title (figure 7.5). You can change LexisNexis' default retrievals display using the "Sort" and "Show" pull-down menus, respectively, on the top left side of retrievals. The user has to read full-texts to learn about the various "impacts" of screen time on children; examples are obesity, heart disease, and disliking one's parents. Along the left side of the page, LexisNexis displays clusters that users can explore. Choosing the *Subject* cluster and scanning its values yields more hints about excessive screen time consequences such as "Physical Fitness," "Chronic Diseases," "Cardiovascular Disease," "Mental Health," and "Violence & Society."

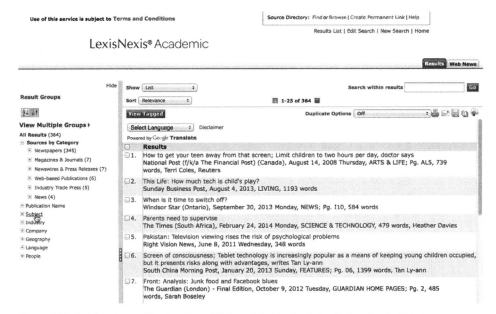

Figure 7.5. Retrievals and Clusters for a FT Search in the LexisNexis Academic Database. Source: LexisNexis, a registered trademark of Elsevier, B.V., image retrieved on 15 March 2015.

Searching Extended-Boolean Search Systems

Long before search systems were available to end users, the late Gerard Salton at Cornell University criticized the Boolean model for its complexity, especially its reliance on arcane and complicated searching languages that only librarians had the patience to learn and opportunity to use on a day-to-day basis. Salton sought an alternative approach that would respond with relevant retrievals to the natural language queries that everyday people use to express their queries. He developed the vector-space model of information retrieval and demonstrated its effectiveness in searches of small, full-text databases in his experimental SMART search system (Salton 1975). That it took another quarter of a century for Google and other Web search engines to build on Salton's approach was due to the high cost of computer memory and storage during his lifetime. Eventually costs plummeted, putting computers in the hands of everyday people and making it possible for today's system developers to improve on Salton's approach and apply it to gargantuan-sized databases.

Urging the information industry to implement Salton's approach in Boolean search systems, Hildreth (1989, 107–8) asserted that "extended-Boolean retrieval methods can be used quite effectively with conventional inverted file structures to enhance the retrieval performance of Boolean search systems." Salton's approach helps to power how today's Boolean search systems rank retrievals, and it is particularly apparent in Google and other Web search engines that respond very effectively with relevant retrievals to the natural language queries end users enter into them.

How Extended-Boolean Retrieval Works

Underlying extended-Boolean search systems is the Boolean OR operator. In response to a user query, the system conducts a Boolean OR operation, retrieving sources bearing any one or more words in the search statement. What retrieved sources the system displays first, second, third, and so on, depends on a host of rules that are programmed into the system. The simplest rule would be to display sources bearing all matching words first, sources bearing all but one search word second, sources bearing all but two search words third, and so on, until all retrieved sources are displayed or the searcher transitions to something else.

Here's how an extended-Boolean search system would search for the natural language query "How do child soldiers adjust to normal life?" It would eliminate punctuation and parse the query into separate words or word stems: how, do, child, soldier, adjust, to, normal, life. Then it would retrieve sources bearing one or more of these eight stems using this Boolean search statement:

```
how OR child OR soldier OR adjust OR to OR normal OR life
```

Because extended-Boolean systems combine retrievals using the Boolean OR operator, they retrieve hundreds of thousands and even millions of retrievals. They rank order retrievals, displaying the most relevant ones first. How extended-Boolean systems determine which sources to rank first, second, and so on is governed by weights that increase and decrease based on how well a source performs relative to criteria such as these (Liddy 2001):

- Occurrence of search terms in texts. Matching search terms in a full-text's title or lead paragraph receives higher weights than in other paragraphs.
- Occurrence of search terms in retrieved sources. Sources bearing all search terms in queries receive higher weights than sources bearing fewer than all search terms.
- The frequency of search terms across all sources in the database. Search terms that occur infrequently in sources receive higher weights than frequently occurring search words.

- Frequency of search terms in each source. The more frequently search terms occur in sources, the higher weights given to the sources.
- Proximity of search terms. Sources bearing search terms adjacent or near one another receive more weight than sources in which search terms are separated by a sentence, paragraph, or more.
- Order of search terms in search statements. The initial search term in a search statement receives higher weights than the trailing search terms.
- Search terms occurring in frequently cited sources. Matching terms in frequently cited sources cited by other frequently cited sources receive higher weights than less frequently cited sources.

Some extended-Boolean systems perform automatic vocabulary assistance, enhancing search statements with co-occurring synonyms. How systems establish co-occurring synonyms is done algorithmically. Each word in a source is compared to every word in the database to determine how likely they are to co-occur. The comparison yields a measure between 0 (not likely to co-occur) and 1 (very likely to co-occur). For example, the word "religious" probably has a high measure, around 0.8, with the word "belief," and a low measure, around 0.0, with the word "duck." The extended-Boolean system considers co-occurring words synonyms. A search that yields few retrievals might automatically trigger vocabulary assistance, and the system would add highly co-occurring words to the search statement to boost retrievals.

Extended-Boolean systems do not publish their indexing, ranking, or vocabulary assistance algorithms. They are proprietary; however, Google's founders published a technical report describing the system's PageRank algorithm that gives higher weights to frequently cited sources cited by other frequently cited sources (Page et al. 1999). Even though anyone can read the report to find out how PageRank works, it is now one of "more than 200 unique signals or cues" that Google uses to rank order retrievals (Google 2015), making it almost impossible for anyone to replicate Google's ranking algorithm.

The relevance-ranking and vocabulary-assistance algorithms of extended-Boolean systems do automatically what expert searchers do manually. "They look for terms that can distinguish one document from another, they ask for the terms to appear close together in the document, they stem words, and count words that appear in the title more heavily than those appearing in the rest of the text. . . . Some systems also try to match query concepts. . . . They enlarge a search beyond the boundaries that the query originally defined" (Feldman 1998). About the only thing that searchers have to do is articulate the queries they enter into extended-Boolean systems. In this context, articulation means performing a facet analysis for the query and expressing each facet in a word or phrase.

Formulating Search Statements for Extended-Boolean Search Systems

Demonstrated here is a Google search for the Child Soldiers query. This query has three facets and these salient search terms:

    A. Child soldiers: child soldiers, child combatants, child conscripts
    B. Adjustment: adjust, readjust, settle, resettle, reintegration, live
    C. Normal life: normal life, everyday life, daily life, civilian life, live normally

Formulating a search statement for an extended-Boolean search engine is simple. Choose one search term per facet, putting the most important search term first. Here are examples of search statements for this query. Enter them into your library's WSD system or your favorite Web search engine. See for yourself whether they produce relevant retrievals:

```
child soldiers adjust normal life
child combatants reintegration civilian life
child soldiers live normally
```

You could enclose the search words child soldiers in quotes, indicating to the search engine that it is a phrase. Extended-Boolean systems give higher weights when search words occur close together in sources, so you can expect systems to retrieve sources with these two words and all the others occurring in the text as close to each other as possible. Thus, enclosing these search words in quotes might not be necessary. Try it with and without quotes around phrases.

By the way, search statements for extended-Boolean systems bear only one search term per facet because these systems don't perform automatic facet recognition; that is, they cannot recognize which search terms belong to which facet. Thus, if you entered all six search terms above for the **Adjustment** facet along with one search term for the **Child Soldiers** facet and one search for the **Normal Life** facet, extended-Boolean systems might rank sources bearing the six **Adjustment** synonyms atop the retrievals list even though their texts don't bear search terms for the other two facets.

The Building Block Search Strategy's À la Carte Edition

Underlying your search for the Child Soldiers query is the Building Block Search Strategy. You conceive the three facets **Child Soldiers**, **Adjustment**, and **Normal Life**; however, your search statement contains only one salient search term per facet. This is the À la Carte Edition of the Building Block Strategy, and it features *one* search term per facet. You use the most salient search term per facet, and for most queries, this means entering the names of the query's facets. Figure 7.6 depicts the À la Carte Edition visually, bearing one selection per course from the menu.

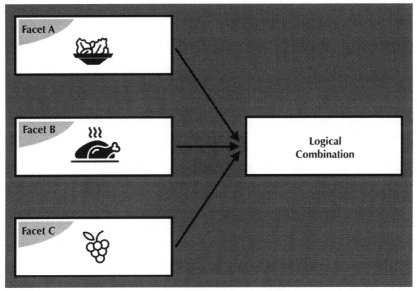

Figure 7.6. À la Carte Edition of the Building Block Strategy. Created using symbols from the Noun Project (http://thenounproject.com): "Salad" symbol by Peter Chlebak; "Turkey" symbol by Quan Do; "Grapes" symbol by Thomas Hirter.

Here's another Google query for the À la Carte Edition of the Building Block Strategy, "How did President Johnson convince conservative lawmakers to pass his War on Poverty legislation?" Its facets are **Lyndon Johnson**, **Leadership**, and **War on Poverty**, and because they are particularly salient, use them to compose a search statement:

```
lyndon johnson leadership war on poverty
```

Ranked high on Google's listed retrievals is an essay entitled "Lyndon B. Johnson and the War on Poverty" that accompanies audio recordings from the Johnson White House recordings pertaining to the War on Poverty and other aspects of his domestic policy. The essayist writes, "Through these recorded conversations, listeners gain a sense of Johnson's famous skill as a legislative tactician and of his ability as a deal maker and a flatterer who understood the ways of Washington, and especially of Congress, at an intimate level" (McKee 2014), and this is exactly the type of analysis that the user is seeking.

The reason why you use only one search term per facet is the inability of extended-Boolean search systems to perform automatic facet recognition on your entered search terms. If they did, they could parse synonymous terms in your search statements into facets and give higher weights to sources matching one or more search terms *per facet* than to sources matching search terms from fewer than all facets. Since they can't, your only option is to formulate queries bearing one search term per facet, forcing the system to rank sources matching all search terms higher than sources matching fewer than all search terms. To find more retrievals, you might have to enter multiple search statements into the system, substituting synonyms for each facet as demonstrated in these search statements and experimenting with and without quotes around phrases:

```
lyndon johnson "negotiation skills" "war on poverty"
lyndon johnson "horse trading" "war on poverty"
lyndon johnson strategy "war on poverty"
```

Entering multiple search statements into extended-Boolean search systems is inefficient. Until extended-Boolean search systems can perform automatic facet recognition, the burden will be on the searcher to bear the inefficiency of extended-Boolean searching in this regard. Using the À la Carte Edition of the Building Block Strategy to represent your search should lighten the load.

Relevance Feedback for Furthering Searches

Retrieving additional relevant retrievals based on one's Boolean or extended Boolean search results is accomplished by special system functionality that system designers have put in place for this very purpose. The technical name for this is *relevance feedback*. Here are three relevance feedback searches called find-like, bibliography scanning (also called backward chaining), and cited reference (also called forward chaining) searches.

Find-Like Searches

One or more of these events are likely to trigger the searcher's desire to conduct find-like searches—a low posted search, the retrieval of an exceptionally relevant source, and the availability of a find-like search in the system you are searching. The search statement for the find-like search is the terminology in a retrieved source. The command for triggering a system's "find like" search accompanies brief or full surrogate record displays and has many different names such as "Find Similar Results," "Find Like," and "Related Articles."

EBSCOhost is most forthcoming about how its find-like search works. Start with a relevant retrieval. Click on the "Find Similar Results Using SmartText Searching" link accompanying the retrieval's full surrogate record display. EBSCOhost pastes the source's title, abstract, and index terms into the search box. Click on the "Search" button and EBSCOhost's SmartText searching responds with an extended-Boolean search and ranks retrievals. By the way, if you don't like one or more of the search words EBSCOhost pastes into the search box, delete them before clicking the "Search" button. You can even edit the original abstract, writing the *perfect abstract* for the sources you want to retrieve.

ProQuest's "find like" is especially versatile. While displaying a surrogate record for a search on Television Violence in the ERIC database, the searcher clicks on "More like this," and ProQuest uses the displayed source's terminology to find similar ones. It maintains results of the current search in the center of the screen while displaying the first five "similar" titles under the "See similar documents" heading on the far right of the screen (figure 7.7). Mousing over a similar title's "Preview" link opens a pop-up window bearing a surrogate record. Thus, the searcher can pursue one or more similar sources without the ongoing search's results disappearing from the page.

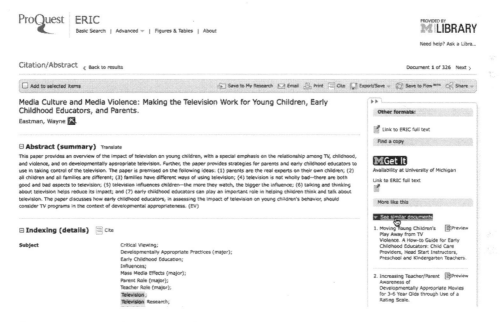

Figure 7.7. Using a Relevant Retrieval in ProQuest's ERIC Database to "See similar documents." The screenshots and their contents are published with permission of ProQuest LLC. Further reproduction is prohibited without permission. Inquiries may be made to: ProQuest LLC, 789 E. Eisenhower Pkwy, Ann Arbor, MI 48106-1346 USA. Telephone (734) 761–4700; Email: info@ proquest.com; Web page: http://www.proquest.com.

Bibliography Scanning Searches (Backward Chaining)

Bibliography scanning is simple. Find one relevant source, display or download its full-text, then scan the sources its author cites in the source's footnotes or bibliography for additional relevant titles. Bibliography scanning yields additional relevant retrievals because authors cite sources that lay the groundwork for their research, support their hypotheses or arguments, and/

or supplement their work. Thus, the sources an author cites may be as relevant as the relevant source you have in hand. Bibliography scanning goes *back in time*, finding sources on the desired topic that were published *before* the one in hand.

The Web of Science (WoS) is the go-to database for backward chaining, automating bibliography scanning for a relevant source you retrieved in a subject search of the WoS database. WoS retrievals are surrogates bearing each source's title, abstract, and bibliography. Finding a relevant source, scan the cited sources in its bibliography. When a cited source has promise, click on its accompanying resolver links to display its full-text. This is *push-button* bibliography scanning, plain and simple!

Typically, you find a relevant source in another database that doesn't have push-button bibliography scanning. As long as the relevant source is published in a scholarly journal, there's a good chance that conducting a WoS title search for it will retrieve the source's surrogate. Searches for the Eating Disorder query are always low-posted, so relevant retrievals from your subject searches of the PsycINFO database should be triggers that prompt you to conduct follow-up bibliography scanning searches in WoS. A relevant PsycINFO title is "Risk Factors for Bulimia Nervosa: A Controlled Study of Parental Psychiatric Illness and Divorce." In figure 7.8, the searcher searches WoS, entering this title into the search box, choosing "Title" from the fields pull-down menu, and clicking the "Search" button. (The search statement is longer than the search box so only its trailing portion is visible in this box.)

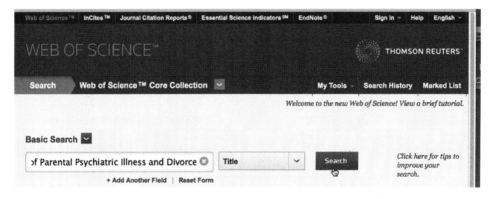

Figure 7.8. Conducting a Title Search in the Web of Science Database. Data included herein are derived from the Web of Science prepared by Thomson Reuters, Inc. (Thomson), Philadelphia, Pennsylvania, USA: Copyright Thomson Reuters 2015. All rights reserved.

WoS retrieves the one title that interests the user. Clicking on its title displays a brief surrogate. Clicking on the brief surrogate's title displays a full surrogate that includes a "Cited References" link (to the right of the surrogate) (figure 7.9). Finally, clicking on the "Cited References" link displays the source's bibliography bearing resolver links so that obtaining a full-text for a cited reference is almost instantaneous.

When WoS title searches for your desired titles fail, bibliography scanning becomes a mostly manual process. Here's what's involved. Consider the handful of relevant sources you retrieved in CV and FT searches for the Eating Disorders query. You'll have to download their full-texts, manually checking each source's footnotes and bibliographies for relevant cited sources. Keep a list of relevant cited sources. When you are done, conduct a title search for each relevant cited source on your list in one or more of these databases: *all* EBSCOhost databases, *all* ProQuest databases, or your library's WSD system. When a title search succeeds, download its full-text by

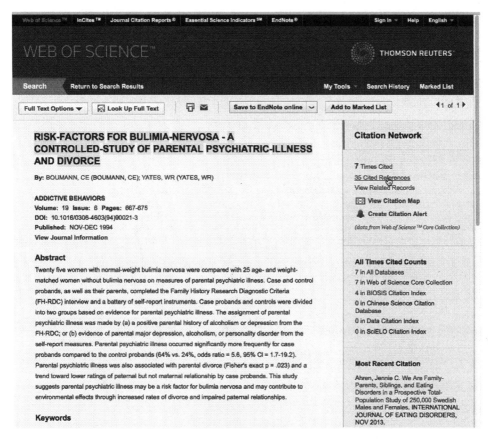

Figure 7.9. Clicking on the Full Surrogate's "Cited References" Link to Display the Source's Bibliography in the Web of Science Database. Data included herein are derived from the Web of Science prepared by Thomson Reuters, Inc. (Thomson), Philadelphia, Pennsylvania, USA: Copyright Thomson Reuters 2015. All rights reserved.

clicking on the accompanying resolver link. By the way, keeping track of retrieved cited sources and full-texts is complicated so consider using a citations management system (pages 234–37).

Cited Reference Searches (Forward Chaining)

Cited reference searching goes *forward in time*, finding sources on the desired topic published *after* the one in hand. Find one relevant source, and search this source in databases that support cited reference searching to find authors who have cited it. Don't expect the most recently published sources to have cited references because it takes several years for researchers to build on the work of their peers and cite them in their publications.

Cited reference searches are a push-button operation in databases and systems that support it. For example, perform cited reference searches in WoS exactly like bibliography scanning searches, entering a title into the search box, choosing "Title" from the fields pull-down menu, and clicking the "Search" button (figure 7.8). Display your desired title's full surrogate, and click on the "Times Cited" link (above the "Cited References" link in figure 7.9). In response, WoS displays citing references bearing resolver links so that obtaining a full-text for a cited reference is almost instantaneous. All along the right side of the page, WoS provides more information about citing sources including a direct link to the most recent one (bottom right).

Cited reference searching is subject searching, but it requires known-item searching skills to search for and verify the relevant source that interests you so that you can follow up with cited reference searches. To avoid this, see if the database where you found relevant sources has a cited reference search capability. EBSCOhost's PsycINFO has such a capability. When your PsycINFO subject searches produce a relevant retrieval, click its accompanying "Times cited in this database" link, and PsycINFO responds with a list of sources that have cited the original source (figure 7.10). Scan citing titles and when one interests you, click on it to display its surrogate and download its full-text.

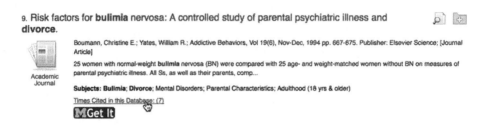

9. Risk factors for **bulimia** nervosa: A controlled study of parental psychiatric illness and **divorce**.

Boumann, Christine E.; Yates, William R.; Addictive Behaviors, Vol 19(6), Nov-Dec, 1994 pp. 667-675. Publisher: Elsevier Science; [Journal Article]

25 women with normal-weight **bulimia** nervosa (BN) were compared with 25 age- and weight-matched women without BN on measures of parental psychiatric illness. All Ss, as well as their parents, comp...

Subjects: Bulimia; Divorce; Mental Disorders; Parental Characteristics; Adulthood (18 yrs & older)

Times Cited in this Database: (7)

Figure 7.10. Clicking on a Surrogate's "Times Cited in This Database" to Display Sources Citing It in EBSCOhost's PsycINFO Database.

The PsycINFO database is limited to psychology and so too are its cited references. Google Scholar and the licensed WoS and Scopus databases feature cited reference searches and their databases are encyclopedic. When your Google Scholar, WoS, and Scopus subject searches produce a relevant retrieval, click on the retrieval's accompanying "Times Cited: N," "N Times Cited," and "Cited by N document" links, respectively, and the database responds with a list of sources that have cited the original source. (By the way, N refers to the number of citing references.)

Unfortunately, few users are systematic about checking "Times Cited" links while conducting subject searches. They realize some time afterward that they have too few relevant retrievals and come to you needing more. When they do, ask them for a list of their relevant retrievals. Then conduct title searches in Google Scholar, WoS, or Scopus for them, and clicking on retrieved surrogates' "Times Cited" links connect users to cited references. For example, your CV search for the Eating Disorders query probably retrieves "Characteristics of Family Background in Bulimia." Launch Google Scholar through your library's database hub and type this title verbatim into Google's search box (figure 7.11). Clicking on the "Cited by 17" link produces two promising cited

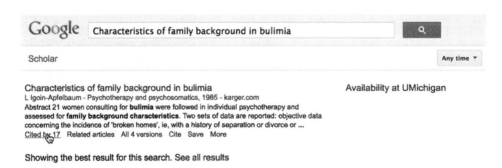

Figure 7.11. Clicking on a Surrogate's "Cited by" Link to Display Sources Citing It in Google Scholar. Google and the Google logo are registered trademarks of Google Inc., used with permission.

references: "Early Family Experiences of Women with Bulimia and Depression" and "Parental Variables Associated with Bulimia Nervosa."

Benefits of Free Text Searching and Extended-Boolean Searching

The benefits of FT searching center on using terminology that is not represented in a database's thesaurus and producing comprehensive search results. Of course, some databases have no CV so FT searching is your only recourse. You can check other databases' CVs for search term ideas, but you will have to search them using your chosen database's FT search functionality—proximity operators, truncation, and nested Boolean logic. In databases with CVs, searchers can supplement CV terms, adding FT words and phrases to one or more facets of the search using the end user's terminology or the words and phrases that experts writing in the discipline or field of study use to describe the idea.

Lexicographers don't add new index terms for new phenomena immediately to their CVs. They wait until experts in the field have published enough information about the phenomenon. The "waiting period" in between the time a new phenomenon arises and a new index term is established in a CV is called *literary warrant*. During the waiting period and for a period of time after the CV bears an authorized index term for the phenomenon, searchers must represent their searches for it using FT to retrieve all relevant information.

FT searching yields comprehensive results, also known as high recall. When you help end users, high recall results are usually the exception rather than the rule. Doctoral students researching their dissertation's literature review, attorneys preparing a case for a lawsuit, researchers writing a systematic review, and inventors preparing a patent application are examples of information seekers concerned with high recall results. If you are in doubt about a user's search objectives, ask him whether and why full recall is desired. By the way, high recall is impossible to accomplish in practice. There are so many different ways authors write about phenomena and formulating FT searches to retrieve them also produces so much non-relevant information that sorting through all of it would be too time-consuming. Plus, in the meantime, new information is being published including new developments that are expressed in subtly different ways that the original search failed to retrieve. At best, searchers may strive for comprehensive search results, covering all the issues and representative reactions to the issues.

Extended-Boolean searching has been a boon for both end users and intermediary searchers. No longer burdened by this or that searching language, they can enter natural language queries into search systems. Finding a relevant source can also lead to additional retrievals using the search system's "find like" functionality that uses the source's terminology as a search statement to query the database.

Comparing Free Text Functionality Across Search Systems and Databases

This chapter's examination of FT search functionality covers basic functionality that you can expect most systems to have. Be prepared for FT search functionality to vary across systems especially in terms of the syntax that search systems use for proximity operators and truncation. Table 7.1 compares FT searching functionality across five search systems.

Questions

Conduct FT searches for the same queries you searched in chapter 6 with these few exceptions: (a) replace the PubMed query with this query and search it in the JStor database, "The role of the railroads in the adoption of standard time," (b) search the College Athletes query in LexisNexis, and (c) search the Wandering Mind query in Google Scholar.

Table 7.1. Comparing Free Text Searching Functionality

BOOLEAN OPERATORS			
Search system	**Boolean OR operator**	**Boolean AND operator**	**Boolean NOT operator**
EBSCOhost	OR	AND	NOT
ProQuest	or	and	not
LexisNexis	or	and	and not
JStor	OR	AND	NOT
Engineering Village	OR	AND	NOT
Google	OR		−
			−chipmunk (eliminates the word chipmunk from Google retrievals)

PROXIMITY OPERATORS			
Search system	**Adjacency, word order matters**	**Nearby, word order matters**	**Adjacency, word order does not matter**	**Nearby, word order does not matter**
EBSCOhost	w0 |"[phrase]"	wN	n0	nN
	world w0 problem consumer w0 behavior "self help"	world w2 problem consumer w2 behavior	jeffrey n0 archer youth* n0 offend*	job n2 satisf* world n2 problem
ProQuest	pre/0 | p/0 | "[phrase]"	pre/N | p/N	near/0 | n/0	near/N | n/N
	world pre/0 problem consumer p/0 behavior "self help"	world pre/2 problem consumer p/2 behavior	jeffrey near/0 archer youth* n/0 offend*	job n/2 satisf* world near/2 problem
LexisNexis	pre/1 | "[phrase]"	pre/N	w/1	w/N
	world pre/1 problem "self help"	world pre/3 problem	jeffrey w/1 archer youth! w/1 offend!	job w/3 satisf! youth! w/3 offend!

(continued)

Table 7.1. Comparing Free Text Searching Functionality *continued*

PROXIMITY OPERATORS *continued*				
Search system	**Adjacency, word order matters**	**Nearby, word order matters**	**Adjacency, word order does not matter**	**Nearby, word order does not matter**
JStor	`"[phrase]"`			`"[word] [word]"~N`
	`"world problem"`			`"moon land- ing"~5`
Engineering Village	`ONEAR/0 |` `"[phrase]" |` `{phrase} |`	`ONEAR/N`	`NEAR/0`	`NEAR/N`
	`lunar ONEAR/0 bases` `"garbage disposal"` `{neural nets}`	`lunar ONEAR/2 bases`	`problem NEAR/0 solving`	`moon NEAR/2 landing`
Google	`"world problems"`	Accomplished by relevance ranking	Accomplished by relevance ranking	Accomplished by relevance ranking

TRUNCATION					
Search system	**Default**	**Unlimited**	**Variable**	**Wildcard**	**Embedded**
EBSCOhost	Simple singu- lars, plurals, and possessives	`observ*`		`cat?` `observ??`	`wom?n` `cent#fold`
ProQuest	Simple singu- lars, plurals, comparatives, and possessives	`*graph` `observ*`	`$5beat` `observ$3` `truck$2`	`cat?` `observ??`	`wom?n` `cent$2fold` `c*tion`
LexisNexis	Simple singu- lars, plurals, and possessives	`observ!`		`cat*` `observ**`	`wom?n`
JStor	Add & to singular to find simple and ir- regular plurals	`observ*`		`cat?`	`wom?n` `cent*fold`
Engineering Village	Turn on auto- stemming to retrieve the stem plus suffixes	`*graph` `observ*`		`cat?` `observ??`	`wom?n` `cent*fold` `c*tion`

Note: Google has no explicit truncation symbols.

Transitioning from CV searching to FT searching may be daunting, so replace your original CV terms for these queries with FT search terms, then dress them up in proximity operators, truncation, and nested Boolean operators. Here's how to do it. Start with the original index term "Problem Youth," and make up sentence fragments in which the two words in this index term retain its meaning. Examples are these made-up fragments:

- youths who have problems
- problematic youths
- youths who have serious problems
- problems specific to youth

Then analyze these fragments to choose between the adjacency and nearby proximity operator and to set its N. In this case, choose the search system's nearby operator and set it to three intervening words, for example, `youth near/3 problem` for ProQuest searches. Need inspiration for more FT terms? Check the database's thesaurus for UFs, then apply proximity operators and truncation.

Suggested FT search formulations for all seven queries are given at the end of the chapter.

Summary

Enter http://www.onlinesearching.org/p/7-free.html into your Web browser for a video on free text searching.

FT searching begins with the facet analysis and logical combination. Search term formulation involves consulting the database's thesaurus in search of relevant index terms and UFs, other databases' thesauri, and even a free thesaurus on the open Web. Having identified enough search terms per facet, dress your search terms up in proximity operators, truncation symbols, and nested Boolean operators. Formulate FT search statements for Boolean search systems by inserting the Boolean OR operator in between synonymous search terms. When searching *surrogates* in Boolean systems, combine search statements for facets with the Boolean AND or NOT operators. When searching *full-texts* in Boolean systems, combine search statements for the query's several facets with the nearby operator.

Extended-Boolean searching is characteristic of Web search engines and web-scale discovery (WSD) systems. Extended-Boolean searches start like all other searches—with the facet analysis and the searcher giving especially salient names to the query's facets. To formulate a search statement for an extended-Boolean search engine, simply enter the names of the facets, putting the most important facet name first. Free text searching tools aren't needed because extended-Boolean systems rank retrievals according to the relative usage of search terms across the database, accomplishing implicitly what expert searchers do explicitly in Boolean systems.

Associated with high recall, FT searching is embraced by expert searchers who aim to retrieve as much relevant material on a topic as they can. FT searching is the only way to retrieve information on new phenomena. Even after literary warrant kicks in and an index term is established for the phenomenon, some searchers will want to search retrospectively for early material and FT is the only way to do it.

Bibliography

Feldman, Susan. 1998. "Where Do We Put the Web Search Engines?" *Searcher* 6, no. 10: 40–57.

Google. 2015. "Algorithms." Accessed March 26, 2015. http://www.google.com/insidesearch/howsearchworks/algorithms.html.

Hildreth, Charles R. 1989. *Intelligent Interfaces and Retrieval Methods for Subject Searching in Bibliographic Retrieval Systems.* Washington, DC: Cataloging Distribution Service, Library of Congress.

LexisNexis. 2015. "LexisNexis Academic." Accessed March 26, 2015. http://www.lexisnexis.com/en-us/products/lexisnexis-academic.page.

Liddy, Elizabeth. 2001. "How a Search Engine Works." *Searcher* 9, no. 5: 38–45.

McKee, Guian A. 2014. "Lyndon B. Johnson and the War on Poverty: Introduction to the Digital Edition." Accessed 2 June 2015, http://presidentialrecordings.rotunda.upress.virginia.edu/essays?series=WarOnPoverty.

Page, Lawrence, Sergey Brin, Rajeev Motwani, and Terry Winograd. 1999. "The PageRank Citation Ranking: Bringing Order to the Web." Accessed March 26, 2015. http://ilpubs.stanford.edu:8090/422/1/1999-66.pdf.

Salton, Gerard. 1975. *Dynamic Information and Library Processing.* Englewood Cliffs, NJ: Prentice-Hall.

Suggested Readings

Badke, William. 2011. "The Treachery of Keywords." *Online* 35, no. 3: 52–54. This article's keyword searching scenarios are spot-on.

Ojala, MaryDee. 2007. "Finding and Using the Magic Words: Keywords, Thesauri, and Free Text Search." *Online* 31, no. 4: 40–42. Useful advice for finding the right search terms.

Rowley, Jennifer. 1994. "The Controlled versus Natural Indexing Languages Debate Revisited: A Perspective on Information Retrieval Practice and Research." *Journal of Information Science* 20, no. 2 (April): 108–18. A literature review that examines the debate between CV and FT searching. Compare her conclusions with Tenopir's (see below).

Tenopir, Carol. 1987. "Searching by Controlled Vocabulary or Free Text?" *Library Journal* 112, no. 19: 58–59. A real classic that gives straightforward answers to this question. Compare her conclusions with Rowley's (see above), then take both into consideration the next time you conduct an online search.

Jacsó, Péter. 2008. "How Many Web-Wide Search Engines Do We Need?" *Online Information Review* 32, no. 6: 860–65. Such a provocative question! Read the author's answer, then discuss in class how you'd go about answering this question.

Answers

Tables under each question bear FT search statements for direct entry into the search system. The remaining rows cover combining intermediary sets for each facet into a final results set and examples of relevant titles. Your search formulations may be different due to the many different ways to conduct FT searches for topics and various sources from which you culled FT terms.

1. ERIC: Bullying . . .

Facets	Choosing Terms for Search Statements (in ProQuest)
Bullying	bullying or bully or (peer near/1 (intimidat* or harass*))
Intervention	intervention or (feasibility pre/0 study) or (behavior near/2 modif*)
Program Effectiveness	(program near/1 (evaluat* or implement* or develop*)) or (comparative pre/0 analysis) or prevention or (outcomes near/1 education[$2])
To combine sets:	Choose "Search history." Checkmark set numbers for these three facets and click on the "Search with AND" button.
New titles not in CV searches:	"Bullying among Young Children: Strategies for Prevention," and "Effective and Ineffective Coping with Bullying Strategies as Assessed by Informed Professionals and Their Use by Victimized Students"

2. PsycINFO: Eating disorders . . .

Facets	Choosing Terms for Search Statements (in EBSCOhost)
Eating Disorders	(eating n0 disorder*) OR bulimi? OR anorexi? OR (eating n0 binge) OR hyperphagi? OR pica OR (kleine w0 levin w0 syndrome) OR (appetite n2 disorder)
Broken Homes	divorc* OR (broken w0 home) OR (marital n2 conflict) OR (marital n0 separat*) OR (marriage n2 problem*) OR (child w0 support) OR (joint w0 custody) OR (parent n2 absen*) OR (mother n2 absen*) OR (father n2 absen*)
Adolescents	teen* OR youth* OR (high w0 school*) OR (middle w0 school*) OR adolescen*
To combine sets:	Choose "Search history." Checkmark set numbers for the three facets and click on the "Search with AND" button.
New titles not in CV searches:	"A Retrospective Exploration of the Childhood and Adolescent Family Mealtime Environment of Women with Binge Eating Disorder" and "The Role of the Father-Daughter Relationship in Eating Disorders"

3. LexisNexis: College athletes . . .

Facets	Choosing Terms for Search Statements
College athletes	((college w/2 athlete) or (college w/2 player) or (student pre/1 athlete))
Payment	(pay or salary or wages or (sherman pre/1 act) or anti-trust or antitrust or (anti pre/1 trust) or stipend)
To combine sets:	Enter both statements separating them with the nearby operator set loosely at **w/15**.
New titles not in CV searches:	"Should Players Punch In?," "Pay Student-Athletes Because It's the Right Thing to Do," and "Don't Pay College Athletes"

4. JStor: The role of the railroads in the adoption standard time

Facets	Choosing Terms for Search Statements
Standard Time	(("standard time") or ("time zone?"))
Railroads	(train? or railroad? or railway?)
To combine sets:	Enter both statements separating them with the Boolean **AND** operator.
New titles not in CV searches:	"The Adoption of Standard Time" and "Standard Time in the United States"

5. COMPENDEX: Hockey helmets . . .

Facets	Choosing Terms for Search Statements
Hockey	hockey
Helmets	helmet or (face near/2 protector) or headgear
Testing	test or inspect or safety or standard
To combine sets:	Choose "Search History." Checkmark set numbers for these three facets. The system automatically inserts the Boolean AND operator in between set numbers in the "Combine Searches" search box and click on the "Search" button.
New titles not in CV searches:	"A Longitudinal Study of Ice Hockey Helmet Shelf Life" and "Analysis of the Impact Performance of Ice Hockey Helmets . . ."

6. **Google Scholar: Wandering mind . . .**

Facets	Choosing Terms for Search Statements
Wandering Mind	wandering mind, uncontrolled mind
Unhappiness	unhappy, negative, happy, positive
To combine sets:	Enter one term per facet in a single search statement minus Boolean operators. Two examples are wandering mind unhappy and uncontrolled mind unhappy.
New titles not in CV searches:	"A Wandering Mind Is an Unhappy Mind" and "Shifting Moods, Wandering Minds: Negative Moods Lead the Mind to Wander"

7. **ERIC: Parents setting limits . . .**

Facets	Choosing Terms for Search Statements (in EBSCOhost)
Social Networking	((social w0 network*) or facebook or myspace or twitter or texting or instagram or youtube or snapchat)
Parent Participation	(parent* n1 (participat* or (child w0 relationship) or role or style or skill or influence or involv*)) or (child n0 rearing)
Limit	(limit* or restrict* or reduc* or monitor*)
To combine sets:	Choose "Search history." Enter set numbers for these three facets into the "Combine searches:" search box and click on the "Search" button.
New titles not in CV searches:	"Net Cetera: Chatting with Kids about Being Online," "A Review of Online Social Networking Profiles by Adolescents . . ."

8

Known-Item Searching

Chapter 8's focus is known-item searching. A known-item search is a request for a specific source that you know exists—it is a particular journal article, book, conference paper, blog, organization, film, magazine or journal, author, advertisement, or television program. Basically, known-item searching boils down to finding *one* source among all the billions of sources in the vast and varied information universe. Known-item searching stands in sharp contrast to subject searching with its emphasis on casting a broad net.

Your decision to conduct a subject or known-item search is the result of typecasting the user's query—step 3 of the online searching process (pages 82–84). Typecasting gets you ever more closer to your ultimate search objective—representing the search as input to the retrieval system so that the search system produces relevant retrievals.

This chapter examines in-depth the two most common types of known-item searches—authors and titles. Citation verification and full-text fulfillment searches are also for known-items. Knowing how to perform them will enable you to help users complete a citation for a known-item, get their hands on its full-text, or find a source someone recommended to them. Known-item searches also pave the way for the journal run. Get past its funny name because it may be the subject search of last resort, producing relevant retrievals when all other subject searches fail. Database detective work is all about searching databases using a combination of subject and known-item searches to answer the offbeat questions users ask.

Title Searches

Your typecasting reveals that a title search is needed for one of these reasons:

- Users want to read, scan, listen to, look at, or watch the source. The title they have in hand could come from just about anything—a book, research report, dissertation, thesis, journal article, conference paper, encyclopedia entry, photograph, film, television special, ad, music, work of art, or map.

- They want to scan the source's contents because they know that it has published, issued, or broadcast information in the past on their topic of interest. They think that by browsing what the source has published, issued, or broadcast since then they might find more like it. Ultimately, this is a subject search in which the user browses the source's contents to find more like a particular article or program he read, scanned, listened to, looked at, or watched in the past. This is the *journal run*, and you'll initiate it with a title search.

Impetus for the Title Search and Journal Run

The impetus for the title search is an exact or not-quite exact title that the user knows exists. Here are sample scenarios that describe how the source's existence came to the user's attention:

- Someone else such as a colleague, instructor, friend, relative, or librarian recommended the title.
- The user culled the title from the footnotes or bibliography of a book, a journal article, encyclopedia entry, or credits from a film or television program.
- The user conducted a database search and noticed the title listed more than once among the retrievals.
- The user conducted a database search, found one or more relevant sources, and, wanting to read the full-text, clicked on resolver links that didn't work.

In all four scenarios, the exact title may not make the trip intact from its point of origin to your interaction with the user—maybe the person who suggested the title got it wrong, the citation was incorrect, the user omitted, added, or transposed title words, or the user was relying on his or her memory of a search conducted one day, one week, one month, or even one year ago! As a result, always be skeptical about the titles users convey to you.

To find the title that the user wants, you must get the title and more information about it from the user. Be attuned to:

- The user's confidence in the title's correctness or how it might be incorrect so that you can experiment with various titles and title searches.
- The title's genre so you know what database to search. If the title is a serial, ask the user whether he intends to browse individual issues to ascertain whether your title search initiates the journal run (pages 58–61).
- The title's subject discipline so you can target the title in a discipline-based database.
- Where the user got the title so you can retrace the user's steps to find it.

Here's a reference interview from a chat transcript in which the user describes her desire for a particular title but her uncertainty about the title makes this an exceedingly difficult search. In fact, a known-item search for this title might have to morph into a subject search because the user provides so little information about the title even though she had the electronic book "in hand" a week earlier.

| User | 15:09 | Hi . . . I contacted you last week and someone gave me an online ebook name to help me write a practicum report. I am looking for guideleines in writing practicum reports. I did another search and couldn't find anything. Do you happen to know of the online book I can access? |

Librarian	15:10	Hi. Searching now. Are you an Ed[ucation] student?
User	15:12	yes Im getting my MSED in FACS to be a teacher.
Librarian	15:15	. . . Still searching . . .
User	15:16	I am still going to look as well. The funny thing is the title didn't have the word practicum in it (I think) that's why I cant find it. Thanks anyway for any help you can give me.
Librarian	15:20	Still looking. Checking with the Education Librarian . . .

Selecting Relevant Databases

Find out what the user knows about his desired title and put it to work selecting a database. Consult your library's catalog for monographs, journal titles, annual conference proceedings, films, musical compositions, and maps. Follow up with searches of the Open WorldCat database to verify the source's existence and correct bibliographic information. If the title is a journal article, conference paper, or unpublished working paper, search your library's WSD system or Google Scholar (launching the latter through your library's database hub). Follow up with searches in database aggregator databases such as EBSCOhost, Gale Cengage Learning, and ProQuest, then in journal aggregator databases such as ProQuest Research Library, SpringerLink, and ScienceDirect. If title searches in encyclopedic databases such as JStor, Scopus, or Web of Science fail, your last resort may be to research databases in the same discipline as the desired title.

Users who are under time constraints might not wait for interlibrary loan (ILL) to supply the desired source, so follow up failed title searches with subject searches in your library's databases to produce comparable sources. You won't be able to fulfill the user's request for a journal run through ILL because libraries won't loan a range of journal volumes. You'll have to continue the reference interview, finding out what the user wants and fulfilling his request with sources in your library.

Facet Analysis

The facet analysis for the title search is simple, consisting of one facet for the desired title. No logical combination of facets is necessary in a one-faceted search.

Representing the Search as Input to the Search System

Find the desired title by browsing the database's alphabetically ordered title index or by conducting a FT search of the database's title fields. With respect to research databases, OPACs almost always have both search types, and indexes, A&I databases, and full-text databases may be limited to FT searches of the title field.

To browse the database's title index alphabetically, choose this option from the fields pulldown menu and enter the title's first few words. What systems call this search varies considerably:

- Indexes | (Mouse down on the accompanying pull-down menu and choose the title index)
- Title-begins-with
- Title-index
- Browse titles
- Look up titles
- Title phrase

To browse the title index of the Classic Mirlyn OPAC, the searcher chooses the "Title begins with . . ." search and enters the initial title words struggles for poland into the search box. In response, Mirlyn lists titles in the alphabetical neighborhood of this title, giving the searcher buttons for paging forward and backward to find the desired title (figure 8.1). Personally, I find the title-begins-with search almost effortless because it requires a minimal amount of data entry, and finding the title on the first page of listed titles is a recognition task that takes a few seconds.

To execute a FT search of title fields, choose this option from the fields pull-down menu and enter most distinctive title words or the ones that you are sure about. OPACs usually refer to this as a title-keyword search. Word order doesn't matter nor should Boolean operators; however, if your FT searches fail, reenter them, inserting the Boolean AND operator in between title words. Title search statement examples are struggles for poland and struggles AND poland.

In response, the search system lists titles bearing the words in your search statement. Enter too few words or very common words and the retrievals list could be very lengthy. On occasion, users recall very little about the titles that interest them. An example is the user who initiates the chat-based reference interview on page 142. You have no recourse other than to perform a subject search using the words they provide you: "guidelines," "writing," and "reports."

Extended-Boolean search systems expect natural language searches so enter the title as is into the search box. If these systems have a fields pull-down menu, choose "title" search to limit the search to titles only. Extended-Boolean systems stem title words and rank retrievals, matching as many title words as possible, the proximity of title words to each other, and so on.

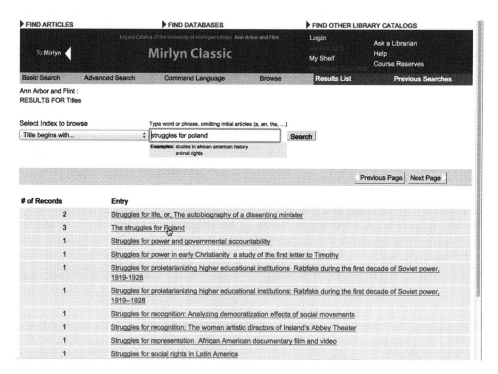

Figure 8.1. Conducting a Title-Begins-With Search in the Classic Version of the Mirlyn OPAC. Screenshots made available under the Creative Commons Attribution license by the University of Michigan Library.

When it comes to extended-Boolean searching, it doesn't matter whether a title word is missing from, incorrect, or added to your search statement; however, retrievals may be numerous, requiring users to browse many titles to find the one they want.

Author Searches

Your typecasting reveals that an author search is needed for one of these reasons:

1. Users want to read, scan, listen to, look at, or watch a particular source that a person wrote, edited, illustrated, photographed, scripted, painted, performed, sculpted, produced, and so on. This is an author search.
2. They want to scan a list of sources that a particular person wrote, edited, illustrated, etc., because they like what the person writes about and they want to find more like it. Calling it an author-bibliography search here distinguishes it from the author search above.

Impetus for the Author and Author-Bibliography Searches

The impetus for author and author-bibliography searches is an author name that is known to the user from past experience or others' recommendations. These sample scenarios that describe how the author's name came to the user's attention are not unlike those for titles:

- Someone else such as a colleague, instructor, friend, relative, or librarian recommended the name.
- The user culled the name from the footnotes or bibliography of a book, journal article, encyclopedia entry, or credits from a film or television program.
- The user conducted a database search recently or in the past where the name was listed among retrievals or in their footnotes and bibliographies.

In all three scenarios, the name may not make the trip intact from its point of origin to your interaction with the user—maybe the person who suggested the name got it wrong; the user omitted, added, or transposed characters in the given, middle, and/or family name elements; or the user is relying on his or her memory of a search conducted long ago. Maybe the name has changed due to a myriad of events that happen to persons or organizations over time. As a result, always be skeptical about the names users convey to you.

To find one or more works connected with the name that interests the user, you must get the name and more information about it from the user. Be attuned to:

- Whether the user seeks a particular *title* written, edited, illustrated, etc., by this person. By the way, this is the *first* information you should get from the user. If the user knows the title, then several avenues are open to you for finding the source—title, author, or a combination of the two. Also, research demonstrates that people are *more successful* searching for *titles* than authors when both are known (Lipetz 1972; Wildemuth and O'Neill 1995; Kilgour 2004). With both author and title information in hand, conduct a *title* search first!
- The user's confidence that the name is correct or clues about how it might be incorrect so that you can experiment with various names in your author searches.
- Who is the person behind the name so you know what database(s) to search.
- Where the user got the name so you can retrace the user's steps to find the name.

Problems Searching for Author Names and Proper Nouns Generally

Names of people, organizations, places, programs, projects, and proper nouns generally are especially problematic. People's names change due to marriage, divorce, remarriage, Anglicization, stage names, pseudonyms, sex changes, and deliberate changes of name (legal or otherwise). Some publishers apply strict editorial rules about the names on their title pages, for example, representing them as the first and middle initials followed by a single or hyphenated surname. Names of organizations change due to mergers, acquisitions, buy-outs, Anglicization, image campaigns, acronyms, splits, and the decisions publishers make about how organization names appear on their title pages. Family names and names of places change. Names of projects, programs, legislation, roads, buildings, monuments, brand names, governments, and other proper nouns change and are known by nicknames, shortened forms, and/or acronyms. They also adopt one-word names that are words used in common everyday language, e.g., castle, design, leader, miracle, meter, miter, peak, and snap. Names also bear numbers that could be written out or represented in Roman numerals or Arabic numbers.

Proper nouns figure prominently in both known-item and subject searches. When they do, consider whether and how your searches should accommodate name changes, variant names, acronyms, and so on so that you can satisfy the user's query.

Authority control is the editorial process used to maintain consistency in the establishment of authorized index terms and relationships between them. When library catalogers and database publishers practice name authority control for known-items, they assume the burden of establishing authorized names for persons, corporate bodies, and families, linking all the unused, synonymous names to the authorized names, and building a syndetic structure into their databases to refer searchers from unused names to authorized names. For example, in an OPAC governed by authority control, you can expect it to respond to your entry of the name "babe didrikson" with a reference to the database's authorized name "Use Zaharias, Babe Didrikson, 1911-1956."

The library catalogers who build OPACs maintain a record of their authority control decisions in the Library of Congress Name Authority File (LCNAF). When you think a name may be problematic, search LCNAF for alternate names (http://authorities.loc.gov/). If you aren't familiar with the MARC (Machine-Readable Cataloging) format, LCNAF records may be difficult to understand, so choose the "Labeled Display" when consulting LCNAF. Figure 8.2 shows such a

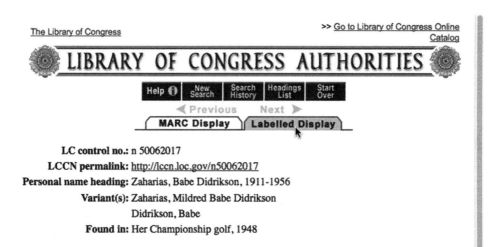

Figure 8.2. LCNAF'S Labeled Display of a Name Authority Record. Courtesy of the Library of Congress.

display of Babe's authority record. In an OPAC, users who enter the variant names "Didrikson, Babe" or "Zaharias, Mildred Babe Didrikson" would be directed to the surrogate records bearing the authorized personal name heading "Zaharias, Babe Didrikson, 1911–1956."

Clicking on the "MARC Display" tab in figure 8.2 displays a MARC-encoded record. Catalogers use MARC to designate the context of LCNAF records, that is, the fields that make up LCNAF records and the types of information that they can encode in these fields. MARC uses three-digit tags to label individual fields and breaks fields up into smaller unit called subfields with single letters and/or numbers preceded by a pipe symbol (|a, |b, or |2) or a dollar sign ($a, $b, or $2). When a user poses a query bearing the name of a person, an organization, and/or a place, check LCNAF for alternate names by examining the names in LCNAF fields beginning with the numbers 1, 4, and 5. Then use the names you find there to search relevant databases. If you are an indexer tasked with authority control, consult MARC Format for Authority Data at http://www.loc.gov/marc/authority/, which details the meaning of individually tagged fields and subfields and the types of authority data that cataloguers are authorized to encode in them.

LCNAF includes names of organizations, places, projects, programs, titles, and proper nouns generally. Other name authority files are the Getty Thesaurus of Geographic Names (TGN) at http://www.getty.edu/research/tools/vocabularies/tgn/ and the Union List of Artist Names (ULAN) at http://www.getty.edu/research/tools/vocabularies/ulan/. Biographies such as Marquis Who's Who and American National Biography Online may trace the many names a person is known by (pages 66–67).

Except for OPACs, authority control is the *exception* rather than the rule. Don't expect authority control in most databases. By the way, the problem of multiple names is not limited to women's names only due to marriage, divorce, or both. Check LCNAF for these men whose authority records list multiple names: John Creasey, Pope Francis I, Prince, Barack Obama, and Stephen King.

Authority control solves the problem of multiple names for an author. It doesn't help with misspelled author names or variants. To be comprehensive about retrieval, formulate search statements bearing as many variant forms of the name as you can think of. Consider initials, initials only, missing name elements, punctuation, symbols, and so on. Whether you are conducting a known-item search for works *by an author* or a subject search for works *about the author*, consider all the possibilities, then formulate your search statements accordingly.

Web search engines such as Google and Yahoo! are able to detect queries bearing names that are affected by both problems. They even detect users' misspelled author names embedded in phrases:

```
books by rosamund smith
ruth rendle's latest mystery
writings of harald robens made into movies
```

Selecting Relevant Databases

As soon as you establish the user's interest in a particular name, ask her for clarification. For a person, ask who this person is, in what discipline he is active, or what he is known for. For an organization, ask what kind of organization or business this is, what type of work or business does it or did it do, or what is it known for. In a pinch, consult an encyclopedia article to learn more about the proper nouns that figure into user queries.

If the user wants everything written by the person, she may be conducting an author-bibliography search—a subject search in disguise. Such searches may be for names of modern-day researchers connected with academic institutions or not-for-profit laboratories, research centers, and think tanks, or for names of writers whose literary works interest the user. Search the Web using your favorite Web search engine, looking for the person's Web page where their curriculum vitae is posted, providing you with a comprehensive list of their publications. Follow up with author searches of encyclopedic databases such Google Scholar, your library's WSD system, Scopus, and Web of Science, then one or more discipline-based databases.

With regard to writers of various literary genres, searches of your library's OPAC will determine whether the library owns a particular writer's works. Follow up with searches of the Open WorldCat database, suggesting that the user request relevant retrievals that your library doesn't own through interlibrary loan. Alternatively, inquire about the writer's genre and recommend writers in the same genre.

Facet Analysis

The facet analysis for both author and author-bibliography searches is simple, consisting of one facet for the author's name. No logical combination of facets is necessary in a one-faceted search.

Representing the Search as Input to the Search System

Formulating search statements for both author and author-bibliography searches is the same. Differences between the two pertain to the user's handling of retrievals. For the former, suggest users scan retrievals in search of the one particular title that was the impetus for their search. For the latter, suggest users scan retrievals in search of one or more on the same topic as the author's work that was the impetus for the search.

Find the desired author name by browsing the database's alphabetically ordered author index or by conducting a FT search of the database's author fields. What systems call the former varies considerably:

- Author index
- Author (last name first)
- Author (last name, first name)
- Browse authors
- Look up authors

In figure 8.3, the searcher browses the Classic version of the Mirlyn OPAC for an author's name. She mouses down on the fields pull-down menu, choosing the "Author (last name first)" option and entering the name brown, dan. Because this is a common name, she enters both surname and given name. It might take her a half minute to browse forward and backward in the alphabetical list, selecting this and that Dan Brown entry to find the Dan Brown that interests her (i.e., the author of *The Da Vinci Code*) among the half dozen Dan Browns listed (figure 8.3).

To execute a FT search of author fields, choose this option from the fields pull-down menu and enter the author's given name and surname. OPACs usually refer to this as an author-keyword or author-words search. In Mirlyn Classic, the searcher chooses the "author words" option from the fields pull-down menu and enters the author's given name and surname. Word order doesn't matter and Boolean operators shouldn't be needed; thus, the search statement dan brown should produce the same results as brown dan. OPACs like Mirlyn Classic respond with a list of sources bearing these names in the author fields of surrogate records. Enter very common names

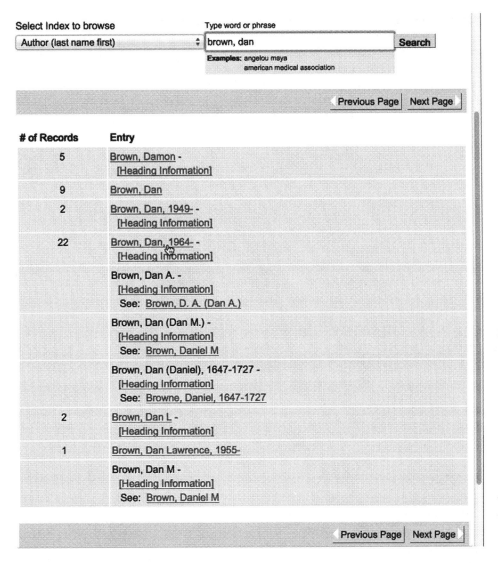

Figure 8.3. Browsing the Alphabetical Author Index in the Classic Version of the Mirlyn OPAC. Screenshots made available under the Creative Commons Attribution license by the University of Michigan Library.

and the retrievals list could be very lengthy. For example, Mirlyn Classic produces a whopping 177 retrievals for *dan brown*! Many are not relevant but they are retrieved because one author's name matches the search term *dan* and a second author's name matches the search term *brown* or Mirlyn retrieves records for a Dan Brown that is not the Dan Brown that interests the user. Examples are:

- The soundtrack to the film *13* with music and lyrics by Jason Robert **Brown** and the book by **Dan** Elish and Robert Horn
- A book on North American Forests by Thomas **Brown** and **Dan** Binkley
- A picture book about George Washington Carver illustrated by (a different) **Dan Brown**

If a search system gives you a choice between browsing the alphabetical author index and conducting a FT search, *always* do the former because you can scroll backward and forward in the alphabet selecting the many variant forms of the author's name. Thanks to authority control, variant forms of names shouldn't be problematic in OPACs; instead your browsing should reveal cross references on which you can click to navigate to the author's authorized name where the author's sources are posted. Additionally, browsing the alphabetical author index allows for precision, keeping name elements in close proximity, so that you can use qualifiers such as birth-and-death dates and roles (e.g., editor, illustrator, photographer, etc.) accompanying listed names to distinguish between persons with the same name (figure 8.3).

Extended-Boolean search systems feature natural language searching so you can enter the author name as is into the search box, no need to invert it. Some such systems feature a fields pull-down menu from which you can choose the "author" search. Extended-Boolean systems have relevance ranking algorithms that weight word proximity very high in author searches, and thus listed first should be retrievals bearing the names "Dan" and "Brown" in close proximity. Figure 8.4 shows an extended-Boolean search for **dan brown** in the U-M Library's VuFind version of the Mirlyn OPAC. This Mirlyn retrieves about 130 sources and places sources bearing these two search terms in close proximity at the top of the list.

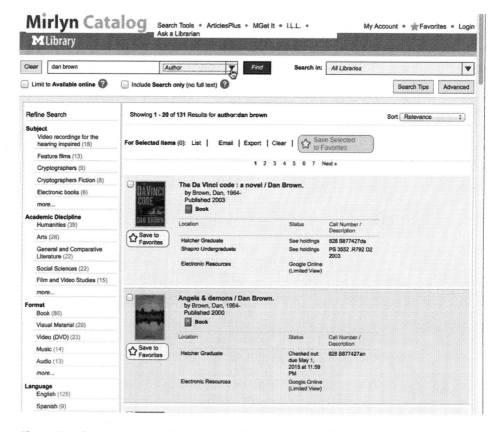

Figure 8.4. Conducting an Author Search for Dan Brown in the VuFind Version of Mirlyn with Relevance Ranked Retrievals. Screenshots made available under the Creative Commons Attribution license by the University of Michigan Library.

Searches for names confuse users. They aren't always sure whether the person figures into their search as an author or a subject. Consider this problematic chat:

| User | 18:55 | How do I find a journal on a specific person? The title is Philosophical Studies, the person is Aristotle. |
| Librarian | 18:57 | Under the first box type in Aristotle and then in the second box type in Philosophical Studies. |

Unfortunately, this chat is doomed from the start because the librarian doesn't bother to find out what the user really wants. Consider the negotiation that is needed to help this user. You have to determine whether the user actually has a citation in hand for a journal article about Aristotle published in the journal named *Philosophical Studies*. If so, conduct a citation verification search. If not, search the Ulrichsweb database to see if there really is a journal named *Philosophical Studies* and what databases index its articles, then proceed accordingly. Most likely, the user's instructor gave her and other students in the class a directive to use sources from scholarly journals. The user is unsure what to do, so she posits her question to the librarian in a way that elicits a response that remains faithful to her professor's directive about using sources from scholarly journals. Most likely, this user should search a database that specializes in philosophy, choosing "subject" from the fields pull-down menu, entering aristotle into the search box, and reviewing clusters in search of a particular aspect about Aristotle that interests her.

Citation Verification and Full-Text Fulfillment Searches

A citation verification search is a known-item search that verifies the citation data the user has in hand for a source or completes it for citation purposes. What style sheet the user is following for citing sources depends upon the disposition of the piece she is writing, so be prepared not only to verify the citation but to help the user formulate a citation that is faithful to a particular style sheet's conventions.

Very similar to the citation verification search is the full-text fulfillment search, a user's request for assistance finding a full-text for a desired source. Because you must have in hand a source's citation to find its full-text, it makes sense to lump the two searches together here.

Impetus for Citation Verification and Full-Text Fulfillment Searches

Initiating the citation verification or full-text fulfillment search is the information users have in hand about a known source that they need verified to complete a citation for the source and/or to obtain the source's full-text. Find out exactly what the user wants because verifying citation data is usually quick and straightforward, whereas obtaining full-texts requires the added steps of finding and downloading the source from a database. Users who are under time constraints might not wait for interlibrary loan (ILL) to supply the source, so you end up helping them find something like the source they originally wanted.

Don't expect the citation data users have in hand to be correct. Even if they copied and pasted it from a digital source such as a full-text's bibliography, a Web page's text, or a database's surrogate record, inaccuracies are typical in original citations, everything from misspelled title words or author names to an incorrect year of publication, volume, or issue number.

Users who verify citations are usually missing or uncertain about one or more citation elements—that's why they're asking for your help. Users wanting full-texts often have in hand full citations. Although you can verify citations and retrieve full-texts with a few elements in hand, the more elements that you have in hand to experiment with, the more likely it is that your search will succeed.

Selecting Relevant Databases

Database selection recommendations for citation verification and full-text fulfillment searches are the same as for title searches (page 143).

Facet Analysis

The facet analysis for the citation verification or full-text fulfillment search depends upon the citation information that the user provides. If the user only has a title or author name in hand, then the facet analysis involves one element—title or author name. No logical combination of facets is necessary for a one-faceted search, and your only course of action would be to conduct a title (pages 141–44) or an author (pages 145–51) search.

For the most part, citations can be boiled down to a title, author name, journal title or publisher, and date elements, and thus, search statements for most verification queries could be represented by a maximum of four facets—one each for each of these elements; however, enter as few facets as possible because errors or inaccuracies may prevent you from retrieving the citation the user wants. Deciding how to proceed depends on your assessment of the situation:

- How sure the user is about the correctness of his citation's elements
- How unique each citation element's terminology is
- Whether your chosen database features Boolean or extended-Boolean searching

Representing the Search as Input to the Search System

When searching an extended-Boolean system, you can copy and paste all available citation elements into the system's search box and let the system do the heavy lifting, so to speak, producing retrievals and ranking them so that retrievals matching all or almost all search terms are ranked higher than retrievals matching one or a couple of search terms. If the desired citation isn't popping onto page 1 of the retrievals list, limit elements to titles and publishers for books or to titles and journal titles for journal articles. Extended-Boolean systems simplify citation verification and full-text fulfillment searches considerably, because they have a certain "forgiveness" factor that allows one or more search terms in search statements to fail without torpedoing the entire search.

When searching Boolean systems, you have to do the heavy lifting, deciding which elements are likely to quickly and efficiently produce the desired citation. Consider starting with one or two elements and adding more until you have a manageable number of retrievals. If you are stumped about how to get started, remember research findings that demonstrate that the title element alone is usually effective for retrieving the desired citation.

Searches may fail because of the ways in which citation data are represented in the surrogate record and indexed in the database. For example, databases might represent journal titles, conference proceedings, book and anthology titles in full form, acronym, or abbreviated forms. Below are PsycINFO's indexed forms for the journal *Psychiatric Quarterly*:

psychiat. quart
psychiat. quart.
psychiatric quarterly
psychiatric quarterly supplement

These forms deviate due to abbreviations, punctuation, and written-out title elements. Much the same happens to indexed forms for the *Journal of the American Helicopter Society* in the Compendex database:

j am helicopter soc
j amer helicopter soc
journal of the american helicopter society

If a citation verification or full-text fulfillment search fails, the problem may be that your search statement fails to accommodate for the variant forms of a journal's title. The solution is to browse the database's journal-title index, scanning for full form, acronym, or abbreviated forms, selecting them, and combining their retrievals into one combined set using the Boolean OR operator. Unfortunately, not all search systems allow you to browse journal-title indexes, so you might have to guess at variant forms, entering them directly and/or using truncation to get the job done. Like people and organizations, journals change their titles. Search their authority records in the Ulrichsweb Global Serials Directory database, opening the database's "Title History Details" tab for a list of previous names.

Personally, I am partial to index browsing, especially when author names, book titles, and journal titles are involved (figures 8.1 and 8.3). It is much easier to recognize the desired names or titles in an alphabetical list than it is to guess at their various forms and dress them up in truncation symbols to retrieve all the possibilities. When a citation verification or full-text fulfillment search leaves you stumped, activate index browsing and scan the alphabetical list to find what you are looking for.

Database Detective Work

Databases are able to answer questions that are different from the subject and known-item queries that they were originally designed for because database fields document a wide range of information such as author affiliations, publisher names, grant names and numbers, methodologies, target audiences, study locations, and types of illustrations, and you can search for them. Scrutinize the databases you search on a daily basis, becoming familiar with the purpose and content of each and every field. Take stock of the fields that you can search above and beyond the usual subject and known-item fields. Think about the questions that users might ask that could be answered by searching these fields, alone or in combination with subject and known-item fields, pre-search qualifiers, and clusters. This type of searching requires searchers to excel in investigation, data collection, ingenuity, and deductive reasoning so it is called "database detective work." Here are a couple of searches that are conducive to this type of work.

Case Study 1: Identifying Hot Themes and Future Research

You conduct a reference interview with an upperclassman who is contemplating her senior thesis. She has written about the "Effect of television violence on children" in several classes in the past. She knows that the amount of research on this topic could fill an Olympic-sized swimming pool but the topic still interests her. She asks you to help her identify this topic's hot themes and where television-violence research may be headed in the future.

One approach to answering this negotiated query is finding recently published literature reviews on this topic. Doing so paves the way for a second approach that requires detective work, using clusters to characterize past and present research.

Discipline-specific databases in education, psychology, communication, sociology, and encyclopedic databases such as Scopus and Academic OneFile are likely to produce relevant retrievals. This is a subject query with four facets: (A) **Television**, (B) **Violence**, (C) **Children**, and (D) **Literature Reviews**, and this logical combination: A and B and C and D. In ProQuest's ERIC database, conduct a CV search for this topic using ERIC index terms (descriptors) to represent each facet, even the **Literature Review** facet. A CV search for all four facets produces a dozen retrievals. Unfortunately, the most recently published review is almost twenty years old. It's too bad this ERIC search is a bust, but all is not lost. Back up, combining this query's three subject facets—**Television** AND **Violence** AND **Children**. Then play with the nine clusters that accompany the over 325 or so retrievals. An analysis of both *Subject* and *Date* clusters could give the user clues about future research trends. Show the user how she can manipulate the *Date* cluster, limiting retrievals to three-year or five-year date ranges. After doing so, open the *Subjects* cluster so that you can study ERIC descriptors assigned to large numbers of retrievals.

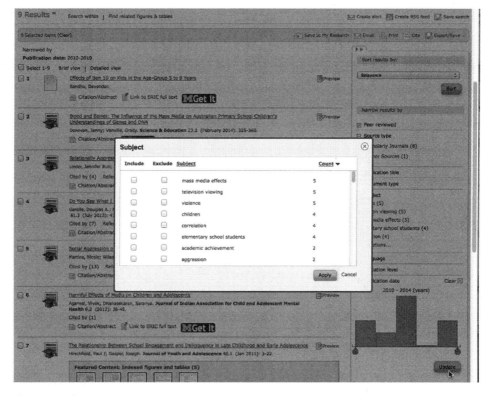

Figure 8.5. Scrutinizing High-Posted Descriptors in ProQuest ERIC's *Subjects* Cluster for Clues about the Future of Television Violence Research. The screenshots and their contents are published with permission of ProQuest LLC. Further reproduction is prohibited without permission. Inquiries may be made to: ProQuest LLC, 789 E. Eisenhower Pkwy, Ann Arbor, MI 48106-1346 USA. Telephone (734) 761–4700; Email: info@proquest.com; Web page: http://www.proquest.com.

Ignore the descriptors in your search statements—they should be high posted because you used them to search for this query. Here are the results. From 2005 to 2009, high-posted descriptors are "Mass Media Effects," "Mass Media Role," and "Mass Media Use," and from 2010 to 2014, they are "Mass Media Effects," "Video Games," and "Academic Achievement" (figure 8.5). A cursory examination of these results could lead one to believe that television-violence research is becoming more inclusive, adding video games to the discussion and emphasizing academic achievement; however, the user should double check her results with what the expert researchers who write literature reviews have to say.

The encyclopedic Scopus database might have literature reviews for this topic. Switch to Scopus. Scopus defaults to searching article titles, author-supplied keywords, and abstracts for your entered search statements. In a way, author-supplied keywords function like a CV, but Scopus and the many other databases displaying author-supplied keywords in their surrogate records don't establish broader-narrower relationships between them. Thus, FT searches are appropriate for subject searches in Scopus.

The FT search statement (televis* AND (violen* OR aggressi* OR antisocial OR (anti PRE/0 social)) AND (child* OR youngster OR youth OR adolescen*)) produces over nine hundred Scopus retrievals (figure 8.6).

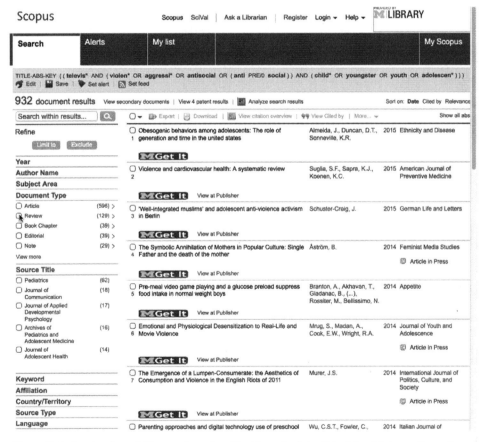

Figure 8.6. Retrievals and Clusters for a Free Text Search of the Television Violence Query in the Scopus Database. Source: Scopus, a registered trademark of Elsevier, B.V., image retrieved 16 March 2015.

Choosing "Reviews" from the *Document Type* cluster eliminates all but an eighth of Scopus retrievals and they are all reviews (figure 8.7). This is exactly what you want! Displaying them reveals several lengthy literature reviews citing many sources.

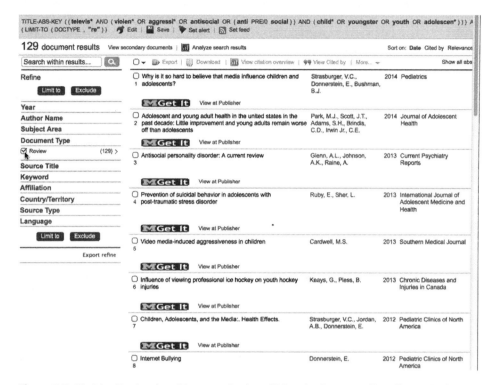

Figure 8.7. Limiting Retrievals to Literature Reviews Using the *Document Type* Cluster in the Scopus Database. Source: Scopus, a registered trademark of Elsevier, B.V., image retrieved 2015 March 16.

Despite using the one truncated search term, `televis*`, to represent this query's **Television** facet, retrieved are recent reviews that address media and video generally. There's even a recent review centered on bullying. Perhaps the clues about future television violence research trends that emerged from your analysis of high-posted ERIC descriptors are actually on target. To confirm these suspicions, the user must read the literature reviews she retrieved in Scopus to learn what the experts have to say about this topic's future.

Case Study 2: The Secrets That Clusters Reveal

Whenever clusters accompany search results, check them to determine what secrets they reveal about your topic. Figure 8.6 shows the ten clusters that accompany the nine hundred or so Scopus retrievals for the Television Violence query. Open are clusters for *Document Type* and *Source Title* revealing each cluster's top-ranked values and "view more" links. Here are the secrets this search's clusters reveal and how searchers can put clustered values to work for them:

- *Subject Area.* Check the top three- to five-ranked subject areas for clues about the disciplines that study this topic. Select databases in these disciplines for follow-up searches.
- *Author Name.* Check the top-ranked authors writing on this topic. If their writings are relevant, then follow up with author searches for them in this and other databases.

- *Source Title.* Check the top three- to five-ranked journal titles. Search these titles in your library's OPAC, then browse recent issues of these journals for articles on this topic. (This is the journal run search that this chapter examines next.)
- *Year.* In high-posted searches, limit retrievals to only the most recent years or use year-clustered retrievals combined with keyword-clustered retrievals to find themes that prevailed during certain time periods. You performed this analysis on the Television Violence topic in the ERIC database (pages 153–56).
- *Keyword.* The contents of keyword (also called subject) clusters help users determine what subtopics co-occur with a topic that interests them. Alternatively, apply both date and keyword clusters to determine trending topics.
- *Affiliation.* Notice the top three- to five-ranked affiliations. If the top-ranked affiliations name research centers, laboratories, or think tanks that produce research on the topic that interests the user, then follow up with known-item searches for these organizations in this and other databases.
- *Document Type.* Figure 8.7 demonstrates how to put the "Review" document type to work identifying future research trends. Become familiar with the full range of Scopus document types in case you need to apply them to help other users.
- *Country.* If this database's retrievals come from one country, follow up as needed with subsequent searches in databases that strive for international coverage.

Select the "Analyze Search Results" link on the Scopus search results page and Scopus presents clustered data in attractive tables and charts. In figure 8.8 is a pie chart for the *Subject Area* cluster that shows medicine (45.1%), psychology (18.8%), and the social sciences (18.8%) accounting for over 80% of the over nine hundred retrievals for the Television Violence query.

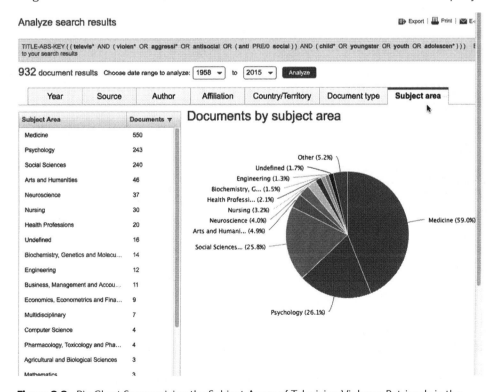

Figure 8.8. Pie Chart Summarizing the Subject Areas of Television Violence Retrievals in the Scopus Database. Source: Scopus, a registered trademark of Elsevier, B.V., image retrieved 16 March 2015.

Few beginning searchers are naturals at database detective work. It takes time and experience to familiarize yourself with the databases at your library's database hub; develop a sixth sense of the usefulness of database fields and their content; and apply your knowledge, searching skills, and ingenuity to answer the question at hand. Put on your detective hat to answer this chapter's questions (pages 163–64).

The Journal Run

The journal run has a funny name until you realize what it is all about. By whatever means, the user identifies a relevant journal, then retrieves the journal with the intention of scanning one or more issues or volumes to find relevant sources. Clusters make it easier than ever to identify journals that publish articles repeatedly on certain topics. Unfortunately, high-posted searches aren't the right candidates for follow-up journal runs, because users are overwhelmed with relevant retrievals and have little incentive to conduct journal runs to find even more. Instead, *low-posted searches* are the *best* candidates for follow-up journal runs.

It's quicker to perform the journal run when the results of a subject search are at hand, clicking on accompanying resolver links to navigate to journal publisher and journal aggregator databases where full runs of journals reside. Unfortunately, you don't know little is written on a topic until you've run the gamut, conducting subject searches in several discipline-based and encyclopedic databases and following up with relevance feedback searches. To show for your efforts, you might only have a handful of relevant full-texts and their citations. Now it's time to initiate the journal run and you'll have to perform it manually. Most libraries offer two basic approaches for finding online journals: browsing the library's alphabetical journal titles list or FT searches of the library's journal titles list.

Both approaches are procedural, requiring users to take a series of steps that starts at their library's database hub or OPAC and ends at a full-text database where they can browse recent and archived issues of the desired journal and downloads full-texts.

Browsing the Library's Alphabetical Journals List

Figures 8.9 to 8.12 walk through browsing the U-M Library's alphabetical journals list for the journal named *Canadian Journal of Experimental Psychology* that has published a handful of articles on a user's low-posted topic. Follow along at your library's hub, but expect the process to be different because of the different ways hubs index journal titles and allow you to browse and search for them.

Navigate to your library's homepage or database hub, and scan it for a link to online journals. The link may be hidden under a pull-down menu, and the terminology used for this link will vary from library to library. Examples are:

- Digital journals list
- E-Journals
- eJournals A–Z
- Electronic journals list
- Journal titles
- Journals
- Online journals

In the U-M Library's Search Tools, the user clicks first on "Online Journals," then on "Browse Online Journals Alphabetically" to navigate to an alphabetical list of the library's online journals (figure 8.9).

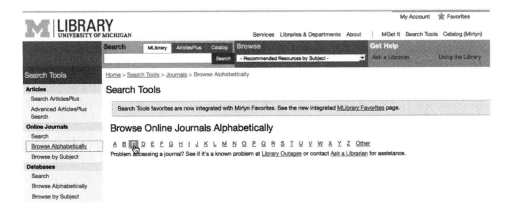

Figure 8.9. Links to an Alphabetical List of the U-M Library's Online Journals through Search Tools. Screenshots made available under the Creative Commons Attribution license by the University of Michigan Library.

In response, Search Tools displays linked letters of the alphabet. Clicking on the letter "C" opens the alphabetical journals list with journals beginning with this letter. Browsing forward in the alphabet eventually produces a holdings record for the journal *Canadian Journal of Experimental Psychology* (figure 8.10).

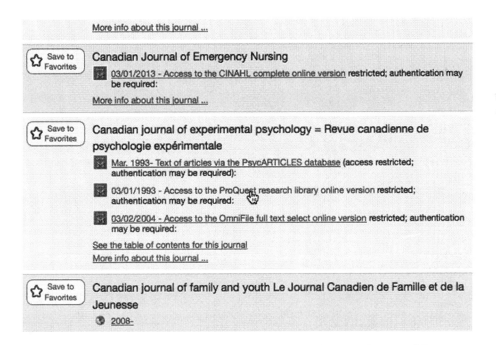

Figure 8.10. A Journal Holdings Record in Search Tools Revealing Suppliers of Full-Texts. Screenshots made available under the Creative Commons Attribution license by the University of Michigan Library.

The holdings record reveals three suppliers of full-text for the *Canadian Journal of Experimental Psychology*, and their entries bear their names and the date ranges of journal issues that they supply. Click on ProQuest, the second-listed entry, a journal aggregator with a familiar name that offers uninterrupted access to issues published from 1993 to the present. In response, ProQuest displays its publication information page for the *Canadian Journal of Experimental Psychology* where the user can click on ranges of years, displaying numbered volumes and issues (figure 8.11).

When conducting a journal run, the user isn't interested in one particular journal article. He wants to scan issue after issue in search of journal articles on a topic that interests him. Thus, he'd click open all years in figure 8.11, displaying volumes and issues and scanning each issue for relevant content. ProQuest is especially helpful in this regard, accompanying article titles with "Preview" links over which the user can hover his computer's cursor to display abstracts and

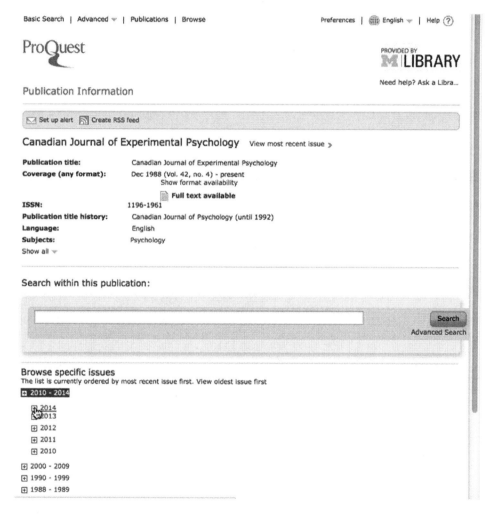

Figure 8.11. Displaying a Journal's Years, Volumes, and Issues in the ProQuest Research Library Database. The screenshots and their contents are published with permission of ProQuest LLC. Further reproduction is prohibited without permission. Inquiries may be made to: ProQuest LLC, 789 E. Eisenhower Pkwy, Ann Arbor, MI 48106-1346 USA. Telephone (734) 761–4700; Email: info@proquest.com; Web page: http://www.proquest.com.

make a quick relevance assessment (figure 8.12). When he does find a relevant source, he can display its full-text in his Web browser's window by clicking on the "Full text" link or download the full-text to his personal computer by clicking on the "Full text—PDF" link.

Figure 8.12. Browsing a Journal Issue's Contents in the ProQuest Research Library Database. The screenshots and their contents are published with permission of ProQuest LLC. Further reproduction is prohibited without permission. Inquiries may be made to: ProQuest LLC, 789 E. Eisenhower Pkwy, Ann Arbor, MI 48106-1346 USA. Telephone (734) 761–4700; Email: info@proquest.com; Web page: http://www.proquest.com.

Searching for a Journal in the Library's OPAC

A second approach to finding online journals involves a search of the library's OPAC. Figures 8.13 and 8.14 walk through this approach using U-M Library's VuFind version of the Mirlyn OPAC. Follow along at your library's OPAC but expect differences for the same reasons mentioned earlier (page 158). Most OPACs default to the basic interface. If a fields pull-down menu accompanies the search box, pull it down and look for a journal title search. Again, the name will vary across OPACs:

- Journal/serial name
- Journal/serial name begins with

- Journal/serial name word(s)
- Journal title
- Journals and magazines

If no journal title search is listed, click the OPAC's advanced search link and look for it there. Many OPACs lump the journal title search into the title search so selecting it may be your only option. If you have a choice between browsing the library's alphabetical journal titles list or conducting FT searches of this list, choose the former, entering as much of the journal name as you think is necessary for the OPAC to place you as close as possible to your desired journal title. The VuFind version of Mirlyn features FT searches of the library's journal titles list only. In figure 8.13, the Mirlyn searcher enters canadian journal of experimental psychology into the search box and chooses "Journal/Serial name" from the fields pull-down menu to limit retrievals to the journal titles list. In response, this Mirlyn retrieves thirty-one titles and lists the desired title second (figure 8.13).

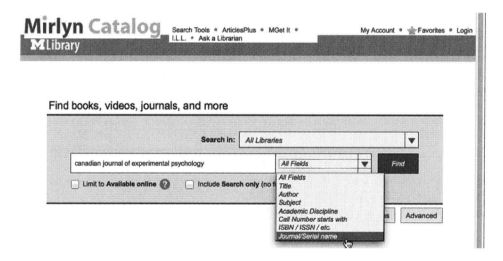

Figure 8.13. Searching for a Journal Title in the VuFind Version of the Mirlyn OPAC. Screenshots made available under the Creative Commons Attribution license by the University of Michigan Library.

Selecting the second-listed title opens this Mirlyn's journal holdings record that lists three suppliers of full-texts (figure 8.14). These three suppliers are the same three aggregators as the Search Tools list (figure 8.10). Click on ProQuest, the second-listed entry, and ProQuest displays a publication information page for the *Canadian Journal of Experimental Psychology* (figure 8.11). The user conducting this journal run then proceeds with journal title review, relevance assessment, and downloading activities (figure 8.12).

Because browsing individual issues takes time, effort, concentration, and perseverance, the journal run is for serious, motivated researchers whose interests are on the cutting edge and who may have trouble finding relevant information. It is not for the casual inquirer who needs a handful of refereed journal articles to write a paper that is due tomorrow afternoon. If neither approach—searching the library's alphabetical journals list or the OPAC—yields the desired journal title, your library probably does not subscribe to it. This ends your journal run search because an interlibrary loan requires known-items, not entire runs of journals.

Figure 8.14. A Journal Holdings Record in the VuFind Version of Mirlyn Revealing Suppliers of Full-Texts. Screenshots made available under the Creative Commons Attribution license by the University of Michigan Library.

Become familiar with the various ways to find online journals on your library's homepage because you will help many users find journals, issues of journals, and journal articles on a daily basis. By the way, when you are positioned at a journal aggregator's or journal publisher's database (figure 8.11), you can enter search statements to retrieve issues bearing certain search terms; however, you do *not* want to do this for the journal run because it enlists the user's recognition—scanning article titles and reviewing the contents of promising ones—to pinpoint relevant sources.

Questions

When finding answers to these questions, keep a record of the steps that you took to answer them.

1. A user needs the full citation for a source entitled "Competitive Sports Activities for Men." She can't remember the database where she found the source. She had trouble downloading the source so she copied and pasted the source's text into a three-page Word document. She doesn't even know its author's name. In response to your question about the source's contents, she tells you that it talks about sports for elderly men suffering from memory problems. Find the source's full citation.

2. A local organization has received large gifts from several donors to help support its 50th anniversary celebration. Alice Walker and Phyllis Chesler are the favorites topping the organizing committee's guest speakers list. Anticipating controversy as a result of their selection, the chair of the organizing committee asks you to search online for information on their recent activism and report back to him with your results.

3. A library user tells you he has read all the library's books by Dan Chernenko and wants to know whether the library has more recent books by this author. Help him find them.

4. A library user vaguely remembers a source published in the journal *Visual Studies* around the turn of the millennium. The library's electronic subscription to this journal starts in 2002, and missing from the library shelves are print volumes from 1998 to 2001. Help him find articles written in *Visual Studies* between 1998 and 2001 so he can scan them in search of the one he remembers.

5. A library user is searching for a photo of Sarajevo citizens avoiding sniper fire in the streets during the 1990s war in Yugoslavia.

6. I need a complete bibliography of all items written by the late great Jerry Salton from Cornell. He taught for many years in Cornell's computer science department.

7. Find me everything on Salton's SMART search system that was the precursor to today's web-based retrieval systems including Google.

Summary

Enter http://www.onlinesearching.org/p/8-known.html into your Web browser for a video on known-item searching.

When you conduct a search for a known-item, you expect to retrieve a source that you know exists. Examples are a journal article, book, conference paper, blog, organization, film, magazine or journal, or author. This chapter spotlights the two most common known-item searches—title searches and author searches. Often, these known-item searches are subject searches in disguise. For the latter, the user wants to scan an author's works in case the author has produced more works like the ones the user knows about. For the former, the user wants to scan a particular title's contents because it has published relevant information in the past and he thinks that by browsing what else the source has published that he might find more like it. This describes the journal run, and it requires the user's full attention, patience and perseverance, methodically and systematically reviewing a particular title's contents. Save the journal run for the most serious researchers or as the search of last resort for very low-posted queries.

Known-item searching is problematic as a result of the original citing source's published inaccuracies, the faulty memories of the persons recommending known-items to users, and the incomplete information users provide you with. Database publishers could ameliorate the situation by performing authority control—the editorial process used to maintain consistency in the establishment of titles and authors and the relationships between them. Authority control is expensive to implement and maintain. Except for the OPAC, few databases perform authority control. The burden is on you, the searcher, to overcome the limitations of databases bereft of authority control in the course of finding what the user wants.

Extended-Boolean systems streamline some known-item searches because they have a certain "forgiveness" factor that allows one or more search terms in search statements to fail without torpedoing the entire search. Google and Web search engines generally might also be able to correct author names so that you can apply what you learn in follow-up searches of full-text databases.

Database searches are able to answer questions that are different from the subject and known-item queries that they were originally designed for. *Online Searching* calls this database detective work. Eventually a user will pose an unconventional user query and your familiarity with the wide range of a database's fields, pre-search qualifiers, and post-search clusters will pay off.

Bibliography

Kilgour, Frederick G. 2004. "An Experiment Using Coordinate Title Word Searches." *Journal of the American Society for Information Science & Technology* 51, no. 1: 74–80.

Lipetz, Ben-Ami. 1972. "Catalog Use in a Large Research Library." *Library Quarterly* 41, no. 1: 129–39.

Wildemuth, Barbara M., and Ann L. O'Neill. 1995. "The 'Known' in Known-Item Searches: Empirical Support for User-Centered Design." *College & Research Libraries* 56, no. 3 (May): 265–81.

Answers

1. Finding a full citation for a source using only its title.

Based on what the user tells you about the source, you should establish a pecking order with respect to searching databases likely to provide a citation. This appears to be a journal article so search your library's WSD system first, then Google and Google Scholar (launching the latter through your library's database hub). If your searches fail, continue searching, choosing database aggregators such as EBSCOhost, Gale Cengage Learning, and ProQuest, then journal aggregator databases such as ProQuest Research Library, ScienceDirect, or SpringerLink. Consider also current newspaper databases such as LexisNexis, InfoTrac Newsstand, ProQuest News & Current Events, and Access World News.

A title search of all EBSCOhost databases and a Google search of the title words enclosed in quotes `"competitive sports activities for men"` retrieves the full citation: Tolle, Ellen. 2008. "Competitive Sports Activities for Men." *Activities Directors' Quarterly for Alzheimer's and Other Dementia Patients* 9, no. 3: 9–13.

2. Find information by and about contemporary persons.

Conduct known-item searches for Walker and Chesler in current newspaper databases such as LexisNexis and ProQuest's News & Current Events. For Walker, LexisNexis clusters named "Families & children," "Israel," "Maternal and child health," and "Palestinian Territory, Occupied" may reveal potentially controversial aspects. For Chesler, ProQuest clusters named "Muslims," "Islam," "Domestic violence," and "Murders & Murder attempts" describe issues that fuel her activism. By the way, display retrievals in reverse chronological order (i.e., most recent first) to see the latest press about each person. Also, your search statements should use the nearby operator to retrieve their names in direct and inverted forms, for example, `alice w/1 walker` and `phyllis w/1 chesler` in LexisNexis and `alice near/0 walker` and `phyllis near/0 chesler` in ProQuest.

3. Find more titles written by a contemporary author.

Check LCNAF for this author's authority record (http://authorities.loc.gov). Dan Chernenko is a pseudonym for Harry Turtledove, an author who writes under his real name (Dan Chernenko), Mark Gordian, Eric G. Iverson, and H. N. Turteltaub. Follow up with author searches in your library's OPAC for each name, showing the user your library's holdings for each and suggesting he pursue ones that interest him.

4. Find articles published in certain issues of an academic journal.

Search for `visual studies` in Ulrichsweb, a database of bibliographic and publication information for serials. Open its "Abstracting & Indexing" tab and scan the list in search of databases that index this journal's turn-of-the-millennium volumes. *Visual Studies* is "core" in two ProQuest databases—Sociological Abstracts and International Bibliography of the Social Sciences—meaning that these databases index *all* articles in this journal. Choose the former, click on the "Advanced" link, then choose "Publication title—PUB" from the fields pull-down menu. Click on the "Look Up Publications" link, enter visual studies, scroll down and under the "Search Options" heading, set the "Publication date" option to "Before this date" and "January 2002," and search the database. Put the list in reverse chronological order by choosing "Publication date (most recent first)" from the "Sort" results pull-down menu in the middle center right of the page. Invite the user to scan the list for the desired source(s).

5. **Find a famous image.**
   Launch AP Images or the Google Image database. Into the search box, enter the most salient terms in the user's description, sarajevo sniper. Hovering your cursor over retrieved AP images produces a pop-up description. In Google, you'll have to click on the image, then on the "Visit page" link in search of their descriptions.

6. **Find an academic's bibliography.**
   If you don't know who Salton is, search him on Google and take note of his various names: Gerard Salton, Jerry Salton, Gerry Salton, and Gerald Salton. Check LCNAF also. Identify computer science databases at your library's hub and search *all* of them using *all* forms of this author's name. Search your library's OPAC for his books also.

7. **Find information about a system bearing a name that is a common noun.**
   This is a difficult query because the search term smart is used in so many different contexts. If you enter smart, you must add subject terms as a hedge to give it context. Search the Inspec database using its "Quick Search." Enter smart into the search box. Retrieved are one hundred thousand retrievals! Choose the "Thesaurus" tab and enter information retrieval into the search box. This phrase is a CV term so click on it to display its syndetic structure. Choose relevant index terms such as "Information Retrieval," "Information Retrieval Systems," "Information Retrieval System Evaluation," "Bibliographic Systems," "Relevance Feedback," "Query Processing," and "Query Formulation," and limit results to the years 1957 (one year before Salton received his PhD) to 1997 (two years after his death). Combine sets using the Boolean AND operator for the smart free text term and the **Information Retrieval** facet, that is, #1 AND #2. This reduces the initial one hundred thousand retrievals to about ten dozen, and you can quickly scan their titles, distinguishing relevant sources, e.g., "Implementation of the SMART Retrieval System," from non-relevant ones, e.g., "Smart Catalogs and Virtual Catalogs." Eventually you'll encounter a source that reveals SMART's full name—Salton's Magical Automated Retriever of Texts—so you can follow up with known-item searches in Inspec and other databases using the name's most salient terms, magical automated retriever.

9

Databases for Assessing Research Impact

This chapter focuses on publication-level and article-level metrics that are used to assess research impact. These metrics come from the well-entrenched library and information science (LIS) area of study called bibliometrics and the fledgling enterprise called altmetrics. Because these metrics pertain to known authors and titles, it makes sense to discuss them here, following on the heels of the known-item searching chapter. Interested in research impact are college and university faculty who use these metrics to decide where to publish their research; administrators at research centers, laboratories, think tanks, and academic institutions who use these metrics to inform employment, tenure, and promotion decisions; and representatives of professional associations, learned societies, national academies, and funding agencies who use these metrics to aid in decision-making regarding committee selection, editorial boards, elected boards and positions, awards, nominations, grants, and much more.

Bibliometrics

Bibliometrics is the statistical analysis of the written products of academic inquiry, scholarship, and research, especially in the form of journal articles, books, dissertations, theses, and conference papers. Eugene Garfield (1955), one of the founders of bibliometrics, applied promising research findings about citation data into the design of the Science Citation Index (SCI). Initially a print publication, SCI was converted into an online database in the 1970s, and it enabled users who had a known-item in hand to find published sources that cited it in subsequent years (pages 131–32). Over the years, Garfield and his colleagues introduced new citation indexes for the arts, humanities, and social sciences. Eventually these citation indexes were combined, forming the Web of Science (WoS) database (Thomson Reuters 2014). While remaining focused on citation searching, WoS evolved into an A&I database with encyclopedic coverage.

Cited-reference searches in WoS produce citation counts for individuals and for specific publications. The citation count is the number of times a person's publications have been cited in other publications or the number of times a specific publication has been cited. Researchers aim for high citation counts, proving to their colleagues that their research is important.

Assembling an Author's Citation Count in the Web of Science Database

Determining a researcher's citation count is procedural in WoS compared to the more straightforward and direct process in Scopus and Google Scholar. When you help users conduct cited-reference searches, ask them about the person they are searching—the author's discipline and their specific research interests—because what you learn will help you search citation databases, distinguishing between persons with the same or similar names. You must also take name changes into account. Check for them in the Library of Congress Name Authority File (LCNAF) and in published biographies, then use the author's current and previous names to assemble all WoS citation entries.

Search WoS using Cliff Lampe, one of my University of Michigan colleagues, who teaches computer-human interaction (CHI) and conducts research on social media and online communities. Launch the WoS database and choose "Cited Reference Search" from the pull-down menu to the right of the "Basic Search" label (figure 9.1).

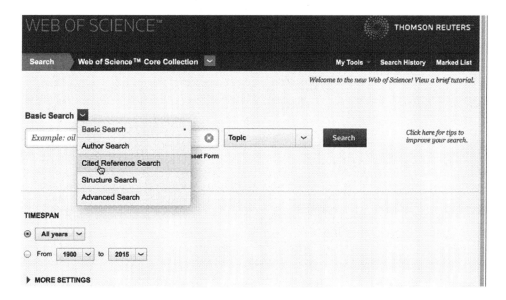

Figure 9.1. Choosing the Cited Reference Search in the Basic Search Interface of the Web of Science (WoS) Database. Data included herein are derived from the Web of Science prepared by Thomson Reuters, Inc. (Thomson), Philadelphia, Pennsylvania, USA: Copyright Thomson Reuters 2015. All rights reserved.

The cited reference search interface opens. Wait! Don't enter Cliff's name into the search box yet because of the problems of multiple names and variant forms of author names (pages 146–47). Instead, click on the "Select from Index" link (figure 9.2).

WoS responds by opening its "Cited Author Index" where you enter the surname lampe and first initial c into the search box and click on the "Move To" button (figure 9.3).

In response, WoS displays names from its cited author index in the alphabetical neighborhood of this author's name. Scroll through the full list and choose listed names even if you're unsure about them; you'll get a second chance to eliminate their postings from the author's citation count in WoS. In figure 9.4, the searcher chooses seven names for Cliff, five bearing various

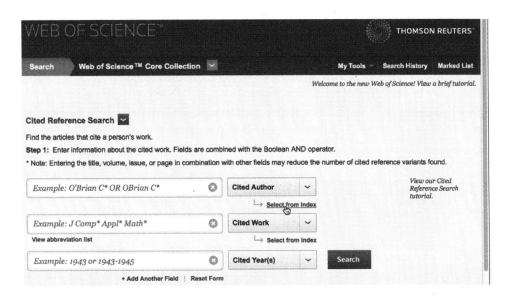

Figure 9.2. Choosing the Cited Author Index in the Web of Science Database. Data included herein are derived from the Web of Science prepared by Thomson Reuters, Inc. (Thomson), Philadelphia, Pennsylvania, USA: Copyright Thomson Reuters 2015. All rights reserved.

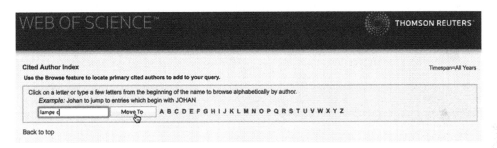

Figure 9.3. Entering an Author's Surname and First Initial into the Web of Science's Cited Author Index. Data included herein are derived from the Web of Science prepared by Thomson Reuters, Inc. (Thomson), Philadelphia, Pennsylvania, USA: Copyright Thomson Reuters 2015. All rights reserved.

initials for his first and middle names, one bearing his whole first name, and one bearing a likely misspelling of his first name. As you select them, WoS lists them at the bottom of the page.

Click on the "OK" button and WoS searches for sources that have cited the author and reports results in a huge "Cited Reference Search" table spanning eight Web pages. Figure 9.5 shows a very small portion of this table. The cited reference search table's columns from left to right are: (1) "Select" checkbox, (2) this cited author's name along with his co-authors, (3) an abbreviated form of the publication in which the cited work was published, (4) year, (5) volume, (6) issue, (7) cited page number, (8) the cited work's unique identifier, (9) number of citing articles to this work, and (10) a link to display this cited work. Each row records one or more cited references to one of this author's sources. Expect multiple entries for the same source because WoS indexes cited references right down to the *page number.*

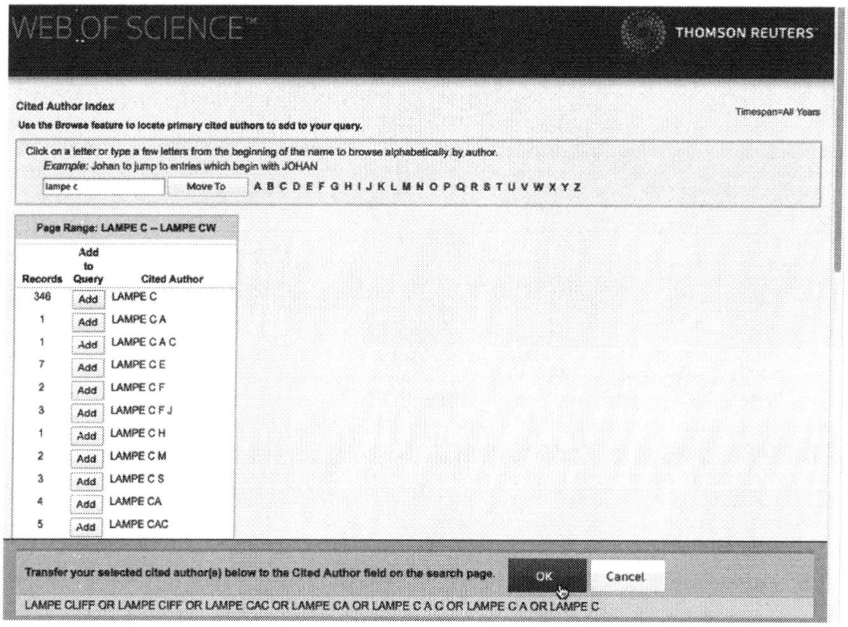

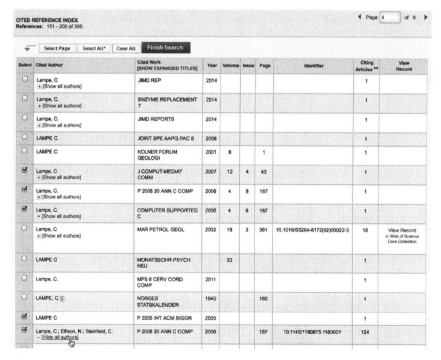

Figure 9.4. Selecting Alphabetized Names from the Cited Author Index in the Web of Science Database. Data included herein are derived from the Web of Science prepared by Thomson Reuters, Inc. (Thomson), Philadelphia, Pennsylvania, USA: Copyright Thomson Reuters 2015. All rights reserved.

Figure 9.5. Cleaning Up Entries in Your Selected Author's Cited Reference Index Table in the Web of Science Database. Data included herein are derived from the Web of Science prepared by Thomson Reuters, Inc. (Thomson), Philadelphia, Pennsylvania, USA: Copyright Thomson Reuters 2015. All rights reserved.

Your job is to "clean up" this eight-page table, reducing it to entries that Cliff wrote on his own and with his co-authors. To do so, scan each entry and check its "Select" checkbox in column 1 for entries that Cliff and his co-authors wrote. Usually the abbreviated source names in column 3 give you enough information to make a decision; for example, entries in figure 9.5 bearing the words and phrases ENZYME REPLACEMENT T, KOLNER FORUM GEOLOGI, MAR PETROL GEOL, and MPS 6 CERV CORD COMP are ones you can leave unchecked in this ongoing search because they do not represent the disciplines where Cliff publishes his scholarship. If you are unsure, hover your cursor over the "View Record" link in column 10 to see the source's title or click on the "Show all authors" link in column 2 to see this author's co-authors.

By the way, Cliff's cited reference search table takes *eight pages* to display so don't jump the gun and click the "finish search" button at the bottom of each page until you have checked all eight pages!

At long last, your cleanup effort results in a cited reference search table bearing thousands of references to articles citing Cliff's works (figure 9.6). In winter 2015, Cliff's WoS citation count is 1,746 but it increases every few days or so. More important than the 175 pages of the cited references to Cliff's publications are the sixteen accompanying clusters because they give the

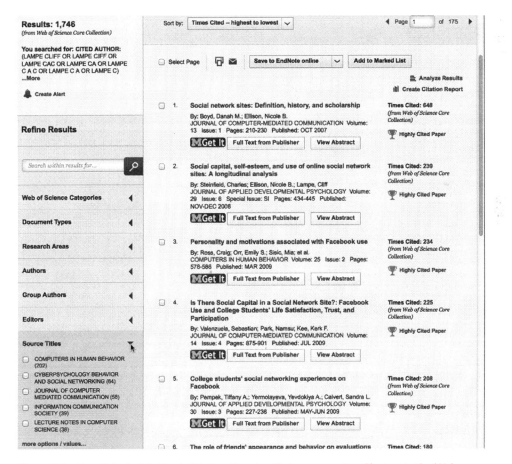

Figure 9.6. Your Selected Author's Citation Count with Accompanying Clusters in the Web of Science Database. Data included herein are derived from the Web of Science prepared by Thomson Reuters, Inc. (Thomson), Philadelphia, Pennsylvania, USA: Copyright Thomson Reuters 2015. All rights reserved.

big picture of Cliff's publication record—the disciplines Cliff's research spans (*WoS Categories* cluster), who cites him the most (*Authors* cluster), what journals cite him the most (*Source Titles* cluster), whether citations to Cliff's works are increasing or decreasing over time (*Publication Years* cluster), and more. Figure 9.6 displays seven of sixteen clusters in which the *Source Titles* cluster is open, revealing the top five journals citing Cliff's publications. Click on the "Analyze Results" link trailing the sixteenth cluster (not shown in figure 9.6) for ways to further refine cluster values.

Searching for an Author's Citation Count in the Scopus Database

To search for Cliff's citation count in Scopus, switch from Scopus' default "Document search" to its "Author search" by clicking on the "Author search" tab. Then, enter lampe into the "Author Last Name . . ." search box and cliff into the "Author Initials or First Name . . ." search box (figure 9.7). Because Cliff's name may be common, enter University of Michigan into the "Affiliation . . ." search box and click the magnifying-glass search icon.

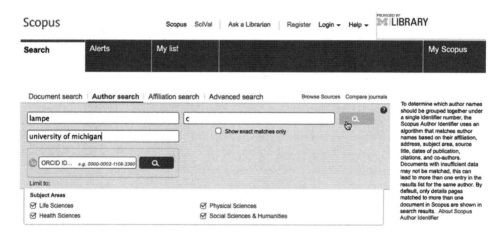

Figure 9.7. Entering an Author's Name to Initiate a Citation Count Search in the Scopus Database. Source: Scopus, a registered trademark of Elsevier, B.V., image retrieved 17 March 2015.

Scopus responds with a list of names. Scan this list using its accompanying author affiliation and disciplinary information to distinguish between people with the same name. Figure 9.8 displays Cliff's Scopus-based bibliometrics.

By Saint Patrick's Day 2015, Cliff's fifty-five sources had spawned 3,173 citations in 2,436 sources. Scopus performs authority control on *author-name variants*, so your retrievals won't be dogged by the variants you found in WoS such as Lampe, C, Lampe, C A, and Lampe, Cliff. Its authority control does *not* extend to *name changes*. Authors (like me) have to contact Scopus asking this database publisher to combine citations for multiple names under their preferred form of name. If authors don't contact Scopus, they'll have more than one author entry, citation count, and h-index requiring users who search for such authors to combine multiple entries for the same author manually.

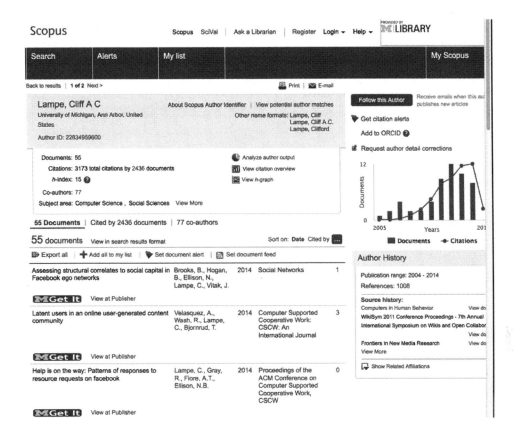

Figure 9.8. An Author's Citation Count and Related Information in the Scopus Database.
Source: Scopus, a registered trademark of Elsevier, B.V., image retrieved 2015 March 17.

Searching for an Author's Citation Count in the Google Scholar Database

Finally, there is Cliff's citation count in Google Scholar. Enter `cliff lampe` into Google Scholar's search box and click on the magnifying-glass icon. Google Scholar responds with a retrievals list and the link "User Profile for Cliff Lampe." Clicking on the link produces this author's Google Scholar user profile (figure 9.9). Topping this profile is his citation count—10,433—almost six times as many citations as WoS (figure 9.6) and more than three times as many citations as Scopus (figure 9.8)!

The main reason for disparities between the three citation counts is that each database uses a different set of sources from which to generate cited references (Bar-Ilan 2008; Meho and Yang 2007; Harzing and Wal 2008). WoS limits its core set to journals, book-based proceedings, and selected books and anthologies. Scopus is less stringent, indexing serial publications such as scholarly journals, trade journals, book series, and conference publications bearing an ISSN (International Standard Serial Number). Google is the least stringent, indexing the full range of academic publications. Boosting Cliff's Google Scholar citation count is this database's comprehensiveness covering the many conference proceedings where Cliff publishes his research. Because researchers in his field of study communicate their findings primarily through conference

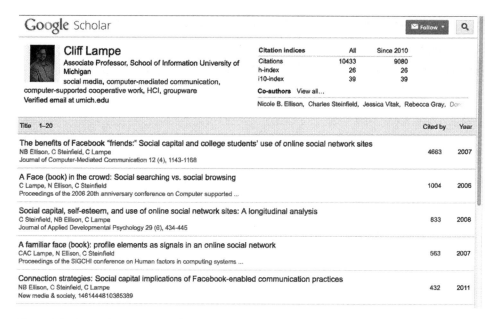

Figure 9.9. An Author's User Profile in Google Scholar Bearing His Citation Count and Related Information. Google and the Google logo are registered trademarks of Google Inc., used with permission.

proceedings, Google Scholar may be the best source for Cliff's citation count. When you assist users with queries that involve citation counts, suggest that they search all three databases and choose results from the one that best represents how scholars in the particular field of study communicate their research to their peers.

Like Scopus, Google Scholar performs authority control on *author-name variants*, not on name changes. If you are searching an author (like me) who has written under more than one name over the years, be prepared to search Google under all of the person's names, combine retrievals, and calculate bibliometrics manually.

Don't expect to find user profiles for every author you search in Google Scholar. No Google Scholar user profile means that the searcher has to calculate an author's citation count manually.

Journal-Level Metrics

A by-product of WoS is Journal Citation Reports (JCR), a database that uses its proprietary *impact factor* metric to rate the twelve thousand journals that WoS indexes. JCR calculates this metric by determining the number of times that articles in a journal are cited by other journals over a two-year period, divided by the total number of citable pieces in the journal. You can use the impact factor to evaluate *Computers in Human Behavior* (CHB), the journal that WoS reports as having the most cited references to Cliff Lampe's works (figure 9.6). Choose JCR from your library's database hub. Fill in the radio buttons for "JCR Social Sciences Edition" and "Search for a specific journal" and click on the SUBMIT button. Into the search box, enter computers in human behavior. An abbreviated report displays CHB's impact factor and several other metrics. Clicking on the CHB link in the "Journal Title" column reveals the full report. It is quite lengthy so figure 9.10 only shows the portion of the report before the fold.

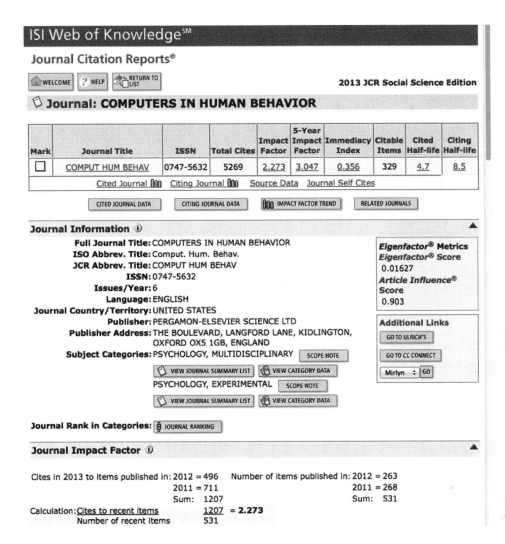

Figure 9.10. Journal Entry Featuring the Impact Factor in the Journal Citation Reports Database. Data included herein are derived from the Journal Citation Reports prepared by Thomson Reuters, Inc. (Thomson), Philadelphia, Pennsylvania, USA: Copyright Thomson Reuters 2015. All rights reserved.

In figure 9.10, JCR categorizes CHB into two fields of study: (1) multidisciplinary psychology and (2) experimental psychology. Clicking on the VIEW JOURNAL SUMMARY LIST button for multidisciplinary psychology produces an alphabetized list of 129 journals in this field of study. Sorting the list for each metric reveals CHB's various rankings—12th in total citations, 24th in impact factor, 22nd for five-year impact factor, 10th for Eigenfactor, and so on. Using this list in conjunction with two or more journals of interest enables you to make comparisons between journals in a particular field. Overall, CHB appears to be smack dab in the middle of the top 25% of journal titles in the multidisciplinary psychology field of study.

The Eigenfactor, the Journal Status, and the Scimago Journal Rank are new journal-rating metrics that bibliometrics researchers have developed to account for prestige, able to boost a journal's rating when it is cited by articles published in prestigious journals. Interestingly, CHB benefits from the prestige element built into the Eigenfactor, leaping from 24th place for the older impact factor metric to 10th place for the newer Eigenfactor metric.

Academics do and should use journal-level metrics to decide where to publish their research, but when they use them for peer review, problems arise because these metrics rate journals. They do *not* rate individual journal articles or the scholars who publish in these journals (Seglen 1997).

By the way, Scopus and Google Scholar publish journal-level metrics on the open Web in their Journal Metrics (http://www.journalmetrics.com/) and Metrics (http://scholar.google .com/citations?view_op=top_venues) databases, respectively.

Using Article-Level Metrics to Compare Two Authors' Publication Records

The h-index is an article-level metric that Scopus and Google Scholar report for cited authors. For example, Cliff's Scopus h-index is 15 (figure 9.8). This means that of the total sources that Scopus considered to calculate Cliff's h-index, fifteen sources were cited fifteen times or more. Cliff's Google Scholar h-index is 26 (figure 9.9), thus, of the total sources that Google Scholar considered, twenty-six sources were cited twenty-six times or more. Google Scholar adds the i10-index to its metrics for cited authors (figure 9.9). Cliff's i10-index is 39, the number of sources he has written that have been cited ten or more times.

The usefulness of article-level metrics becomes apparent when they are used to compare two authors' publication records. When Cliff was evaluated for promotion and tenure (P&T) in 2013, perhaps his P&T committee was tempted to compare his citation counts, h-index, and i10-index with those of a recently tenured colleague at a peer institution. I asked Cliff for suggestions, and he told me he is usually compared with Associate Professor Darren Gergle at Northwestern University who received tenure and promotion in 2011. Table 9.1 compares their publication records using Scopus and Google Scholar (GS) article-level metrics.

Both researchers received their PhD in 2006. Cited references to Cliff's publications are three to four times higher than to Darren's publications; however, a large proportion (55.5% in Scopus and 45.0% in Google Scholar) of them come from a paper Cliff co-authored with first author Nicole Ellison on the hot topic "Facebook Friends." According to Google Scholar, Darren has written a few more papers than Cliff. All things considered, these two academics have very similar publication records. Notice that Table 9.1 is limited to article-level data. His P&T committee could have enhanced this table with index factors and Eigenfactors for the journals in which these two scholars publish alongside average metrics for all the journals in their field of study, but these

Table 9.1. Comparing Two Academics' Publication Records Using Article-Level Metrics

Data Type	Cliff		Darren	
	Scopus	GS	Scopus	GS
Number of publications	55	86	53	93
Citation count	3,173	10,433	642	2,920
h-index	15	26	13	25
i10-index	NA	39	NA	41
Year awarded PhD (from vita)	2006		2006	

would be journal-level data that rate journals, not the publication records of the academics who publish in them. (By the way, Cliff received tenure and promotion to associate professor at the University of Michigan in 2013.)

Altmetrics

Article-level metrics are based on researchers citing other researchers' works. Because it takes the academic publishing cycle almost a half decade to come full circle, such data are not very useful for evaluating researchers in the *short term*. More immediate and granular than the traditional benchmarks are new article-level metrics (ALMs) that can be generated from the online systems that come into contact with new sources as they enter the academic publishing cycle and bring them to people's attention (Tananbaum 2013; Priem et al. 2011). Cave (2013) characterizes this contact and the data sources used to quantify each contact:

- *Usage:* Are people reading the source? Data sources are journal publisher and journal aggregator systems that log how many times full-texts and their supplemental data (if available) have been displayed and downloaded.
- *Captures:* Are people keeping the source and sharing it with like-minded people? Data sources are recommender systems such as CiteULike and Mendeley that cite how many times sources have been bookmarked or shared in their systems.
- *Social Media:* Is the source piquing people's interest? Data sources are social networking services such as Facebook, LinkedIn, and Twitter that count how many people have acknowledged sources.
- *Mentions:* What are people saying about the source? Data sources are blogs, Wikipedia, and journal aggregators where people discuss the scholarly sources they read.

The creation and study of new metrics for quantifying the reach and impact of an academic article that includes mentions in social media is called altmetrics (Tananbaum 2013). Into the BioMed Central, Nature Publishing Group (NPG), and Scopus databases are incorporated ALMs tools developed and marketed by the company Altmetric. Using ALMs tools is simple. Find a source that interests you in one of these databases, scan the source's surrogate looking for the Altmetric "donut" that summarizes ALMs, and click on the "see details" link for more information.

To determine the "buzz" surrounding Cliff's most recent journal article, check its Altmetric report in Scopus. Perform an author search for c lampe. Sorting retrievals by date puts his "Assessing Structural Correlates to Social Capital in Facebook Ego Networks" at the top of the list. Clicking on its title reveals a summary Altmetric report on the bottom right of the page. Click on "see details" to display a three-tabbed report. Figure 9.11 shows the content of the report's "Score" tab. Altmetric assigns weights to the different sources that mention the source, that is, news, blogs, Q&A forums, Twitter, Google+, and Facebook likes are weighted 8, 5, 2.5, 1, 1, and 0.25, respectively. Not factored into the score are reader counts from Mendeley or CiteULike or citation counts. His article has generated thirteen tweeters, forty-five Mendeley shares, and one CiteULike save, earning it a 7.70 Altmetric score.

Altmetric suggests that the Altmetric score quantifies attention—whether people have noticed the article, what they are saying about it, and how much people notice the article relative to its peer articles (Altmetric 2015). The Altmetric score does not quantify whether the attention is good, bad, or indifferent. Such an assessment is the user's job based on reading comments enumerated in the Altmetric report.

That research databases are investing in altmetrics functionality is evidence that the information industry has high expectations for it. Presently, altmetrics is in a research and development

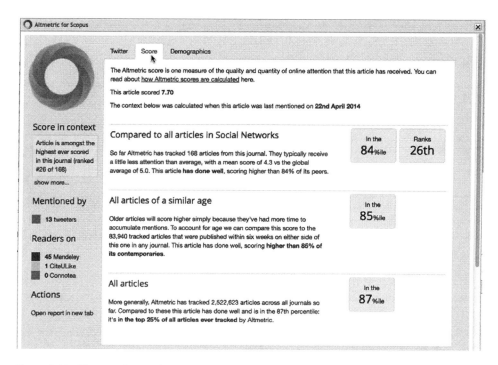

Figure 9.11. Altmetric Report for a Very Recently Published Source in the Scopus Database. Source: Scopus, a registered trademark of Elsevier, B.V., image retrieved 17 March 2015.

phase that may be followed by a shaking down period in which altmetrics providers, methods, and metrics expand and consolidate, giving way to the development of best practices and standards across the information industry. The time is right for you to carve out your role, introducing and interpreting altmetrics to end users, including experimenting with their potential as a source credibility strategy for domain novices.

Social Media Websites for Academic Researchers

Academic.edu (http://www.academia.edu) and Research Gate (http://www.researchgate.net) are social media websites for academics. Registered participants can use these sites to disseminate their profile, share publications, monitor their publications' impact, receive immediate notification of newly posted publications on their topics of interest, send public and private messages, review and discuss articles, ask and receive answers to questions, and much more. Register at these websites to avail yourself of their content and social media services. In fact, the more registrants are proactive about disseminating their published research in this way, the bigger these websites will become, making them a go-to destination for finding the latest research.

Questions

These questions give you practice searching WoS, Scopus, and Google Scholar to help library users find relevant sources and assess the research impact of individual sources and publication records.

1. Help a user who wants to search WoS for cited references to James Paul Gee's book entitled *What Video Games Have to Teach Us about Learning and Literacy*.
2. In a follow-up interview, the first user asks you to show him how to use the Scopus database to find relevant cited references to James Paul Gee's book entitled *What Video Games Have to Teach Us about Learning and Literacy*.
3. Help a user who wants to search the Scopus database find relevant cited references to Joseph LeDoux's article "Emotion, Memory, and the Brain" published in *Scientific American*.
4. You have written an awesome manuscript that is in keeping with the content that the journals *portal: Libraries and the Academy, Journal of Academic Librarianship* (JAL), and *College & Research Libraries* (C&RL) publish. Which is the most prestigious journal and why?
5. Your dean gives you the table below, telling you to complete it with metrics for my publications in Scopus and Google Scholar. Hint: You might have to compute some metrics manually; however, don't go overboard, comparing entries on successive pages in search of duplicates, then combining duplicates into single entries. Instead, jot down notes describing how you'd handle duplicates.

Data Type	Karen Markey	
	Scopus	GS
Number of publications		
Citation count		
h-index		
i10-index	NA	

Summary

Enter http://www.onlinesearching.org/p/9-impact.html into your Web browser for a video on assessing research impact.

Library users search citation databases not only to find relevant sources on topics but to assess the research impact of a particular journal, a particular journal article, or a particular researcher's publication record. Especially interested in research impact are college and university faculty who participate in employment, tenure, and promotion decisions. Three databases provide citation count data: Web of Science (WoS), Scopus, and Google Scholar. Of the three, Web of Science is the most complicated because it places the burden of disambiguating citation entries bearing same-named authors on the searcher. Searching Scopus and Google Scholar for citation count data is simple and straightforward for authors who publish under one name. When they publish under multiple names, the searcher might have to search under each name and manually combine results into a single citation count.

Academics use journal-level metrics to decide where to publish their research and to determine whether the colleagues they review for employment, promotion, and tenure are publishing in the best journals. Journal Citation Reports (JCR) is the go-to licensed database for journal-level metrics, and there are open access alternatives from Scopus and Google Scholar.

When it comes to research impact metrics, altmetrics is the new kid on the block, quantifying the "buzz" that accompanies the publication of new scholarly sources. Generated from journal aggregator logs, recommender systems, social networking services, and much more, altmetrics provides immediate feedback compared to the half decade or so that it takes for citation data to accumulate. Altmetrics is in a formative period right now. Monitor what's happening so that you can advise your library's users with regard to the usefulness of altmetrics for evaluating sources and the people who write scholarly papers.

Bibliography

Altmetric. 2015. "Article-Level Metrics: Here Are the Basics." Accessed March 26, 2015. http://www.altmetric.com/article-level-metrics.php.

Bar-Ilan, Judit. 2008. "Which H-Index? A Comparison of WoS, Scopus and Google Scholar." *Scientometrics* 74, no. 2: 257–71.

Bauer, Kathleen, and Nisa Bakkalbasi. 2005. "An Examination of Citation Counts in a New Scholarly Communication Environment." *D-Lib Magazine* 11, no. 9. http://www.dlib.org/dlib/september05/bauer/09bauer.html.

Cave, Richard. 2013. "Finding Insights in ALMS for Research Evaluation." Last modified November 7, 2013, accessed March 26, 2015. http://www.slideshare.net/rcave/finding-insights-in-articlelevel-metrics-for-research-evaluation.

García-Pérez, Miguel. 2010. "Accuracy and Completeness of Publication and Citation Records in the Web of Science, PsycINFO, and Google Scholar." *Journal of the American Society for Information Science and Technology* 61, no. 10: 2070–85.

Garfield, Eugene. 1955. "Citation Indexes for Science: A New Dimension in Documentation through Association of Ideas." *Science* 122: 108–11.

Harzing, Anne-Wil K., and Ron van der Wal. 2008. "Google Scholar: A New Source for Citation Analysis." *Ethics in Science and Environmental Politics* 8: 61–73.

Jacsó, Péter. 2006. "Deflated, Inflated and Phantom Citation Counts." *Online Information Review* 30, no. 3: 297–309.

Markey, Karen. 2015. "Researcher: Vita." Last modified June 1, 2015. http://ylime.people.si.umich.edu/researcher.html.

Meho, Lokman I., and Kiduk Yang. 2007. "Impact of Data Sources on Citation Counts and Rankings of LIS Faculty: Web of Science versus Scopus and Google Scholar." *Journal of the American Society for Information Science and Technology* 58, no. 13: 2105–25.

Priem, Jason, Dario Taraborelli, Paul Groth, and Cameron Neyland. 2011. "Altmetrics: A Manifesto." Last modified November 28, 2011, accessed March 26, 2015. http://altmetrics.org/manifesto.

Seglen, Per O. 1997. "Why the Impact Factor of Journals Should Not Be Used for Evaluating Research." *BMJ: British Medical Journal* 314, no. 7079: 498–502.

Tananbaum, Greg. 2013. *Article-Level Metrics: A SPARC Primer.* Chicago: Association of Research Libraries. Accessed March 26, 2015. http://www.sparc.arl.org/sites/default/files/sparc-alm-primer.pdf.

Thomson Reuters. 2014. "50th Anniversary of Science Citation Index." Accessed March 26, 2015. http://wokinfo.com/sci-anniversary.html.

Suggested Readings

Brigham, Tara J. 2014. "An Introduction to Altmetrics." *Medical Reference Services Quarterly* 33, no. 4: 438–447. This introduction defines altmetrics, reviews altmetric tools, and discusses the benefits and drawbacks of this new technology.

De Bellis, Nicola. 2009. *Bibliometrics and Citation Analysis.* Lanham, MD: Scarecrow. Written before the altmetrics movement, this textbook is standard fare in the LIS field's bibliometric and citation courses.

Lapinski, Scott, Heather Piwowar, and Jason Priem. 2013. "Riding the Crest of the Altmetrics Wave: How Librarians Can Help Prepare Faculty for the Next Generation of Research Impact Metrics." *College & Research Libraries News* 74, no. 6: 292–94, 300. The title says it all.

Answers

Because of the open-endedness of these questions, these aren't hard-and-fast answers, but they explain how to proceed and what you're likely to find.

1. **Search WoS for cited references to a book.**
   Search your library's OPAC for a correct bibliographic citation for the book (Gee, James Paul. 2003. *What Video Games Have to Teach Us about Learning and Literacy.* New York: Palgrave Macmillan). Launch the WoS database and choose "Cited Reference Search." Click on the "Select from Index" link" where you enter the surname gee and first initial j in the search box and click on the "Move To" button. Choose listed names even if you're unsure about them. WoS lists them at the bottom of the page. Click on the OK button and WoS returns you to the "Cited Reference Search" page. Enter 2003 into the "Cited Year(s)" search box, and click on the "Search" button. Then clean up WoS' Cited Reference Search table so that your selected entries refer only to Gee's book. Don't be surprised if your selected entries only vaguely resemble the book's title, e.g., FFHAT VIDEO GAMES HA, VIDEOGAMES HAVE TEA, WHAT VID GAM HAV, and PALGRAVE MACMILLAN.

   WoS reports over 1,235 cited references for this book and lists them in reverse chronological order. When assisting users, show them how clusters reveal authors, publications, and document types that cite this book repeatedly, and how to use WoS' "Results Analysis" to produce graphical reports of retrievals.

2. **Search Scopus for cited references to a book.**
   Scopus is limited to journal articles. Find cited references to books in WoS and Google Scholar.

3. **Search Scopus for cited references to a journal article.**
   Use the Scopus default "Document Search," entering the source's title enclosed in quotes into the search box and clicking on its magnifying-glass search icon. Scopus reports about three hundred cited references. Again, show the user how to sort the results and produce reports.

4. **Choose the most prestigious journal.**
   Choose JCR (Journal Citation Reports) from your library's database hub. Under "Select a JCR edition and year," select "JCR Social Sciences Edition" and the most recent year; under "Select an option," choose "View a group of journals by Subject Category," and click the SUBMIT button. Scroll down the list, choose INFORMATION SCIENCE & LIBRARY SCIENCE, fill in the "View Journal Data" radio button, and click the SUBMIT button. JCR responds with the "Journal Summary List," a multipage spreadsheet of journal names and metrics in alphabetical order. Choose a metric to sort the list using "Sorted by" on the top left, then see where your three journals rank. For example, 2013 metrics for "Total Cites" and "Impact Factor" yield these ranks for portal (52 and 44), JAL (30 and 48), and C&RL (31 and 24), respectively. You could base your decision on one, two, or more JCR metrics. Finally, which journal would you choose and why?

5. Use metrics for an academic with a name change.

This exercise involves Scopus and Google Scholar searches for an academic who publishes under two names. A search of LCNAF reveals that I have written using these two names:

- Karen Markey (KM), before 1990 and after 2003, and
- Karen Markey Drabenstott (KMD), from 1990 to 2003.

Scopus takes my name changes into account. Google doesn't. Search Scopus for KM and copy its metrics into the table. Search Google for KM and KMD, finding and eliminating duplicates, and combining results. Thus, your manual calculations of Google Scholar's h- and i10-indexes will be estimates.

The table below displays Scopus and Google Scholar metrics on March 17, 2015. The table divides Google Scholar metrics into columns for sources attributed to the KM and KMD names. Estimated Google metrics involves adding the KMD metrics indicated with plus (+) signs to the KM metrics. Doing so approximates the number of publications on my vita (Markey 2015). Interestingly, this table displays the same disparity between Scopus and Google metrics as table 9.1 displays for Cliff and Darren. When you calculate these metrics, presumably they will be even higher because more people have cited the sources I've written.

Data Type	Scopus	Google Scholar	
		KM	KMD
Number of publications	56	123	+16
Citation count	452	1931	+183
h-index	11	23	+2
i10-index	NA	40	+5

In the absence of another academic's metrics for comparison, my metrics are meaningless. Choose a faculty member from another school whose teaching and research interests overlap my own (e.g., organization of information, online searching, or subject access), but when you do, choose an academic who has published under one name so you don't have to estimate their metrics. Then expand the table above, placing the person's metrics side by side with mine. Finally, make up a story such as making a decision regarding a promotion, an honor, a nomination, or an invitation; compare the two academics' publication metrics; and make a decision or describe what other information you'd seek to make a decision.

10

Search Strategies

The definition of search strategy is "a plan for the whole search" (Bates 1979, 206). Authors of the first online searching textbooks and manuals owe a debt of gratitude to Charles P. Bourne, Barbara Anderson, and Jo Robinson, who were the first to propose search strategies for Boolean systems based on their research building a practice ERIC database for the Dialog search system (Markey and Atherton 1978; Meadow and Cochrane 1981; Harter 1986). Except for Drabenstott's (2000) additions to accommodate searching Web search engines in the pre-Google era, the original strategies have stood the test of time. Once again, it's time to take stock of these strategies because, in the intervening time period, so much has changed, particularly the migration of search systems to the Web and the success of Web search engines.

This chapter presents six search strategies that should suffice for almost all of the online searches that you conduct in Boolean and extended-Boolean search systems. When choosing a search strategy, there are several factors to take into account. Some are straightforward, such as whether the user's query is single- or multifaceted and whether the search system has this or that functionality, and others are more complex, requiring your judgment about the importance of the query's facets relative to one another and the user's overall grasp on his topic. At the end of the chapter is a search strategy selection flowchart that will help you choose the right search strategy for the job.

Building Block Search Strategy

The Building Block Search Strategy is for multifaceted subject queries. It requires the searcher to develop each facet of the query separately as if it were a subsearch on its own, then make the final logical assembly of the individual subsearches. Figure 6.9 diagrams this strategy using three separate blocks, one atop the other, to represent sets of retrievals for the individual facets, and arrows protruding from the three blocks' right sides, all meeting at a single block representing the final set of retrievals.

The Building Block Strategy comes in two editions: (1) the Buffet Edition for Boolean search systems (figure 6.10), and (2) the À la Carte Edition for extended-Boolean systems (figure 7.6). These names are analogies for the ways in which searchers represent search terms in their search statements. The Buffet Edition is reserved for Boolean systems, equating the buffet to the database, the buffet tables to the query's facets, and the various foods that you choose from the buffet tables to the several search terms that make up your search statements for each facet. You choose several items per buffet table, arrange everything onto your plate, and chow down. Choosing several food items per buffet table is like choosing an index term and its relevant BTs, NTs, and RTs from the database's thesaurus displays to construct search statements for each of the query's facets. Demonstrating the Buffet Edition are searches for the Humor, Farm Women, and Screen Time queries on pages 89–94, 118–120, and 122–24, respectively.

The À la Carte Edition is meant for searching extended-Boolean systems. These systems aren't yet capable of distinguishing which search terms belong to which facets. They choke over queries that are suited to the Buffet Edition; that is, when they are unable to produce retrievals for all entered search terms, they rank retrievals bearing as many search terms as possible. As a result, your retrievals may address fewer than all of your query's facets. To effect better results in extended-Boolean systems, use the À la Carte Edition of the Building Block Strategy, entering search statements composed of *one* search term per facet. Use the most salient search term per facet, and for most queries, this means entering the names of the query's facets. Demonstrating the À la Carte Edition are searches for the Child Soldiers and Lyndon Johnson queries on pages 125–28. The benefits of the Building Block Strategy are:

- It produces a clear search history that is easy to follow while you are conducting the search, easy to review and understand later, and explain to the user; in fact, its search history should read like the actual negotiated query.
- Its retrievals address all aspects of the topic that interest the user.
- Once the searcher scripts a search that conforms to the Building Block Strategy, executing it requires less judgment on the part of the searcher, and thus, this strategy appeals to aspiring intermediary searchers who are less confident about their ability to make spur-of-the-moment adjustments online.

The drawbacks of the Building Block Strategy are:

- The searcher enters and combines search statements for all facets of the query when, in fact, fewer facets may be needed to produce relevant retrievals.
- The searcher has no idea how many retrievals she will retrieve until the search's final moment when she combines sets for each facet using Boolean AND or NOT operators.

The Building Block Strategy deserves emphasis as a satisfactory strategy for multifaceted subject searches generally. You could apply this strategy to all multifaceted queries but you will encounter queries for which there are better strategies, and they deserve your consideration.

Can't Live Without This Facet First Search Strategy

The Can't Live Without This Facet First Search Strategy is also for multifaceted subject queries. Over the years, it has been known by other names—Most Specific Facet First, Lowest Posted Facet First, Successive Fractions, or Big Bite Strategy. Basically, it requires the searcher to assess the query, determining which facet *must* be represented in the retrievals for the user to consider them even marginally relevant.

The Can't Live Without This Facet First name is particularly vivid, and it has caught on with my students more readily than this strategy's other names: Most Specific Facet First or Lowest Posted Facet First. The most specific facet is one that is not likely to suffer from any vagueness of indexing. It may be a proper noun such as a piece of legislation or a person's name or a concept that is limited in the ways in which you can express it using free text (FT) or controlled vocabulary (CV). The lowest posted facet is the one that is the lowest posted of the query's several facets. You'll have to draw on your online searching experience to determine which facet is the lowest-posted. The Can't Live Without This Facet First Search Strategy works in the same way no matter which name is used.

Figure 10.1 depicts the Can't Live Without This Facet First Search Strategy. At first glance, it looks like a carbon copy of the Building Block Search Strategy, but it has important differences. The facet analysis may yield several facets, but the searcher has identified one that the user can't live without, that is, the user would be dissatisfied with every retrieval in the final result set if this facet's retrievals were not represented. (Alternatively this facet may be exceptionally specific or the searcher expects it to be low posted.) The searcher builds a set of retrievals for this facet *first*. If he is searching an extended-Boolean system, then he enters the one search term that represents this facet *first* in the search statement followed by as many other search terms as there are facets in the query. Extended-Boolean systems usually place more weight on the first search term, so make it the one that the user can't live without.

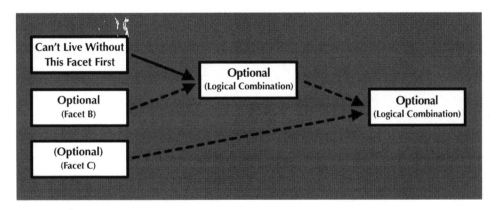

Figure 10.1. Can't Live Without This Facet First Search Strategy.

In a Boolean search system, the searcher builds a set of retrievals for the can't-live-without-it facet first using several synonymous terms combined with the OR operator. The searcher also assesses the number of retrievals, and if few are retrieved, ponders whether more facets are necessary. Making the decision to continue, the searcher builds a set of retrievals for one of the optional facets using several synonymous terms combined with the OR operator, then combines its retrievals using the Boolean AND or NOT operator with retrievals for the can't-live-without-this facet. The searcher's choice between which of the two or more optional facets to search second should not be willy-nilly. Instead, it should be guided by which facet the searcher thinks will be more important in terms of producing relevant retrievals. The searcher combines sets for the can't-live-without-it facet and optional facet using Boolean AND or NOT operators, and again, assesses the number of retrievals, deciding whether more facets are necessary or whether the results can stand on their own.

Taking into account postings for the can't-live-without-it facet and subsequent one(s) may compel the searcher to end the search before all facets have been introduced into the search. Here's an example using the negotiated query "What effect does video game violence have on adolescents?" The query's facets and logical combination are:

Video Games AND **Violence** AND **Adolescents**

Which is this query's can't-live-without-it facet? If you chose **Video Games**, you are right! Build a set of retrievals for the **Video Games** facet first. Having done so in a Boolean system such as ProQuest's ERIC, you find out that the maximum number of retrievals that your search will produce for this topic will be no more than 1,800. This number is still too many to review manually so continue the search, building a set of retrievals for one of the optional facets. Which facet would you tackle next—**Violence** or **Adolescents**? If you are unsure, think about the retrievals that will be produced by the Boolean AND combination of this query's can't-live-without-it and optional facets:

Video Games AND **Violence**
Video Games AND **Adolescents**

If this was your query, which combination's retrievals would you rather have? You have to use your judgment here, weighing which combination to search based on what the user wants. Personally, I would be inclined toward the combination bearing the **Violence** facet because its retrievals would be more likely to address the topic that interests me. Even though the **Adolescents** facet isn't introduced into the combination, reviewing retrievals to determine whether they are or aren't about adolescents would be an easy and straightforward task. In contrast, the combination bearing the **Adolescents** facet could go in so many non-relevant directions, for example, what video games adolescents like, prospects for educational video games for adolescents, the impact of excessive video game playing on adolescents' academic performance, and much more. Definitely prefer the **Video Games** AND **Violence** combination over the **Video Games** AND **Adolescents** combination.

Combining the **Video Games** and optional **Violence** facets reduces ERIC retrievals to about 150. When searching Boolean systems, keep a running total of your retrievals each time you combine search statements using the Boolean AND or NOT operators just in case a combination drops retrievals precipitously. In fact, keep a running total in Boolean searches regardless of the search strategy that governs the search.

Knowing that the two facets **Video Games** and **Violence** result in about 150 retrievals should make the searcher pause and ponder whether the third facet, **Adolescents**, is necessary. Scanning the first page of twenty retrievals reveals several titles bearing the words "youth" or "adolescents" in article titles or journal titles. Does it make sense to stop here, casting a wide net and advising the user to scrutinize retrievals for evidence that they study adolescents? Should the searcher continue searching, entering search terms for the **Adolescents** facet? What information could the user provide you with to help you make this decision? The benefits of the Can't Live Without This Facet First Strategy are:

- It requires less time and effort on the part of the searcher.
- It permits the search to be completed at an earlier point in time than the Building Block Strategy.
- It retrieves relevant sources that may be missed when all of the query's facets are represented in the search.

The drawbacks of the Can't Live Without This Facet First Strategy are:

- Sometimes the query has no obvious can't-live-without-it, most specific, or lowest posted facets that make this strategy possible.
- Determining the lowest posted facet may be difficult in the absence of search aids like print thesauri with postings notes or the searcher's experience with a database.
- Failing to represent all facets in the search may result in many postings that the user must scan to find relevant ones.

Citation Pearl Growing Search Strategy

The Citation Pearl Growing Search Strategy is a series of searches that the searcher conducts to find relevant search terms and incorporate them into follow-up searches. It is the most interactive of all the search strategies, requiring your full attention scanning retrievals for relevant terms, distributing them into the facets to which they belong while you make on-the-spot decisions about representing them as CV or FT, formulating search statements, and combining these statements to produce relevant results. Fit for both Boolean or extended-Boolean systems, the Citation Pearl Growing Strategy is a very effective strategy when you have little time to prepare for the search in advance.

Not only is the Citation Pearl Growing Strategy a *series of searches*, it is a *series of search strategies*. You may start with the Can't Live Without This Facet First Strategy, transition to the Citation Pearl Growing Strategy to find more retrievals, and conclude with the Building Block Strategy as a result of finding several relevant search terms per facet through Citation Pearl Growing.

To initiate the Citation Pearl Growing Strategy, enter a search that is faithful to the À la Carte Edition of the Building Block Strategy. Do so regardless of the Boolean or extended-Boolean nature of your chosen search system. Enter *one* search term per facet using the most salient search term per facet, and for many queries, this means the names of the query's facets. Review retrievals, identifying relevant terms in the CV, author-supplied keywords, and abstract fields of surrogate records, distributing them into their respective facets, and formulating everything into search statements. If you fall short on relevant terms, cull them from full-texts too. Then follow up with a search using the Building Block or Can't Live Without This Facet First Strategy and the search terms you gathered from surrogate and full-text retrievals. Figure 10.2 depicts the Citation Pearl Growing Strategy—an arrow that expands outward in a circular motion and becomes wider as it gathers additional relevant retrievals from the series of searches you conduct.

Figure 10.2. Citation Pearl Growing Search Strategy.

Let's walk through an online search that enlists the Citation Pearl Growing Strategy. The negotiated query is "Whether religious practice is a necessary ingredient to prevent alcoholics from relapsing." This query has three facets: A. **Religion**, B. **Alcoholism**, and C. **Prevention**, and its logical combination is:

Religion AND **Alcoholism** AND **Prevention**

Choose EBSCOhost's PsycINFO database and conduct a FT search using this query's three facet names. Such a search enlists the À la Carte Edition of the Building Block Strategy. The EBSCOhost system gives you several ways to gather search terms from this search's forty-four retrievals:

- Clicking on the accompanying *Major Subjects* and *Subjects* clusters' links to display frequently occurring PsycINFO index terms
- Clicking on the accompanying *Classification* cluster's link to display frequently occurring PsycINFO classification captions
- Scanning titles, PsycINFO index terms, and abstracts in surrogate record displays
- Searching PsycINFO index terms from relevant retrievals in the thesaurus, gathering relevant BTs, NTs, and RTs, and adding them to the search

Table 10.1 shows relevant search terms collected from the *Major Subjects, Subjects,* and *Classification* clusters. It distributes them into facets and identifies them as index terms (IT) or classification captions (CC).

Table 10.1. PsycINFO Index Terms Extracted from Retrievals Using the Citation Pearl Growing Search Strategy

Facet	Search Term	CV or FT
Religion	religion	IT and CC
	spirituality	IT
	religious beliefs	IT
Alcoholism	drug & alcohol usage (legal)	CC
	alcoholism	IT
	alcohol intoxication	IT
	alcohol rehabilitation	IT
	alcoholics anonymous	IT
	alcohol drinking patterns	IT
Prevention	health & mental health treatment & prevention	CC
	drug & alcohol rehabilitation	CC
	prevention	IT
	sobriety	IT
	drug rehabilitation	IT
	drug abuse prevention	IT

There are so many relevant PsycINFO index terms and classification captions for each facet, that it seems pointless to bolster Table 10.1's list with FT terms. Other in-depth queries might present more of a challenge, requiring the searcher to cull search terms from titles and abstracts, possibly full-texts. With the experience of the initial À la Carte search under your belt, you know that there is plenty of information on this Religion topic and proceeding with a full-fledged search governed by the Building Block Strategy may be appropriate. Alternatively, you might decide that the Can't Live Without This Facet First Strategy is more appropriate, beginning with a search statement bearing classification captions and index terms for the **Religion** facet first because this facet should be present in all retrievals for the user to consider them even marginally relevant, continuing with the **Alcoholism** facet and, lastly, the **Prevention** facet.

Figure 10.3 shows the search history for a follow-up CV search for the Religion query that is governed by the Can't Live Without This Facet First Strategy. Based on PsycINFO index terms generated from relevant retrievals and searches of these index terms in the PsycINFO thesaurus, it retrieves almost 250 retrievals, many of which are relevant.

The Citation Pearl Growing Strategy is often used as a follow-up to low-posted searches. A perfect example is the Eating Disorder query, a search topic that consistently produces few relevant retrievals for CV, FT, backward and forward, and find-like searches (pages 110, 129–32, and 138). You should be able to double this query's relevant retrievals using the Citation Pearl Growing

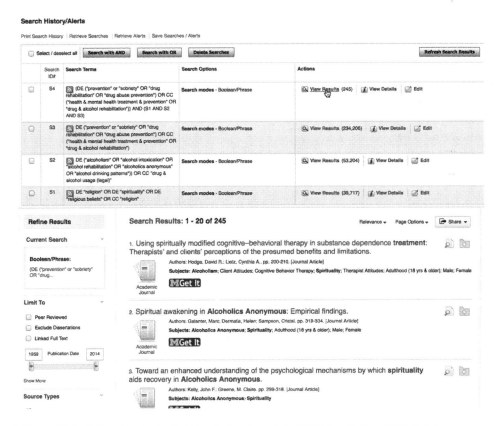

Figure 10.3. Follow-Up Controlled Vocabulary Search in EBSCOhost's PsycINFO Database Using Index Terms Culled from the Retrievals of a Citation Pearl Growing Search.

Strategy, then put your new relevant retrievals to work at finding more relevant retrievals using follow-up cited reference, author-bibliography, and find-like searches. By the way, the extensive searching that you have done across several chapters for the Eating Disorders query is unusual, more characteristic of the type of assistance given to a doctoral student, faculty member, or researcher who is investigating a new research topic for which there is little written in the published literature or conducting a comprehensive search for a literature or systematic review. The benefits of the Citation Pearl Growing Strategy are:

- It has the potential to find additional relevant retrievals for searches conducted in both Boolean and extended-Boolean systems.
- It can stand on its own two feet for finding relevant sources, or it can be one or more follow-up searches to increase the results of low-posted searches governed by the Building Block or Can't Live Without This Facet First Strategies.
- When conducting a Citation Pearl Growing search from scratch, little pre-search preparation is needed, beyond entering facet names using FT search terms.

The drawbacks of the Citation Pearl Growing Strategy are:

- You must be a confident searcher, knowledgeable about online searching and thoroughly familiar with the search system's capabilities to accomplish the on-the-spot thinking and search formulation that the Citation Pearl Growing Strategy entails.
- Following fruitless paths could result in greater use of the search system and more time spent online than you or the end user had expected. For example, if you head down a blind alley, you might have to save results, ponder them offline, then return to the search.
- Using relevant retrievals to find additional ones can get complicated, requiring the full spectrum of the searcher's experience and knowledge of the search system and database at hand and online searching generally.
- Experience, patience, and perseverance are required for conducting effective Citation Pearl Growing searches.

Shot in the Dark Search Strategy

The Shot in the Dark Search Strategy is for one-faceted queries. Figure 10.4 depicts this strategy using a rifle sight that takes aim in the dark.

The Free Dictionary gives two definitions for the phrase "shot in the dark": 1. A wild unsubstantiated guess, and 2. An attempt that has little chance at succeeding. Let's examine one-faceted queries to determine what is going on with this strategy's name. Some queries that are candidates for the Shot in the Dark Search Strategy consist of one word:

- Norway
- Fashion
- ADHD
- Subway
- Madonna
- Oracle

Others are expressed in several words that form a phrase so familiar and commonplace that it has come to represent a single big idea, concept, or theme. Examples are:

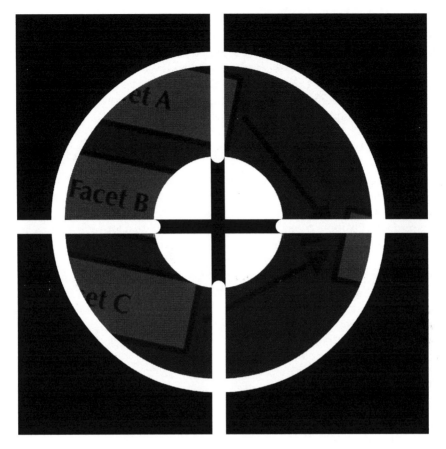

Figure 10.4. Shot in the Dark Search Strategy.

- Acid Rain
- Capital Punishment
- A Cut Above
- Nevil Shute Norway
- Cerebral Palsy
- Panera Bread

Scanning these queries should leave you puzzled, wondering what it is about Norway, Fashion, Acid Rain, and so on that interests the user. You might even say to yourself that these queries are impossible, that even if you searched for Norway there would be so much information that the user couldn't possibly read it all, that the reference librarian didn't do his job, conducting a thorough interview to find out what aspects of these topics interest users.

Let me share an experience with you regarding an end user's one-faceted query that happened almost forty years ago, just as online searching began. In the academic library where I worked, my late colleague, Ed Terry, was in charge of the online searching service. Because online searching was so expensive, only librarians with special training were allowed to do it. Costs associated with the search such as connect-time and royalties for displaying and printing surrogate records were usually charged to a grant or departmental account (there were no full-texts back then and retrieved surrogate records were printed on computer paper and given to users). Members of the general public paid out of pocket for the costs associated with the search. One day, Ed interviewed a user who wanted a search performed on "Norway." Ed probed, "What is it about Norway that interests you?" The person assured Ed that he wanted information on "Norway." Ed persisted asking, "What do you want to know about Norway—its climate, trees, mountains, culture, rats?" The user replied, "Everything on Norway." When Ed advised him that the search would be very expensive, the user was unperturbed. Ed conducted the search in whatever database made sense back then (there were hardly more than two dozen available). The user returned a few days later, Ed gave him the printout in the form of a stack of computer paper about twelve inches high, and he paid out of pocket. Ed never saw the user again. Perhaps he is still reading the sources cited on the printout!

I told this story to emphasize that one-faceted *subject* queries *are* impossible to answer. Forty years ago, they retrieved thousands of citations; they would retrieve so many more today; in fact, the stack of computer paper would probably start at your office and reach to faraway Norway! Thus, when you detect a one-faceted *subject* query, negotiate the query and if the user insists on sticking with his one-faceted query, transition to Getting a Little Help from Your Friends Strategy (pages 193–96).

One-faceted *known-item* queries can be answered; however, before proceeding with them, you have to continue the negotiation, finding out exactly what the user wants. Doing so helps you determine what database has potential for providing answers. Examine the queries listed above starting with the name Nevil Shute Norway. Ask the user what interests her about Norway, his novels, one particular novel, films based on his novels, his published works in engineering, his life generally? You would consult your library's OPAC for his novels and films, engineering-specific databases for his engineering works, and biographical dictionaries for his biography.

If the user's interest in Cerebral Palsy involves the major charitable association for this disease, then this is a known-item search; alternately, if he wants to know about this disease, then this is a subject search for the Friends Strategy.

The Oracle query is vague. In the reference interview, find out whether it means Oracle Inc., or the oracle that past and present cultures consult for advice or prophetic opinions. If the latter, then Oracle is a subject query for the Friends Strategy. If the former, then ask the user to tell you more about her interest in Oracle. Perhaps she wants to learn about Oracle database products, trade news about Oracle in the business electronics industry, how to get a job at Oracle, or something else. When you enter names or proper nouns into Google, it responds very accurately, ranking the official websites of well-known people, organizations, jurisdictions (places), programs, and projects at or close to the top of the list. For example, Google searches for `oracle`, `madonna`, `subway`, and `panera bread` rank the official websites of Oracle Inc. (the company), Madonna (the popular entertainer), Subway (the fast-food chain), and Panera Bread (the casual restaurant) at the top of the heap of millions of websites. Search the Mergent Online database for names of companies and its name-authority control functionality helps you match company names with ones indexed in the database so that you can retrieve their entries along with financial information and trade and industry news.

Adding a facet to provide context for a one-faceted query that is a proper noun may be the only way to find relevant information when the noun is a common word or phrase. The query A Cut Above applies to beauticians, clothing, landscaping, meats, trees, video production, and more. Adding a facet that describes the service performed by a business bearing this name and/or the geographical area it serves is almost absolutely necessary to zero in on the business that interests you, that is, `a cut above denver`.

Maybe Cerebral Palsy, Madonna, Oracle, and Subway but definitely Norway, Fashion, ADHD, Acid Rain, and Capital Punishment are *subject* queries. All are candidates for the Friends Strategy. The benefits of the Shot in the Dark Strategy are:

- Its criteria for predicting which queries are likely to succeed as one-faceted searches are simple to apply.
- It acknowledges that this strategy is most successful when applied to known-item queries bearing one facet.
- It diverts one-faceted subject queries to the Friends Strategy where they have a greater chance of success as a result of this strategy's tools to help users further develop their queries.

The drawbacks of the Shot in the Dark Search Strategy are:

- It is not appropriate for one-faceted subject queries.
- One-faceted queries for known-items that are one-word titles or common author names might be high-posted, requiring searchers to introduce a second facet to reduce retrievals to a manageable size.

Getting a Little Help from Your Friends Search Strategy

When the reference interview reveals a one-faceted *subject* query, this is a sign that more negotiation is necessary to find out what exactly the user wants. If the user is still clueless, call on your "friends" to help the user out. Friends refers to system features or specialized reference databases that have been designed with this very purpose in mind—helping users whose interests are undefined, unsettled, or vague. Figure 10.5 depicts the Friends Strategy—a central figure locking the two figures on either side of him in a friendly embrace, all three poised to solve difficult searching problems.

Figure 10.5. Getting a Little Help from Your Friends Search Strategy. Friends symbol by Moriah Rich from the Noun Project (http://thenounproject.com).

Which friend you recommend to the user depends upon your assessment of the situation and your library's available sources. Consider how queries for ADHD, Norway, Cerebral Palsy, Acid Rain, Capital Punishment, Subway, and Fashion would benefit from the one or more friends that follow.

Dictionaries and Encyclopedias

If users cannot get a foothold on their topics, it may be because they don't know much about them. Recommend a dictionary, biography, or encyclopedia that discusses broad-based topics at a basic level, defining topics, summarizing state-of-the-art knowledge, and citing sources for more in-depth information (pages 64–71). These reference sources may be encyclopedic or disciplinary, depending on which treatment you think matches your user's understanding and technical expertise with the topic.

Clusters

When users are having trouble finding a focus, get them started with a CV search for their one-faceted query, then invite them to review the clusters accompanying the results. Review the several searches in which clusters were used to help users add specificity to their broad topics (pages 101–103 and 153–57). Clusters are a new feature of databases and search systems so don't expect them all the time.

Certain Gale databases feature a topic finder that produces a circular or tiled array of related terms. For example, in Academic OneFile, the search statement adhd produces the array displayed in figure 10.6 along with terms such as "Behavior," "Drugs," "Parents and Teachers," "Mental Health," and "Symptoms" that might pique the user's interest. In figure 10.6, the searcher has clicked on the array's "Drugs" term, which prompts the system to display retrievals on both subjects, ADHD and drugs, to the right of the array that the user can browse for relevant ones.

Classifications

Incorporated into a minority of discipline-based databases is a classification system, used to represent the discipline's knowledge and provide subject access points for searchers. With regard to the latter, selecting a classification caption, code, or number enables searchers to retrieve and display sources assigned to the particular class. Examples of databases enhanced with classifications are ACM Digital Library, Biosis, Embase, and PsycINFO. Users can browse the classification, selecting relevant classes and combining them with Boolean operators and/or accompanying clusters. On its own or in conjunction with clusters, the classification is a means for users to conduct a subject search almost entirely on the basis of recognition so it may appeal to users who know what they want but cannot express it in words.

Web Subject Directories

Web subject directories classify websites according to subject. These directories consolidate all indexed websites under a dozen or so broad topics. Clicking on a broad subject leads to lists of subtopics that become increasingly narrower in scope every time the user clicks on a listed subtopic.

Browsing topics and subtopics is helpful for users who can't quite put their particular interest in words but will know it when they see it. Below are listed the most well-known directories along with some notes to help you select the right one. The list of directories has shrunk considerably

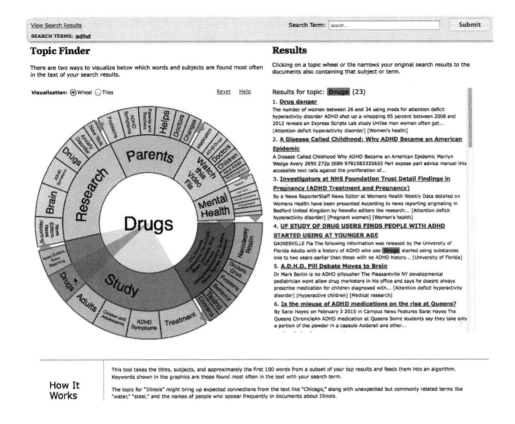

Figure 10.6. Topic Finder and Retrievals for a Selected Cluster Term in the Academic OneFile Database from Gale Cengage Learning. Courtesy of Gale Cengage Learning.

over the years because directory services rely on human editors to classify websites and keep their directories up to date and support for editorial staff is expensive over the long term.

AcademicInfo at http://www.academicinfo.net/subject-guides. Scroll below the advertisements where the subject guide resides. AcademicInfo selects websites useful to faculty, students, and researchers at colleges and universities. Accompanying websites are useful, informative annotations, sometimes as long as a paragraph.

DMOZ at http://www.dmoz.org. Navigate from broad topics to increasingly specific subtopics (with postings) ending in website titles with one-sentence descriptions. DMOZ and Yahoo! Directory are the largest of all the directories.

Yahoo! Directory at http://dir.yahoo.com. Navigate from broad topics to increasingly specific subtopics (with postings) ending in website titles with one-sentence descriptions. Includes commercial topics. Yahoo! Directory and DMOZ are the largest of all the directories.

The benefits of the Getting a Little Help from Your Friends Strategy are:

- It acknowledges that users might not be able to articulate their queries and provides them with tools to further develop their queries.

- Its tools organize knowledge in systematic ways that users can explore to further develop their queries.

The drawbacks of the Getting a Little Help from Your Friends Strategy are:

- Not all search systems and databases are equipped with the full or partial sets of online tools that enable the Friends Strategy.
- Because Friends tools require time, know-how, effort, and perseverance on the part of users, some users might not want to use them, preferring more direct and immediately gratifying approaches to finding information.
- Editorially based Friends tools are costly to develop, maintain, and apply to newly published sources because they require human intervention. That the number of Web subject directories continues to shrink may herald more problems for Friends tools in the years ahead.

Choosing a Search Strategy

When you choose a search strategy, five external factors help you make the decision:

1. If the user's query bears one facet, this is a query for the Shot in the Dark Strategy, where you determine whether the user wants a known-item or subject. In the case of a subject, pass it on to the Getting a Little Help from Your Friends Strategy that enables the user to further develop his topic. Remaining one-facet queries should be for known-items that involve searches of citation fields of surrogate records such as author, title, or publication title fields.
2. If the query has a can't-live-without-it facet, choose the Can't Live Without This Facet First Search Strategy. In a Boolean system, this means building a set of retrievals for the can't-live-without-it-facet first, evaluating search results, and entering one or more remaining facets if needed. In an extended-Boolean system, this means formulating search statements in which terms for the can't-live-without-it facet come first.
3. If you are searching a Boolean system, choose the Building Block Strategy's Buffet Edition, and if it is an extended-Boolean system, choose this strategy's À la Carte Edition.
4. If searches from your Building Block or Can't Live Without This Facet First Strategies are low-posted, extract relevant search terms from retrievals and enhance your search statements with them. This is the Citation Pearl Growing Strategy.
5. If you have little time to prepare in advance, conduct a subject search using the Building Block's À la Carte Edition. Then extract relevant search terms from retrievals and enhance your search statements with them, following up with a search using the Can't Live Without This Facet First Strategy or one of the two Building Block editions for more relevant retrievals. Again, this is the Citation Pearl Growing Strategy.

Figure 10.7 is a flowchart to help you choose a search strategy. Strategies for some searches morph into others; for example, a low-posted search from a Building Block Strategy becomes a candidate for a Citation Pearl Growing Strategy and a search for a Shot in the Dark Strategy becomes a candidate for the Friends Strategy. Right now search strategy selection might look complicated, but in time, you will find yourself moving between strategies with the ease of an Olympic figure skater practicing her routine with all its required moves and jumps.

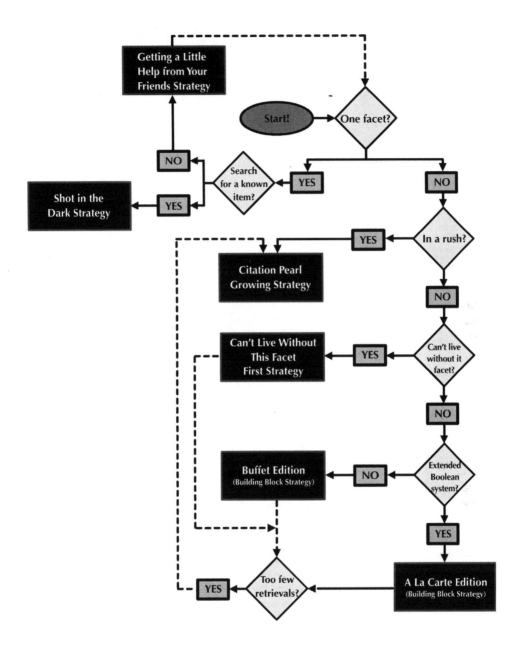

Figure 10.7. Search Strategy Selection Flowchart.

Questions

Below are negotiated queries. You've encountered some in previous chapters and others are new. Conduct a facet analysis and logical combination for each query (or reuse this pre-search preparation from previous chapters), taking into consideration the suggested databases. Then choose one or more search strategies, providing a rationale that describes why you chose it.

1. Compendex database: Testing ice hockey helmets to make sure they are safe.
2. ERIC database. A teacher who teaches social studies at the high school level wants instructional materials to help him teach a unit on cultural awareness to his students.
3. Environmental Sciences and Pollution Management database: Agent Orange.
4. ProQuest Research Library: How should high school coaches and trainers, parents, and the players themselves respond to possible incidences of sports-related concussions?
5. LexisNexis: Recent press about and sources written by Phyllis Chesler so that the user can assess her suitability as a guest speaker for a local celebratory event.
6. ERIC: Parents setting limits on their children's use of social networking sites and the Internet generally.
7. Google: Making Money as a Travel Blogger.
8. PsycINFO: Are college students who get enough sleep more successful academically than students who don't?
9. PubMed: Does mindfulness meditation reduce the stress of pregnancy?

Summary

Enter http://www.onlinesearching.org/p/10-strategies.html into your Web browser for a video on search strategies.

This chapter presents six search strategies that should suffice for almost all of the online searches that you conduct in Boolean and extended-Boolean search systems. Defined as "a plan for the whole search" (Bates 1979, 206), search strategy requires the searcher to take stock of the number of facets in the query, the importance of these facets relative to the user's interests, the closeness of these facets with respect to the database's discipline, the system's Boolean or extended-Boolean nature, and the user's knowledge and understanding of both his topic and its underlying discipline. Search strategy deployment demands "all the knowledge one can gain about online searching systems and all one can learn about indexing vocabularies and the conventions practiced in . . . data base construction" (Meadow and Cochrane 1981, 133).

For the foreseeable future, you might feel comfortable sticking with the Building Block Strategy for the majority of in-depth subject queries. When you've got the Building Block Strategy down pat, entertain other strategies using this chapter's search strategy selection flowchart that boils search strategy selection down to the number of facets in negotiated queries. As your confidence grows, experiment with other strategies, particularly the Can't Live Without This Facet First and Citation Pearl Growing Strategies, because they will enable you to increase your efficiency and effectiveness as an expert intermediary online searcher.

Bibliography

Bates, Marcia J. 1979. "Information Search Tactics." *Journal of the American Society for Information Science* 30 (July): 205–14.

Drabenstott, Karen M. 2000. "Web Search Strategies." In *Saving the Time of the Library User Through Subject Access Innovation: Papers in Honor of Pauline Atherton Cochrane*, edited by William J. Wheeler, 114–61. Champaign, IL: University of Illinois.

Harter, Stephen P. 1986. *Online Information Retrieval: Concepts, Principles, and Techniques.* San Diego, CA: Academic Press.

Markey, Karen, and Pauline Atherton. 1978. *ONTAP: Online Training and Practice Manual for ERIC Database Searchers.* Syracuse, NY: ERIC/Information Resources Clearinghouse. ED 160109.

Meadow, Charles T., and Pauline A. Cochrane. 1981. *Basics of Online Searching.* New York: Wiley.

Answers

1. **Compendex database: Testing ice hockey helmets . . .**
   Facets: A. **Hockey**, B. **Helmets**, C. **Testing**
   Logical combination: **A** AND **B** AND **C**
   Can't Live Without This Facet First Strategy. Start with the **Hockey** facet because it is key to the user's interests. Then add **Helmets** in a Boolean AND combination with **Hockey** to focus retrievals on that aspect of the sport. If too many retrievals, then proceed with facet C.
   Citation Pearl Growing Strategy. All searches stand to benefit from this strategy. Initially, get the search started with an À la Carte Edition, entering one FT term per facet, scanning relevant retrievals' index terms, and using them to populate the search statements you enter in the follow-up searches using the Can't Live Without This Facet First Strategy.

2. **ERIC database: Cultural awareness . . .**
   Facets: A. **High school**, B. **Social Studies**, C. **Cultural Awareness**, D. **Instructional Materials**
   Logical combination: **A** AND **B** AND **C** AND **D**
   Buffet Edition of the Building Block Strategy. This query requires all four facets for retrievals to be relevant. In the ERIC thesaurus there are at least a handful of descriptors for representing each facet. Too few retrievals means following up with the Citation Pearl Growing Strategy.

3. **Environmental Sciences and Pollution Management database: Agent Orange.**
   Facets: A. **Agent Orange**
   Logical combination: **A**
   Shot in the Dark Strategy. The user's query bears one facet for a subject search. One-faceted *subject* queries *are* impossible to answer because there is so much information available for them. Divert to the Friends Strategy.
   Getting a Little Help from Your Friends Strategy. Search this database's thesaurus for an index term to represent this query's lone facet, then show the user this database's clusters for focusing his query on a more manageable subtopic.

4. **ProQuest Research Library: Sports-related concussions . . .**
   Facets: A. **Concussions**, B. **Athletics**, C. **High School**, D. **Reporting**
   Logical combination: **A** AND **B** AND **C** AND **D**
   Can't Live Without This Facet First Strategy. Start with the **Concussions** facet because it must be present for retrievals to be even marginally relevant. If too many retrievals, then combine it with the **High School** facet to provide context. Assess retrievals in case the **Reporting** and **Athletics** facets are not necessary. Too few retrievals means following up with the Citation Pearl Growing Strategy.

5. **LexisNexis: Phyllis Chesler . . .**
   Facets: A. **Phyllis Chesler**
   Logical combination: **A**

Shot in the Dark Strategy. The user's query bears one facet for a known-item search. Search for newspaper articles by Chesler.

Getting a Little Help from Your Friends Strategy. Search for newspaper articles about Chesler, then apply one or more clusters to reveal themes that may shed light on her suitability.

6. **ERIC database: Children's use of social networking sites . . .**
   Facets: A. **Social Networking**, B. **Parent Participation**, C. **Limits**
   Logical combination: **A** AND **B** AND **C**
   Can't Live Without This Facet First Strategy. Start with **Social Networking** because that's key to the user's interests. Then enter **Parent Participation** to temper the **Social Networking** retrievals. Add facet **C** to the mix only if retrievals produced by the first two facets are not relevant or too many in number. Too few retrievals means following up with the Citation Pearl Growing Strategy.

7. **Google: Travel Blogger . . .**
   Facets: A. **Travel Blogging**, B. **Monetization**
   Logical combination: **A** and **B**
   À la Carte Edition of the Building Block Strategy. Successively enter search statements bearing one term per facet, e.g., travel blogging monetization, travel blogging revenue, travel website make money.

8. **PsycINFO database: College students who get enough sleep . . .**
   Facets: A. **College Students**, B. **Sleep**, C. **Academic Performance**
   Logical combination: **A** and **B** and **C**
   Can't Live Without This Facet First Strategy. Start with **Sleep** facet first because it must be present for the user to consider retrievals even marginally relevant. Then proceed with **Academic Performance**. Add facet **A** to the mix only if retrievals produced by the facets **B** and **C** are not relevant or too many in number. Too few retrievals means following up with the Citation Pearl Growing Strategy.

9. **PubMed database: Does mindfulness meditation reduce the stress of pregnancy?**
   Facets: A. **Mindfulness Meditation**, B. **Stress**, C. **Pregnancy**
   Logical combination: **A** AND **B** AND **C**
   Buffet Edition of the Building Block Strategy. This query requires all three facets for retrievals to be relevant. MeSH features several main and subdivided index terms for representing each facet. Too few retrievals means following up with the Citation Pearl Growing Strategy.

11

Displaying and Assessing Retrievals and Responding Tactically to the Search System

This chapter discusses the seventh and final step of the online searching process—displaying and assessing retrievals and responding tactically to the system throughout the course of the search. Displaying retrievals may sound pedestrian and straightforward, but in recent years, search systems have become more sophisticated about displaying the most relevant ones first. Thus, users have come to expect relevant sources in response to their queries, rarely venturing beyond the first or second page of retrievals. Some search systems are going so far as to use the personal information that they glean from your use of their systems and services to rank retrievals and show you additional information that generates revenue for them, advertisers, and website sponsors. The race for your eyeballs is so intense that some website providers engage in deceptive practices so that Web search engines rank their sites at the top of the retrievals. While dubious practices are characteristic of the open Web, you should also be on guard when you search the licensed Web, scrutinizing a search system's output to make sure its retrievals correspond to your search statements, and if they don't, asking vendors to describe what's happening and why.

Search tactics come to the fore the moment the reference interview begins and continue until the search ends, usually with retrievals that are likely to satisfy the user's query. A search tactic is "a move to further the search" (Bates 1979, 206). Search tactic deployment depends on the judgment of the searcher who is engaged in an ongoing search and, while monitoring what is happening, recognizes that an adjustment is needed to keep the search on track and responds with the use of one or more system features that effect the adjustment. There is seldom a one-to-one correspondence between making adjustments and the use of the system's features. Adjustments almost always require a series of deliberate moves on the part of the searcher involving the manipulation of several features. Search tactics help you characterize and power through the situation. Like search strategies, successful search tactic deployment requires thorough knowledge of online searching concepts and mastery of online searching skills.

Displaying Retrievals

Most databases give users several options for displaying retrievals:

- Relevance. Displaying the most relevant retrievals first based on the system's relevance ranking algorithms.
- Publication date descending or ascending. Displaying the most recently published or oldest sources first.
- Main entry or author. Displaying retrievals alphabetically by author or by title when authorship is diffuse or anonymous.
- Title. Displaying retrievals alphabetically by title.
- Classified. Displaying retrievals by subject using a classification scheme.
- Times cited. Ordering the retrievals display by the most to the least cited or vice versa. This option is limited to databases with cited-reference searching.

Users have become so accustomed to the relevance-ranked retrievals displays of Web search engines, which are quite accurate at listing relevant sources at the top of the list that many licensed search systems are now using relevance as their default display mode.

The phenomenon of users limiting their review of retrieved sources to only the first one or two pages is well documented (Spink et al. 2001; Jansen and Spink 2006; Markey 2007; Pan 2007). When users don't find what they want there, they enter new search statements, re-enter their original search statements (dubbed "incredulous repetitions" by more than one researcher [Sandore 1993; Peters 1989]), or project relevance onto the first-listed retrievals.

When you help users get their searches started, mouse down on the retrievals-display pull-down menu, showing them what options are available and suggesting that they be thorough in their retrievals review because other display options are likely to serve up relevant retrievals that relevance-ranking misses. Additionally, point out the clusters that accompany retrievals, likening them to an outline or table of contents for retrievals and suggesting that they apply this and that cluster to filter retrievals.

The propensity of users to focus almost exclusively on the highest-ranking retrievals is particularly problematic when they search the open Web. In fact, Google uses "fifty-seven signals—everything from where you [a]re logging in from to what browser you [a]re using to what you searched for before—to make guesses about who you [a]re and what kinds of sites you'd like" (Pariser 2011, 2). At least Google is up front, telling you that it's using personalized information about you to order its retrievals display. With other systems, you just don't know.

Accompanying retrievals displays from Web search systems and directories are ads. You have to pay attention to labels such as "ads," "sponsored advertising," or "paid advertisement" and/or visual cues such as borders, background colors, and three-dimensional beveling to distinguish Web retrievals from ad retrievals. Distinguishing between the two is difficult because everyone receives personalized retrievals; consequently, there really is no set of "legitimate" Web retrievals. The next time you are together with friends, family, or classmates, search your favorite Web search engine and compare your retrievals for various topic classes to determine whether the ads and "legitimate" content you retrieve are the same as theirs. Here are some topics to search:

- Academic: `television violence children, alcoholism spirituality relapse, windmills birds`
- Consumer health: `diabetes obesity, knee injuries women, peanut allergies`
- News, sports, and popular culture: `gaza reconstruction, lebron james, ebola`
- Shopping: `diesel jeans, new car, modest clothes`

Sebastian (2014) reports that web-based content providers are deliberately toning down distinctions between substantive content and paid ads because advertisers bristle when distinctions between the two are obvious. This tactic is called native ads or native advertising, and it is "meant to draw readers to ads by making them more or less resemble the surrounding editorial content. A bit of reader confusion over what's an ad is inherent."

Thinly disguised as substantive content are the Web pages that content farms publish, bearing easy-to-read essays on popular topics and advertising for which the farms receive revenue every time a Web user lands on the page or clicks on an accompanying ad. When Google adjusted its retrieval algorithms so that websites with substantive content such as research, in-depth reports, and thoughtful analysis achieved higher rankings, it was thought to have been a response to reduce content-farm manipulation of search-result rankings (Guynn 2011).

Search engine optimization (SEO) is the deliberate process of jumping the queue to effect a higher ranking for one's website. Acceptable to search engines are "white hat" techniques that use SEO to bring a website's content to the attention of like-minded users. Web search engine developers do not tolerate deceptive (black hat) techniques and are constantly tweaking their systems' ranking algorithms so that retrievals are not adversely affected by these techniques. Unfortunately, even respected companies participate in the subterfuge (Cutts 2006).

Critics of white-hat SEO, personalized search results, and retrievals-ranking generally argue that their long-term effect will stifle our experience of the world, putting content that complements our interests, opinions, and personal viewpoints in front of our eyeballs while distancing us from opposing views. "Ultimately, the proponents of personalization offer a vision of a custom-tailored world, every facet of which fits us perfectly. It's a cozy place, populated by our favorite people and things and ideas" (Pariser 2011, 12). One could be cavalier about the manipulation of Web search results, believing that the World Wide Web is the search domain of the masses and that no serious researcher would rely on it entirely; however, people *do* rely on the Web's information for serious and less-than-serious pursuits, and because they do, your interaction with them should include a warning about the importance of evaluating information, especially what they find on the open Web.

What about the search systems that access licensed databases? No one knows how their retrieval-ranking algorithms work because they are trade secrets. What is stopping them from programming their algorithms to give greater weights to:

- Sources written by higher-cited researchers
- The highest-cited sources
- Sources with higher altmetrics
- Sources published in journals with higher journal-level metrics
- The most popular sources in terms of numbers of views or downloads

On one hand, one could argue that it makes good sense for the search system to apply such weights using the logic that sources that garner greater interest among researchers deserve greater exposure to others active in the field. On the other hand, one could point out the chilling effect this could have on research generally. Research that receives little attention but is important could get swept under the rug because no one notices it buried deep in the middle- or tail-end of high-posted retrievals. This could put undo pressure on researchers, especially brand-new, never-cited researchers, to abandon research that isn't likely to pay off in the long term in favor of pursuing research that they know will have an immediate payoff. It is not out of the question to imagine a future in which scholarly publishers require researchers to pay white-hat SEO editors who would rework their manuscripts to maximize their retrievability. Would it ever come to publishers or researchers themselves paying a premium to search systems to boost their rankings? Would it become an acceptable practice if boosted retrievals were designated as such in a search system much like Web search engines do for paid ads? Would a publisher who hosts search services for its own sources as well as those of other publishers be inclined to give greater weight to its own retrievals than to other publishers' retrievals?

Addressing the underlying issues that these questions raise concerned librarians with regard to the newest technology in libraries—web-scale discovery (WSD) systems. In response, librarians have been proactive, participating side-by-side with publishers and WSD-system providers in the National Information Standard Organization's (NISO) Open Discovery Initiative (ODI) that "address[es] perceptions regarding bias and concern about the possibility of bias in discovery services" (NISO 2014, 2). The NISO report that publishes best practices for WSD systems speaks directly to fair linking, recommending that "discovery services should not discriminate, based on business relationships, among content providers or products (especially their own) in the methods that are used to generate results, relevance rankings, or link order" (NISO 2014, 25). That WSD-system providers agree to these best practices is expected in the form of voluntary conformance statements that they issue. "In the absence of [such] voluntary statements, libraries can use the presence or absence of these factors to infer conformance" (NISO 2014, vi).

At the present time, search systems that access licensed databases appear to be straightforward, weighting retrievals algorithmically based on Boolean or extended-Boolean criteria. To have a hand in determining whether these systems remain faithful to these criteria, scrutinize Boolean retrievals where you have total control of retrievals based on the CV, FT, truncation, proximity, and Boolean operators you enter. Telltale signs that a Boolean system is straying from its focus are retrievals that exceed the constraints of your search criteria, new genres that you haven't seen before, or the same publications appearing atop retrievals lists. Extended-Boolean retrievals may be more difficult to assess. When you find retrievals that don't make sense, save the search and discuss the situation with a vendor representative. If vendor explanations aren't satisfactory, perhaps the time has come for an ODI-like initiative for licensed search systems.

Assessing Retrievals

Assessing retrievals for relevance and credibility may seem like a straightforward task but it really isn't, especially for users who are unsure of their topics. In addition to recommending such users start with an encyclopedia, get them started with the right search terms, facets, and search logic, pointing out relevant sources that are appropriate for their basic level of understanding. While you are at it, ask them what guidelines their instructor gave the class regarding cited sources. If users must cite a quota of scholarly sources, then demonstrate the database's scholarly presearch qualifier. If they have no such guidelines, then recommend a database that would be too basic for a domain expert but appropriate for someone new to the topic or the discipline.

Assessing retrievals is an important component of many academic institutions' information literacy training. The actual content of your information literacy training pertaining to source evaluation is beyond *Online Searching*'s scope. Plenty of books address information literacy generally, and you should consult them for more information (Grassian and Kaplowitz 2009; Ragains 2013; Buchanan and McDonough 2014). Taking a master's level information literacy course should be in your academic plans. You'll want to prepare now for your new job where your information literacy duties may range from plugging into an existing information literacy instruction program to helping your colleagues revamp and deploy a redesigned program.

Assessing Relevance

High-posted searches may be overwhelming to users, especially international students for whom English is a second language. Encourage them to be systematic about retrievals, reading each retrieval's abstract and saving promising ones using the database's save functionality (pages 232–33). By the way, some users think that abstracts are the actual articles themselves, so make sure they know that abstracts are summaries and that they will have to follow up, downloading full-texts for their most promising retrievals (Cull 2011). Finding full-texts isn't always straightforward (pages 151–53), so encourage users to ask you for help when they have full-text fulfillment difficulties.

Because users are likely to experience shifts in their topic as they review surrogate records, their second pass through retrieved sources should be more decisive, eliminating saved surrogates that they deem no longer promising and downloading full-texts for the rest. Suggest that users save downloaded full-texts on their personal computers in a folder named for their project so they will be able to find them later. Alternatively, introduce users to citation management systems where they can store everything about their retrievals—citations, abstracts, keywords, downloaded full-texts, and notes (pages 234–37).

Reading full-texts may be a daunting task for users. Compounding the situation may be the quota their instructor imposed on them, requiring them to cite so many *research* articles. For users unfamiliar with the research genre, they will be doubly in the dark about how to proceed. Advise users that they don't have to read every single source from start to finish. Instead, they can perform a technical reading that limits reading to those portions of sources that are the most important for understanding overall content. For research sources, this means scanning the source's

- Title and abstract to get an overall sense of its content
- Introduction for the researcher's objectives and why the research is important
- Methods section to find out how the researcher conducted the experiment
- Conclusions where the researcher states his most important findings

Non-research articles are more varied, making it difficult to give hard-and-fast rules about which sections to read. At the very least, users should scan the source's

- Title and abstract to get an overall sense of its content
- Headings and subheadings, treating them like a table of contents that orients them to the source as a whole
- Introduction, especially the author's purpose for writing the article
- Discussion where the author puts his most important points in a real-world context
- Summary or conclusion that spotlights the most important content

Often users are seeking sources that map entirely onto their interests, perhaps even writing their paper for them. Impress on them that it is rare to find such sources, and instead, they have to read promising sources to determine whether and how their content addresses their interests and synthesize what they learn from reading sources into a piece that fulfills the requirements of their assignment or into an answer that satisfies their queries. Suggest to users that their chosen topics and the relevance assessments they make for retrieved sources are moving targets as a result of their exposure to new information and its consolidation into their knowledge base, shifting their point of view on the many details that go into a project right up until the moment they complete it, and, possibly, beyond.

Assessing Credibility

With relevant Web sources in hand, users know that they should assess their credibility, but few actually do it, and when they do, they have little desire to take a rigorous approach to credibility assessment (page 5). Research findings that enlist experimental online systems to elicit credibility ratings and assessments from users have been promising. These systems shadow users while they search for information, prompting them to rate a source's credibility and relevance and describe the reasons for their ratings. Their evidence for their credibility ratings usually pertains to authors, author credentials, or the source's genre, and their evidence for their relevance ratings usually pertains to the source's content or its closeness to their chosen or assigned topic (Leeder 2014; Markey, Leeder, and Rieh 2014).

Comparable to these experimental systems is the operational NoodleTools platform that supports students while working through the academic research process (NoodleTools 2015). It just may be the type of online system that is needed to motivate students to think deeply about the sources they use for their papers, getting them in the habit of taking notes from sources, outlining their written reports, staging their notes from sources in their outline, and citing their sources using a well-known style sheet. For example, NoodleTools transforms the very process of a student entering citation data for retrieved sources into a preliminary evaluation of source credibility. Specifically, it connects the various elements of a citation (i.e., date, the user's annotation about relevance, author, the user's annotation about accuracy, and publisher) with the elements of the CRAAP credibility checklist (i.e., currency, relevance, authority, accuracy, and purpose), respectively.

Your institution's information literacy training should include source credibility evaluation. Of the various information literacy venues, stand-alone courses and course-integrated instruction may give librarians ample time to cover credibility in depth. For example, let students perform a "taste test," so to speak, retrieving sources on a topic from the open Web and licensed databases, comparing these sources side-by-side using a CRAAP-like credibility test that elicits their credibility assessments and rates the two sources. Consolidating the results for the whole class to see whether students give higher ratings to sources from open Web or licensed databases and deliberating on the results would make the exercise more vivid for everyone. It doesn't matter which source type wins. What is important is that students are exposed to and get experience answering the types of questions they should ask about a source's credibility.

Information literacy instruction may be more important in public libraries than in academic libraries because public library users search for information to help them make decisions about health, finance, retirement planning, job seeking, and much more, that is, decisions that not only affect their lives but the well-being of family members also. On-the-spot reference interviews may be the only opportunity for librarians to impress on such users the importance of source evaluation; however, they may be particularly sensitive to what you have to say in this regard because their decision-making affects loved ones.

Search Tactics

Search tactics describe the many ways available to online searchers to maneuver during the ongoing search. Marcia Bates (1979; 1987) defined search tactics many years ago, when online searching was limited to expert intermediary searchers, and expanded on them a few years later, when online searching was first being introduced to end users through their library's OPAC. In the interim, search systems have changed considerably so it makes sense to update search tactic names and definitions, eliminate superseded and unnecessary tactics, and add new ones that are in keeping with today's full-featured Boolean and extended-Boolean systems.

Search tactics are the strategic moves searchers make to further the ongoing search (Bates 1979). To perform the search tactic, the searcher may wield several system features to get the job done. Not necessarily co-occurring with one or two particular steps of the online searching process or a particular search strategy, search tactics are cross-cutting—searchers execute them when it is appropriate to do so during the course of the online search.

Table 11.1 classifies search tactics into five types, defines them, and lists steps of the search process where the searcher is most likely to perform these tactics. (The capital letter B accompanying definitions refers to tactics that have made the trip from Marcia Bates' original lists into the table, but new names may be used.)

Table 11.1. Search Tactics, Adapted from Bates (1979; 1987)

Tactic	Definition	*Steps of the Search Process
Search Monitoring Tactics: Keeping the search on track and efficient		
Weigh	Assess current and anticipated actions (B)	All
Trail	Pay attention to both fruitful and less-than-fruitful trails contemplated, planned, anticipated, or taken (B)	All
Check	Compare the negotiated query with the ongoing search (B)	3, 4, 5, 6, 7
Correct	Correct spelling, logical, and strategic errors (B)	All
History	Review the online search	3, 4, 5, 6, 7
Search Formulation Tactics: Assembling and revising the search formulation		
Exhaust	Search all of the query's facets (B)	3, 4, 5, 6, 7
Discriminate	Search selected facets of the query (B)	3, 4, 5, 6, 7
Block	Eliminate search term(s) or facets from the search (B)	3, 4, 5, 6, 7
Precision	Retrieve only relevant retrievals	All
Recall	Retrieve all relevant retrievals	All
Reduce	Reduce retrievals while maintaining high-precision output (B). Partner tactics: Equate, Subdivide, Sub, and Cluster	3, 4, 5, 6, 7
Gain	Increase retrievals (B). Partner Tactics: Equate, Neighbor, Pseudonym, Contrary, Super, Relate, Space & Symbol, Pearl Growing, and Find Like	3, 4, 5, 6, 7
Search Term Selection Tactics: Selecting relevant search terms for the query's facets		
Equate	Select synonymous terms that are as specific as the facet they represent (B)	3, 5, 7

(continued)

Table 11.1. Search Tactics, Adapted from Bates (1979; 1987) *continued*

Tactic	Definition	*Steps of the Search Process
Search Term Selection Tactics: Selecting relevant search terms for the query's facets		
Neighbor	Select terms in the same alphabetical neighborhood (B)	3, 5, 7
Pseudonym	Select pseudonyms for a name	3, 5, 7
Contrary	Select terms that are opposite in meaning (B)	3, 5, 7
Subdivide	Select subdivisions of main terms	3, 5, 7
Auto-Term Add	Let the system automatically add statistically co-occurring terms to the search	3, 5, 7
Search Term Representation Tactics: Formulating search statements		
Field	Designate the fields in which search terms reside	2, 5, 7
Proximate	Designate how close together search terms should be	2, 5, 7
Truncate	Apply truncation to search terms or let the system perform it automatically	5, 7
Spell	Select spelling variants (B)	5, 7
Space & Symbol	Select variants that are one-word/two-word variants, or bear hyphens, slashes, and other symbols (B)	5, 7
Nickname	Select acronyms, initialed, or nicknamed variants	5, 7
Search Term Revision Tactics: Improving on retrievals		
Super	Select terms that are hierarchically superordinate to the facet (B)	5, 6, 7
Sub	Select terms that are hierarchically subordinate to the facet (B)	5, 6, 7
Relate	Select related terms that are not in a hierarchical relationship (B)	5, 6, 7
Pearl Growing	Select relevant terms from retrievals to enhance the ongoing search (B)	5, 6, 7
Cluster	Qualify retrievals with co-occurring subject and non-subject terms	5, 6, 7
Find Like	Select a relevant retrieval to find additional ones like it	5, 6, 7

*The seven steps are: (1) conducting the reference interview, (2) selecting a relevant database, (3) conducting a facet analysis and logical combination, (4) typecasting the negotiated query as a subject or known-item, (5) representing the negotiated query as input to the search system, (6) entering the search and responding strategically, and (7) displaying retrievals, assessing them, and responding tactically.

Search monitoring tactics pertain to all or most steps of the search process, and with good reason, because they keep the search on track and efficient. Pay attention to the various trails that you have taken and expect to take during the course of an online search through the Trails tactic. For example, you might make a mental note of the havoc several marginal search terms may introduce to the formulation so that you are prepared to rectify the situation later (with the Block tactic) should the retrievals deviate from the topic due to these terms. Check is an important tactic that doesn't require search functionality, but it does require your attention on both the negotiated query and how the ongoing search is faring beginning with facet analysis (step 3) through the display of retrievals (step 7). On occasion, a disparity arises between the negotiated query and the search, due to interruptions, search term selections, search logic, and much more, so you will want to rectify the situation as soon as you notice it.

Also independent of search functionality is Correct. When retrievals aren't as expected, diagnose the problem—is it connected with database selection, typecasting, facet analysis, logical combination, search term selection, search strategy, or a combination of these, and what corrections need to be done? Do you have to touch base with the user to confirm or clarify your understanding of her query? History is one of the few search tactics embodied as a standalone feature of search systems.

When assembling and revising search statements, the searcher wields search formulation tactics. Your decisions to include all, some, or deliberately omit some query facets pertain to the Exhaust, Discriminate, and Block tactics, respectively. For example, the Eating Disorders query has been a prime candidate for the Can't Live Without This Facet First Strategy in which are included some (i.e., **Eating Disorders** and **Broken Homes**), not all (i.e., **Adolescents**), facets in the search formulation, and thus, it enlists the Discriminate tactic in which some but not all facets are searched. Interestingly, this is a case in which a strategy and tactic overlap.

Precision and Recall tactics are named for the precision and recall measures that our field uses to assess a search's success. High precision characterizes a search bearing mostly relevant retrievals, and high recall characterizes a search that is comprehensive in its retrieval of as many relevant sources as there are in the database. These measures are inversely proportional—when recall is low, precision is high and vice versa—making it impossible (using today's online searching systems) for a search to achieve both. These measures come to the fore when users express their search objectives during the reference interview, for example, one user wants a handful of relevant articles to write a paper that is due tomorrow and a second wants a comprehensive search on a topic that he might pursue for his senior thesis. Their objectives now become your goals, formulating a high-precision search to satisfy the first user's objective and a high-recall search to satisfy the second user's objective. To satisfy the first user, these search term selection tactics come to the fore:

- Equate: Select CV terms that are specific to each query facet.
- Neighbor: Browse and select CV terms from alphabetical indexes.
- Contrary: Select CV terms that are opposite in meaning.
- Subdivide: Select subdivided forms of CV terms.

Additionally, apply the Field and Proximate search term representation tactics to limit the scope of the above tactics to CV because CV search formulations produce high-precision retrievals. Should revision be necessary, these tactics are in keeping with high-precision CV search formulations:

- Sub: Add narrower CV terms to your search statements.
- Pearl Growing: Scan retrievals for relevant CV terms and add them to your search statements.

- Cluster: Explore accompanying clusters for relevant co-occurring subject and non-subject terms to add to your search statements, the former for changing the search's direction and the latter for reducing retrievals.

To satisfy the second user, you'll use several of the same search term selection tactics you used for the first user but your focus will be on formulating a FT search:

- Equate: Formulate FT terms that are specific to each facet of the query.
- Neighbor: Browse alphabetical indexes for search term variants and represent them as FT.
- Pseudonym: Include pseudonyms for names. These won't be in alphabetical indexes. You'll have to consult authority files and biographical dictionaries for them.
- Contrary: Formulate FT terms that are opposite in meaning.
- Truncate: Apply truncation to search variant forms of terms.
- Spell: Add spelling variants to your FT search statements.
- Space & Symbol: Add one-word/two-word variants and variants bearing symbols such as hyphens, slashes, and hashtags to your FT search statements.
- Nickname: Add variants that are nicknames, acronyms, or initialed forms of terms.
- Auto-Term Add: Especially in extended-Boolean systems, turn on this feature so that the system adds statistically co-occurring terms to the search.

Additionally, apply the Field, Proximate, and Truncate search term representation tactics to expand the scope of the above tactics to FT because FT search formulations cast a wide net, resulting in high-recall searches. Should revision be necessary, these tactics are in keeping with high-recall FT search formulations:

- Super: Add broader terms to your search statements.
- Relate: Add related terms, that is, terms that are not hierarchically related, to your search statements.
- Pearl Growing: Scan retrievals for relevant FT terms and add them to your search statements.
- Find Like: Select a relevant retrieval to prompt the systems to find additional ones like it.

All these search tactics may leave you feeling confused and overwhelmed. That's to be expected. In fact, you are probably already confusing them with search strategies and the many features of this and that search system. Search tactic deployment demands all the knowledge you have accumulated about online searching. In time, you'll find yourself at an impasse while conducting an online search, wanting to accomplish something. Reviewing these tactics might help you determine what to do next. This chapter's questions and answers challenge you to break the impasse with search tactics.

For the time being, orient yourself to online searching through the seven steps of the process. Initially, rely on the Building Block Strategy, making the choice between Buffet and À la Carte Editions contingent on whether you are searching a Boolean or extended-Boolean system. As your confidence increases, ask yourself whether the Can't Live Without This Facet First Strategy makes sense for the query in hand over the Building Block Strategy. When a low-posted search sparks your interest in search tactics, review the search tactics list, realizing you've been there all along, wielding search system functionality to monitor the ongoing search, select search terms, and revise them.

Questions

1. With a laptop in hand, sit next to a friend and search Google for shopping, consumer health, popular culture, and academic topics that interest you. Compare retrievals. If retrievals differ, describe how they differ, what Google is factoring into its personalization algorithm for you that differs from your friend, and whether this is a fair assessment of you. When would you want to turn off Google's personalization algorithm?

2. Search Google (http://google.com), Bing (http://www.bing.com), and Ask (http://www.ask.com). Where do these Web search engines place ads and what visual and verbal cues do they add to help you distinguish ads from retrieved content?

3. Search ABI/Inform, Public Library of Science (PLoS), and your library's WSD system. What pre-search qualifiers and post-search clusters do they give you to limit retrievals to the most credible, scholarly, and trustworthy ones?

4. Conduct a high-precision search in a discipline-specific A&I or full-text database for a topic that is very familiar to you, perhaps one that you researched for a course last semester or even more recently. Review the first two pages of retrievals, assessing relevance on a 0-1-2 scale for not relevant, possibly relevant, and relevant, respectively. Exchange your laptop with a friend, describing your search topic to him and asking him to assess these same retrievals using the same results. Compare your results. Whose relevance assessments are higher? After talking about the relevance assessments on which you do not agree, decide which one of you is a more positive judge of relevance and why. Switch roles.

5. In a search of the ERIC database for parents setting limits on their children's use of social networking sites and the Internet generally, you retrieve two sources ED542901 ("Parents, Children & Media: A Kaiser Family Foundation Survey") and ED507549 ("Net Cetera: Chatting with Kids About Being Online"). Enter these two accession numbers into the ERIC database and download full-texts. Perform a technical reading of each source, and, based on this reading, decide which is the more high-quality source. Then submit each source to the CRAAP Test, rating each source using these questions:

    Currency: Does this topic require current information, and if it does, is the source's information current? (Rate: 0 = not current, 1 = somewhat current, 2 = very current)

    Relevance: Does the information relate to the query? (Rate: 0 = not relevant, 1 = possibly relevant, and 2 = relevant)

    Authority: Who wrote the source? What are the author's credentials and do they qualify the author to write on this topic? (Rate: 0 = not qualified, 1 = somewhat qualified, 2 = qualified)

    Accuracy: What claims does the author make? Does he support his claims with evidence? (Rate: 0 = no evidence, 1 = some but not enough evidence, 2 = enough evidence)

    Purpose: Is the author's purpose to inform, teach, sell, entertain, or persuade? (Rate: 0 = entertain or sell, 1 = persuade, 2 = inform or teach)

    Calculate CRAAP scores for each source. Which source achieves a higher CRAAP Test score? Does your initial assessment agree with your CRAAP Test score? If it doesn't, why doesn't it? Is the CRAAP Test a more rigorous way to assess quality than your initial assessment? Why or why not? Would you recommend the CRAAP Test to students enrolled in an information literacy course? Why or why not?

6. Finding yourself at an impasse while conducting a search is not unusual. Below are examples of typical impasses. Consider each, then select one or more search tactics that you would exercise to break the impasse. Tell why you chose the tactic(s) to break the impasse.

- My retrievals address the topic but they seem really broad.
- This person wrote much more than I'm retrieving here.
- Why does this non-relevant theme constantly pop up in my retrievals?
- I know I've chosen the right database, so why can't I find anything on this topic?
- Why aren't my retrievals expressing the _____ facet?
- I'm working with a four-faceted search that produces thousands of retrievals and so many of them are relevant.
- Despite plenty of CV terms for this facet, it seems so underposted in this database.
- This legislation was pivotal. Why am I finding so little about it?

Summary

This chapter covers the seventh and final step of the online searching process—displaying and assessing retrievals and responding tactically to system responses throughout the course of the search. Users have come to expect systems to display the most relevant sources first, so they rarely display more than the first or second page of retrievals. Encourage users to reorder the retrievals display, selecting another display option from the "sort" pull-down menu and scanning its retrievals for relevant ones. It's much simpler than what users usually do—enter a new search statement, re-enter their original search statement, or project relevance onto the first-listed retrievals.

Searching the Web for free and reading retrieved content actually comes with a price—putting advertising in front of your eyeballs that's tailor-made to your interests. It's your job to impress this on users so they evaluate the information they glean from the Web. To date, licensed search systems have been aboveboard with respect to the search and display of retrievals. Because of the possibility of bias in web-scale discovery (WSD) systems, everyone involved in their deployment—librarians, publishers, and WSD-system providers—have joined forces, hammering out best practices for these systems to avoid potential problems in the future.

Search tactics describe the many ways available to online searchers to maneuver during the ongoing search. There are five tactic types for: (1) search monitoring, (2) search formulation, (3) search term selection, (4) search term representation, and (5) search term revision. Initially, you may be overwhelmed by the many search tactics available to you and confuse them with the seven steps of the online searching process and six search strategies. Start simple, orienting yourself to the online searching process through its seven steps and relying on the Building Block Strategy for most searches. Should you find yourself at an impasse with respect to finding relevant retrievals, review search tactics (table 11.1) and when you do, you'll notice that you've been wielding them all along.

Bibliography

Bates, Marcia J. 1979. "Information Search Tactics." *Journal of the American Society for Information Science* 30, no. 4: 205–14. Accessed March 26, 2015. http://pages.gseis.ucla.edu/faculty/bates/articles/Information Search Tactics.html.

Bates, Marcia J. 1987. "How to Use Information Search Tactics Online." *Online* 11, no. 3 (May): 47–54.

Blakeslee, Sarah. 2004. "The CRAAP Test." *LOEX Quarterly* 31. Accessed March 26, 2015. http://commons.emich.edu/cgi/viewcontent.cgi?article=1009&context=loexquarterly.

Buchanan, Heidi E., and Beth A. McDonough. 2014. *The One-Shot Library Instruction Survival Guide.* Chicago: ALA Editions.

Cull, Barry W. 2011. "Reading Revolutions: Online Digital Text and Implications for Reading in Academe." *First Monday* 16, no. 6. Accessed March 26, 2015. http://firstmonday.org/ojs/index.php/fm/article/view/3340/2985.

Cutts, Matt. 2006. "Ramping Up on International Webspam." *Gadgets, Google, and SEO* (blog). Accessed March 16, 2015. https://www.mattcutts.com/blog/ramping-up-on-international-webspam/.

Grassian, Esther S., and Joan R. Kaplowitz. 2009. *Information Literacy Instruction.* 2nd ed. New York: Neal-Schuman.

Guynn, Jessica. 2011. "Google Makes Major Change in Search Ranking Algorithms." *LA Times*. Accessed March 26, 2015. http://articles.latimes.com/2011/feb/26/business/la-fi-google-search-20110226.

Jansen, Bernard J., and Amanda Spink. 2006. "How Are We Searching the World Wide Web? A Comparison of Nine Search Engine Transaction Logs." *Information Processing & Management* 42, no. 1: 248–63.

Leeder, Christopher Alan. 2014. *Scaffolding Students' Information Literacy Skills with an Online Credibility Evaluation Learning Tool.* PhD diss., University of Michigan.

Markey, Karen, Chris Leeder, and Soo Young Rieh. 2014. *Designing Online Information Literacy Games Students Want to Play.* Lanham, MD: Rowman & Littlefield.

Markey, Karen. 2007. "Twenty-Five Years of End-User Searching, Part 1: Research Findings." *Journal of the American Society for Information Science and Technology* 58, no. 8: 1071–81.

NISO (National Information Standard Organization). 2014. *Open Discovery Initiative: Promoting Transparency in Discovery.* Baltimore, MD: NISO.

NoodleTools. 2015. "NoodleTools: Smart Tools, Smart Research." Accessed March 26, 2015. http://www.noodletools.com/.

Pan, Bing. 2007. "In Google We Trust: Users' Decisions on Rank, Position, and Relevance." *Journal of Computer-Mediated Communication* 12, no. 3: 801–23.

Pariser, Elliot. 2011. *The Filter Bubble: What the Internet Is Hiding from You.* New York: Penguin.

Peters, Tom. 1989. "When Smart People Fail: An Analysis of the Transaction Logs of an Online Public Access Catalog." *Journal of Academic Librarianship* 15, no. 5 (Nov.): 267–73.

Ragains, Patrick. 2013. *Information Literacy Instruction That Works.* 2nd ed. Chicago: ALA Neal-Schuman.

Sandore, Beth. 1993. "Applying the Results of Transaction Log Analysis." *Library Hi Tech* 11, no. 2: 87–97.

Sebastian, Michael. 2014. "New York Times Tones Down Labeling on Its Sponsored Posts." *Advertising Age.* Accessed March 26, 2015. http://adage.com/article/media/york-times-shrinks-labeling-natives-ads/294473/.

Spink, Amanda, Dietmar Wolfram, Bernard J. Jansen, and Tefko Saracevic. 2001. "Searching the Web: The Public and Their Queries." *Journal of the American Society for Information Science and Technology* 52, no. 3: 226–34.

Suggested Readings

Ojala, Marydee. 2003. "When Bad Searches Happen to Good Searchers." *Online* 27, no. 1 (Jan./Feb.): 58–60. Although the article's references to specific databases and searching languages are outdated, its advice about diagnosing why searches fail and what to do is still spot-on.

Answers

1. **Personalized retrievals in Google**
    Discuss your findings with your friend. When students discuss their experiences in class, we tally results for the whole class with respect to personalization producing different retrievals for searches on shopping, consumer health, popular culture, and academic topics, whether students think that Google's personalization algorithm represents them fairly, and whether and when they want to turn off Google's personalization algorithm.

2. **Visual and verbal cues that a search engine's retrievals are ads**
    Search engines change these cues all the time. Here are some things to look for:

    -   Sandwiching retrievals in between ads, placing ads above the fold and "legitimate" content below it, placing ads on the left where your vision falls naturally and content on the right
    -   Thin horizontal lines, ads spread atop pale grayish backgrounds or the same-colored background as "legitimate" retrievals, boxes outlined with thin lines
    -   Headings named "Ad," "Shopping," "Sponsored," "Ads related to [insert your search statement]"

3. **Choosing clusters for credible, scholarly, and trustworthy retrievals**

    -   *ABI/Inform.* Toggle the *Peer Reviewed* cluster on. Choose the "Scholarly Journals" from the *Source Type* cluster. Also *Source Types* such as "Trade Journals," "Dissertations and Theses," "Books," and "Conference Papers and Proceedings" may undergo peer review and editorial scrutiny.
    -   *PLoS.* PLoS has no post-search clusters; however, of its seven journals, six are peer-reviewed and one is controlled by an editorial board. Thus, quality is built into the PLoS database.
    -   *WSD system.* Check your library's WSD system for clusters similar to ABI/Inform's.

4. **Assessing relevance**
    When students discuss their experiences in class, we tally results for the whole class with respect to who is the more positive judge of relevance. We find that friends are more positive than query originators but not always. We've hypothesized that the originator knows exactly what is and isn't relevant because of his experience using retrievals to complete the assignment connected with the query. In contrast, friends are more positive because they don't have this experience and prefer to leave things wide open so query originators can use retrieval results as they see fit.

5. **Assessing credibility and trustworthiness**
    Debrief in a class discussion. The CRAAP Test you administered is my abridgement of a longer version (Blakeslee 2004). If you wouldn't recommend the CRAAP Test to students in an information literacy class, what is a comparable alternative?

6. **Choosing tactics when you find yourself at an impasse**

    -   *My retrievals address the topic, but they seem really broad.* Sub tactic, adding narrower search terms to one or more facets. Subdivide tactic, adding subdivided forms of CV terms that express aspects of the unsubdivided main heading in one or more facets.

- *This person wrote much more than I'm retrieving here.* Neighbor tactic, browsing the database's alphabetical author index and choosing variant forms of this person's name. Pseudonym tactic, checking LCNAF and biographical databases for pseudonyms.
- *Why does this non-relevant theme constantly pop up in my retrievals?* Block tactic, using the NOT operator to eliminate specific search terms or entire facets of search terms.
- *I know I've chosen the right database so why can't I find anything on this topic?* Gain tactic, increasing retrievals by adding more search terms to the formulation. How the searcher accomplishes Gain may be manual, for example, the searcher chooses search terms that are synonymous (Equate), alphabetically nearby (Neighbor), opposite (Contrary), or broader (Super), or it may be algorithmic, for example, the system calculating statistical associations between sources or terms to find additional retrievals (Find Like or Auto-Term Add).
- *Why aren't my retrievals expressing the _____ facet?* History tactic, reviewing previous search statements and logic for errors. Correct tactic, correcting search logic. Spell tactic, correcting spelling errors. Neighbor, Space & Symbol, Nickname, Pseudonym, and Equate tactics, adding variants to search statements.
- *I'm working with a four-faceted search that produces thousands of retrievals, and so many of them are relevant.* History tactic, reviewing previous search statements and logic. Correct tactic, making sure search logic is correct. Cluster tactic, limiting retrievals by one or more non-subject clusters such as language, publication date, or peer reviewed.
- *Despite plenty of CV terms for this facet, it seems so underposted in this database.* Contrary tactic, for adding CV terms that are the opposite in meaning. The combination of Field, Proximate, and Truncate tactics, for adding free text terms.
- *This legislation was pivotal.* Why am I finding so little about it? Nickname, Neighbor, Spell, or Space & Symbol tactics, for representing variant forms of this legislation's name. (This is an impasse you might experience when searching any type of proper noun—a company, organization, place, event, test, and so on.)

12

Performing a Technical Reading of a Database and Its Search System

Helping users satisfy their information needs will require you to select from among the potentially hundreds of databases available through your library's database hub and the World Wide Web. This chapter gives you a methodology for quickly and efficiently familiarizing yourself with a database and the system you use to search it.

Called performing a technical reading of a database, this methodology involves answering ten questions about the database and its search system. Because you will almost always be pressed for time at the reference desk, it will be impossible for you to first search the database to answer the ten questions, then search the database to satisfy the user's query. Instead, you need to do both, keeping these ten questions in mind while searching the database to find relevant information for the user.

The Ten Questions

To quickly and efficiently familiarize yourself with a database, answer ten questions about the database and its search system. This chapter uses the Compendex database and its Engineering Village (EV) search system to demonstrate how to perform a technical reading of a database.

1. Will This Database Yield Information That Satisfies the User's Query?

When you choose a database to answer a user's query, use *Online Searching*'s database classification (figure 4.1) to classify it as:

- A surrogate or source database for producing retrievals and for supplying the actual sources themselves (page 51)
- An encyclopedic database or a database specializing in a particular subject or supporting the research of domain experts in a particular discipline or field of study (pages 49–50)
- Text, media, numeric and spatial data, or a digital library (pages 51–56)
- A research or reference database and its specific *research* form (e.g., bibliography, catalog, or full-text) (pages 57–64) or its specific *reference* genre (e.g., almanac, biography, or encyclopedia) (pages 64–71)

At the very least, you want to match the database's subject coverage with the user's topic of interest. In an academic setting, this can be easy—just ask the user for more information about the class he is taking or the name of the academic department that offers the class. In a public library setting, this may be more difficult. You might have to probe, asking the user to clarify the impetus for her query. For example, if a user's query addresses abortion, ask her whether she is interested in the biological, ethical, religious, medical, political, or psychological aspects of the topic, then choose a database that addresses this topic from the desired perspective.

Consider also the database's intended audience. Recommend databases to users that are in keeping with their level of sophistication vis-à-vis their topic of interest. For example, if the user is a surgeon looking for a source on a new surgical procedure, recommending that he search a database that specializes in consumer health information isn't going to cut it.

The Compendex (also called Engineering Index) database is the "gold standard" for engineering professionals in the applied sciences, specifically, chemical, civil, electrical, mechanical, mining, and general engineering (Elsevier 2015). Begun in 1884 as a print-based A&I reference source, it was one of the first abstracting and indexing (A&I) sources to automate. Since 1998, Compendex has been published by Elsevier, which applies the Engineering Village (EV) search system to Compendex. Compendex's content comes primarily from scholarly journals, conference proceedings, and trade journals. Compendex is a research database, specifically an A&I database, that searches and retrieves surrogates, supplying some full-texts through its publisher Elsevier and others through the library's resolver links.

2. Does This Database's Search System Respond with Boolean or Extended-Boolean Searches to My Search Statements?

Knowing whether a search system responds with Boolean or extended-Boolean searches to your entered search statements drives how you represent the search as input to the search system and what search strategies are available to you (i.e., steps 5 and 6 of the searching process).

To determine a search system's Boolean or extended-Boolean status, do a visual check first, launching the system's default and advanced interfaces and looking for evidence of these Boolean searching conventions:

- Two to three separate search boxes
- Pull-down menus in between search boxes, one listing Boolean operators, and possibly, a second listing database fields
- Tips that show sample searches with Boolean operators
- A sets capability
- A search history capability

Figure 12.1 shows the Compendex database's default interface. It features all five Boolean searching conventions above. Thus, a visual check is all that is needed to confirm that Compendex performs Boolean searches in response to the search statements you enter into its default interface.

The EBSCOhost system is more complicated. Using the Index Islamicus database, start with a visual check. EBSCOhost's default (or basic) search interface enlists a single search box that prompts the user to "Enter any words to find books, journals, and more" (figure 12.2). Under this box are these four options with the first-listed option being the default:

1. Boolean/phrase
2. Find all my search terms
3. Find any of my search terms
4. SmartText searching

Figure 12.1. Default Interface for Conducting Boolean Searches in the Compendex Database on Engineering Village. Source: Engineering Village, a registered trademark of Elsevier, B.V., image retrieved on 18 March 2015.

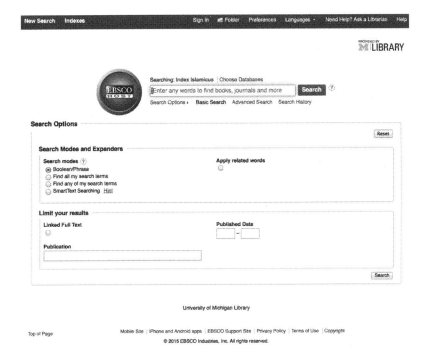

Figure 12.2. Default (or Basic) Interface for Conducting Searches in the Index Islamicus on EBSCOhost.

Clearly, the first option is a Boolean search because it is labeled as such. So is the second because to retrieve sources bearing all your search terms, the system has to perform a Boolean AND operation. A visual check is insufficient for the second option, so follow up with a test, entering black muslims nationalism and expecting EBSCOhost to insert an implicit AND operator in between each search term, which it does.

EBSCOhost's third option is an extended-Boolean search, inserting an implicit Boolean OR operator in between each search term, black OR muslims OR nationalism, and producing one hundred thousand retrievals. That the user is able to find relevant retrievals is due to EBSCOhost's retrievals-relevance ranking. By the way, search each term individually and combine their results with the Boolean OR operator. Retrieved are the same one hundred thousand retrievals. SmartText is EBSCOhost's brand name for its extended-Boolean search (page 129). No matter which of the four search options you choose, EBSCOhost's relevance ranking algorithm kicks in, placing the most relevant retrievals atop the list.

Short on time, you could follow a few rules of thumb. Interfaces bearing multiple search boxes interspersed with pull-down menus of Boolean operators probably respond with Boolean searches to your search statements. Interfaces bearing a lone search box could go either way, so play it safe, entering search statements using the À la Carte Edition of the Building Block Strategy into them and visually inspecting first- and last-listed retrievals for occurrences of your search terms.

3. What Document Representation Does My Query Search?

Answers to question #3 might require visual inspections of first- and last-listed retrievals to determine whether matches are limited to surrogates or extend to full-texts. The answer to question #3 governs your decisions regarding facets, Boolean operators, and proximity operators. If your searches are limited to surrogates, you won't need a facet for relationships (if the query calls for one), and to combine search results for individual facets, you'll use Boolean operators. If your searches extend to full-texts, then you can add a causality facet (if the query calls for one) and to combine facets, you'll use proximity operators. (See pages 78 and 120–23 for more discussion about the relationship facet and substituting proximity for Boolean operators in searches of full-text databases.)

If you don't have time to scrutinize retrievals, mouse down on the database's fields pull-down menu accompanying the search box. (Such a menu is almost always present in a system's advanced search interface.) See if there is a field label named something like full-text, document text, all text fields, or entire document, and if there is, it's a sure sign that your search statements extend to full-texts. Additionally, you might consider an inordinate number of retrievals for multifaceted queries to be a sign that your search statements extend to full-texts, but it could also mean that you are searching an extended-Boolean system.

4. What Types of Searches Does This Database Support?

Knowing what types of searches the database supports gives you a jumpstart on typecasting the user's query and representing the search as input to the search system. Table 12.1 lists the wide variety of subject and known-item searches that are characteristic of today's search systems and clues that the system you are searching supports this particular search type. Don't expect every system to "have it all," and should you find one that does, how sweet it is!

To determine the searches a search system supports, scan the database's searchable fields by mousing down on the fields pull-down menu in the system's search interface, scrutinize its pre-search qualifiers, and check the system's various interfaces for links to alphabetical indexes. Doing so in Compendex reveals the database's subject and known-item searches (table 12.2).

Table 12.1. Subject and Known-Item Searches

Subject Searches	
Specific Search Type	**Clues That This System Supports This Search Type**
CV searches	The search system provides functionality for the searcher to display the CV's syndetic structure and/or select relevant CV terms that it enters directly into the search.
FT searches	The database has no CV and no functionality for displaying the CV's syndetic structure or selecting relevant CV terms.
Combination CV-FT searches	The system provides both CV and FT search functionality.
Find-like searches	Accompanying a source is a link named "find like," "related articles," or "find similar" that uses the source's terms to find more like it.
Bibliography scanning (backward chaining) searches	Accompanying a source is a link such as "N Cited References" that displays older sources when selected.
Cited reference (forward chaining) searches	Accompanying a source is a link such as "N Times Cited" or "Cited by N documents" that displays more recent sources when selected.
Known-Item Searches	
Title searches	The system's fields pull-down menu bears a title option.
Author searches	The system's fields pull-down menu bears an author option.
Combination author-title searches	The system provides the searcher with multiple search boxes and their accompanying pull-down menus list options for author and for title.
Author-bibliography searches	The system's fields pull-down menu bears an author option and/or its search results include an Author cluster.
Citation verification and full-text fulfillment searches	The system provides the searcher with multiple search boxes and their accompanying pull-down menus list options for author, title, publisher, and publication name.
Journal run searches	The system's fields pull-down menu bears a publication name option and/or its search results include a Publication Name cluster.
Journal-assessment searches	The system provides journal impact metrics.
Author-assessment searches	The system provides citation, bibliometrics, and/or altmetrics data for individual sources.

Table 12.2. Subject and Known-Item Searches in the Compendex Database on Engineering Village

Subject Searches	
Specific Search Type	**Field Name, Pre-Search Qualifier, Index Type, or Cluster**
CV searches	Choose the "Thesaurus search," then search Compendex's online thesaurus
	Ei classification code
	Ei main heading
	Ei controlled term (field search or alphabetical index browse)
FT searches	FT searches apply to subject, title, and author fields
Bibliography scanning (backward chaining) searches	Identify relevant sources and follow up with known-item searches in the Web of Science
Cited-reference searches (Forward chaining)	Click on the "Cited by in Scopus (N)" link to open Scopus at a display of the N cited references
Known-Item Searches	
Title searches	Title
	Conference information
	Conference code
	Source title
Author searches	Author (field search or alphabetical index browse)
	Author affiliation
	Country of origin
Combination author-title searches	Into the first search box enter the author's name and choose "Author" from the pull-down menu, and into the second search box enter the title and choose "Title" from the pull-down menu
Author-bibliography searches	Author (field search, alphabetical index browse, post-search Author cluster)
Citation verification and full-text fulfillment searches	CODEN
	ISSN
	Any title fields above
	Author
	Any journal run fields below
	Date (choose as a pre-search qualifier)
Journal run searches	Source title (field search, alphabetical index browse, post-search cluster)
	Publisher (field search, alphabetical index browse, post-search cluster)
Author-assessment searches	Click on the author-name links accompanying surrogates to open Scopus at a display of the N cited references

Compendex offers a wide array of subject and known-item searches. Backward chaining is performed manually with the searcher retrieving relevant sources in Compendex, then following up with known-item searches in the Web of Science, which, if successful, display the sources that the relevant source cites along with resolver links for full-texts. Compendex partners with Scopus to automate forward chaining and author-assessment searches. For the former, it adds links to surrogates specifying the number of times the retrieval is cited in Scopus; searchers merely click on the link to launch Scopus where they conduct forward chaining. For the latter, it adds links to surrogates for author and co-author names; again, searchers merely click on a link to launch Scopus, which displays the author's h-index and the number of times others have cited the author's works. For the time being, Compendex has no find-like search.

You'll be surprised by the questions you can answer using combinations of the fields. For example, a user tells you his instructor recommended an article by Carlos Maltzahn from a recent conference on gamification. To find it in Compendex, browse the author index selecting various forms of this author's name, search the conference information field for the truncated stem gamif*, and combine the results in a Boolean AND operation. Doing so retrieves the surrogate displayed in figure 12.3.

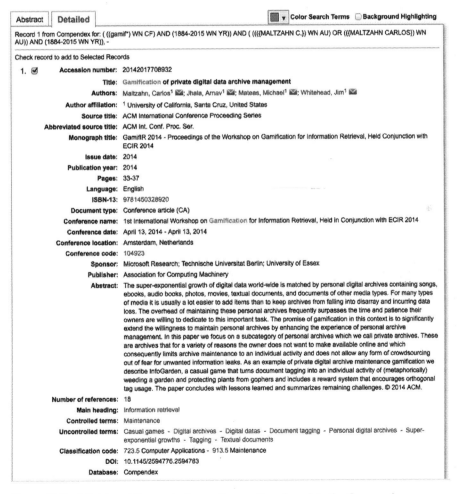

Figure 12.3. A Retrieved Surrogate from a Known-Item Search in the Compendex Database on Engineering Village. Source: Engineering Village, a registered trademark of Elsevier, B.V., image retrieved on 18 March 2015.

Sometimes, a database has unusual search types. In the case of Compendex, you can search its author affiliation and country of origin field. Most likely, you would have your database detective hat on when searching these fields alone or in combination with other fields.

5. Does This Database Search the Controlled Vocabulary's Syndetic Structure?

To determine whether a database features syndetic structure searching of a CV, look for a link or tab named "Thesaurus," "Thesaurus Search," "Search Tools," or bearing the word "classification," "tree" or "hierarchy." EV enables syndetic structure searching of the Compendex database through the "Thesaurus Search" tab (figure 12.1). Use it to quickly and efficiently formulate a CV search that produces high-precision results.

Some databases have a CV with a syndetic structure but their search systems don't feature syndetic structure searching. You have to create a work-around, for example, displaying CV terms, entering them directly, creating ORed sets for each facet, then combining these sets in one final Boolean AND combination. Other databases have a CV with a flat structure, devoid of BTs, NTs, and RTs. Searching these databases is limited to browsing alphabetical lists of CV terms, selecting at least one relevant CV term per facet, and combining search statements for each facet with the Boolean AND operator.

6. Can I Combine Previously Created Sets?

Sets functionality comes in three different flavors: (1) no sets creation, (2) sets creation and display only, or (3) sets creation, display, and combination. Flavor #1 is hardly useful because the system provides you with no record of previously entered search terms and logic. Flavor #2 overcomes the limitations of flavor #1, enabling you to review previously entered search terms, check your logic, and display previously retrieved sources. Flavor #3 is the most flexible, allowing you to do everything flavor #2 allows plus combining previously created sets with Boolean and/or proximity operators.

To determine whether your selected database creates previously created sets, look for a link or tab entitled "Search History," "Previous Sets," or "Previous Searches." Typically, combining sets involves clicking on the search history link to display previously created sets, checkmarking their set numbers, and choosing the Boolean AND, OR, or NOT operators from a nearby pull-down menu to combine them. Alternatively, enter a Boolean expression directly into the search box with a pound sign # or set abbreviation letter s appended to the set number:

```
#1 and #2
(s1 or s2 or s3) and s4
```

7. What Pre-Search Qualifiers Are Available?

Many systems accompany search boxes with pre-search qualifiers. At the very least, they feature qualifiers for date of publication and language. Figure 12.1 shows Compendex's four pre-search qualifiers: *Document Types* (e.g., journal article, conference article, book chapter), *Treatment Types* (e.g., economic, review, theoretical), *Languages*, and *Date of Publication*.

Pre-search qualifiers are database dependent. EBSCOhost's Index Islamicus and PsycINFO databases feature four and over twenty pre-search qualifiers, respectively. PsycINFO is unusual in that it features several pre-search subject qualifiers: *Age Group, Classification Code, Population Group,* and *Methodology*. Prefer *subject* pre-search qualifiers over building retrieval sets using CV and FT terms because they are time-savers—you select one blanket term instead of browsing and selecting multiple search terms.

Applying non-subject pre-search qualifiers along with your search statements may reduce retrievals to zero. Because you will almost always encounter a database's pre-search qualifiers in the form of its post-search clusters, wait until you know how many sources your search retrieves to apply them. For example, you wouldn't have guessed that the Eating Disorders query would have retrieved so few sources until you conducted CV and FT searches for it in the course of answering questions in chapters 6 and 7. Had you applied non-subject pre-search qualifiers such as *Language* or *Peer-reviewed*, you would have had to backtrack to determine whether so few retrievals were the result of combining this query's three facets, applying pre-search qualifiers, or a combination of the two.

8. What Is This System's Free Text Searching Language?

To learn a search system's free text searching language, you really have to consult its online help. Granted, you could learn from the system's feedback, that is, the searching language it displays in response to your entered terms; however, not knowing a search system's unique syntax for adjacency, nearby, or truncation may turn your interpretation of the system's feedback into a guessing game. Table 12.3 summarizes the free text searching language of the EV search system for its collection of engineering databases.

Remembering the fine details connected with a system's searching language is difficult unless you search the system on a daily basis. Consider consolidating its searching language into

Table 12.3. Engineering Village's Free Text Searching Language

BOOLEAN OPERATORS		
Operator Name	**Search Syntax**	**Sample Search Statement**
Boolean OR	OR	waste OR debris OR refuse
Boolean AND	AND	plastics AND space AND radiation
Boolean NOT	NOT	(#1 AND #2) NOT #3
PROXIMITY OPERATORS		
Explanation	**Search Syntax**	**Sample Search Statement**
Adjacency, word order matters	Quotes or curly brackets	"space shuttles" {garbage disposal}
	ONEAR/0	space ONEAR/0 shuttles
Nearby, word order matters	ONEAR/N	space ONEAR/3 debris
Adjacency, word order does not matter	NEAR/0	spacecraft NEAR/0 shielding
Nearby, word order does not matter	NEAR/N	debris NEAR/2 cloud

(continued)

Table 12.3. Engineering Village's Free Text Searching Language *continued*

TRUNCATION		
Explanation	**Search Syntax**	**Sample Search Statement**
Default (called autostemming, it is on by default; turn it off under the search interface's "Sort by" link)		argument retrieves variant forms such as argue, argued, arguing, argument, arguments, argumentation, argumentative
Unlimited truncation, (right) retrieving words starting with same letters up to the symbol and any letters afterward or (left) retrieving words with any letters up to the symbol and ending with same letters after the symbol	*	argument* retrieves argument, arguments, argumentation, argumentative
	*	*sorption retrieves absorption, adsorption, biosorption, chemisorption, desorption, electroabsorption, sorption, thermosorption, thermoabsorption
	$	When autostemming is turned off, preface the search term with $ to retrieve the stem and suffixes, e.g., $argument retrieves argue, argued, arguing, argument, arguments, argumentation, argumentative
Wildcard, retrieving words with as many letters as there are wildcard symbols	?	cat? retrieves cats, cato, catv, etc. observ?? retrieves observer, observed, observes
Embedded truncation, retrieving any one letter in place of the symbol or any number of letters in place of the symbol	? *	wom?n retrieves woman, women, womyn c*tion retrieves contraption, caution, caption, computerization, etc.

cheat sheets and filing them into a print-based or electronic notebook that accompanies you to the reference desk and the information literacy classes you teach. More cheat sheet examples are tables 6.2, 6.3, and 7.1. By the way, when search systems give you more than one approach to effect proximity or truncation, record on your cheat sheets the way that is typical of the majority of the search systems you use so you'll have less to remember.

9. What Post-Search Clusters Are Available?

Not all search systems accompany retrievals with post-search clusters (also called facets, limits, or qualifiers). If you search a database repeatedly, compare its pre-search qualifiers with its post-search clusters to determine how much they overlap. When there is significant overlap between the two, put off applying non-subject qualifiers until you've conducted the search. Three of Compendex's four pre-search qualifiers—document types, languages, and publication dates—reappear as post-search clusters; only treatment type is missing from its post-search qualifiers (left side of figure 12.4).

Post-search clusters benefit users whose search topics are unfocused, diffuse, or broad (pages 100–103). Compendex's subject clusters—*Controlled Vocabulary* and *Classification Code*—may reveal ideas users hadn't thought of previously or describe an aspect of their topic that piques their interest. Non-subject clusters such as *Document Type, Language*, and *Year* may be useful for reducing high-posted searches using criteria that won't change the subject. Other non-subject clusters such as *Author, Source Title, Publisher,* and *Author Affiliation* may reveal authors, journal titles, publishers, or research centers pursuing the research, topic, or line of inquiry that interests the user. For example, open in figure 12.4 are *Country* and *Source Title* clusters showing countries (e.g., U.S., China, and Japan) and publications (e.g., *SAE Technical Papers* and *Automotive Engineer*) connected with automobile air bag research and development.

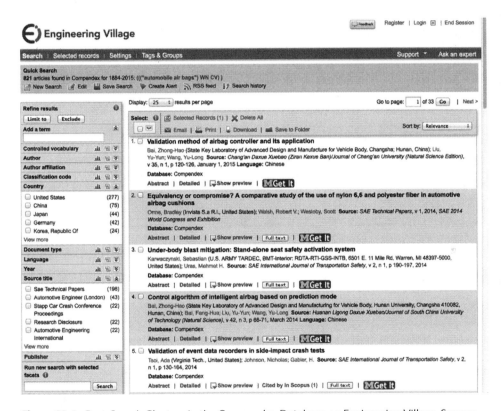

Figure 12.4. Post-Search Clusters in the Compendex Database on Engineering Village. Source: Engineering Village, a registered trademark of Elsevier, B.V., image retrieved on 2015 March 18.

10. What Fields Can I Browse?

Browsing the indexed values in a database's fields enables you to determine the exact values used to express ideas, concepts, objects, events, and names. Index browsing is mandatory in databases devoid of authority control to gather all variant forms, particularly in the case of authors, journal titles, publisher names, and author affiliation information. The OPAC is one of the few remaining database types in which authority control is the rule rather than the exception. For all other databases, compensate by browsing indexes (when available).

The only downside to index browsing is doing so in a search system that displays index values but doesn't allow you to select them. You'll see systems that do the same for their thesaurus displays. It's hard to believe that search systems would implement browsing in such a half-baked manner but it happens. When you encounter browsing implemented in this way, your only alternative is to copy and paste or jot down relevant values on a notepad, then follow up, entering these values directly into the system's search box.

In figure 12.1, Compendex's default interface lists five indexes for browsing (top right): (1) author, (2) author affiliation, (3) CV, (4) journal titles, and (5) publisher names. Click on Compendex's expert interface and another five indexes join these original five: (6) language, (7) document type, (8) treatment type, (9) discipline, and (10) IPC code. Click on the "Indexes" link in EBSCOhost's PsycINFO database, and you can choose from a menu of twenty-six indexes! Both databases' search systems—EV and EBSCOhost—are especially comprehensive with respect to allowing searchers to browse indexes and select indexed values. When searching databases, pay attention to their index browsing capabilities and use them to ensure that your searches are composed of relevant values for the ideas, concepts, objects, events, and names that make up user queries.

Epilogue: The Benefits of This System's Unique Features

Your answers to the technical reading's ten questions will reveal the most important search system functionality that you need to know to search databases for relevant information for user queries. On occasion, you'll find a system feature that the ten questions don't cover. Experiment with it to determine its benefits, including how, when, and why you'd use it.

The vast array of a search system's functionality for a particular database might not be immediately apparent to you or you might be too busy to experiment with it. Make a mental note, and follow up after you've completed the reference interview at hand or have a few spare moments later on to investigate more thoroughly.

Responding to the Ubiquitous Nature of Search

Search is everywhere! When confronted with a search box on a website or in an application, how do you respond, especially when instructions aren't available or the search is so fleeting or integral to the online experience that you hardly notice that you are searching? One approach is to "go with the flow," that is, respond spontaneously with the idea or intention you had in mind that brought you to this electronic destination. Typically that means entering a phrase enclosed in quotes or a couple of salient words with or without Boolean AND operators inserted between them. If you don't find what you want, review your retrievals to determine how your search statements were processed, then reformulate your search statements so that subsequent results are on target. If you still fail to find what you want, scrutinize your search terms. Do they express what you want or do they skirt the issue? Revise your search statements and be precise, entering exactly what interests you.

Search statements that are in keeping with the À la Carte Edition of the Building Block Strategy almost always have promise. Because they are made up of salient one-word terms and phrases that express each one of the facets that interests the searcher, there should be no holding back on your part. Even the most sophisticated search function on an especially complex website can't read the searcher's mind, so let it all hang out, populating your search statements with search terms that describe your interests.

Alternatively, you could be a minimalist, entering one unique word or phrase in quotes, scrutinizing retrievals to determine how your search statements are processed. Then build them up, adding one word or phrase at a time, until you find what you are looking for. A useful variation of the minimalist approach is to avoid entering subject words altogether, building a search from the search system's non-subject qualifiers and reviewing retrievals. In fact, this is a particularly productive approach for searching the brief entries that characterize many reference databases.

Keep in mind that most web-based search functions are secondary to the website you are visiting or the application in which they reside. Rarely will they have online tips or help so that you can figure out how to search them correctly and effectively. Don't expect feedback either such as post-search clusters to jog your memory or to give you ideas about how express your interests in words. Instead, you have to be forthcoming in your search statements, expressing exactly what interests you, and scrutinizing retrievals, figuring out for yourself how searching is done.

On a personal note, I recall hearing a sacred piece by Henry Purcell on the radio and making a mental note of its title so I could search for it on YouTube later that day. Forgetting to do so, I searched YouTube several weeks later, remembering only the composer's name. My searches for Purcell failed due to too many retrievals. Adding a **Choral** facet (sacred OR choral OR choir) produced more promising results in the form of retrieval lists that described the *class* of music that interested me. Although I'm still looking for the Purcell piece, my experience demonstrates a typical searching problem—a searcher who is able to express the class of phenomena but not the specific instance that interests her. YouTube excels in the latter but not the former. Wikipedia, OPACs, and shopping sites do both. For example, online grocery stores typically double and triple post their merchandise, indexing items under *classes* such as "vegetables" or "fruits," *specific instances* such as "peas" and "pineapple," and even *brand names* such as Green Giant Sweet Peas and Dole Pineapple Chunks in 100% Juice, respectively. Shopping sites want you to purchase their goods so they should index them in multiple ways that characterize how people remember and talk about merchandise.

That search has become commonplace does not mean that you respond willy-nilly, entering whatever pops into your head. Give search the respect it deserves, responding thoughtfully with search terms that express your interests. When results are non-relevant, don't jump the gun, firing off new search statements without a moment's hesitation; instead, scrutinize retrievals to determine how search works and building on what you've learned in the formulation of subsequent search statements.

Database Poster Project

In place of the usual end-of-chapter questions and answers is a description of the Database Poster Project. The purpose of the Database Poster Project is twofold:

1. Apply the ten-step technical reading process so that you learn how to search one particular database and its search system and
2. Increase your familiarity with the technical reading method so that you know how to deploy it when you find yourself searching a particular database or search system for the first time.

Recruit one or two classmates, choose an online database that interests you, and perform a technical reading of the database. This involves answering the technical reading's ten questions and unique-features epilogue question. Then document your answers both verbally and visually on the poster. Although the blank poster's white space looks huge to begin with, it fills up very quickly with answers, so limit what you say to the most salient aspects of your database. For example, a poster showcasing PubMed would emphasize CV searching, and a poster showcasing

LexisNexis would emphasize FT searching because these databases specialize in these searching approaches. If you gear your poster's content to end user searching in PubMed, you would dedicate lots of poster real estate to PubMed's automatic term mapping feature because users will enter natural language terms instead of MeSH. Make sure your poster shows a typical, run-of-the-mill query in this database.

My online searching class dedicates two class periods to oral presentations of posters to enable some students to stand by their posters while others visit them. Poster authors share the task of briefing visitors on their technical reading, demonstrating database searching with their poster's contents and answering visitors' questions. Authors give visitors a two-page cheat-sheet on which they put the most important information about their technical reading including a sample search. They also sum up their database's strengths and weaknesses, telling visitors when they'd deliberately seek out or avoid this database.

Summary

This chapter gives you a methodology for quickly and efficiently familiarizing yourself with a database and the system you use to search it. Called performing a technical reading of a database, this methodology requires you to answer ten questions about the database and its search system. For the databases you search all the time, spend your downtime answering these ten questions thoroughly, and possibly, recording your answers on cheat sheets. Over time, you will find yourself asking these questions on your own, without referring to your cheat sheet to remind yourself of them. When you do, you've become an expert intermediary searcher!

Rarely will you experience all of a database's features the first few times you use it. Repeated usage, however, will expose them to you. Once you feel thoroughly familiar with this and that database, either the database publisher or search system introduces something new, changes, or takes something away. Prepare accordingly, using the few free moments you have from time to time to experiment searching databases and reading trade magazines such as *Information Today* and *Online Searcher* to keep up with the latest information industry news.

Bibliography

Elsevier. 2015. "Engineering Village: History." Accessed March 26, 2015. http://www.elsevier.com/online-tools/engineering-village/history.

13

Interacting with Library Users

This chapter refocuses the spotlight on your interaction with library users in the reference interview where you enlist their assistance, making sure the search is on track and retrieving relevant information to satisfy their queries. Eventually, you will transfer your ongoing searches and their retrievals to users so that they can use them as they see fit. Search systems have all sorts of transfer functionality. This chapter not only explores this functionality and its usefulness during your reference interview interaction with users, but it urges you to use the occasion of the reference interview to alert users to the wide range of retrieval-handling functionality available. This includes citation management systems (CMSs), specialized software that helps users manage their retrievals.

Beginning with sources management, this chapter walks through the steps of the online searching process, identifying content that is appropriate for your teaching efforts. It also suggests that you prepare for sustained teaching events, especially half- and full-semester courses and workshop series with a syllabus, lesson plans, and teaching materials.

Retrievals for the Long Haul

At the academy, users might not perceive the benefits of saving, organizing, and reusing online sources until they commit to a discipline or decide on a career path that involves a culminating experience such as a capstone project, portfolio, or thesis. Then they find themselves scrambling, trying to find sources that they used for previous projects in the folders of their personal computers or among their many Web browser bookmarks. Failing that, they backtrack, searching the open Web or the library's web-scale discovery (WSD) system for sources they've seen before. Reuse also concerns public library users—they want to send a friend or family member an online source that they read months ago or they are working on a long-term project such as a family history and genealogy, business plan, invention, or patent application. In such cases, saving online sources becomes almost mandatory so that users can refer to them repeatedly during the course of their projects and long afterward. Saving sources comes in all different flavors. It varies from system to system, and it even goes beyond search systems, extending to third-party software applications called citation management systems (CMSs).

Saving Features in Search Systems

Saving begins with you, the reference librarian, sharing an ongoing search with a user. You get the user started, conduct an entire or partial search for him, then send him a link to your search. In some systems (e.g., ScienceDirect), saving may be as simple as copying the URL in a Web browser's address bar and pasting it into an email message to the user. In other systems, a few extra steps may be necessary. For example, in EBSCOhost, click on the system's "Share" link on the top right side of the retrievals list, copy the URL in the rectangular box labeled "Permalink," and paste it into an email message to the user (figure 13.1). When permalinks are encoded with your institution's proxy server, clicking on the link should launch the database and restore the search so that the user can pick up where you left off.

Figure 13.1. Copying a Retrieval's Permalink in an EBSCOhost Database for Pasting and Sending It to a User in an Email Message.

Saving the search is also an option for the user who is searching at his own personal computer or at a public workstation. The user signs on to the search system, and if he doesn't have an account, he signs up for one right there on the spot, usually establishing a username and password. Signed on to the system, he is now able to select the "save search" option, name his search, and save it permanently or for a certain amount of time. The advantage of saving the search is that it resides in the search system where links to full-texts also reside. When the user has time to resume the search, he signs on to his account, recalls the saved search, executes it, resumes the process of reviewing retrievals, and downloads full-texts. Because the logistics connected with saving searches are different from system to system, familiarize yourself with how to save searches in the systems you use and recommend to others on a regular basis.

Given the option between saving searches or saving retrievals, it is more efficient to save the search because the search resides in the search system where it is accessible at a later time to users from any computer. They can see what search statements have been entered, revisit their retrievals, or pick up from where they left off. For example, JStor allows the user to save sources in a folder along with the options to sort them chronologically by date of publication or by save date and to request an email message from JStor when it detects a new source citing your saved source (figure 13.2).

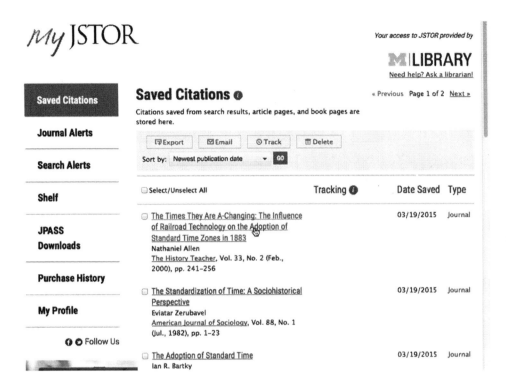

Figure 13.2. A User's Saved Sources in the JStor Database. Reprinted courtesy of JSTOR. JSTOR © 2013. All rights reserved.

The search alert is a special type of saved search that the search system executes per your instructions, sending you newly retrieved sources that meet your search criteria on a regular basis. Search alerts are a cinch to set up. You conduct a search, then save your search statements, choosing the system's search alert option. The system responds with a form, asking you to name and describe your saved search. Figure 13.3 shows the bottom half of EBSCOhost's form where you schedule how frequently and for how long you want the system to execute the saved search, how you want the system to send you newly retrieved sources (usually your choice between email or RSS), and in what format you want to receive sources. Thereafter, sit back and wait for the system to send you retrievals.

When your reference interviews reveal users whose information needs are long-term, suggest the search alert to them. Use the search you are formulating for them as the basis for the search alert or invite them to set up an appointment where you can set up one or more search alerts in relevant licensed and open Web databases. Even Google and Google Scholar feature

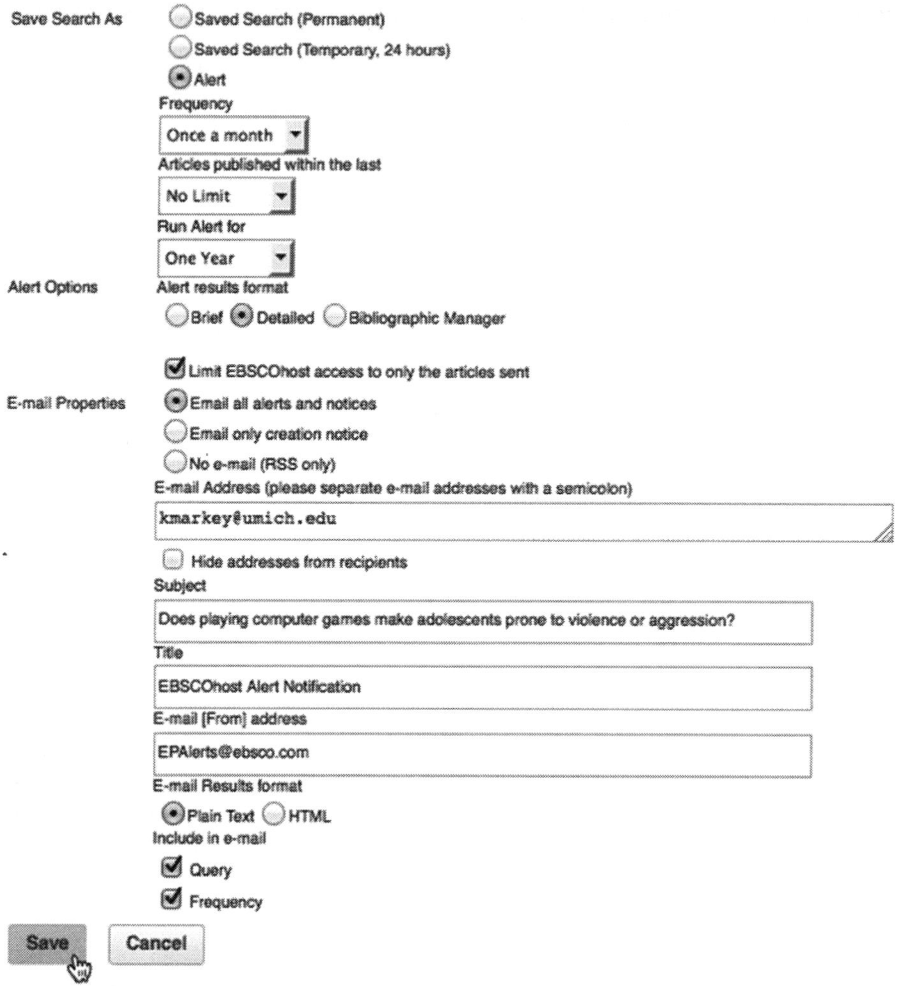

Figure 13.3. Completing EBSCOhost's Search Alerts Form.

search alerts. Keep a diary of the search alerts you set up for users, messaging them periodically, offering to update their search alerts. Finding alerts useful, university faculty may become favorably inclined to libraries generally, inviting you to brief their students on searching for information online.

Managing Saved Sources in Citation Management Systems

Designed specifically to facilitate the library research process are citation management systems (CMSs), which function as both libraries for the user's saved sources and suites of automated tools to help the user manage these sources and cite them in written works. For the most part, the CMS lies dormant on the user's Web browser until the user saves a source from a licensed database or the Web. The CMS senses the saved source, either acknowledging the user's saving action in a temporary pop-up message or opening its interface in a new tab or window where

CMS-based tools are available to the user to manage this source in particular or vis-à-vis the other sources that the user has saved in the CMS. Using CMS-based tools, users can:

- Edit the CMS' automatically generated citations and abstracts (when available) for saved sources
- Attach full-texts, read them, take notes, add tags, and file everything connected with a source together
- Create and name new folders for their projects including nesting folders within folders
- File saved sources into a different folder
- Search citations, abstracts, and even full-texts of saved sources
- Insert footnotes, endnotes, and in-text citations for CMS-saved sources and a bibliography into their paper, formatting everything in a style sheet of one's choosing
- Share saved sources with friends, colleagues, or a research group

The leading CMSs are EndNote, Mendeley, RefWorks, and Zotero. Here's a quick look at the open source Zotero CMS.

The Zotero CMS

Zotero is an extension to the Firefox Web browser that operates in a separate three-paned work-space atop a Web page. Anyone can download Zotero for free at http://www.zotero.org. Figure 13.4 shows the Zotero workspace. You can adjust how much of the Web browser's window Zotero takes up, dismiss Zotero, and recall it in a split second with the click of a few keys. On the left pane are several folders (also known as collections) that the Zotero user has named for various projects past and present. When you start a new project, create and name a new folder, and use it to store promising sources you have retrieved from licensed and open Web databases that pertain to this project. In figure 13.4, the Zotero user has enabled the "Future of Online Searching" folder;

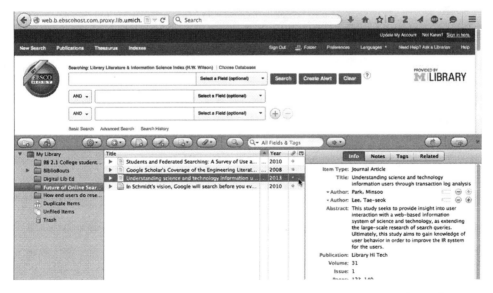

Figure 13.4. Zotero's Three-Paned Workspace. Courtesy of the Roy Rosenzweig Center for History and New Media.

that is, she has moused down on this folder (indicated by the dark-gray bar on the left pane), revealing its contents in the center pane in the form of four sources and their titles, creators, publication dates, and a dot indicating an attached full-text. The third-listed source is enabled, that is, the Zotero user has moused down on its title (indicated by the medium-gray bar on the center pane), revealing the source's citation and abstract in the right pane. While reading the source, the Zotero user can take notes, clicking on the "Notes" link on Zotero's right pane and entering them into the window.

In figure 13.4, EBSCOhost's Library Literature & Information Science database lies underneath Zotero, and it is open to the source entitled "The Declining Value of Subscription-Based Abstracting and Indexing Services in the New Knowledge Dissemination Era" that is cited in chapter 14. To save this source to your Zotero library, hover your computer's cursor over the rectangular "page" icon in the Web browser's address bar and mouse down on it. Zotero responds with a "Saving to . . ." pop-up message (bottom right) and transfers the source's metadata (i.e., citation and [when available] index terms and abstract) and full-text (when technically available) to this Zotero user's "Future of Online Searching" folder. Zotero updates the user's workspace instantaneously, listing the title "The Declining Value of Subscription-Based Abstracting and Indexing Services in the New Knowledge Dissemination Era" in the center pane and displaying its citation and abstract (when available) in the right pane (figure 13.5).

Notice that the center pane bears dots in the far right column under the paper clip icon for all but this newly added source. This means that Zotero wasn't technically able to automatically

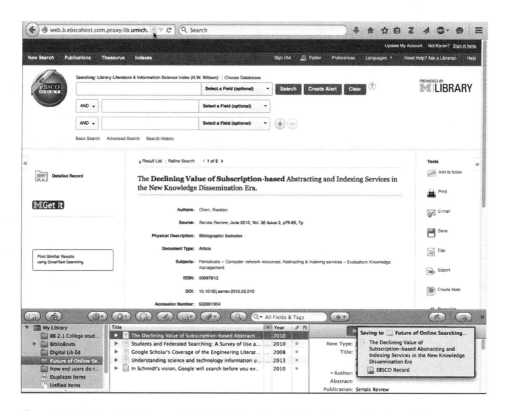

Figure 13.5. Zotero's Workspace Updated with a Newly Added Source. Courtesy of the Roy Rosenzweig Center for History and New Media.

download this source's full-text when it claimed the source's citation and abstract from the database. You can attach it manually, downloading the full-text from the database to a folder on your personal computer and telling Zotero in which folder this full-text resides on your personal computer. A multistep process, it is best understood by watching a video (Zotero 2015). When Zotero senses an attachment for an added source, it adds a dot in the center pane's far right column designating the availability of an attachment, presumably a full-text PDF. Zotero users are not limited to PDFs but can add snapshots of webpages, images, audio and video files, spreadsheets, text files, and much more to entries in their Zotero folders.

Install the free Zotero plug-in for Microsoft Word to facilitate citing sources and producing bibliographies in your written work. On a Mac, a successful installation of this plug-in adds a fully featured Zotero submenu to the Applescript icon (it looks like a scroll or a three-dimensional capital S) in Microsoft Word's main menu. When writing a passage where you cite a saved Zotero source, mouse down on the Applescript icon and choose the Zotero submenu and the "Add Citation" option from the menu. If this is the first time you are adding a citation to your written piece, Zotero will ask you to choose a style sheet, then prompt you to choose the title from your Zotero library. Adding a bibliography to your written piece is as simple as choosing the "Add Bibliography" option from the Zotero submenu, then sitting back and letting Zotero do all the heavy lifting, that is, producing a bibliography for all the sources you cited in your text.

Selling Users on Citation Management Systems

CMSs serve as clearinghouses for users' saved sources and assist them when they cite sources in their written papers, helping them format sources as in-text citations, footnotes, or endnotes, generating a bibliography for the paper and formatting everything according to the user's chosen style sheet.

Having used both RefWorks and Zotero for writing projects both big and small, I am impressed with their versatility, flexibility, and time-savings potential; however, you may be hard-pressed to convince students especially at the high school and undergraduate levels to use a CMS because these systems assume students have a working knowledge of databases, surrogates, full-texts, cited sources, style sheets, and they are comfortable using new technologies. Students especially might not feel the need to save sources until they undertake a major project or develop a serious and potentially long-term interest in a topic, discipline, or field of study. Should you conduct reference interviews with library users who are beginning major projects, you might mention to them in passing that using a CMS may streamline their efforts. If you pique their interest, then invite them to the library's CMS workshops where you and your colleagues show attendees how to use this or that CMS to save and cite sources and produce bibliographies. You could also invite them to make appointments for one-on-one training where you walk them through saving sources in the CMS, then invite them back after they've saved a CMS library of relevant sources so that you can walk them through the process of adding in-text references and generating a bibliography.

Many students aren't ready for a CMS. Perhaps their exposure to information literacy concepts and skills in the grade school levels was limited. To ramp students up in this regard is the NoodleTools research companion, ushering students through the research process while they work on their own or in groups on an actual writing assignment (NoodleTools 2015). NoodleTools isn't limited to students in schools and colleges but appeals to veteran authors who use its organizational tools to document citations, take notes, outline their written works, sequence their notes within the outline, and compose their written pieces.

Teaching Users during the Reference Interview

Reference interviews conducted via email, chat, and phone aren't necessarily naturals for the teachable moment. In the absence of visual cues, the user is left hanging on every word you say or write. Inserting an information literacy tip that deviates significantly from answering the question may confuse the user. Thus, you may prefer to stay on topic when conducting a reference interview via these modes of communication. At the very least, you can walk the user through the steps you take to answer the question. If you sense an impatient user whose sole interest is the answer to his question, perhaps the only information literacy tip that you leave him with is a closing that invites him to contact you or your colleagues anytime in the future.

In-person reference interviews are much more suited to teaching users about online searching and information literacy concepts and skills generally. You will still have to judge how far afield you can go. Limiting your ability may be a host of show-stoppers such as other users who are waiting for your assistance; an impatient user who is pressed for time; or a user who is too preoccupied with a mobile device, an intimate friend, or a crying child to give you their full attention. At the very least, you can swivel your computer monitor around and walk users through what you are doing. You may find yourself giving them the keyboard more than once during the face-to-face reference interview so that they can further the search.

Introduce users to surrogate records and full-texts so that they are able to distinguish between the two in the future. Whether users don't know that the abstract serves as a brief summary of a much longer full-text or they are trying to shortcut their writing assignments, all too often, they limit their interaction with digital texts to surrogate records. Set the record straight so that users understand that securing the full-text is their search objective, not the surrogate record.

Consider making a practice of leaving each and every user with one information literacy-oriented tip above and beyond the information that satisfies their information need. Here are a few ideas to get you started. Choose one or more based on your assessment of the particular situation at hand.

- Showing users how to apply clusters to explore aspects of broad topics or to put into words ideas that they may be struggling to articulate
- Limiting to quality retrievals (usually designated by the database as peer-reviewed, scholarly, or journal articles)
- Linking to full-texts
- Preferring databases at the library's hub over Google and the World Wide Web
- Alerting users to a database's pre-search subject qualifiers that map onto the big ideas (i.e., facets) in their queries
- Inviting users to revisit you and your colleagues in person or via phone, email, or chat

Sustained Teaching Events

Information literacy classes, workshops, and in-service training are sustained events that should provide you with ample opportunities for teaching attendees about online searching. Post your teaching materials online so that attendees can consult them later and refer them to their friends. Bring your business cards to one-shot workshops and workshops series, telling users that it is your business to help them and inviting them to contact you when they get stuck. Promote future information literacy venues and urge users to complete your evaluation forms, telling them that you and your colleagues incorporate their input into future events. Also establish a site where you and your colleagues share your teaching materials so that you can reuse content and coordinate your efforts.

Course Design and Deployment Documentation

Formalize your preparation for sustained teaching events in a course syllabus, lesson plans, and teaching materials. At the highest level of granularity is the course syllabus. It gives everyone—prospective registrants, attendees, you, and your colleagues—an overview of your workshop series or half- or full-semester course. Publish your syllabus on the Web and draw from its contents to generate publicity statements. At the next level of granularity are lesson plans in which you detail what you expect attendees to learn, how you will deliver content, and what methods you will use to check for attendees' understanding (Milkova 2014). At the lowest level of granularity are the course materials and activities you prepare to deploy during class. These might include a LibGuide to which attendees can refer after your presentation ends, providing them with one-stop access to all of the sources you discussed in class along with notes that annotate sources and tell them how they'd benefit from using them. Table 13.1 describes the specific contents of the syllabus, lesson plans, and teaching materials, designates their target audience, and suggests others, including yourself, who would benefit from access to your documentation.

Table 13.1. Course Design and Deployment Documentation

Target Audience	Access	Contents
Syllabus		
Your institution's library users, prospective registrants, course attendees	Your institution's library users, prospective registrants, course attendees, you, and your colleagues	Vital information. Lists course specifics, e.g., instructor's name and contact information, course name, number, etc.
		Description. Describes course content and how attendees will benefit in the long term.
		Organization. Describes how the course will be conducted.
		Learning objectives. In bullet points, describes what attendees will learn as a result of taking the course.
		Schedule of topics. Into a two-column table, schedules course content for the dates that the course meets.
		Reading list, equipment, supplies, etc. Into a two-column table, schedules, readings, equipment, supplies, etc., on the dates that the course meets.
		Grading. For credit-bearing venues, describes graded assignments. Insert them in a four-column table bearing assignment names, brief descriptions, distribution dates, and due dates.
		Expectations. Cites your expectations of attendees, e.g., handling personal emergencies, advice about how to succeed in the course, and rules of conduct.

(continued)

Table 13.1. Course Design and Deployment Documentation *continued*

Target Audience	Access	Contents
Lesson Plans for Each Workshop or Class Period		
You	You and your colleagues	Learning objectives. Describes what you want attendees to learn in this particular workshop or class period.
		Teaching and learning activities. Describes content and content-delivery methods.
		Evaluation strategies. Describes how you will check for attendees' understanding.
Teaching Materials for Each Interaction		
You and course attendees	You, course attendees, and your colleagues	A wide range of actual materials are possible, e.g., notes, outlines, PowerPoint slides, instructional videos, demonstrations, games, journals, role-playing scenarios, case studies, simulations, concept maps, LibGuides, and so on.

Despite your many years being a student on the receiving end of a teacher's instruction, you may find it daunting to be the one doing the teaching. Enroll in an information literacy course in your library school or iSchool where you will learn how people learn, study best practices for integrating library-user instruction with faculty partnerships, and get actual teaching experience where you'll have to draft a syllabus, lesson plans, and teaching materials.

Online Searching Content

To learn about online searching, you took a for-credit, graduate-level course, and your performance, especially with regard to formulating searches that retrieved relevant information, was tested. Few, if any, end users will do the same; in fact, when a select group of university professors were given the same training that you received (minus the tests), they reverted back to their original behavior within six months, querying search systems using natural language search statements (Bates, Wilde, and Siegfried 1995). Thus, expecting end users, even those with expert knowledge in their chosen discipline, to learn and apply Boolean searching techniques or the searching language of the go-to database in their selected discipline may be a pipe dream. Using the steps of the online searching process as an outline, here is online searching content that is appropriate for teaching users in sustained information literacy events.

SELECTING A DATABASE (STEP 1)

When it comes to selecting a database, expect end users to glom onto the Internet, and when they have exhausted the basic stuff they find there, come to you to find specialized information. Promote your library's database hub as *the* source of reliable and trusted information. If users want a Wikipedia-like experience that will provide them with easy-to-understand information, suggest hub-based encyclopedias such as the World Book and Encyclopedia Britannica or encyclopedia databases such as Oxford Reference and the Gale Virtual Reference Library. Qualify the sources that they'll find there, telling them that disciplinary experts have written the encyclopedia's entries and cited the most important sources written on the topic at the end of their articles. When an encyclopedia article says something that is spot-on, instruct users to check the passage for cited references and follow up with searches for the cited reference's full-text because it is likely to provide more detail that they can use in their assignments.

Encyclopedic databases such as Academic OneFile, ProQuest Research Library, and Reader's Guide Abstracts may be the next step up from encyclopedias, yielding sources that don't require mastery of disciplinary knowledge to understand. News databases such as Factiva, LexisNexis Academic, NewsBank, and ProQuest Newsstand also have basic content.

At the academy, users are likely to receive directives from their instructors regarding the use of scholarly or peer-reviewed sources, so bring to their attention pre-search qualifiers that enable them to limit content in this regard. Because users can't count on every database having such qualifiers, instruct users on how to differentiate between scholarly and non-scholarly sources. Eventually, academic instructors will require students to search for information in their discipline's go-to database for domain experts. Demonstrate your library's database hub where users can search databases by subject. Additionally, many libraries use LibGuides to organize and provide access to their digital resources, creating electronic cheat-sheets that enumerate and annotate the full array of digital resources in a discipline or on a topic so that users understand when and why they'd use them for their research. Consider doing the same for your library's users.

TYPECASTING THE QUERY (STEP 2)

Although most users will conduct subject searches, on occasion they will seek known-items. Because searching for known-items is different from subject searching, users must be able to distinguish between the two. Define the two search types. In a subject search, the user wants information *about* a topic, person, place, organization, and so on. In a known-item search, users want a specific source they know exists such as a book, an article, film, etc., that *is called* "[insert title]" and/or *is by* [insert author's name]. Give users sample queries to typecast, letting them work with classmates so that they can deliberate on typecasting together.

CONDUCTING THE FACET ANALYSIS AND LOGICAL COMBINATION FOR SUBJECTS (STEP 3)

In subject searches, facet analysis is critical to online searching. When users get the facet analysis "right," their chances of finding relevant information increase substantially. What prevents them from getting it right is their failure to express their interests fully. Perhaps they haven't given their topics much thought, their lack of knowledge about the discipline underlying their topics affects their ability to fully specify things, or they are self-conscious about revealing their true interests. Whatever the reason, the facet analysis is not the time for users to hold back. Emphasize to users that they must be forthcoming about their interests in the statements they enter into search systems. Reading minds isn't something search systems are able to do. Users have to "let it all hang out." Failing to specify one or more facets means that retrievals aren't likely to specify the missing facet(s), and if they do, it's purely by chance.

When you talk about the facet analysis with users, you might want to substitute the phrase "big idea" or "concept" instead of "facet" because some users won't know what "facet" means. Use your judgment, inserting terminology you feel is understandable to your library's users.

Define the facet analysis for users. A facet is a separate aspect (i.e., idea, set, notion, part, component, object, or entity) of a query. It represents one idea. It can be expressed in one word, e.g., insurgency, automobile, ivory, or norway, and it can be expressed in a phrase that through the years has come to mean one idea, e.g., lung cancer, zebra mussels, jack pine, or genetically modifiable crops.

Advise users to conduct the facet analysis *before* they start searching. If they have trouble conducting the facet analysis, invite them to write down their queries, choosing the one prompt below that "feels right" to them and completing the sentence with their query:

- I want to know whether _____.
- I am interested in _____.
- I need information on _____.
- I want to know about _____.
- I am researching _____.

Table 13.2 shows how five different users responded to the above prompts, inserting their queries into the right column. Before proceeding with the next step, ask users to review what they've written. Does it really express their interests? Have they "let it all hang out," saying what's *really* on their mind? Give them a moment to revise what's there, even choosing another prompt and completing it with their query.

Table 13.2. Using Prompts to Elicit Queries from Users

I want to know whether	genetically modifiable crops affect people's health.
I am interested in	the collapse of the Soviet Union.
I need information on	cyanobacteria as a source of alternative energy.
I want to know about	going to college, does it change people's behavior?
I am researching	why one should not take life too seriously.

Next, instruct users to dissect their query into single words and phrases that express the big ideas that interest them. Two or three big ideas are usually enough. Five big ideas are too many. The easiest way to do this is to underline single words or phrases in their sentences. Table 13.3 shows such underlined words and phrases for the five queries.

Table 13.3. Inviting Users to Dissect Their Queries into Big Ideas

I want to know whether	genetically modifiable crops affect people's health.
I am interested in	the collapse of the Soviet Union.
I need information on	cyanobacteria as a source of alternative energy.
I want to know about	going to college; does it change people's behavior?
I am researching	why one should not take life too seriously.

Finally, ask users to scrutinize their queries. If their underlined phrases exceed two words, ask them to simplify them. For example, if an underlined phrase is an adjectival phrase made up of three or more words, challenge them to reconceive it as two big ideas or reduce it to two words without losing meaning or sacrificing specificity; if one of their underlined phrases is a prepositional phrase, suggest that they consolidate their interests into a single noun or two-word adjectival phrase. In table 13.4, three users have revised their big ideas under their original underlined words and phrases: (1) breaking up "genetically modifiable crops" into "genetic modification" and "crops," (2) restating "change people's behavior" as "behavior change," and (3) restating "not take life too seriously" as "conduct of life."

Table 13.4. Advising Users to Break Up or Restate Wordy Big Ideas

I want to know whether	genetically modifiable crops affect people's health.
	genetic modification crops health
I am interested in	the collapse of the Soviet Union.
I need information on	cyanobacteria as a source of alternative energy.
I want to know about	whether going to college effects a change in people's behavior.
	college behavior change
I am researching	why one should not take life too seriously.
	conduct of life

If users underline only one word or phrase, ask them to rethink their interests, digging deep inside themselves for the wherewithal to describe in written or spoken words what is only a vague notion right now inside their heads. If they still come up empty handed, then that's fine. Their query is a candidate for the Friends Strategy and searches in a database that features post-search clusters. For example, the Conduct of Life query might benefit from clusters in a psychology, sociology, or religion database, even in an encyclopedic database.

Getting users to specify their subject queries, break them into facets, and transform them into search statements to which Boolean and extended-Boolean search systems respond with relevant retrievals is difficult to do. The University of Texas Libraries has developed a computer-assisted approach to help users with Boolean searching (University of Texas at Austin 2013). Called a keyword-generator, it uses a three-step process to script user queries into Boolean search statements.

REPRESENTING THE SUBJECT SEARCH AS INPUT TO THE SEARCH SYSTEM (STEP 4)

Users' underlined words and phrases or their restated words and phrases are the search terms that they should enter into their selected database(s). If the search system offers separate search boxes connected with the Boolean AND operator, advise the user to enter one underlined/restated word or phrase per search box. If the user runs out of search boxes, she could add a row or begin her search with what she thinks are the most important big ideas, entering the remaining big ideas only if her retrievals are too broad, too many, or a combination of the two. Even better than entering these remaining big ideas is browsing the database's clusters in search of subjects or classification captions that are satisfactory representations of one or more remaining big ideas and applying them.

In figure 13.6 the user enters the search terms collapse and soviet union into two separate search boxes in the ProQuest Research Library. The user has to exercise her judgment, deciding whether to add quotes to phrases. Doing so may stop search systems from performing automatic stemming, for example, retrieving plural and singular forms and forms bearing different word endings, e.g., -ed, -ing, -ation. In this case, adding quotes to the search term soviet union may be warranted to limit retrieval to this particular place only. In a search for the Going to College query, it makes sense to omit quotes from the restated search term behavior change so that retrieval extends to phrases such as changes in behavior, behavioral changes, and changing one's behavior.

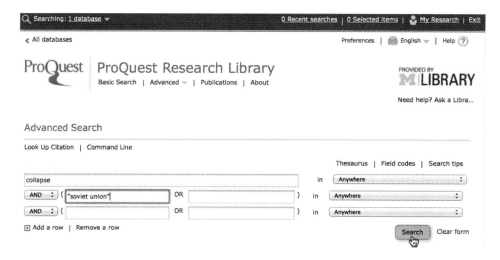

Figure 13.6. Entering Search Terms into Separate Search Boxes Combined by the Boolean AND Operator into the ProQuest Research Library Database. The screenshots and their contents are published with permission of ProQuest LLC. Further reproduction is prohibited without permission. Inquiries may be made to: ProQuest LLC, 789 E. Eisenhower Pkwy, Ann Arbor, MI 48106-1346 USA. Telephone (734) 761-4700; Email: info@proquest.com; Web page: http://www.proquest.com.

If the database offers a single search box, advise the user to switch to the advanced interface. If the single search box is still there, then trial and error may be in order. The user should enter her search terms, entering the most important big idea first (with or without quotes in the case of a phrase) and placing the Boolean AND operator in between the terms that represent each big idea:

genetic modification AND crops AND health

If retrievals are relevant, then the user should pursue them. If the system produces too few or no retrievals, then advise the user to enter her search terms minus the Boolean AND operator:

genetic modification crops health

This second search statement is for an extended-Boolean system. If it fails to produce retrievals the second time around, perhaps the user should choose a different database.

Personally, before switching to a different database, I would browse the database's thesaurus (if it has one), searching for CV terms that are synonyms for one or more of my search terms; however, I am an expert searcher who knows how to use a database's thesaurus. Use involves several actions—spotting a database's thesaurus on the search system's interface, browsing the thesaurus for appropriate search terms, interpreting term relationship designations, and substituting my search terms for more appropriate thesaurus terms. Furthermore, thesauri are not standard issue across all databases, they designate term relationships in different ways, and they are implemented differently in search systems. Whether to teach end users about the role of the thesaurus in online searching is a judgment call on your part because of the complexity that the thesaurus adds to the searching process. Before making a hard-and-fast decision about introducing students to a database's thesaurus, experiment in sustained interactions with upperclassmen and graduate students who are studying in a discipline with a go-to database that features a thesaurus to determine whether students glom onto the thesaurus, it confuses them, or they opt to ignore it.

CHOOSING A SUBJECT SEARCH STRATEGY (STEP 5)

Recommend the À la Carte Edition of the Building Block Strategy for multifaceted topics. This means entering one salient search term per facet. Because users won't know whether they are searching a Boolean or extended-Boolean search system, they might have to enter their search statements twice, the first time with Boolean AND operators in between their search terms, and if retrievals aren't satisfactory, the second time without the Boolean AND operators. When you present this strategy to users, explain the analogy behind its name and use *Online Searching*'s visual representation of this strategy so that it is vivid to them (pages 127–28), making it likely that they'll remember it and execute it in the future.

The À la Carte Edition of the Building Block Strategy isn't much different from how users conduct subject searches now. Calling their search terms keywords, users enter the first words that pop into their minds. À la Carte adds discipline and deliberation to the search term selection and entry tasks:

- Urging users to be forthcoming about the full scope of their interests
- Expressing these interests in a sentence
- Extracting the big ideas from the sentence
- Repackaging their big ideas: Dividing complex big ideas into two facets and/or consolidating wordy ones into shorter adjectival phrases or simple nouns

REDUCING TOO MANY AND INCREASING TOO FEW RETRIEVALS (STEP 6)

The Citation Pearl Growing Strategy helps users whose subject searches produce too few retrievals find additional ones. To execute this strategy, users must scrutinize few retrievals, looking for synonyms for their search terms. For example, retrievals for the Crops and Cyanobacteria queries use the terms "transgenic plants" and "reusable energy" instead of "genetic modification" and "alternative energy," respectively. Substituting the former for the latter is likely to increase the number of relevant retrievals because the former are the CV terms that science databases use to refer to the latter.

Three other approaches for increasing retrievals are find-like searches, backward chaining, and forward chaining. Find-like isn't available in all search systems and databases but when it is, it requires a minimum of effort on the user's part. The user only has to identify a relevant source among his retrievals, then click on the accompanying find-like link to trigger the search system to find more like it. Find a relevant source in any licensed or open Web database, switch to WoS, and conduct a known-item search for the source. When you find it, clicking on its "N Cited References" or "M Times Cited" initiates backward or forward chaining, respectively. Scan cited references and times-cited references for relevant ones, and full-texts are a click away via accompanying resolver links. This is push-button research. What could be easier?

Clusters aren't available for every database and search system, but when they are, they characterize retrievals from a variety of perspectives, providing users with a means of reducing high-posted searches using non-subject criteria such as date of publication, language, and genre. Additionally, the subject clusters that systems construct from co-occurring index terms and classification captions help users who are uncertain about their topics, giving them ideas for subtopics they might pursue. Benefiting the most from subject clusters are users whose facet analysis bears one facet. Encourage them to browse subject and classification clusters in search of interesting subtopics. For example, the user who poses a Conduct of Life query is definitely a candidate for a search in a psychology, sociology, or religion database that features clusters.

EVALUATING RETRIEVALS (STEP 7)

Because users gravitate to the World Wide Web where anyone can author, sponsor, and publish information, it is important to dedicate some of your sustained interaction with users to source credibility, possibly engaging them in an activity in which they experience source credibility from the perspective of the people putting the message on the Web and the people receiving it. For example, challenge them to generate strategies that they would use to persuade website visitors about an issue, purchase a product, or support an organization. Then turn the tables, so to speak, challenging them to generate strategies that they would use to expose a website's persuasive tactics and counter them so that they could use the information that they find there instead of entirely dismissing it out of hand. Check out the wide range of approaches that library practitioners devised to instruct users about source credibility (Abilock 2012; Baildon and Baildon 2012; Gardner, Benham, and Newell 1999; Myhre 2012; Schrock 2009; Zhang, Duke, and Jiménez 2011).

Asked to provide evidence of why a source is relevant, users overwhelmingly point to specific subject matter that the source contains or to the overlap between their topic of interest and a particular source's contents (Markey, Leeder, and Rieh 2014, 144). When users have difficulty assessing relevance, they usually don't have a firm grasp on their topic of interest. On a personal note, I recall floundering over a literature search—I just couldn't put into words what I wanted. A colleague recommended that I read a particular article, but I failed to see how this article related to my ill-defined interests. It took me over a year to firm up my topic, and when I did, that very article was the linchpin in my understanding of the topic.

That relevance is a moving target subject to users' knowledge about a topic and their exposure to newly retrieved sources is built into the Berrypicking Model of information retrieval (pages 30–31). When you discuss relevance with users, comment on this as well on the research that demonstrates people's propensity to depend on the first few ranked retrievals to the exclusion of all other retrievals and to project relevance on them (page 202). As much as users would like there to be a "little man" inside the computer who makes intellectual decisions about the closeness of their ranked retrievals vis-à-vis the queries they have in mind, no such little man exists in search systems. Relevance ranking is little more than a numbers game, wholly dependent upon matches between a user's search terms and the terms in titles, abstracts, and index terms; their closeness in written text; their occurrences in more important fields (usually titles and index terms) over less important fields (usually full-texts); and much more. As a consequence, advise users to be circumspect about retrievals lists, going beyond the first few listed ones in pursuit of useful information and taking retrievals at face value instead of reading into them what they want them to say. Finally, talk to users about their unspoken desire to find the perfect source that matches exactly what they want to say. Rarely does such a source exist. Instead, users who are engaged in an in-depth project should expect to synthesize the information they find, drawing on qualified others for insight, knowledge, and understanding to complete an assignment, form an opinion, make a decision, or take decisive action.

MANAGING RETRIEVALS (STEP 8)

Walk users through surrogate records, showing them the citations that they'll use later to cite in their written works and the titles, index terms, and abstracts that are helpful for determining a source's relevance and convincing them that securing the source's full-text is their next step. Too many users terminate their search at the surrogate—they think that the surrogate is the full-text, securing full-texts is difficult, the abstract is sufficient for their needs, or they have too many other things to do to bother with full-texts.

Demonstrate how to find full-texts. This includes artifacts from the library's physical collection such as books, journals, and films. Make sure users understand that the surrogate record is just that, a surrogate, and that they'll want to secure the full-text to read what the author has to say about the subject.

Reading full-texts from cover-to-cover isn't necessary for the majority of retrievals. Instruct users on how to perform a technical reading of a lengthy text so they can invest the time they save reading full-texts for the most relevant sources (page 205). Refer them to how-to guides on reading scientific papers (Fosmire 2015; Madooei 2014).

The sustained interaction is the right venue for introducing users to citation management systems (CMS) for managing their retrievals. Schedule the CMS workshop when users are beset with research assignments and receptive to methods for organizing their retrievals and citing them in their written works. Your workshop publicity should suggest that they come to the workshop with a handful of retrievals so they can get started, populating the CMS with these retrievals and using them to insert footnotes, cited references, and a bibliography into a paper they are writing.

CONDUCTING SEARCHES FOR KNOWN-ITEMS (STEPS 1 TO 8)

Facet analysis is critical to known-item searches too. What the user knows about the source—its title, author, publisher, the journal it's published in—are the facets of the known-item search. Because extended-Boolean systems are forgiving about inaccuracies, misspellings, and incomplete data, it makes sense for end users to search there first. Advise them to copy and paste as much of the citation that they have in hand into the WSD system to see if it retrieves the desired source. Failing to find the desired source, users should truncate their copied citations to author and title, then to the title only. Follow up in Google Scholar (entering it through your library's database hub), Google, and Open WorldCat, entering the full copied-and-pasted citation, then truncating it to author and title, then to the title only.

In a Boolean search system such as your library's OPAC, it's more efficient searching for one facet at a time, first searching the known title and scanning retrievals for the desired one, then replacing the title with the known author and scanning retrievals for the desired one. Most Boolean search systems feature a "fields" pull-down menu adjacent their search box. Pull down and choose the "title" field for known title searches or "author" field for known author searches.

In OPACs, browsing the system's title index or its author index for the known title or known author should quickly and efficiently produce the desired source. Follow up in a database aggregator's search system, searching all EBSCOhost, all Gale, or all ProQuest databases in one fell swoop, or in a journal aggregator's search system, searching all Springer (SpringerLink database), all Taylor & Francis (Taylor & Francis Online Journals database), or all Elsevier (ScienceDirect database) publications.

Failed known-item searches eventually become subject searches. On a personal note, I sought a fifty-year-old advertisement for my Visual Persuasion course. Knowing only the advertiser (Kodak) and a few words from its song ("Turn Around"), I entered them into Google, kodak turn around, and voilà, Google's first-listed retrieval was spot-on.

Teaching Tips

Going hand-in-hand with teaching people how to be effective online searchers is understanding how people learn. For all the detail, supplement your school's information literacy course with elective courses on learning in your institution's education department.

Eventually, you will find yourself teaching library users in a variety of venues, and you will want to do your best. Here are teaching tips to keep in mind as you prepare for the big moment.

- *Be the epitome of organization.* Compose a syllabus for half- and semester-long classes and workshop series. Distribute an agenda that enumerates major class-period activities. If you lecture, begin with an outline that summarizes the content you expect to cover. Review your lectures in advance, making sure you haven't crammed too much into the allotted time period and your content is ordered logically.
- *Know your audience.* Do some research about your audience in advance. Here are some examples. If an academic instructor invites you to his class, interview her in advance to learn about the course, for example, the course assignment that is the impetus for your presentation to students, and the instructor's special instructions to students about the sources and databases she expects them to use. If you are conducting a reference interview, ask the user tactfully about his comfort level with technical or advanced material so you can select a database that bears sources that he is likely to understand. If you are conducting a one-shot class, check evaluation forms that attendees completed the last time it was offered to see their suggestions for improvements.
- *Don't overwhelm users.* If you are teaching a class, limit your teaching objectives to what you can accomplish in the time allotted, leaving ample time for questions, evaluations, and minimal deviations from your lesson plan. Librarians always want to be comprehensive, and that includes overwhelming users with too many relevant retrievals and databases. Cool it! Less is more. If faculty assign you more than you can cover, you'll have to be frank with them, negotiating how much and what you can cover in the allotted time period.
- *Substitute active learning for lecturing and demonstrations.* Online searching is a natural for active learning because users *do* online searching. They interact with an online system that produces results instantaneously, allowing them to experiment in a penalty-free environment and save what they do for post-search debriefings and analyses. Whether you are teaching young people or older adults, devise situations where they experience online searching firsthand and have opportunities to share their observations about their searches and search results with others.
- *Don't jump the gun.* If you ask attendees a question or ask for volunteers to share their online searching experiences, wait for an answer. People hesitate because they know they'll feel bad if they give a wrong answer or their participation isn't up to snuff. This is especially apparent

with older learners who don't want to lose face. On a personal note, I tell students that I prefer wrong over right answers because we get to languish over a search that went awry, brainstorming on what went wrong and what we'd do to improve things.

- *Admit when you don't know the answer to someone's question.* To be honest, most people's body language reveals when they don't know an answer, so don't bother faking one. Promise to follow up with the answer at the next class meeting or via email. If you don't have time to follow up, give everyone one minute to find an answer right then and there, or, in a credit-bearing course, offer extra credit to the first person who messages you the right answer. Always commend the inquirer whose question has you stumped.

- *Expect the unexpected.* The database, search system, or user-authentication system goes down. The projector breaks. There's a fire drill. You go farther afield than you want to go answering a student's question. Instead of losing your cool, take a few deep breaths, and relax your shoulders, jaw, or wherever you tense up under stress. Then consider the situation and respond accordingly. If you lose a significant amount of time to unexpected events, you could consider a make-up class or contact users to inform them when the class repeats in the future.

- *Be reflective about your assistance to users.* Debrief mentally about your assistance to users. Initially, this means everything—how you greet them, how you elicit what they really want, how you put your knowledge of the information universe to work to answer their questions— so you can develop a modus operandi with which you are comfortable. Then turn your attention to reference interviews that you think went really well or really badly. With regard to the latter, be honest with yourself about what you did, what you wish you would have done, and how you'll respond more effectively to a similar situation in the future. This isn't about beating yourself up, it's about learning from your experiences and priming yourself so that you do better in the future. Balance your debriefing with reflecting on the former so that you can build on your successes in future interactions. Revisit your modus operandi from time to time, tweaking it as needed.

- *Ask your colleagues.* It's impossible to know everything about online searching, teaching, information literacy, and library science generally. If you are stumped, consult your colleagues, telling them where you've checked when you ask for their help. When it comes to interpersonal interactions, group dynamics, in-class policies, and the like, check with your more experienced colleagues because they've probably encountered much the same and experimented with and instituted solutions that work. When you are new on the job, your colleagues will expect you to ask questions and seek their advice. Use this initial "honeymoon" period to test your colleagues, observing whom you can trust and take into your confidence.

- *Prepare in advance, and practice, practice, practice!* Preparing well in advance gives you the opportunity to stew over your presentation, filling in gaps, improving on your original plans, and checking points that you are unsure of. Take advantage of every opportunity to make oral presentations so that you become accustomed to speaking to groups, expressing yourself extemporaneously, answering questions, handling the unexpected, and much more. Most of all, you want to overcome the jitters. It won't happen overnight, but one day, you'll notice several hours after your presentation is over that you didn't even think about getting nervous.

Questions

Questions 1 to 5 give you hands-on experience saving searches and retrievals and sharing them with another person, just like you'll have to do at the reference desk. So, with your laptop in hand, pair up with a friend or classmate, making sure that either one or the two of you have signed up for a CMS account on EndNote, Mendeley, RefWorks, or Zotero. Sit side-by-side, choose a database, and conduct a multifaceted search for a topic of your own choosing or a topic that you have encountered in *Online Searching*. Examples are Television Violence, Wandering Mind, Eating Disorders, and Reducing Bullying. If the database's search system allows sets and Boolean operators, enter multiple search terms for each facet, then combine intermediate results into a final answer set using the Boolean AND operator. Now you are ready to answer these questions.

1. Often, you'll conduct a search that gets the library user started, then send her your search so she can pick up where you left off. Using the search you just conducted, share it with your friend using the system's search-sharing capability. By the way, you might have to register for an account to share searches in your chosen database's search system.
2. Alternatively, checkmark potentially relevant retrievals, then use this system's retrievals-sharing capability to send them to your friend via email.
3. There are many reasons for saving a search. For example, you don't have time to finish the search, you aren't getting the results you expected and need to give it more time and thought, or you expect more users to approach you asking for your help with the search you just conducted. Save your ongoing search. By the way, you might have to register for an account to save searches.
4. Now that you have an account in this search system, what else can you do with your saved searches and retrievals?
5. Which CMS do you use? Demonstrate it to your friend, showing him or her how to save a retrieval, both its citation and its full-text, into the CMS. While the CMS is open, show your friend other retrievals you've saved and tell him or her when and why you use this CMS.

Here are more questions. In addition to checking your answers with those concluding this chapter, discuss them in class with your classmates.

6. In a face-to-face reference interview, what verbal or non-verbal cues might reveal that the user would be receptive to information literacy instruction right then and there, especially instruction that is related to but goes beyond your answers to the user's query? Do you think that there is ever an opportunity to provide information literacy training during phone or chat interviews? Tell why or why not, and if you've had experiences in this regard, share them with your classmates.
7. A user asks an in-depth query that snowballs into a series of unsuccessful searches across multiple databases including your library's OPAC and WSD system. You are stumped. What do you do next?
8. Upon a colleague's unexpected resignation to take a new job, you are tasked with teaching her new half-semester information literacy course. You hardly have a month to prepare. How can you streamline your preparation before the course starts?
9. How do you know that you've not only answered the user's question but you've saturated him with too much information?

Summary

Enter http://www.onlinesearching.org/p/13-interacting.html into your Web browser for a video on searching for information online.

This chapter comes full circle, back to your interaction with users, surveying what you should teach them about online searching. The framework for this chapter's recommendations about specific online searching content for information literacy instruction is the online searching process. Such content is appropriate for sustained teaching events—information literacy classes, workshops, and in-service training. These events may also warrant the preparation of a course syllabus, lesson plans, and teaching materials.

Make the most of the reference interview, teaching users what you can sandwich into the short period of time that you have with them. You may be inclined to stay on topic when conducting reference interviews via chat, email, or phone because users can't see you, and thus, they are left hanging on every word you say or write. At the very least, you can walk users through the steps you take to answer their questions. Good listeners may catch on, able to answer comparable questions on their own in the future. Always close the interview with an invitation to contact you or your colleagues anytime in the future.

In-person reference interviews, personal appointments, the one-shot information literacy class, the standalone workshop or workshop series, and the half- or full-semester courses are much more suited to teaching users about online searching and information literacy concepts and skills generally. If you are pressed for time due to the number of users who are queued for reference service, turn your computer monitor toward the user and explain what you are doing at each step of the way. Make a habit of adding at least one kernel of wisdom above and beyond what the user wants but that is intimately connected with what he wants, and if you fail to achieve this goal with each and every user, be confident that backing off was the right thing to do.

Punctuating the searching process is retrievals management. For most users, managing retrievals is a one-time event connected with the project at hand and the save-retrievals functionality in the one system they search may be sufficient. Reusing sources may appeal to users who are close to committing to a discipline or involved in a long-term endeavor such as a capstone project, senior thesis, book, business plan, or patent. Such users may be favorably inclined to exploring the potentials of third-party software applications called citation management systems (CMSs). Not only do CMSs enable users to save sources, they provide tools to help users organize, find, share, and cite their sources in written papers.

Bibliography

Abilock, Debbie. 2012. "True—Or Not?" *Educational Leadership* 69, no. 6: 70–74.

Baildon, Mark, and Rindi Baildon. 2012. "Evaluating Online Sources: Helping Students Determine Trustworthiness, Readability, and Usefulness." *Social Studies and the Young Learner* 24, no. 4: 11–14.

Bates, Marcia J., Deborah N. Wilde, and Susan Siegfried. 1995. "Research Practices of Humanities Scholars in an Online Environment: The Getty Online Searching Project Report No. 3." *Library and Information Science Research* 17 (Winter): 5–40.

Fosmire, Michael. 2015. "Tutorials—Scientific Paper." Accessed March 26, 2015. https://www.lib.purdue.edu/help/tutorials/scientific-paper.

Gardner, Susan A., Hiltraut H. Benham, and Bridget M. Newell. 1999. "Oh, What a Tangled Web We've Woven! Helping Students Evaluate Sources." *The English Journal* 89, no. 1: 39–44.

Madooei, Ali. 2014. "The Art of Reading Research Papers." Accessed March 26, 2015. http://www.sfu.ca/~amadooei/files/ReadingAdvice.pdf.

Markey, Karen, Chris Leeder, and Soo Young Rieh. 2014. *Designing Online Information Literacy Games Students Want to Play.* Lanham, MD: Rowman & Littlefield.

Milkova, Stiliana. 2014. "Strategies for Effective Lesson Planning." Accessed March 26, 2015. http://www.crlt.umich.edu/gsis/p2_5.

Myhre, Sarah K. 2012. "Using the CRAAP Test to Evaluate Websites." Presented at the *17th Annual Technology, Colleges, and Community Worldwide Online Conference,* April 17. Accessed March 26, 2015. http://hdl.handle.net/10125/22479.

NoodleTools. 2015. "NoodleTools, a Powerful, Integrated Platform for Research & Literacy: Product Info." Accessed March 26, 2015. http://www.noodletools.com/tools/index.php.

Schrock, Kathy. 2009. "The Five W's of Web Site Evaluation." Accessed March 26, 2015. http://www.schrockguide.net/uploads/3/9/2/2/392267/5ws.pdf.

University of Texas at Austin. 2013. "How to Generate Keywords." Last modified March 25, 2014, accessed March 26, 2015. http://www.lib.utexas.edu/keywords/index.php.

Zhang, Shenglan, Nell K. Duke, and Laura M. Jiménez. 2011. "The WWWDOT Approach to Improving Students' Critical Evaluation of Websites." *Reading Teacher* 65, no. 2: 150–58.

Zotero. 2015. "Adding Items to Your Zotero Library." Last modified February 2, 2015, accessed March 26, 2015. https://www.zotero.org/support/getting_stuff_into_your_library.

Suggested Reading

Dobbs, Aaron W., Ryan Sittler, and Douglas Cook, eds. 2013. *Using LibGuides to Enhance Library Services.* Chicago: American Library Associations.

Answers

Specific answers to questions 1 to 5 are not given because they depend on the particular databases you have chosen. Add to this chapter's suggested answers to questions 6 to 10 with ideas generated from in-class discussions.

1. **Search-sharing capability**

   Not all systems have a search-sharing capability. "Share" is the name Gale and EBSCOhost use for this on their search-result pages. Other links named "export," "save," or "email" usually pertain to retrievals, *not* to the *search*. If you cannot find an appropriate link, copy the search-result page's URL and paste it into an email message. Send it to your friend, asking him or her to make sure it works.

   When you are successful finding a way to share your search with a friend, check whether it reports intermediate sets or just the final result set that is a Boolean combination of two or more sets. Which would you prefer, intermediate sets or one final result set, and why?

2. **Retrievals-sharing capability**

   Almost all systems have a retrievals-sharing capability. One challenge is figuring out what link triggers sharing. Test the system's links called "email," "save," "share," and "export" with your friend until you find the right one. Your tests should reveal the many ways search systems enable you to share retrievals. A second challenge is deciding whether to send all retrievals to the user or to review them, sending only the most relevant retrievals. Time constraints usually force the issue, and when they do, add a note to your email message telling the user to scan retrievals for relevance.

3. **Search-saving capability**

   Not all search systems allow users to save their searches. When they do, you have to register for an account so the system knows how to connect you with your saved retrievals now and in the future. Use a mnemonic name for your saved searches and make notes that tell why you saved it as a reminder in the future.

4. Your search-system account

What you can do with your account depends on the search system in which you registered. Check to see if this system allows you to do the following, and if it can do more, add to this list:

- Edit a saved search
- Save retrieved sources in custom folders, name folders, move sources between folders, copy sources into other folders, and delete sources from folders
- Add notes to retrieved sources and edit or delete your notes
- Add more custom folders, nest folders within folders, and delete folders
- Add a search alert, edit an existing one, or delete it
- Add a journal alert, edit an existing one, or delete it

5. CMS demonstration

Almost all search systems have a CMS save-and-export capability. The challenge is figuring out what system link triggers it. A dead giveaway that you've found the correct link is a menu prompting you to export the retrieval into a CMS and naming specific CMSs such as EndNote, RefWorks, or Mendeley. Zotero is different from these CMSs. Because it is a pervasive presence on your browser, whenever you display retrievals in the browser window, a "Save to Zotero" icon appears in the browser's address field, allowing you to click on the icon to download the source(s) into your Zotero library without ever leaving the database or webpage from which you retrieved it. Since you've got your CMS open, give your friend a tour, telling him or her what you like and don't like about it.

6. Information literacy training

- Cues that users are receptive in this regard are their lingering after you've answered their question, their follow-up questions that go beyond your answers, their return visits for assistance related to their original question, and the depth that you're able to achieve in the course of answering their questions.
- Of the two interview types, phone interviews have more promise. When a user asks for clarification, you may be able to back up, giving more background information or explaining in simpler terms than you intended. If the user asks an in-depth query, you might ask if she could visit you in the library so that she can follow along and make sure your research is on the right track.

7. You are stumped

Admit to the user that you are having difficulty answering the question. Users facing immediate deadlines may change their topic right then and there. Users less concerned about time constraints are usually willing to give you their email address so you can do some research on your own, including consulting your colleagues.

8. Streamlining new-course preparation

- Before your colleague leaves, ask him to share what he has prepared to date.
- Draft a syllabus, breaking course content into smaller modules and scheduling it into each class period.
- Reuse course content from your previous courses.

- Show your syllabus to colleagues, asking them to share their materials with you.
- Formulate lesson plans only for content that is entirely new to you or that you feel unsure about.
- Search ERIC, Library Literature, Inspec, and other databases for course materials.

9. **Saturating the user with too much information**

   When you notice one or more of these verbal and non-verbal cues, the user is saturated and it's time for you to stop:

   - The user rustles or gathers up her laptop, papers, backpack, purse, and coat.
   - The user no longer maintains eye contact with you.
   - The user starts looking around the room instead of at you.
   - The user keeps nodding her head in agreement with what you are saying.
   - The user grabs her phone to check a text or incoming call.
   - The user starts to move away.
   - The user crosses her arms or moves from an open to a closed body stance.

14

Online Searching Now and in the Future

This final chapter discusses several important online searching issues, some probing the milieu in which expert intermediary searchers conduct their work and others speculating on the factors that are likely to shape online searching in the years to come. *Online Searching* concludes with a wish list of improvements to today's search systems and databases.

Current Trends and Issues

Here is a discussion of seven current trends and issues that are bound to play an important role in how online searching evolves over the next three to five years.

Satisficing in the Age of the Information Explosion

Beginning in the 1960s, the term *information explosion* came to be associated with the explosive growth in scholarship. Recent studies estimate that the volume of scholarly publications doubles every twenty-four years (Bornmann and Mutz 2014; Pautasso 2012). This doubling is both a curse and a blessing. On one hand, it makes it hard for domain experts to keep abreast of the latest developments in their chosen specialties and for aspiring scholars to achieve mastery of theirs. On the other, it means that there is plenty of information available on just about any topic under the sun. For most end users, finding what they want involves entering a few keywords into their favorite search system, scanning the first few retrievals above the fold, and expecting them to link to sources that satisfy their queries. The term *satisficing* has come to be associated with this information-seeking approach. The combination of *satisfy* and *suffice*, satisficing means "setting an acceptable level or aspiration level as a final criterion and simply taking the first acceptable [solution]" (Newell and Simon 1972, 681).

Satisficing is contrasted with *optimal decision-making*—finding the best decision option. Marchionini (1995, 63–64) suggests that satisficing may be the only viable option available to information seekers in view of the herculean effort that would be needed to gather *all* pertinent information for an in-depth query and the time required to fully assimilate it. In short, people *satisfice* with regard to their information needs, finding information that is *good enough* and applying it to the situation at hand.

Good enough may be satisfactory for instructors who task students at the middle school, high school, and undergraduate levels with a research paper. They view the paper as a "meaningful learning experience," wanting students to find and synthesize the information, and at the undergraduate level, to begin to ask themselves, "What can I conclude from the research?" and "How do scholars work?" (Valentine 2001, 110).

Expecting end users to be comprehensive with respect to their information seeking may be more reasonable at the graduate level and beyond, when users are specializing in a discipline, becoming familiar with its most respected writers and mastering the field's methods and techniques. The objective here should be finding sources that are seminal, central, and essential to the user's interests. Identifying such sources starts with the field's systematic reviews, discipline-specific dictionaries, and encyclopedias. If you are the library's subject specialist for one or more areas, identify the field's journals and annual review series that specialize in literature reviews. Backward chaining is useful for checking older sources cited repeatedly in the literature reviews of research publications. Finding the same ones cited in several such publications may mean that you've found the seminal works on the topic.

On a personal note, I needed to find research that "graded" the sources undergraduate students cited in their research papers. I found dozens of studies and most cited three thirty-year-old papers that proposed methodologies for grading students' cited sources and/or applied them. These were *the* seminal works on the topic, and to amass more sources on the topic, I merely had to trace them forward via cited reference searches in Google Scholar, Web of Science, and Scopus. For me, a "critical mass" meant that the new sources I was finding repeated what other sources had to say on the topic and their cited and citing sources failed to reveal new ones. Those are good rules of thumb to apply when making the decision whether to continue or stop searching for new information.

Users who want to go beyond the critical mass, striving for comprehensiveness, are likely to be conducting research for state-of-the-art, literature, or systematic reviews, doctoral dissertations, books, research proposals, patents, business plans, or encyclopedia articles. Their searches should run the gamut, enlisting every type of subject and known-item search (see chapters 6, 7, and 8) in a wide variety of discipline-based and encyclopedic databases. Of all the Boolean search strategies, the Can't Live Without This Facet First Strategy is recommended for high-recall searches because it allows the searcher to stop the searching before all facets are exhausted. Follow up with the Citation Pearl Growing Strategy using search terms in relevant retrievals to find additional ones. Not necessarily a high-recall strategy, the À la Carte Edition of the Building Block Strategy will have to suffice for searching extended-Boolean systems along with follow-up searches governed by the Citation Pearl Growing Strategy.

Monitoring Changes to Database Content and Search System Functionality

Just when you've mastered a search system, the vendor changes its interface or searching functionality. Changes are disruptive and disconcerting for everyone. Users notice and expect you to reorient them to the system and the favorite databases they search there. It's your job to bone up on the system, assessing what the vendor has done and changing what you say about the search system and its databases to users. To avoid surprises and prepare for changes in advance, keep up to date on information industry news and developments; read trade publications such as the monthly *Information Today*, semi-monthly *Online Searcher*, and daily Search Engine Watch (http://searchenginewatch.com); attend conferences specific to online searching such as Electronic Resources & Libraries (http://www.electroniclibrarian.org), Computers in Libraries, and Internet

Librarian; monitor and participate in online discussion groups such as ERIL-L and Liblicense-L; and share what you learn with your expert searcher colleagues via email, staff newsletter, intranet, blog, and/or a private Facebook group. Use in-service training opportunities to brief your colleagues on momentous industry developments, possibly devoting entire sessions to in-depth analyses of new search systems and databases or comprehensive changes to existing ones. The availability of so many search systems and databases makes it impossible for you, your expert searcher colleagues, and users to remember all the details. Document changes on a searching language cheat sheet to which you and your colleagues can refer when they search the search system and database in the future.

Track what you and your library's users are doing at the reference desk using a reference tracking and reporting (RTR) application. Such applications provide forms on which you and your colleagues describe the nature and substance of your reference interviews with users. In figure 14.1, the librarian uses Gimlet for RTR, entering the duration, question, answer, and even more about the interaction (Sidecar Publications 2015).

It may seem burdensome to document every interview, but it could pay off later when you search Gimlet's entries to determine whether your colleagues have encountered the same question and how they've answered it. Gimlet's reporting capability also gives you tools to tally data on completed forms, create graphs and tables that summarize the library's reference activity, and analyze it so that you can develop an in-depth understanding of your library's reference service and fine tune it as necessary.

Analyze COUNTER-compliant data to find out what databases your library's users are searching and what online journals they are reading. If you think better databases and journals are underutilized, rethink their presentation at your library's database hub, mount a publicity campaign to increase awareness among users most likely to benefit from using them, and revise your information literacy efforts so that instructional materials, LibGuides, and your one-time and

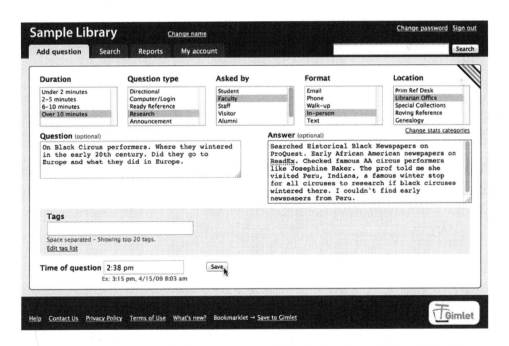

Figure 14.1. Characterizing a Reference Interview in Gimlet. Courtesy of Sidecar Publications.

sustained interactions with users promote them. Gingerly touch base with instructors, making sure they are aware of better sources so that your recommendations don't contradict theirs. In short, you want to stay one step ahead of the game, knowing what resources your library's users gravitate toward, what questions they are likely to ask, and anticipating changes to the search systems and databases you use all the time so that you are prepared the moment something changes.

Disambiguating Legitimate Retrievals from Everything Else

Google and other Web search engines routinely personalize search results, passing retrievals including ads and paid content through a *filter bubble* in search of retrievals best suited to your interests based on the data-laden cookies and personal tracking beacons it installs into your Web browser (Pariser 2011). The filter bubble means that Web search engines are programmed to deliver content that is biased toward your point of view, likes, and preferences. When you search for something ephemeral, trivial, and superficial, you might want Web search engines to personalize results, delivering retrievals that pertain to your personal interests and desires. When conducting research, you probably want search systems and databases that are objective and immune to bias so that they deliver retrievals that take all viewpoints into consideration. At the very least, these engines should give you a button to turn filtering on or off or a slider to reduce its strength.

When you search the open Web, keep in mind that Web publishers are always trying to trick the Web search engine's relevance-ranking algorithm into listing their content first. Of the many techniques they use, here are three that result in what looks like legitimate content:

- *Content farms.* Employing large numbers of freelance writers who write light, easy-to-understand essays on topics that Web searchers like to search, and are designed for maximal retrieval by Web search engines.
- *Article (or content) spinning.* Using a software program to rewrite an article so that a Web search engine will think that it is a different article.
- *Scraper sites.* Publishing a website that copies texts from several other websites and pastes them into a new website of amalgamated texts.

Web publishers use these techniques to put your eyeballs on their website, not necessarily for the legitimate content that matches your search terms, but because they want to sell you something or persuade you to embrace their point of view on a topic, issue, or situation. To root out offenders, Google in particular employs a webspam team who use both computer algorithms and human reviewers to detect the latest techniques that unscrupulous Web publishers have devised to trick the system's retrieval-ranking algorithm (Google 2014).

Ultimately, the burden is on *users* to be proactive, evaluating the information they find on the Web. Cautioning users about Web content and teaching them how to evaluate the sources they glean from the Web should be a key component of your library's information literacy program.

Thankfully, search systems that access licensed databases do not engage in deceptive practices that give precedence to certain content. These systems do, however, perform relevance ranking, and because they don't publish specifics about their search algorithms, they leave searchers in the dark about the criteria they use to rank retrievals. Thankfully, again, these search systems provide alternatives to ranked retrievals such as listing them chronologically in ascending or descending order or alphabetically by author or title. Encourage users to experiment with different display modes. If they find relevant retrievals from other modes on a consistent basis, users might begin to question relevance ranking in search systems generally, sampling other display modes and making a habit of browsing beyond the first page of ranked retrievals.

Sensing the potential conflict of interest that faces web-scale discovery (WSD) systems, their stakeholders have participated in the Open Discovery Initiative (ODI), drafting standards and best practices to ensure that the retrieval and display of WSD content is not subject to the perceptions and possibilities of bias (page 204). Should bias become an issue in the retrieval and display of sources from licensed databases, ODI may serve as a model, inspiring online searching stakeholders to join forces and hammer out comparable standards and best practices.

Personally, no matter what system I search, I treat their first-listed retrievals as suspect. I pay attention to subtle cues that may be tip-offs that something is not right with their retrievals. You should be skeptical too, making sure that the licensed online systems and services your library provides to users are free of potential bias, treating sources objectively and on their own merits.

Subsidizing the Cost of Searching the Web

If you've ever wondered about how "free" web-based services generate revenue to remain in business, Pariser (2011, 6) sums up the secret to their success as follows: "You're getting a free service, and the cost is information about you." Your personal data are the search statements you enter into search engines, the travel dates and destinations you submit to travel aggregators, the photographs you share on image hosts, the stories you like on social news sites, the players you trade in fantasy football, and much more. Everyone who surfs the Web subsidizes search with the personal data they enter into websites.

How services collect personal data is subtle, stealthy, and slick. For example, let's say I search for a flight at a "free" web-based travel aggregator agency. Whether I purchase the flight or not, the agency places a cookie on my Mac saying, "She wants cheap flights to Albany, New York, in late September." The agency sells my Albany-flight data to companies that harvest web-generated personal data, which auction them to the highest-bidding company. For the sake of example, let's say Delta Airlines wins the auction. Delta then shows me ads for relevant flights—not just on the travel aggregator's website but on the subsequent websites I visit. "The whole process—from the collection of [my] data to the[ir] sale to [Delta]—takes under a second" (Pariser 2011, 44).

Underlining Google's confidence about its ability to predict your future searches is its CEO, who expects search to become "autonomous, meaning that it will offer you search results even before you've looked for them" (Gaudin 2010). That a search system could be clairvoyant (serendipity was the term Google's CEO used) may seem to be the stuff of science fiction. Yet, considering how spot-on Google's search and relevance-ranking are, it isn't difficult to imagine that this search engine could generate accurate queries that are likely to pop into your head based on the data you enter into its many "free" applications—calendar, contacts, email, maps, search, spreadsheet, translate, word processing, and so on. On one hand, users may welcome system-generated queries because, of the several steps of the searching process; they consider search statement formulation to be one of the most difficult steps. On the other, they may feel that Google is invading their privacy.

If you are uncomfortable with the reach that web-based services have in what you do or think next, there are alternatives, for example, searching the DuckDuckGo search engine (https://duckduckgo.com) instead of Google, Bing, or Yahoo!, or entering a query into Google via Startpage (https://startpage.com). See where your fellow classmates stand on privacy concerns by discussing these points in class:

- Cite evidence convincing you that Google and other Web services (e.g., travel, sports, social networking, shopping sites) are using your personal data.
- Have you or your friends ever avoided Google and other Web services because you knew they were tracking you? If you are willing to share, describe the information you or your friends were seeking, why you avoided certain services, and alternative strategies you employed.

- What responsibilities do you have regarding the personal data you enter into web-based services for your library's users?
- How would you advise your library's users about personal data they enter into web-based services?

The Future of Boolean Search Systems

Boolean searching languages are complicated. Perhaps the only people who use the full range of a system's Boolean searching language are expert intermediary searchers, who have taken for-credit, graduate-level online searching courses and search these systems on a daily basis at the reference desk, and search system representatives, who give on-demand demonstrations and tutorials to prospective and current clients. In the mid-1980s, a NISO (National Information Standards Organization) committee defined a common command language for Boolean search systems but the common language never really caught on (Hildreth 1986).

Despite similarities in functionality, Boolean search systems have sported their own unique searching language, a practice that continues to the present day. In the 1990s, the combination of graphical user interfaces (GUIs) and Web browsers simplified searching languages, replacing the formulation and entry of complicated command-bound search statements with a series of simple point-and-click actions; however, to assemble these series requires an understanding of facet analysis, indexing languages, thesaurus relationships, Boolean operators, and search strategy. Few end users have such an understanding. Thus, it should not come as a surprise that analyses of search statements entered into today's search systems conclude that the search statements end users enter into search systems are short and simple, and they rarely enlist elements of a system's formal searching language (Park and Lee 2013; Aula, Khan, and Guan 2010).

EBSCOhost is exceptional in its ability to strike a happy medium between Boolean and extended-Boolean searching. The former appeals to expert searchers who are partial to the exactitude of Boolean searching, browsing and selecting CV from a database's thesaurus, entering FT search statements directly, and choosing specific fields especially for known-item searches. The system responds to zero-posted Boolean searches with extended-Boolean (EBSCOhost calls it SmartText searching) searches, displaying relevance-ranked retrievals and clusters that users can explore to narrow their interests. The latter appeals to end users especially when they are limited in their ability to express their queries. They can enter anything—a series of keywords, a rambling statement, or a title or abstract they copied and pasted from a retrieved source into the search box—then click on "SmartText Searching" to divert EBSCOhost from its Boolean default to its extended-Boolean search.

Predicting the Demise of Licensed Databases

Researchers have predicted the demise of licensed databases (Chen 2010; Meier and Conkling 2008). Fueling their predictions are their observations that Google Scholar's coverage is comparable to this and that licensed database's coverage and that most journals post their tables of contents on the open Web where Web search engines index their content. They suggest that libraries could save money, canceling their subscriptions to licensed databases and delegating database searching to Google, Google Scholar, Microsoft Academic Search, and comparable "free" search services.

What these researchers fail to take into consideration is that database publishers make selection decisions about the sources they index in their databases, striving to be comprehensive about the disciplinary literature they cover as well as covering the most respected, highly cited, and top cited sources in the discipline—not only journals but the major genres in which domain experts publish their scholarship. Especially in favor of the current database-search system model is the advanced functionality that search systems offer—a controlled vocabulary that uses domain-expert terminology, an online thesaurus for browsing, selecting, and exploding controlled vocabulary terms, alphabetical browsing indexes, field searching especially for known-item searches, pre-search qualifiers, post-search clusters, and find-like searches. Discipline-based databases also publish lists of the sources to document to domain experts that they index the most important sources in the discipline, and they enable them to use system functionality to limit searches to one or more journals. Finally, domain experts whose searches in their discipline's go-to databases retrieve no new sources on their topics of interest that they aren't already aware of can rest assured that they are keeping abreast of the latest developments.

Consider the ABI/Inform database. It specializes in business exclusively, providing full-text access not only to journals but to dissertations, conference proceedings papers, working papers, and newspapers. ABI/Inform strives to achieve comprehensiveness and depth in its coverage of the world's business literature (ProQuest 2015). Available through the ProQuest search system, ABI/Inform provides searchers with a wide array of CV and FT searching tools. Search ABI/Inform's online thesaurus and classification codes, limiting searches to controlled vocabulary that produce high-precision results. ProQuest searchers can browse special database fields naming companies/organizations, NAICS codes, persons, and locations—criteria that are typical of user queries for business topics. Accompanying ABI/Inform search results are clusters to help users define their interests more specifically. FT searching of full-texts is available to searchers. Finding an especially relevant source, users can click on the accompanying "See similar documents" to trigger ProQuest's find-like search. A shopping analogy is appropriate here. Shopping for specialty items such as bird feeders, purses, and jeans, you can find these items at a mega-discount retailer (e.g., Target, Walmart, or Meijer), but for quality, selection, and personal service, you'd go to a specialty store (e.g., Wild Birds Unlimited, Coach, and True Religion Brand Jeans). The same thing applies to database searching.

Web-Scale Discovery Systems: The New Google for Academic Content

If licensed databases and search systems perceive a threat, it comes from web-scale discovery (WSD) systems. The development of WSD systems is in response to library users who don't know where to start searching for scholarly, professional, and educational information, and when they do choose a database, they can't establish a foothold because searching there is complex, arcane, or unnatural. Baffled and perplexed, users revert to what's familiar to them and what's worked in the past—Google, Wikipedia, and the open Web. To win them back, libraries have implemented WSD systems, one-stop shopping for academic information. Into a Google-like search box users enter their search statement, and the WSD system searches a humongous index bearing content from the OPAC, licensed databases, quality open Web databases, and institutional repositories. It retrieves surrogate records, many bearing abstracts, summaries, tables of contents, full-texts (when available) or links to full-texts, all ranked according to relevance. To build WSD indexes, their developers had to strike deals with their direct competitors. Imagine ProQuest, the developer of the Summon WSD system, asking EBSCO Information Services, developer of the Discovery Service WSD system, for its exclusive and proprietary Historical Abstracts and America: History and Life databases, so that it can index them into Summon. There would be a wide range of reactions to such requests, some competitors wanting to go exclusive with their own databases and search systems, others restricting their competitors to indexing the tables of contents of the journals they publish, and still others successfully bartering for content that would enrich their respective WSD systems.

A half decade of WSD-system deployment in libraries has passed, and there are now studies that shed light on this new system's impact. At Grand Valley State University, Way (2010) attributes the dramatic decrease in the use of A&I databases and increase in downloads from full-text databases to the WSD system. Preliminary results of an ongoing study of all four WSD systems across two dozen academic institutions also report an overall increase in full-text downloads before and after WSD-system implementation, but whether overall and institution-level differences are significant has yet to be determined (Levine-Clark, Price, and McDonald 2014). Korah and Cassidy (2010) survey Sam Houston State University (SHSU) students regarding their use of Web search engines, the library's database hub, and its federated (or meta-) search system. Although federated search is a precursor of today's WSD systems, its goals of unifying search into one search box and merging results from multiple databases into one list of ranked retrievals mirror those of WSD systems. SHSU researchers conclude that students' preference for individual databases or federated search is related to their class, starting at ratios of 1:1 for freshmen, 2:1 for upperclassmen, 4:1 for master's students, and 7:1 for doctoral students, adding that by the time students reach graduate levels, their level of sophistication with their chosen discipline may be more suited for their discipline's go-to databases. Once aspiring students stake their claim to a discipline and "find" disciplinary databases, they stick with these databases, benefiting from their disciplinary specialization and their full-fledged functionality.

Because WSD systems are still relatively new, more studies are sure to follow, eventually reaching a critical mass that may tip the balance one way or another or hold it steady. Repeatedly replicating results from the SHSU study may stave off the demise of the database hub. No doubt faculty will "raise the roof" should librarians cut database subscriptions. Yet librarians have cut journal subscriptions in the past amid faculty protest because there were no funds to renew subscriptions. Whether librarians will ax individual databases because WSD systems access some of the same content is anyone's guess. Possibly, WSD designers are thinking ahead to future iterations of this system that will be a boon for users at all academic levels while database publishers are looking in the rearview mirror, implementing enhancements that ensure their database's uniqueness.

Future Functionality Wish List

Search systems and databases aren't perfect. They continue to evolve. Here's my wish list for future functionality.

1. Automatic Facet Detection in Extended-Boolean Search Systems

Boolean search systems are tremendously efficient because they enable expert searchers to enter multiple synonyms for each facet, create intermediate sets for each facet, then combine intermediate sets into a final result set. Entering a Boolean search bearing three synonyms per facet for a three-faceted query would require the direct entry of twenty-seven separate search statements in an extended-Boolean system! That's really inefficient. Some extended-Boolean systems perform automatic vocabulary control, adding synonyms to search statements, but they don't report back what synonyms they add so searchers never know how such systems enhance their queries.

Extended-Boolean systems should be able to detect the synonyms in search statements, clustering synonyms together in facets, performing searches, and giving greater weights to retrievals matching one or more synonyms for *all* facets in queries. In fact, such an enhancement could use the same technology that fuels article spinning, a black-hat search engine optimization technique. Because this technique detects words and phrases in texts and replaces them with synonyms, it should be able to detect synonyms in a string of words and phrases and group the synonyms together for searching and relevance-retrievals ranking.

Ultimately, an extended-Boolean system enhanced with automatic facet detection has the potential to increase relevant retrievals because it has more search terms to work with. For example, today's extended-Boolean systems are satisfactory for retrieving relevant sources for the search statement `alcoholism spirituality relapse` bearing one search term per facet that is in keeping with the À la Carte Edition of the Building Block Strategy. If extended-Boolean could only process this more complex search statement . . .

> `spirituality alcoholism alcoholics anonymous relapse religion intoxicants re-`
> `covery rehabilitation twelve steps sobriety`

. . . that bears several search terms per facet and is in keeping with the Buffet Edition of the Building Block Strategy. Because there are more search terms for the system to consider, it has the potential to increase relevant retrievals. Plus, sources that match two or three search terms per facet should be criteria that extended-Boolean systems with automatic facet recognition use to boost a source's ranking in retrievals lists.

2. Automatic Source Evaluator

Most users pay lip service to source evaluation, telling anyone who asks that they recognize its importance. In practice, if they evaluate sources at all, they do so in a cursory manner. Why can't systems provide more automatic assistance in this regard? Most A&I and full-text databases already provide pre-search qualifiers and post-search clusters that enable users to limit retrievals to scholarly or peer-reviewed sources. Why not link to bibliometrics and altmetrics so users could check author publication records and discover the latest buzz pertaining to a source?

Getting users to evaluate the information they find on the open Web sources is where the *real challenge* lies. Because Web sources are so variable, an automatic source evaluator could take the form of a computer-based guide that prompts the user as to what questions to ask to evaluate a website. Researchers are beginning to experiment with such guides, displaying the questions users should be asking about the source at hand, for example, *who* wrote it, *what* did they write about, *where* was it published, *when* was it published, and *why* was it published (page 206). Incorporated into automatic source guides should be incentivizing features that encourage users to perform the evaluation. Examples are:

- Allowing the user to score websites with regard to the ease with which he can answer who, what, where, when, and why questions so that he can compare the score that the website at hand has earned against an average score for all websites he has scored and make a decision whether to use the website's information.
- Adding group participation so that a study group, class, or research group can pool their efforts on the same task and learn how their peers evaluate sources.
- Adding a monitoring and reporting capability so that instructors can determine the extent to which students participate in evaluation activities and users can request on-the-spot assistance from librarians.

3. Better Database Selection Tools

The impetus for building WSD systems is Google-like simplicity—one search statement searches a gargantuan pool of sources. No database selection is necessary on the part of the user. To reconnect users to resources at the library's database hub, librarians, database publishers, and online system designers should be brainstorming on and experimenting with ways to do this. Certainly LibGuides and sustained instruction events are two ways to get started, but their reach is limited. What automated tools are possible? A long time ago, searches of Dialindex, Dialog's huge index to its many databases, reported which databases contributed what sources so that searchers could follow up with in-depth searches in databases contributing the most sources. Why can't WSD systems do the same? If users notice one or two particular databases are contributing the best sources, they may be inclined to navigate to that database specifically and benefit from its advanced features such as discipline-specific CV, online thesaurus and alphabetical index browsing, find-like searches, and more.

4. Intelligent Stemming in Boolean Search Systems

Intelligent stemming should be standard issue in all search systems so that searchers don't have to wonder whether their search terms retrieve singular, plural, and irregular nouns or common word endings on verbs that vary due to past, present, future, and conditional tenses. This would relieve expert searchers from having to keep track of two or three truncation symbols per system and of the subtle nuances pertaining to how a search system applies plural-singular retrieval and truncates simple word stems. When searchers need to be explicit about truncation to retrieve exactly what they want, systems should spell out the details in their online help. All too often, such help is sketchy and scant, giving few details and hardly any examples. Also, give searchers controls to turn intelligent stemming on and off.

5. Automatic Technical Reader

While abstracts usually give enough information about a source for users to determine a source's relevance, they are vague about details that would enable users to know exactly how the source applies to their interests. Thus, such a reader would create a representation that is a middle ground between an abstract and a full-text. For research, it would draw attention to the source's title and abstract, then invite the user to read its introduction to determine the problem that the researcher is trying to solve, his objectives, and the research's importance, scan its methods section to determine how the researcher conducted the experiment, and study the source's conclusions where the researcher states his most important findings. Non-research sources would be more challenging for an automatic technical reader to process because they don't have the same predictable structure as do reports of research. Because some users think that abstracts are full-texts, an automatic reader would have to present its middle-ground representation in a way that impresses upon users that they still have to put effort into reading the full-text of their most relevant retrievals.

6. Online Help

Every search system should have online help that users can both browse and search. It should be called "help" on every Web page and the link or button that opens help should be located in a conspicuous location *above the fold* on every Web page. Search systems should submit their online help to usability testing, making sure everyone understands it—end users and expert searchers alike.

7. Personalization That Users Control

This is a no brainer. Let users decide when and whether they want systems to perform personalization. Search systems should give users an on-off switch or let users regulate its strength using a slider. Personally, I like personalization when I'm traveling, wanting to know where the nearest Whole Foods, Toys R Us, or Target is located, but when I'm conducting research, I would turn personalization off, wanting to see *all* retrievals, not just those that agree with my point of view.

Handing You the Baton

Okay, so expert intermediary searchers don't have batons, but they do have to orchestrate a wide array of factors to achieve their goal of helping people satisfy their information needs. So much about people is variable—their knowledge of the topic that interests them, their ability to verbalize what they want to someone else, the depth of their specific knowledge of the topic they seek, their overall knowledge and ability to handle scientific, technical, and scholarly information, and the time and effort they are able (or willing) to put into solving the information problem at hand. At the database hub, the databases that your institution's budget can support to satisfy the information demands of its user base may number in the dozens, hundreds, or thousands. The search systems that access licensed databases and free open Web databases have a wide variety of searching, browsing, selecting, and retrievals-management functionality. Finally, there's you! You have prepared by taking a graduate-level course in online searching, reading *Online Searching* carefully and thoughtfully, answering its end-of-the-chapter questions, comparing your answers with its answers, and discussing them in class. To round out your knowledge, you've probably taken graduate information literacy, reference, education, and one or more discipline-based reference courses. You have your particular subject expertise to draw on as well as your question negotiation and interviewing skills. Add to the foregoing your boundless energy, extraordinary enthusiasm, and an unwavering personal commitment to the field of library and information science, and you are ready to step onto the podium, pick up the baton, and orchestrate the wide array of factors that make up the online searching enterprise in the service of helping your library's users satisfy their information needs.

Bibliography

Aula, Anne, Rehan M. Khan, and Zhiwei Guan. 2010. "How Does Search Behavior Change as Search Becomes More Difficult?" *Proceedings of CHI 2010*: 35–44.

Bornmann, Lutz, and Rudiger Mutz. 2014. "Growth Rates of Modern Science: A Bibliometric Analysis Based on the Number of Publications and Cited References." *Journal of the Association for Information Science and Technology.* Accessed March 26, 2015. http://arxiv.org/abs/1402.4578.

Chen, Xiaotian. 2010. "The Declining Value of Subscription-Based Abstracting and Indexing Services in the New Knowledge Dissemination Era." *Serials Review* 36: 79–85.

Gaudin, Sharon. 2010. "In Schmidt's Vision, Google Will Search Before You Even Ask." *Computerworld* (Sept. 30). Accessed March 26, 2015. http://www.computerworld.com/article/2515965/search/in-schmidt-s-vision--google-will-search-before-you-even-ask.html.

Google. 2014. "Inside Search: Fighting Spam." Accessed March 26, 2015. http://www.google.com/intl/en-US/insidesearch/howsearchworks/fighting-spam.html.

Hildreth, Charles. 1986. "Communicating with Online Catalogs and Other Retrieval Systems: The Need for a Standard Command Language." *Library Hi Tech* 4: 7–11.

Korah, Abe, and Erin Dorris Cassidy. 2010. "Students and Federated Searching: Survey of Use and Satisfaction." *Reference & User Services Quarterly* 49, no. 4: 325–32.

Levine-Clark, Michael, Jason Price, and John McDonald. 2014. "Discovery or Displacement? A Large-Scale Longitudinal Study of the Effect of Discovery Systems on Online Journal Usage." Accessed March 26, 2015. http://docs.lib.purdue.edu/charleston/2013/Plenaries/2/.

Marchionini, Gary. 1995. *Information Seeking in Electronic Environments*. Cambridge: Cambridge University Press.

Meier, John J., and Thomas W. Conkling. 2008. "Google Scholar's Coverage of the Engineering Literature: An Empirical Study." *Journal of Academic Librarianship* 34, no. 3: 196–201.

Newell, Alan, and Herbert Simon. 1972. *Human Problem Solving*. Englewood Cliffs, NJ: Prentice-Hall.

Pariser, Eli. 2011. *The Filter Bubble: What the Internet Is Hiding from You*. New York: Penguin Press.

Park, Minsoo, and Tae-seok Lee. 2013. "Understanding Science and Technology Information Users through Transaction Log Analysis." *Library High Tech* 31, no. 1: 123–40.

Pautasso, Marco. 2012. "Publication Growth in Biological Sub-Fields: Patterns, Predictability, and Sustainability." *Sustainability* 4, no. 12: 3234–47.

ProQuest. 2015. "ABI/Inform Complete." Accessed March 26, 2015. http://www.proquest.com/products-services/abi_inform_complete.html.

Sidecar Publications. 2015. "Gimlet: Staff Your Desk Wisely." Accessed March 26, 2015. https://gimlet.us/.

Valentine, Barbara. 2001. "The Legitimate Effort in Research Papers: Student Commitment versus Faculty Expectations." *Journal of Academic Librarianship* 27, no. 2: 107–15.

Way, Doug. 2010. "The Impact of Web-Scale Discovery on the Use of a Library Collection." *Serials Review* 36, no. 4: 214–20.

Glossary

A&I database. A special type of index enhanced with abstracts (also called summaries) that describe sources' contents.

abstract. A concise and accurate summary of a source's contents.

abstracting and indexing database. *See* A&I database.

adjacency operator. A proximity operator that the searcher incorporates into his search statement to retrieve texts in which the search words are adjacent to one another. The operator also specifies whether or not word order matters.

almanac. "A collection of facts, statistics, and lists" (Bopp and Smith 2011, 440).

altmetrics. New metrics for quantifying the reach and impact of an academic article that includes mentions in social media.

AND. The Boolean operator that searchers insert into the search statements they enter into a Boolean search system to tell the system which search terms should co-occur along with other search terms in retrievals.

article-level metric. A measure that is used to evaluate the impact of an article in a scholarly journal. *See also* h-index.

author. A person, corporate body, or family responsible for creating a source.

author-bibliography search. A subject search in which users want to scan a list of sources that a particular person wrote, edited, illustrated, etc., because they like what the person does and they want to find more like it.

author-keywords. The subject words and phrases that journal editors ask authors to add to their manuscripts when they submit them to the journal for review. Author-keywords do not comply with the rule of specific entry.

authority control. The editorial process used to maintain consistency in the establishment of authorized index terms such as names, titles, subjects, and the relationships between them.

authority file. A database of index terms, usually for names, titles, and/or subjects, that are authorized for use in the known-item and subject heading fields of surrogate records. *See also* authority record.

authority record. An entry that displays an index term's syndetic structure and entry vocabulary plus related information such as a scope note, the date that the index term was authorized in the CV, and a history note. *See also* authority file.

authorized term. *See* index term.

backward chaining. *See* bibliography scanning.

bibliographic database. *See* surrogate database.

bibliography. A systematic listing of citations, usually organized alphabetically by author name, and restricted in coverage by one or more features such as subject, publisher, place of publication, or genre.

bibliography scanning. Finding relevant retrievals among the citations listed in a source's footnotes or bibliography. (Also called backward chaining.)

bibliometrics. The statistical analysis of the written products of academic inquiry, scholarship, and research, especially in the form of journal articles, books, dissertations, theses, and conference papers.

biography. An account of a person's life, often supplemented with one or more other appropriate genres, e.g., bibliography, catalog, discography, filmography, etc., to report their accomplishments.

black hat. A computer programmer who engages in unacceptable search engine optimization techniques.

Boolean logic. The systematic ways in which Boolean search systems produce retrievals in response to search statements bearing Boolean operators.

Boolean operators. The operators OR, AND, and NOT that searchers insert into the search statements they enter into a Boolean search system to tell the system which search terms should be present in retrievals, which search terms should co-occur along with other search terms in retrievals, and which search terms should be deliberately excluded from retrievals, respectively.

Boolean search systems. Search systems governed by Boolean logic to produce retrievals in response to user-entered search statements.

broader term (BT). A hierarchical relationship between two controlled vocabulary terms in a thesaurus that expresses either a whole-part or genus-species relationship, the broader term designating the whole or the genus.

browsing. The act of scrutinizing the system's display of indexed entries such as an alphabetical index, classified list, cluster array, or thesaurus authority record by a user with the intent of selecting one or more entries to further the search.

catalog. A special type of index bearing surrogate records that describe sources contained in a collection, library, or group of libraries and that are organized according to a formal scheme or plan.

cataloger. *See* indexer.

CD-ROM search systems. Stand-alone, single-user search systems that delegated search to a personal computer and database on a CD-ROM (compact disk read only memory).

citation. A reference to a source that gives just enough identificatory information so that a person can find the source in a collection such as a library or a database.

citation count. The number of times a person's publications have been cited in other publications.

citation management system (CMS). A library for the user's saved sources and a suite of automated tools to help the user manage these sources and cite them in written works.

citation pearl growing. The practice of scrutinizing retrievals, both surrogates and the actual sources themselves (when available), for the purpose of finding relevant terms to incorporate in a follow-up search that retrieves additional relevant sources.

citation verification search. A known-item search that verifies the citation data the user has in hand for a source or completes it for citation purposes.

cited reference searches. Finding relevant retrievals among the sources that have cited an older source since its publication. (Also called forward chaining.)

cited references. Sources that the source in hand cites (usually in the form of footnotes or citations in a bibliography). Cited references go back in time. *See also* bibliography scanning.

citing references. Sources that have cited the source in hand since its publication. Citing references go forward in time. *See also* cited reference searches.

classification. Putting sources in order, mostly by subject but sometimes by genre.

classification captions. Broad-based topical headings that make up a classification's outline. In some databases, indexers assign such captions (or codes) to surrogates in ways that are similar to their assignment of controlled vocabulary terms from a thesaurus so that search systems can index the captions to facilitate subject searching.

closed-ended questions. Questions that librarians ask users during the reference interview to elicit yes-no or short answers from them.

clusters. *See* post-search clusters.

command-line interface. Allows users to interact with a computer by entering commands that instruct the computer to perform certain operations.

controlled vocabulary. A carefully selected list of words, phrases, or codes that indexers assign to surrogate records to describe a source's intellectual contents and to facilitate online searching.

controlled vocabulary searching. Utilizing search system features for browsing, selecting, or directly entering a database's controlled terms in the form of words, phrases, or codes, ultimately for the purpose of producing high-precision retrievals.

controlled vocabulary term. *See* index term.

COUNTER-compliant data. Database usage statistics that conform to Project COUNTER standards.

credible. Whether the information at hand is trustworthy and written by a domain expert on the topic.

database. A collection of data or information systematically organized to facilitate retrieval. A database may contain texts, media, and spatial and/or numeric data.

database aggregators. Search services that host databases from a variety database publishers. Such services may also host databases that they themselves publish. (Also called database supermarkets.)

database hub. The centerpiece of the library's virtual services where self-service access to scholarly, professional, and educational information resides, not only access to surrogate records but to the actual sources themselves in the form of digital full-texts, media, and numeric and spatial data. (Also called database gateways, gateway systems, information portals, and scholar portals.)

database publishers. For- and not-for-profit publishers that employ professional staff to select database content, organize it, and deposit it into the database. Some publishers index database content and add search and retrieval services and other publishers license database aggregators to do it for them.

database supermarkets. *See* database aggregators.

descriptor. *See* index term.

dictionary. *See* language dictionary; discipline-based dictionary.

digital libraries. Research databases that provide access to actual sources across a wide range of genres—texts, media, and numeric and spatial data.

direct entry. The searcher's manual entry of search terms and searching language into the system's search box.

directory. A collection of entries for people and organizations bearing contact information and other potentially useful information such as age, gender, and occupation for people, and founding date, number of employees, and contact person name for organizations that bear definitions and explanations.

discipline-based dictionary. A collection of entries for concepts, events, objects, and overarching topics in a discipline, subject, or field of study along with definitions and short explanations.

document representation. The information—surrogate, actual source, or both—that a search system indexes, retrieves, and displays.

domain expert. A person who has earned credentials (e.g., degree, certification, license, experience) that represent her mastery of a discipline, subject, field of study, practice, trade, or profession.

double posting. A database indexing practice in which systems index the words and phrases in surrogate record fields multiple times to maximize the searcher's chances of retrieving information.

encyclopedia. A collection of entries for concepts, events, objects, or overarching topics in a discipline, subject, or field of study that give background information, definitions, detailed explanations, current issues and trends, and include bibliographical references to seminal sources.

encyclopedic. A database that covers a wide range of disciplines, subjects, or fields of study.

end user. A person who uses library resources and services excluding the library staff who provide access to library resources and services. (Also known as everyday people.)

entry vocabulary. Synonyms that link users to authorized index terms in a controlled vocabulary. Also called cross-references, see references, use references, and use terms. *See also* use references.

everyday people. *See* end user.

expert intermediary searcher. A person (usually a librarian) who has received special training in online searching from search system representatives or faculty in schools of library and information science (LIS).

extended-Boolean search systems. Search systems that respond with relevance-ranked retrievals to the natural language queries end users enter into them.

facet. A word or very short phrase that describes a single concept or idea. A facet can also be a word or phrase that is a data element in a citation such as a title or author name.

facet analysis. An analysis of the user's query in which the objective is to express it in no more than a handful of big ideas, major concepts, or facets that should or should not be present in retrievals.

facets. *See* post-search clusters.

fair linking. Search systems giving equal consideration to retrievals in the search and display process.

federated search system. A search system that distributes the user's search statement to a set of disparate databases, merges each database's retrievals into a succinct response with duplicates handled in an efficient manner, and presents retrievals to the user along with functionality for sorting them in various ways.

field. A set of characters in a database that, when treated as a unit, describes a particular kind of data like an author, title, or summary.

field label. The full or abbreviated name of a field that the user chooses from a search system's select-a-field pull-down menu or enters directly into a search statement for the purpose of restricting retrieval to this field.

filter. *See* post-search cluster.

filter bubbles. *See* personalization.

form. The structure of a database.

forward chaining. *See* cited reference searches.

free text (FT) searching. Utilizing a searching language to enter natural language words and phrases into a Boolean search system, ultimately for the purpose of producing high-recall retrievals. (Free text searching that a user conducts in a full-text database is also called free text searching.)

full-text. The text of the actual source itself.

full-text aggregator. *See* journal aggregator.

full-text database. A systematic organization of values (e.g., words, phrases, numbers, or codes) contained in a source database's full-text sources along with the pointers, references, or addresses that the search system uses to retrieve the full-texts in which the values occur.

full-text fulfillment search. Finding a full-text for a desired source.

full-text publisher. *See* journal publisher.

full-text searching. *See* free text (FT) searching.

genre. The nature of the sources contained in a database—what they *are* as opposed to what they are *about*.

h-index. An article-level metric that is used to evaluate the impact of journal articles. An author with an index of h has published h papers, each of which has been cited by other papers h times or more.

handbook. "A handy guide to a particular subject, with all of the critical information that one might need" consolidated into a single source (Bopp and Smith 2011, 443).

high-posted searches. Searches that produce many retrievals.

history note. Information about an index term's representation in a CV such as changes over the years, special instructions for searching this term online, and the range of years an unused term was in use.

hits. The number of retrievals that a search statement retrieves. (Also called postings.)

impact factor. A metric that is used to evaluate the impact of a journal. It is calculated by determining the number of times that the journal's articles are cited by other journals over a two-year period, divided by the total number of citable pieces in the journal.

implicit operators. In response to a search statement, a search system inserts Boolean operators in between search words, usually AND in Boolean systems and OR in extended-Boolean systems.

imposed query. A query that the user poses to a reference librarian that comes from someone else, typically a teacher, family member, boss, neighbor, friend, colleague, et al.

in-depth query. Negotiated queries that usually require subject searches and produce multiple retrievals from which users must synthesize an answer to their questions.

index. A systematic organization of values (e.g., words, phrases, numbers, or codes) contained in a database's surrogate records or full-text sources along with the pointers, references, or addresses that the search system uses to retrieve the surrogates and/or full-texts in which the values occur.

index term. A controlled vocabulary term for a name, subject, or title that is authorized for indexers to assign to controlled vocabulary fields of surrogate records and for searchers to use in controlled vocabulary searches of online databases.

indexer. A human being who assigns controlled vocabulary terms to surrogate records to represent the names, subjects, or titles pertaining to sources.

indicative abstract. A summary that functions like a table of contents, describing a source's range and coverage and making general statements about the source.

indicative-informative abstract. A summary that is part indicative of the source's more significant content and part informative of its less significant content.

information explosion. The rapid increase in the amount of information that became available to people starting at the time of the Cold War and continuing until the present day.

information need. The user's recognition that what he knows is inadequate or incomplete to satisfy an overarching goal.

information retrieval system. *See* search system.

informative abstract. A summary that functions as a substitute for a source, detailing its quantitative or qualitative substance.

institutional repository (IR). A combined search system and online database that a learning institution such as a college, university, or laboratory supports, where institution members (e.g., faculty, students, researchers, administrators) archive digital materials that are the products of their teaching, research, and/or service activities.

intermediary searcher. *See* expert intermediary searcher.

journal aggregators. Search services that deliver full-texts for the journals that they publish and for the journals that other journal publishers outsource to them.

journal holdings record. A listing of the copies of a journal that the library has stored on its bookshelves or online. Listing journal holdings by year, volume, issue, and supplement, the record includes the names of the journal publisher or journal aggregators that supply full-texts.

journal publisher. A publisher that specializes in the publication of one or more journals. When journal publishers offer search services to their journals that include full-text fulfillment searches, they become database publishers; however, due to costs, the majority of journal publishers outsource search services and full-text fulfillment to journal aggregators.

journal run. A subject search in which users want to scan multiple issues of a journal because it has published a relevant article(s) on the topic they seek and they want to find more like it.

keywords. The words and phrases that users enter into search systems to express their queries. The keywords users enter don't necessarily arise from a facet analysis and logical combination, and they vary in form, ranging from single words and phrases to sentences, questions, and even whole paragraphs.

known-item search. A request for a specific source that you or the user knows exists such as a particular journal article, book, conference paper, blog, organization, film, magazine or journal, author, advertisement, or television program.

language dictionary. A collection of entries for acronyms, proper nouns, phrases, or words giving definitions, etymology, foreign-language equivalents, grammar, orthography, pronunciations, regionalisms, synonyms, usage, visual imagery, and/or written-out forms.

LCNAF. *See* authority file.

lexicographer. The person who develops and maintains a thesaurus or classification.

LibGuides. An easy-to-use content management system marketed to librarians who use it to author web-based resource pages for users, putting users a click away from recommended resources on a topic, genre, theme, current event, etc.

library catalog. The physical or virtual index that users search to access a library's collection, consisting mostly of surrogate records for monographs and serial titles. *See also* OPAC.

Library of Congress Name Authority File. *See* authority file.

licensed databases. Databases that database publishers, database aggregators, journal publishers, and journal aggregators license to libraries for a subscription fee. Because authentication is required, access to these databases is limited to a library's cardholders.

licensed Web. The online space in which licensed databases reside.

limits. *See* post-search clusters.

link resolver. A software product that processes the citation data embedded in an OpenURL to determine whether the library holds or owns the actual source itself, and when it does, facilitates the retrieval and display of the source back to the user.

literary warrant. When enough domain experts have written on a topic, the lexicographer establishes an index term for the topic and adds it to the controlled vocabulary.

literature review. An evaluative report of what is known about a subject, theme, current event, issue, etc., that strives to be comprehensive in a certain way(s), for example, covering a certain range of years, a certain genre, a certain methodology, etc. *See also* systematic review.

logical combination. The addition of Boolean operators to the facet analysis to indicate to the search system how it should combine facets during retrieval.

main entry. When main entry governs the display of retrievals, the result is a retrievals list ordered alphabetically by author and, when authorship is diffuse or anonymous, by title.

major index terms. Index terms that indexers assign to surrogate records when the sources are specifically about the subjects described by the major index term.

manual. "A convenient guide to a particular procedure, typically with step-by-step instructions" (Bopp and Smith 2011, 444).

media. Information packages that people experience with their visual, tactile, or auditory senses.

NAICS codes. A classification of businesses called the North American Industry Classification System.

narrower term (NT). A hierarchical relationship between two controlled vocabulary terms in a thesaurus that expresses either a whole-part or genus-species relationship, the narrower term designating the part or the species.

nearby operator. A proximity operator that the searcher incorporates into his search statement to retrieve texts in which the search words are separated by one or more intervening words. The operator specifies whether or not the word order matters. (Also called near operator or neighbor operator.)

negotiated query. The librarian's understanding of what the user wants as a result of conducting a reference interview with the user.

nested Boolean logic. The inclusion of parentheses (or brackets) in a search statement for the same purpose that algebra uses parentheses—to designate which combinatorial operations should be done first, second, third, and so on.

NOT. The Boolean operator that searchers insert into the search statements they enter into a Boolean search system to tell the system which search terms should be deliberately excluded from retrievals.

numeric data. Data expressed in numbers.

online public access catalog. *See* OPAC.

OPAC. The online index that users search to access a library's collection, consisting mostly of surrogate records for monographs and serial titles. *See also* library catalog.

open access. Unrestricted access to peer-reviewed scholarship on the open Web.

open-ended questions. The questions that librarians ask users during the reference interview to elicit anything but a yes-no or short answer.

open Web. The public section of the World Wide Web where anyone with a computer, Internet connection, and Web browser can search, retrieve, display, and publish information.

openURL. A standard for encoding citation data for actual sources into a URL that can be passed to a link resolver that processes the citation data to determine whether the library holds or owns the actual source.

OR. The Boolean operator that searchers insert into the search statements they enter into a Boolean search system to tell the system which search terms should be present in retrievals.

pay-walls. The restrictions publishers levy on users who want to access their web-based sources but have no subscription to or have not placed a firm order for a retrieved source. Pay-walls operate on a soft to hard continuum, with soft allowing some access such as the display of a retrieved source's index terms, abstract, and cited sources, and with hard restricting access almost entirely to citations.

PDF (portable document format). A file format that displays text, media, or numeric data like the printed page so that a person can read, view, print, and/or transmit the file electronically to other(s).

peer-review. The systematic evaluation of scholarship by domain experts in a discipline, subject, or field of study.

personalization. A relevance-enhancement technique that Web search engines perform algorithmically, utilizing personal information that they glean from the Web to influence retrievals for a search, populating them with ones that are specific to the person's interests.

post-coordination. The searcher's deliberate combination of words into search statements *after* the search system has extracted words from texts into its searchable indexes.

post-search clusters. The broad-based categories that search systems use to display salient aspects of retrievals and that are also selectable so users can limit retrievals to these aspects. (Also called clusters, facets, filters, limits, or refinements.)

postings. The number of retrievals that a search statement retrieves. (Also called hits.)

precedence of operators. Rules that govern which Boolean operator the search system processes first, second, third, and so on. Check the system's help to learn its precedence of operators.

precision. A search that yields mostly relevant retrievals. Precision is calculated by dividing the total number of relevant retrievals your search retrieves by the total number of retrievals your search retrieves.

precoordination. The combination of individual concepts into complex subjects before conducting a search for them.

pre-search qualifiers. Broad-based criteria that databases display so that users can select them to limit retrievals at the same time they enter their search statements.

proximity operator. An operator in a search system that specifies two criteria that must be met for retrieval of surrogates and/or full-texts to occur: (1) how close the words should occur in the text, and (2) whether word order matters.

query. The user's immediate expression of his information need.

recall. A search that yields as many relevant retrievals as there are on the topic in the database. Recall is calculated by dividing the total number of relevant retrievals your search retrieves by the total number of relevant retrievals in the database.

reference databases. A systematically organized collection of data or information that people search to find facts and answers to their questions.

reference interview. A conversational exchange between a reference librarian and a library user in which the user is likely to describe something she doesn't know, requiring negotiation between the two so that the librarian is able to determine what the user really wants.

refinements. *See* post-search clusters.

related term (RT). A controlled vocabulary term in a thesaurus that is coordinate to another controlled vocabulary term. Because both terms are at the same level in the hierarchy, they are not related hierarchically. (Also called an associative relationship.)

relationship designator. *See* role.

relevance. User perception that the information at hand has the potential to answer their question or contribute to satisfying their information needs.

relevance feedback. The search system's utilization of one or more retrievals and their cited or citing references to find ones like them.

relevance-ranked retrievals. Retrievals that systems rank algorithmically in order of likely relevance using hundreds of factors including the extent to which they match user-entered search terms, the frequency of such terms across all sources in the database, and the proximity of such terms in retrievals.

research databases. A systematically organized collection of data or information that people search, producing multiple retrievals from which they must synthesize answers to their questions.

resolver links. Links that trigger the release of a retrieval's citation data to link resolvers, software that automatically queries the library's other databases to determine whether they contain the actual source, and when they do, retrieves and displays the actual source to the user.

retrievals. A database's report of the number of sources it has retrieved for a user-entered search statement that sometimes includes a display of the first dozen or so sources in the form of surrogates or the actual sources themselves. *See also* source.

role. A word or phrase that describes the part played by a person, corporate body, or family in a source's creation. Examples are author, calligrapher, editor, illustrator, photographer, and videographer.

saved search. Search system functionality that keeps a search formulation permanently or for a specified time period. *See also* search alert.

scholarship. The process of sharing new discoveries, theories, ideas, information, and data.

scope note. In a controlled vocabulary, an index term's definition and/or explanatory information about the index term's proper usage such as clarifying an ambiguous term or restricting the term's usage.

search alert. A special type of saved search that the search system executes per the searcher's instructions, sending him newly retrieved sources that meet his search criteria on a regular basis. *See also* saved search.

search box. Usually a single-line box into which the user enters a search statement and bearing a search button or magnifying-glass icon on which the user clicks to submit his statement to the search system. (Also called a dialog box.)

search engine. *See* Web search engine.

search engine optimization (SEO). The deliberate process of jumping the queue to effect a higher ranking for one's website.

search history. A search system's functionality for displaying the user's previous search statements, sets (when available), and number of retrievals (when available). Also for combining sets (when available).

search statement. An expression of the negotiated query that the expert intermediary searcher formulates with reference to the search system's searching language and the database's controlled and free text vocabularies and enters into the search system with the expectation that on its own or in conjunction with other search statements, it will produce relevant retrievals.

search strategy. "A plan for the whole search" (Bates 1979, 206).

search system. A computer program that indexes and stores surrogates and/or the actual sources themselves, prompts people to enter search statements that represent their queries, and processes these statements in ways that enable it to respond with surrogates and/or sources that have the potential to satisfy people's queries.

search tactic. "A move to further the search" (Bates 1979, 206).

searching language. System-provided instructions and controls that the searcher wields to tell the system what operations to perform and how to perform them.

see from references. *See* use from (UF) references.

see references. *See* use references.

select-a-field pull-down menu. The pull-down menu in a search system's basic or advanced interface bearing field names that the user chooses for the purpose of restricting retrieval to the selected field.

sets. Temporary storage bins for search results.

SIC codes. *See* standard industrial codes.

source. "A distinct information or artistic creation" (Tillett 2003, 11). (Also called a work.) *Online Searching* uses source to refer in a general way to the surrogates, texts, media, and numeric and spatial data that searches produce and users scrutinize for answering user queries. *See also* retrievals.

source database. A database that both contains and searches the actual sources themselves—full-texts, media, and numeric and spatial data.

spatial data. Numeric values that reference an object, event, phenomenon, etc., to a location on the earth's surface.

specificity. A principle that governs the indexer's assignment of index terms from a controlled vocabulary to surrogates that are as specific as the source's subject matter.

standard industrial codes. A numeric code that classifies industry areas. (Also called SIC codes.)

stemming. The search system's retrieval of variants for words and phrases in search statements. For example, the word *argument* in a search statement retrieves variants such as argue, argued, arguing, argument, arguments, argumentation, and argumentative. (Also called intelligent stemming.)

subject. A topic or area of knowledge that is the content of a source or that interests a person.

subject heading. A subject word or phrase to which all material that the library has on that subject is entered in the catalog or index.

subject search. A request for information about a topic, idea, object, phenomenon, person, organization, etc., that almost always retrieves several sources (e.g., journal articles, books, conference papers, blogs, directory entries, and combinations of these).

subject term. *See* index term.

summary. *See* abstract.

surrogate. A summary version of a source that is full-text, media, or numeric and spatial data. At a minimum, a surrogate is a citation that contains just enough information to enable a person to find the source in a library's collection or database. More comprehensive are surrogates bearing index terms and/or an abstract that summarizes the source's intellectual contents.

surrogate database. A database that bears summary versions of the actual sources; it does not bear the actual sources themselves.

syndetic structure. The thesaurus network of controlled vocabulary term relationships—BTs, NTs, RTs, and UFs.

synonym. A term with the same or similar meaning as one or more other terms. In a controlled vocabulary, only one such term will be authorized and the other(s) designated as use reference(s).

systematic review. A rigorous literature review, usually in the health sciences, that is based on a clearly articulated research question, identifies all relevant published and unpublished studies, assesses each study's quality, synthesizes the research, and interprets and summarizes research findings. *See also* literature review.

technical reading of a database. A methodology for searchers to quickly and efficiently familiarize themselves with a database and the system they use to search it.

technical reading of a source. Reading only those portions of a source that are the most important for understanding overall content.

texts. Written documents.

thesaurus. A controlled vocabulary that designates a subset of a natural language as authorized index terms, expresses the broader and narrower relationships between these terms, and includes related terms and cross-references from synonyms.

title. The word(s) that identify a source but are not necessarily a unique identifier for the source.

truncation. The use of a symbol such as a question mark, asterisk, colon, or ampersand to shorten, limit, or cut off a search word so that the search system retrieves longer and/or differently spelled variants.

typecasting. Scrutinizing the user's query to determine whether a subject search or a known-item will satisfy it.

uniform resource locator (URL). An address for a website, document, or other resource on the World Wide Web.

unused synonyms. *See* use references.

URL. *See* uniform resource locator (URL).

use from (UF) references. In an authority record, a list of unused synonyms for the record's authorized name, subject, or title.

use references. In a controlled vocabulary, a synonym for or variant of a name, subject, or title that guides the user to the authorized index term. *See also* entry vocabulary.

Venn diagrams. Visual representations of Boolean expressions in which the circles are facets and the overlap between two or more circles are relationships between facets that should or shouldn't be present in search results.

Web-scale discovery (WSD) system. A library's Google-like interface to much of its digital content, offering one-stop shopping for academic information. (Also known as discovery systems, library discovery systems, single-search discovery systems, single-source discovery systems, or these same adjectives ending with services or tools.)

Web search engine. A computer program that indexes the World Wide Web, prompts people to enter search statements that represent their queries, and processes these statements in ways that enable it to respond with surrogates for World Wide Web content that link to specific websites that have the potential to satisfy people's queries.

white hat. A computer programmer who engages in acceptable search engine optimization techniques.

World Wide Web. *See* open Web.

WSD system. *See* web-scale discovery system.

yearbook. A review of trends, issues, and events pertaining to a topic, place, or phenomenon in a particular year.

Bibliography

Bates, Marcia J. 1979. "Information Search Tactics." *Journal of the American Society for Information Science* 30 (July): 205–14.

Bopp, Richard E., and Linda C. Smith. 2011. *Reference and Information Services: An Introduction.* 4th ed. Santa Barbara, CA: Libraries Unlimited.

Tillett, Barbara. 2003. "FRBR: Functional Requirements for Bibliographic Records." *Technicalities* 23, no. 5: 1, 11–13.

Index

À la Carte Edition of the Building Block Search
    Strategy, 127-28, 183-84, 187, 188, 189, 196,
    197, 200, 210, 220, 228, 245, 256, 262
A&I databases, 29, *50*, *57*, 59-61, *62*, 211, 218, 262,
    267
ABI/Inform database, 61, *107*, 211, 214, 261
Abilock, Debbie, 246, 251
abstracting and indexing databases. *See* A&I
    databases
abstracts, 15, 22, 23, 51, *52*, *57*, 58-60, *63*, 73, 129,
    187-89, 205, 235, 261, 267
    teaching end users about, 205, 238, 247, 264
Academia.edu, 178
Academic OneFile database, *105*, *107*, 108, 110, 154,
    194, *195*, 241
AcademicInfo web directory, 195
ACM Digital Library database, 194
Acronym Finder, 67
active listening, 30, 40
adjacency operator, 115-17, 120, 122, *134-35*, 136,
    138-40, *225*, 267
Advanced Research Projects Agency (ARPA), 2, 3
advertising, 202-203, 204, 211, 212, 214, 258, 259
affiliation, *86*, 153, 157, 172, *222*, 224, 227, 228
Agricola database, 2
Air University Library's Index to Military Periodicals
    (AULIMP) database, *72*, 74
Alexander Street Press, 52, *53*, 73
All About Birds database, 20, 69
almanacs, *50*, 65, 70-71, 83, 267
Altmetric, 177, *178*, 180
altmetrics, 167, 177-78, 179-80, 203, 263, 267
America: History and Life database, 51, *52*, 261
American Film Scripts Online database, *64*
American National Biography Online database, 147
American Psychiatric Association, 71, 73

American Psychological Association, 89, 108
AND operator, 77-82, 84, 93, *94*, 95, 97, 106, 115,
    119, 120, *134*, 144, 220, 223, *225*, 228, 243,
    244, 245, 267
    in search strategies, 98, 99, 184, 185, 186
Anderson, Barbara, 183
Ann Arbor District Library, 18
AP Image database, 52, *53*, 166
Armstrong, Annie R., 10, 11
article-level metrics, 167, 176-77, *182*, 267. *See also*
    h-index
article spinning, 258, 262
ArticlesPlus web-scale discovery system, 20-22, *23*
arXiv database, 9, 11, *21*, 61, *64*
Ask search system, 211, 214
Associations Unlimited database, 68, *69*
Atherton, Pauline. *See* Cochrane, Pauline A.
audience, *87*, 153, 218, 239, 248
Aula, Anne, 260, 265
authentication, 6, 18, 20, 23, 24, 25
author-bibliography search, 145, 147, 148, 164, 165,
    166, 190, *221*, *222*, 267
author credentials, 31, *86*, 206, 211
author-keywords, 23, *87*, 95, 155, 187, 267
author searches, 83, 141, 145-51, 156, 164, 165, 172,
    177, *221*, *222*
authority control, 146-47, 150, 164, 172, 174, 192,
    227-28, 268
authority file, *146*, 147, 210, 268
authority record, 90-91, *92*, 93, 96, 97, 98, *105*, *106*,
    146, 268
authorized term. *See* index terms
authors, 5, *86*, 95, 129, 133, 141, 145-51, 156, 164,
    165-66, 168, *169*, *171-74*, 176-79, 181-82, 202,
    206, 211, 223, 228, 237, 247, 267
automatic facet recognition, 127, 128, 262-63

automatic vocabulary assistance, 126, *208*, 210, 215, 244, 262

Avery Index to Architectural Periodicals database, 59, *60*

backward chaining. *See* bibliography scanning

Badke, William, 13, 137

Baildon, Mark, 246, 251

Bar-Ilan, Judit, 173, 180

Bates, Marcia J., xx, xxi, 30–31, 45, 63, 73, 98, 108, 109, 183, 198, 201, 206, *207–208*, 212, 240, 251, 278, 279

Battelle, John, 4, 11

Bauer, Kathleen, 180

Berners-Lee, Tim, 3–4, 10, 11

berrypicking model, 30–31, 43, 246

bibliographic database. *See* databases: surrogate

Bibliographic Retrieval Services (BRS), 2–3

bibliographies, *50*, 57–58, 68, 73, 130, *131*, 142, 145, 151, 164, 166, 235, 237, 247, 268

bibliography scanning, 129–31, *221*, *222*, 268

bibliometrics, 167–76, 179, 181–82, 263, 268

Big Bite Search Strategy, 184

big ideas. *See* facet analysis; facets

Bing search engine, 211, 259

biographies, *50, 56, 65*, 66–67, *71, 74*, 142, 168, 192, 268

Biosis database, 194

Birds of North America Online database, 68–69, *70*

Björner, Susanne, 3, 11

black hat, 201, 203, 258, 262, 268

Blakeslee, Sarah, 212, 214

Book Review Index database, 59, *61*

books, 3, 4, 34–35, 38, *39*, 51, 58, *63, 64*, 82, 113, 120, 121, 141, 142, 145, 164, 167, 173, 179, 181, 247, 251, 256

Boolean logic and operators, 77–84, *93*, 109–112, 114, *119*, 122, *134*, 138–40, 185, *207*, 218, 220, 224, *225*, 240, 268. *See also* names of Boolean operators

Boolean search systems, 90–99, *105, 107*, 114–24, *134–35*, 143–44, 148–49, 152–53, 218–220, 240, 262, 268

future of, 260

search strategies for, 183–84, 185, 187, 190, *197*, 198, 210

Bopp, Richard E., 27, 40, 45, 46, 65, 70, 71, 73, 267, 272, 275, 281

Borgman, Christine, 8, 11

Bornmann, Lutz, 255, 265

Bosch, Stephen, 7, 11

Bourne, Charles P., 2, 11, 13, 183

Breeding, Marshall, 23, 24

Brigham, Tara J., 180

broader term (BT), 88–89, 91, *92*, 95, 96, 99, 103, *105, 106*, 184, *208*, 210, 215, 268

Brophy, Jan, 10, 11

browsing, *208*, 210, *222*, 227–28, 247, 261, 269

databases at the hub, 16, 24

directories, 68

for the journal run, 158, *159–61*

in author searches, 147–48, 150, 215, 248

in cited reference searches, 168, *169–70*

in title searches, 142, 143, *144*, 248

index terms, 98, 107, 224

journal names, 153, 158

online thesaurus, 90–93, 104, *105*, 245, 260, 261

BRS search system, 3

Buchanan, Heidi E., 204, 212

Buffet Edition of the Building Block Search Strategy, 99, 183–84, 196, *197*, 199, 200, 210, 263

Building Block Search Strategy, 98–99, 108, 127–28, 183–84, 187, 188, 189, 190, 196, *197*, 198, 199, 200, 210, 212

Cailliau, Robert, 13

Can't Live without This Facet Search Strategy, 184–86, 187, 189, 190, 196, *197*, 198, 199, 200, 209, 210, 256

Cassell, Kay Ann, 27, 45, 46

Catalog of U.S. Government Publications, *64*

cataloger. *See* indexers

catalogs, 2, 29, 34–35, *50, 57*, 58–59, *74*, 143, 269. *See also* OPACs

Cave, Richard, 177, 180

CD-ROM search systems, 3, 5, 269

chat interviews, 34–36, 38, 40, 142–43, *144*, 238, 250, 251

cheat sheets, *105, 107, 134–35, 225–26*, 230, 241, 257

Chen, Xiaotian, 260, 265

citation count, 167–74, *176, 179, 182*, 269

citation indexes. *See* cited reference searches

citation management system (CMS), *131*, 205, 231, 234–37, 247, 249, 251, 253, 269

Citation Pearl Growing Search Strategy, 41, 96, 187–90, 196, *197*, 198, 199, 200, *208*, 209, 210, 245, 256, 269

citation verification searches, 141, 151–53, 163, 165, *221, 222*, 269

citations, 2, 3, 15, 22, 51, 57, 58, 59, *61*, 73, 83, 114, 141, 142, 151–53, 163, 165, 206, 235, 237, 247, 269

cited reference searches, 29, 190, *221, 222*, 223, 269

for authors, 168–74

for individual publications, 131–33, 179, 181, 246, 256

cited references, 23, 114, 129–30, *131, 221,* 246, 247, 269

citing references, 114, 167, 202, 203, *221,* 246, 269

classes. *See* information literacy training

classic model of communication, 28

classification, 58, *87,* 194, 202, 269

classification captions and codes, 89, 100, *188,* 189, *222,* 224, 227, 244, 246, 261, 269

closed-ended questions, 41, 269

closing, 33, 43

clusters, *94,* 124, 202, *208, 222,* 224, 225, 229, 261, 262, 276

    accompanying citation count results, *171, 172,* 181

    age group, 110

    classification, 188, 194, 244, 246

    non-subject, 100, 215, 226–27

    search tactics involving, 210, 211, 214–15

    source title, *156, 157, 158, 171, 227*

    source type, *155, 157, 171,* 227

    subject, 22, 100, *101–103, 124, 154,* 156, 157, 165, *171,* 188, *194,* 227, 246

    teaching end users about, 202, 238, 246

    to articulate unfocused queries, 22, *23,* 47, 100–103, 151, 194, 199, 227, 246, 261

    used in database detective work, 153, 154–57, 165

Cochrane, Pauline A., 98, 109, 183, 198, 199

Cold War, 1, 3, 10

Colón-Aguirre, Mónica, 9, 10, 11

Columbia University, 59, 73

command-line interface, 3, 5, 270

common nouns, 88–89, 166, 192

communication paradigms, 4, 10

Communications & Mass Media Complete database, 104

Compendex database, *107,* 108, 111, 139, 153, 198, 199, 217–28

comprehensive searches, 44, 190, 209, 255–56. *See also* literature reviews; systematic reviews.

conducting a facet analysis and logical combination. *See* facet analysis; logical combination

conducting the reference interview. *See* reference interview

Connaway, Lynn Sillipigni, 10, 11

content farms, 203, 258

controlled vocabularies (CVs), 15, 58, 88–89, 95, 103–104, 113, 133, 261, 270. *See also* index terms; controlled vocabulary (CV) searching

    as sources of free text terms, 114, *115,* 121, 188

    databases without, 114, 133

fields bearing, 86–87, 114

flat, 88, 104, 224

tactics pertaining to, *208,* 209

controlled vocabulary (CV) searching, 85–112, 209–210, *221, 222,* 224, 228, 229, 270

    benefits of, 103–104. *See also* controlled vocabularies (CVs); index terms

    cross-system comparison of, 104–107

    for in-depth queries, 90–98, 108–12

    for unfocused queries, 100–103, 227

    search strategies for, 98–99, 185, 187–89, 194

    sample queries for, 108, 109–112

controlled vocabulary terms. *See* index terms

Cook, Douglas, 252

Cornell Lab of Ornithology, 68, 69, *70,* 73

costs, 6–9, 11, 18, 24, 192, 196, 259

COUNTER-compliant data, 257, 270

CRAAP test, 206, 211, 214

CRC Handbook of Chemistry and Physics database, *71*

CQ Almanac database, 70

CQ Press, 70, 73

credibility, xix, 178, 204, 206, 211, 214, 246, 270

Cull, Barry W., 205, 213

Cummings, Anthony, 7, 11

Cutts, Matt, 203, 213

database aggregators, 2, 7, 15–16, 143, 165, 248, 270

database hubs, xix, xx, 5–6, 7–8, 9, 11, 15–21, 23–25, 49, 63, 72–73, 158, 217, 240–41, 262, 264, 265, 270. *See also* Search Tools

database publishers, xix, 2, 7, 15–16, 20, 22–23, 104, 146, 164, 260, 262, 264, 270

database selection. *See* databases: selection

database supermarkets. *See* database aggregators

databases, 257, 270. *See also* names of databases

    accessing, 15–25

    classification of, 49, *50,* 72–73, 217–18

    discipline-specific, 2, 9, 16–19, 49, *50,* 73, 142, 143, 148, 154, 158, 194, 241, 256, 262

    encyclopedic, 49, 67, 132, 143, 148, 154, 155, 158, 167, 194, 217, 241, 243, 256, 27

    evaluating, xix, 5–6, 15, 16, 24

    familiarizing oneself with. *See* technical reading of a database

    for assessing research impact. *See* altmetrics; bibliometrics

    full-text, *50, 57,* 58, 61–65, 66–71, 73, 125, 211, 214, 220, 262, 272

    future of, 260–61

    genre, 16, 18–19, 25, 49, *50,* 51–56, *65,* 68, *71, 72,* 73, *74,* 217

licensed, xix, 1–6, 8–10, 15–19, 24, 49, *64, 71,* 201, 203, 204, 206, 212, 234, 258, 261, 274
licensing, 5, 6, 7, 16
mastering, 217–28, 230
open-Web, 6, 15, 16, 20, *21,* 24, *61, 64,* 67, 68, 69, 70, *71, 72, 74,* 107
origins of, 1–4
reference, 49, *50,* 64–74, 82–83, 217, 229, 277
research, 49, *50,* 57–64, 72–74, 98, 177, 217, 218, 277
selecting, xx, 16–19, 23–24, 33, 42, 49–74, 78, 84, 143, 147–48, 152, 215, 217, 263–64
source, 49–55, 57, 61–64, 73, 217–18, 279
split between licensed and open Webs, 6–10, 20, *21*
surrogate, 49, *50,* 51, 57–61, *62, 63,* 73, 217–18, 280
teaching end users about, 240–41
types of searches in, 220, *221–22*
dates, *87,* 89, 90, *92, 105, 106,* 154, *155, 156,* 157, 172, 202, 224, 246
De Bellis, Nicola, 180
deceptive Web practices. *See* black hat
descriptors. *See* index terms
detective work, 141, 153–58, 164, 165–66, 223–24
Dewdney, Patricia, 34, 45
Diagnostic and Statistical Manual of Mental Disorders database, 71
dialog box. *See* search box
Dialog search system, 2–3, 183, 264
dictionaries. *See* language dictionaries; discipline-based dictionaries
Dictionary of Opera Characters database, *67,* 68
digital libraries, xix, 49, *50,* 51, 56, 73, 101, 217, 270
direct entry, 96–98, 106, *107,* 123, *124, 134–35,* 144, 148–50, 270
directories, *65,* 67, 68, *69, 71, 74,* 270–71
discipline-based dictionaries, 29, *50,* 65, 66, 67–68, 194, 271
disciplines, 9, 20, 41, 49, 68, 69, 73, 142, 147, 168, 172, 174, 217, 218, 228, 256, 262
displaying retrievals and responding tactically, 33, 42, 43, 201–15, 245–47. *See also* retrievals; search tactics; sources
DMOZ web directory, 195
Dobbs, Aaron W., 252
document representation, 49, 51, 220, 271
document type. *See* sources: genre
Dolan, Rebecca, 5, 11
domain experts and expertise, xix, 6, 11, 194, 204, 217, 240, 255, 261, 271
double posting, 271
Drabenstott, Karen M. *See* Markey, Karen

DuckDuckGo search engine, 259
Durrance, Joan C., 33, 45
dynamic term suggestions, 95

eBird database, 36
EBSCOhost, 51, 52, 90–97, 100–102, 104–107, 109, 110, 112, 115–16, *118, 120, 121,* 122, 129, 130, 132, *134–35,* 138, 140, 143, 165, 188, *189,* 218, *219,* 220, 224, 228, *232,* 233, *234, 236, 244,* 248, 252, 260
Edwards, Richard, 7, 11
Elsevier B.V., *123–24, 155–57, 172–73, 178,* 218, *219, 223, 227,* 230, 248
email interviews, 34, 238, 251
Embase database, 194
Emrich, Barry R., 1, 10, 12
encyclopedias, 29, 49, *50, 65,* 66, 67, 68–70, *71,* 73, *74,* 82, 101, 194, 204, 240–41, 256, 271
end users, xx, xxi, 4–6, 10, 15, 75, 133, 142–43, 145, 147, 151–52, 178, 261, 265, 271
  and search strategies, 184, 185, 193, 195, 196
  conducting research, 49, 133, 162, 190, 237, 255–56, 258, 264
  handling retrievals, 201–204, 212, 231–234, 237, 263
  in reference interviews, 27–47, 209, 237
  knowledge and sophistication of, 3, 29, *41,* 194, 198, 212, 218, 241, 248, 262, 265
  overwhelming, xxi, 158, 205, 248, 250, 254
  teaching about online searching, 205, 206, 238–51, 253–54
Engineering Village, 104–107, *134–35,* 218, *219, 222, 223, 225–26, 227*
entering the search and responding strategically. *See* controlled vocabularies (CVs) searching; free text (FT) searching; known-item searches; search strategies
entry vocabulary, 88, 90, *91,* 271
Environmental Sciences and Pollution Management database, 198, 199
ERIC database, 2, 104, 107, 108, 109, 112, 129, 138, 140, 154, 156, 183, 186, 198, 199, 200, 211, 254
Europa World of Learning database, 68, *71*
everyday people. *See* end users
expert intermediary searchers, xix, xx, xxi, 2–3, 44, 75, 85, 93, 95, 100, 114, 133, 190, 198, 201, 206, 232, 245, 257, 265, 271. *See also* librarians
explode, 91, *92, 105, 106,* 110, 261
extended-Boolean searching, 113, 271, 152, 164, 204, 218–220, 262–63, 271
  for known-items, 144–45, 150, 247

for subjects, 125–29, 133, 136, 244–45
strategies for, 127–28, 183–84, 185, 188, 190, *197*, 198, 210

Facebook, 67, 177, 257
facet. *See* clusters
facet analysis, xx, 33, 42, 185, 188, 198–200, 271
adjusting the, 82
for known-item searches, 143, 148, 152, 247
for subject searches, 75–82, 83–84, 89–90, 114, 120, 122, 136
in extended-Boolean search systems, 126, 127–28
teaching end users about, 241–44, 247
facets, 75–76, 78, 104, 109–112, 138–40, 204, *207–208*, 209, 212, 215, 228, 229, 262, 271
articulating, 229, 241–43
number of facets in queries, 46, 100, 108, 143, 148, 152, 183, 184, 190–93, 196, 220
relationship, 78, 84, 122, 220
in search strategies, 98–100, 127–28, 183, 184, 186, 187, 190–93, 198, 199–200
selecting search terms for, 90–94, 97–98
using clusters to represent, 110, 154
fact-finding, 43, 49, *50*, 64, *65*, 68, 70, 73
faculty. *See* instructors
fair linking, 204, 259, 271
Fast, Carl V., xx, xxii, 5, 10, 12
fastcat, 104
federated search system, 24, 262, 272
Feldman, Susan, 126, 137
field labels, 96, *97*, 106, *107*, 220, 272
fields, 51, 52, 58, *59*, *60*, 61, *62*, 66, 86, *87*, 108, 114, 120, 153, 158, 187, *208*, 209, 210, 215, 220, *222*, 223, 246–47, 261, 272
fields of study. *See* disciplines
Filmmakers Library Online database, 52, *53*
filter. *See* clusters
filter bubbles. *See* personalization
find-like searches, 128–29, 133, 190, *208*, 210, 215, *221*, 245–46, 261
First World War Poetry digital collection, *72, 74*
Fister, Barbara, 10, 12
Folger, Kathleen M., 5, 16, 18
follow-up, 33, 43, 190
form, 49, *50*, 57, 58, 61, 62, *64*, 71, *72*, 73, *74*, 272
format. *See* databases: genre; literary genre; sources: genre
forward chaining. *See* cited reference searches
Fosmire, Michael, 247, 251
Fowler, Kristine K., 9, 12
free text (FT) searching, 104, 113–40, 188, 210, *221*, *222*, 230, 272
benefits of, 133

cross-system comparison of, 133–35
for authors, 148–50
for titles, 144, 162
identifying search terms for, 114–15, 126, 136
language, 114–24, 144, 148–50, 225–26
of Boolean search systems, 114–24, 144, 148–50
of extended-Boolean search systems, 125–29, 144–45, 148–49
of full-texts, 113, 120–24, 136, 272
of surrogate records, 113, 118–20
operators for, 115–17, 121–22
friends, xx, 10, 39, 42, 113–14, 142, 145, 214, 231, 235, 238, 259
Friends Strategy. *See* Getting a Little Help from Your Friends Search Strategy
full-text aggregators. *See* journal aggregators
full-text fulfillment searches, 141, 151–53, 205, *221*, *222*, 272. *See also* full-texts
full-text publishers. *See* journal publishers
full-text searching. *See* free text searching: of full-texts
full-texts, 5, 15–16, *52*, 58, *63*, 100, 114, 136, 187, 205, 261–62, 264, 272. *See also* full-text fulfillment searches
authenticating for, 6, 20, 24, 25
databases of. *See* databases: full text
in citation management systems, 235–37
indexing, 51, *57*, 61, 64–65, 85
resolver links accompanying, 22, 59, 60, 130, 131, 218, 223
searching, 113, 120–24, 136, 220
teaching end users about, 238, 247

Gale Cengage Learning, 61, 68, *69*, 73, *103, 105*, 106, *107*, 143, 165, 194, *195*, 248, 252
Gale Virtual Reference Library, 68, 241
García-Pérez, Miguel, 180
Gardner, Susan A., 246, 251
Garfield, Eugene, 167, 180
gateway systems. *See* database hubs
Gaudin, Sharon, 259, 265
General OneFile database, *105, 107*, 110
genre. *See* databases: genre; literary genre; sources: genre
Geographic Research, 55, 73
Gergle, Darren, 176
Getting a Little Help from Your Friends Search Strategy, 192, 193–96, *197*, 199, 200
Getty Thesaurus of Geographic Names (TGN), 147
Gillies, James, 13
Gimlet reference tracing and reporting application, 257

Google, xix, xx, 4, 5, 6, 11, 61, 137, 165, 166, 174, 177, 233, 259, 261
  end user predilection for, 1, 10, 11, 15, 20, 238, 261
  for developing a working knowledge on a topic, 9
  retrievals in, 202, 203, 200, 211, 214, 258, 259
  searching, 6, 125, 126-28, *134-35*, 147, 164, 192
Google Images database, 52, 166
Google Scholar, 6, 24, 133, 140, 234, 260
  enhanced with resolver links, 20
  for bibliometrics, 173-74, 176, 178-79, 181-82
  for cited reference searches, 132, 256
  for known-item searches, 143, 148, 165, 247
  for quality information, 9, 20, *64*
graphical user interfaces, 5, 10, 89
Grassian, Esther S., 204, 213
greeting, 33-34, 249
Gross, Melissa, 39, 45
Guédon, Claude, 7, 12
Guynn, Jessica, 203, 213

h-index, *173, 174,* 176, 179, 182, 223, 272. *See also*
  article-level metrics
Hafner, Katie, 3, 12
Hahn, Trudi Bellardo, 13
handbooks, *50, 65,* 71, 272
Harmeyer, Dave, 27, 45, 46
Harter, Stephen P., 183, 199
Harzing, Ann-Wil K, 173, 180
Hawkins, Donald T., 98, 108
Hayes, Robert M., 1, 12
Head, Alison J., xx, xxii, 9, 10, 12
help, 104, 118, *119,* 225, 229, 264
Hernon, Peter, 33, 45
high-posted searches, 10, 155, 158, 203, 205, 220, 229, 245-46, 273
  clusters for reducing, 100, 227, 245
  for authors, 149
  for one-facet queries, 192, 193
  for titles, 144
  major index terms for reducing, 91
  tactics for reducing, *207-208,* 209-210
Hildreth, Charles R., 3, 12, 125, 137, 260, 265
Hiremath, Uma, 27, 45, 46
history note, 89, 90, *92,*104, *105,* 273
hits. *See* retrievals
hypertext, 3-4

i10-index, *174,* 176, 179, 182
identifiers, 61, *87,* 89
images, *21, 52, 53,* 55, 56, *64, 65, 71, 74,* 101, 164, 166, 237, 259
impact:
  author's, 167-74, 176, 179, 182, *221, 222,* 223

factor, 174-76, 273
  journal's, 174-75, 179, 181, *221*
  individual publication's, 131-33, 179, 181
imposed queries, *36,* 39, 273
in-depth queries. *See* queries: in-depth
Index Islamicus database, 218-20, 224
Index of Christian Art, *64*
index terms, 2, 3, 22-23, *52,* 76, 82, 96, 99, 108-112, 129, 136, 154-55, 166, 245, 273. *See also*
  controlled vocabularies (CVs); controlled
  vocabulary (CV) searching
  benefits of, 103-104
  browsing in the online thesaurus, 88-96, *105,* 188, *222, 224,* 245
  clusters of, 100-103, 154-57, 188, 269
  direct entry of, 95, 96-98, 106, *107*
  in a controlled vocabulary, 88-89
  in surrogates, 7, 15, 51, 57, 58, 59, *60,* 61, *62, 63,* 85, *87*
  preferring over free text terms, 103-104, 108
  relationships between, 88-89, *92, 106*
  scanning for relevant, 188-89
  transforming into free text, 120, 136
  words in, 97-98, *107*
indexers, 15, 85, 88-89, 90, 95, 103, 108, 146, 273
indexes, *50,* 57-62, 273
indexing, 85, *86, 87,* 88-89
indicative abstracts, 59, 61, *62,* 273
indicative-informative abstracts, 59, 273
information explosion, 1, 10, 255, 273
information literacy training, xxi, 204, 206, 211, 214, 237, 238-51, 253-54, 258, 264
  course syllabus for, 239-40, 248
  lesson plans for, 239-40
information needs, xix, 27-30, 36-37, 42, 44, 45, 256, 265, 273
Information Please Almanac database, 70
information portals. *See* database hubs
information retrieval systems. *See* search systems
information search process (ISP) model, 31-32
information seeking models, 27-32, 45
informative abstracts, 59, 273
InfoTrac Newsstand database, 165
Inspec database, 166
institutional repositories (IRs), 8-9, 23, 25, 261, 274
instructors, 5, 6, 10, 167, 204, 248, 258, 263
  conducting research, 7-9
  their directives to end users, 39, *41,* 142, 145, 151, 205, 223, 241, 256
  their research impact, 167, 171, *173, 174, 178*
interfaces, xxi, 4, 10, 16, 24, 244
interlibrary loan, 59, 143, 148, 151, 162

intermediary searchers. *See* expert intermediary searchers

International Bibliography of the Social Sciences database, 166

International Medieval Bibliography database, *64*

Internet. *See* open Web

Internet Movie Database, *64*

Jacsó, Péter, 137, 180

Jansen, Bernard J., xx, xxii, 202, 213

journal aggregators, 15, 20, 51, 59, 60, 158, 160, 165, 177, 179, 274

journal articles, 51, 59, *60*, 67, 83, 142, 145, 151, 176, 181

Journal Citation Reports database, 174–75, 179, 181

journal holdings record, *159–60*, 274

journal publishers, 4, 7–9, 15, 22, 60, 146, 158, 177, 204, 274

journal run, 141, 142, 158–62, 164, 165–66, *221, 222*, 274

journal titles. *See* source titles

JStor database, 61, 133, *134–35*, 139, 143, 233

Julien, Heidi, 5, 12

Kelly Bluebook database, *72, 74*

keywords, 10, 44, 75, 95, 245, 255, 260, 274. *See also* natural language

Kilgour, Frederick G., 145, 165

King, Douglas, 5, 12

Kirk, Thomas, 29, 45

known-item searches, 132, 141–66, 248, 261, 274

known-items, xx, 82, 83, 192, 193
   disguised as subject searches, 132, 142, 145, 147, 164
   teaching end users about, 241, 247–48

Kolowich, Steve, xx, xxii

Korah, Abe, 262, 265

Kracker, Jacqueline, 32, 45

Kuhlthau, Carol, 31, 32, 45

Lampe, Cliff, 168–78

language clusters, fields, and qualifiers, 22, 59, 87, *124, 155*, 224, *227, 228*

language dictionaries, *50, 65*, 67, *71, 72*, 274

Lapinski, Scott, 181

Leeder, Christopher Alan, 10, 12, 206, 213, 246, 251

levels of question formation model, 29–30

Levine-Clark, Michael, 262, 265

lexicographers, 88, 89, 274

LexisNexis, 121, 137, 198, 230, 241

LexisNexis database, 61, 121–24, 133, *134–35*, 139, 165, 199–200

LibGuides, 25, 239, 241, 257–58, 264, 274

librarians, xx–xxi, 7, 125, 142, 145, 232, 248, 262. *See also* expert intermediary searchers
   dedicated to open access, 8, 9
   evaluating sources, 5, 6, 15, 16, 18, 24, 206
   improving search systems, 5, 6, 204, 212, 264
   negotiating user queries, 29, 33–43
   searching the licensed web, xix
   users consulting, xx, 10, 28–47, 75
   with training in online searching, 3, 125, 191

library anxiety, 10

library catalogs. *See* OPACs

Library Literature database, 236, 254

Library of Congress Name Authority File (LCNAF), *146*, 147, 165, 166, 168, 182, 215

Library of Congress Subject Headings (LCSH), 58, *59*

library users. *See* end users

licensed Web. *See* databases: licensed

Licklider, J. C. R., 3

Liddy, Elizabeth, 125, 137

limits. *See* clusters

link resolver, 22, 275

LinkedIn, 67, 177

Lipetz, Ben-Ami, 145, 165

literary genre, 148, 205, 260

literary warrant, 89, 113, 133, 136, 275

literature reviews, 133, 154–56, 190, 256, 275. *See also* comprehensive searches; systematic reviews

Lockheed Missiles and Space Company, 2–3

logical combination, xx, *33, 42*, 77–84, 89–90, 109–112, 114, 122, 138–40, 154, 185, 188, 198, 199–200, 204, 208, 275
   teaching end users about, 241–43

low-posted searches, 185, 196, 203, 225, 244
   Citation Pearl Growing Strategy for increasing, 189, 190, 199–200 245–46
   journal run for increasing, 158, 164
   tactics for increasing, *207–208*, 209–201
   using cited and citing references to increase, 128, 130, 132

Lowest Posted Facet First Search Strategy, 184, 185, 186

Lynch, Clifford, 7, 8, 9, 12

Madooei, Ali, 247, 251

main entry, 58, 202, 275

major index terms, 90, *91, 92*, 100, *101, 102*, 105, *106*, 188, 275

manuals, *50, 65*, 71, 275

maps, 54, *55*, 56

Marchionini, Gary, 255, 266

Markey, Karen, 3, 10, 12, 98, 109, 180, 182, 183, 198, 202, 206, 213, 246, 251
Marquis Who's Who, 66, 73, 147
Marquis Who's Who database, *66*
McKee, Guian A., 109, 128
Meadow, Charles T., 98, 109, 183, 198, 199
media, xix, 5, 22, 24, 25, 49, *50*, 51-53, 56, 73, 217, 275
Medline database, 2
Meho, Lokman I., 173, 180
Meier, John J., 260, 266
Mergent database, 68, 192
Merriam-Webster Online database, *71*
MeSH (Medical Subject Headings) database, 104-106, *107*, 111, 200, 230
Metzger, Miriam, 5, 12
Michigan eLibrary (MeL), 18
Microsoft Academic Search, 6, 9, 260
Milkova, Stiliana, 239, 251
Mirlyn OPAC, 25, 144, 148, *149-50*, 161, *162-63*
Mischo, William H., 3, 9, 12, 24
misspellings, 10, 96, 97, 147, 151, 207, 208, 210, 215, 247
models, 27-32, 45
Morrill Land-Grant Acts, 7
Most Specific Facet Search Strategy, 184
Munson, Doris M., 74
Myhre, Sarah K., 246, 251

NAICS codes, 261, 275
names, 64, *65*, 66, 68, 145
   author, *57*, 58, 59, *60*, *62*, 65, 145-51, 156, 164, 165, 168-70, 172, 192
   changes of, 58, 145, 146-47, 153, 168, 172, 174, 182
   database, 16, 58, 71
   database hub, 16, 23, 24
   of organizations, 146-47, 192
   of persons, 145-47, 164, 165, 184, 192
   OPAC, 25
   problems searching for, 146-47, 151, 168, 182, 192
   proximity operator for, 117, 165
   web-scale discovery system, 20-21, 23, 24
narrower term (NT), 88-89, 91, *92*, 96, 99, 103, *105*, *106*, 184, *208*, 209, 214, 275
national bibliographies, 58
National Information Standards Organization (NISO), 204, 213, 260
National Library of Medicine, 106, 109
natural language, 10, 21, 133, 144, 150, 230, 240. *See also* keywords
Naxos Music Library database, *64*

nearby operator, 115-17, 122, *134-35*, 136, 138-40, 165, *225*, 275
negotiated queries, xx, 30, 38-39, *42*, 44, 46, 49, 75, 82, 198, *207*, 209, 275. *See also* queries
negotiation, 29-31, *33*, 34-38, 45, 46-47, 151, 192, 193, 265
neighbor operator. *See* nearby operator
nested Boolean logic, 80, 118, *119*, 136, 138-40, 275
Newell, Alan, 255, 266
News & Current Events database, 165
news stories and reporting, 51, 121, 177
Nilsen, Kirsti, 27, *36-37*, 39, 46, 47
non-verbal cues, 34, 40, 43, 250, 254
NoodleTools, 206, 213, 237, 252
NOT operator, 77, 80-83, 89, 94, 120, 122, *134*, 136, 184, 185, 186, 215, *225*, 275
NTIS (National Technical Information Service), 60, 73
NTIS database, 2, 60-61, *62*
numeric and spatial data, xix, 5, 49, *50*, 54-56, 73, 217, 276

OAIster database, 9, *21*
OCLC, 10, 13
Ojala, MaryDee, 137, 213
online public access catalogs. *See* OPAC
online searching, xx, *33*, *42*, 228-29
   conferences, 256-57
   cost of, 3, 6-9, 10
   databases for, 15-24, 49-73
   for assessing research impact, 167-179
   for known-items, 141-64
   for subjects, 85-108, 113-37
   future of, xxi, 255-65
   interviewing users for, 27-45
   origins of, 1-11
   pre-search preparation for, 75-84
   process of, xx-xxi, *33*, *42*, 45, *208*, 210, 212
   retrievals, 201-205, 231-237
   strategies, 183-200
   tactics, 206-10, 214-15
   teaching end users about, 231-48
   trade publications, 230, 256
   using controlled vocabulary for, 85-112
   using free text for, 113-40, 144, 148-49, 155
online thesaurus, 90-94, 188, *222*, 224, 261
Onwuegbuzie, Anthony J., 10, 13
OPACs, 3, 5, 11, 23, 25, 29, 58-59, 83, 192, 227-28, 247, 261, 276. *See also* catalogs
for known-items, 143, *144*, 146-47, 148, *149-150*, 161-63, 164, 165, 166
open access, xix, 8-9, 11, 276
Open Discovery Initiative (OSI), 204, 259

open-ended questions, 38–40, 276
open Web, xx, 3–11, 206, 233, 238, 261, 276
   databases and quality information generally, xix,
      6, 10, 15, 18, 20, *21*, 66–67, 68, 69, 70, *71–72*,
      74, 107, 176
      deceptive practices on the, 201–203, 258–259
      evaluating information on the, xix, 6, 203, 206,
         246–47, 263
openURL, 276
Opposing Viewpoints database, 101
OR operator, 77–83, *92*, 93, 98, 99, 106, *119*,
      125–26, 153, 185, 220, *225*, 276
Orbit search system, 3
organizations. *See* names: of organizations
Oxford English Language Dictionary database, 67
Oxford Islamic Studies Online database, *56*
Oxford Reference, *67*, 68, 241
Oxford University Press, 56, 67, 74

Page, Lawrence, 126, 137
Pan, Bing, 202, 213
Pariser, Elliot, 202, 203, 213, 258, 259, 266
Park, Minsoo, 260, 266
Pautasso, Marco, 255, 266
pay-walls, 6, 9, 11, 20, 24, 276
PDF (portable document format), 15–16, 61, 237,
      276
peer review, 6–9, 11, 176, 238, 241, 276
personalization, 201, 202, 211, 212, 214, 258, 259,
      264–65, 276
Peters, Tom, 202, 213
phone interviews, 34, 40, 238, 250, 251, 253
Piwowar, Heather, 181
Porter, Brandi, 9, 13
post-coordination, 116, 276
postings. *See* retrievals
Powers, Audrey, 16, 24
pre-search qualifiers, 153, 165, 204, 211, 214, 220,
      222, 224–26, 229, 238, 241, 261, 263, 276
precedence of operators, 80, *119*, 277
precision, *41*, 85, 86, 97, 103, *207*, 209, 211, 214, 261,
      277
precoordination, 76, 277
Priem, Jason, 177, 180, 181
process of online searching. *See* online searching:
      process of
promotion and tenure, 7, 177, 167
proper nouns, 65, 88–89, 146–47, 184, 192, 215
ProQuest, 20, 54, *60, 62, 74*, 104–107, 112, 115–18,
      129, 130, *134–35*, 138, 143, *154, 160–61*, 162,
      165, 166, 198, 199, *244*, 248, 261, 266
ProQuest Research Library database, 143, *160–61*,
      163, 165, 198, 199, 241, *244*

proximity operators, 96, 115–18, 122–23, *134–35*,
      138–40, *208*, 209, 210, 215, 220, *225*, 277.
      See also names of proximity operators
PsycINFO database, 89–97, 100–102, 104, 110, 112,
      132, 138, 152, 188–89, 194, 198, 200, 224
Public Library of Science (PLoS) database, 211, 214
publication titles. *See* source titles
publishers, 1, 4–11, 15–16, 22, 57, 58, *59, 87*, 152,
      204, 212, 258
publishing, 4–10, 11, 167
PubMed database, 104–107, 108, 111, 198, 200,
      229–30
Puerto Rico Encyclopedia database, *72, 74*

quality information, xix, 1, 6, 9, 10, 11, 15, 20, 214,
      238, 240, 246–47, 263
queries, xx, 28–31, 34–47, 75, 242, 262, 277.
      See also negotiated queries
   a cut above, 191, 192
   acid rain, 191, 192, 194
   ADHD, 190, 192, 194
   ALS patients, 83, 84, 108, 111
   articulating, 29, *30*, 34–37, 229, 241–42
   capital punishment, 191, 192, 194
   cerebral palsy, 191, 192, 194
   collapse of the Soviet Union, 242–44
   complete a citation for the source entitled
      "Trends in Extreme Apparent Temperatures . . . ,"
      82, 83
   conduct of life, 242–43, 246
   cyanobacteria as a source of alternative energy,
      242, 243, 245
   depression, 100–102, *103*
   does smoking cause lung cancer? 75–77, 78
   eating disorders, 82–83, 84, 108, 110, 130–33,
      138, 189–90, 225
   effect of television violence on children, *129*,
      153–57
   effect of video game violence on adolescents,
      185–86
   entrepreneurial activities of farm women,
      114–21
   escape systems from earth-orbital vehicles, 2–3
   fashion, 190, 191, 192, 194
   flextime, 78–80
   genetically modifiable crops that affect people's
      health, 242–44, 245
   going to college, 242–44
   highest temperature ever recorded in Miami,
      Florida, 82, 83
   hockey helmets, 83, 84, 108, 111, 139, 198, 199
   how do child soldiers adjust to normal life?,
      125–27

humor to treat people who are depressed, 80–82, 84, 89–98

Impact of screen time on children, 82, 122–24

in-depth, 27, 38, 41, 43, 49, 57, 90–98, 108–112, 255–56, 273

initial, *31*, 34–37

K–12 students, 100, 102

local food movement, 100

Madonna, 190, 192

more novels by the author of *The Lovely Bones*, 82, 83

multifaceted, 108, 136, 183–85, 220, 250

Nevil Shute Norway, 191, 192

Norway, 190, 191–92, 194

one-faceted, 46–47, 100, 143, 148, 152, 190–93

Oracle, 190, 192

Panera Bread, 191, 192

parents setting limits, 83, 84, 108, 112, 140, 198, 211

paying college athletes, 83, 84, 108, 110, 133, 139

President Johnson's war on poverty legislation, 82, 83, 128

reducing bullying, 83, 84, 109, 108, 109, 138

role of railroads in the adoption of standard time, 133, 139

Subway, 190, 192, 194

wandering mind, 83, 84, 108, 112, 133, 140

whether religious practice is necessary to prevent alcoholics from relapsing, 188–89, 263

Radford, Marie L., 10, 11, 27, 33, 34, *36–37*, 39, 46, 47

Ragains, Patrick, 204, 213

recall, *41*, 44, 113, 114, 118, 120, 133, 136, *207*, 209, 210, 256, 277

Reference & User Services Association (RUSA), 33, 46

Reference Center Gold database, *105, 107*

reference databases. *See* databases: reference

reference interview, xx, xxi, 27, 28–30, 32–47, 82, 142, 143, 206, 209, 231, 233, 237, 238, 248–49, 257, 277

reference librarians. *See* librarians

Reference USA database, 68

refinements. *See* clusters

RefWorks citation management system, 235, 237, 249, 253

related term (RT), 88–89, 91, *92*, 99, 103, *105, 106*, 184, *208*, 210, 277

relationship designator. *See* role

relaxation, 34, 40, 249

relevance, 22, 32–33, 202, 204–206, 211, 212, 214, 229, 246, 264, 277

relevance feedback, 128–33, 277

relevance-ranked retrievals, 10, 24, 124, 125–26, 128, 150, 202, 203, 204, 220, 246, 258, 259, 261, 263, 277. *See also* retrievals: ranking

representing the query as input to the search system, xx, 33, 42

  for citation verification, 151–53, 163, 165

  for finding journals, 158–63, 164, 165–66

  for full-text fulfillment, 151–53

  in author searches, 148–51, 164, 165, 166

  in subject searches, 85–112, 113–40, 164, 166

  in title searches, *130*, 143–45

  teaching end users about, 243–45

  using controlled vocabulary, 85–112, 164, 166

  using free text, 113–140, 144, 148–49, 164, 166

research databases. *See* databases: research

Research Gate, 178

resolver links, 20, 22, *23*, 24, 25, 51, 59, 60, *61*, 63, 130, 131, 142, 158, 218, 223, 246, 278

results presentation. *See* retrievals

retrievals, 33, 49, 51, 57, 65, 73, 98, 142, 145, 220, 258, 278. *See also* displaying retrievals and responding tactically; search tactics; sources

  displaying, xx, *94*, 201–204, 255, 246–47, 259

  form of, 62, *64*, *71*, *72*, *74*

  evaluating, xx, 201, 204–206, 246–47

  legitimate, 202–203, 204, 258–59

  number of, 184, 186

  ranking, 20, 125–26, 152. *See also* relevance-ranked retrievals

  relevant, 27, *42*, 43, 44, 81, 85, 89, *96*, 103, 114, 118, 125, 128, 129, 132, 184, 187, 190, 201, 205, *207*, 212, 231, 246

  saving, 232–33, 234, 250, 252–53

  teaching end users about, 245–47

  too few. *See* low-posted searches

  too many. *See* high-posted searches

Rieh, Soo Young, 10, 12, 206, 213, 246, 251

Robinson, Jo, 183

role, 245, 278

Ross, Catherine Sheldrick, 27, 34, *36–37*, 39, 46, 47

Rowley, Jennifer, 137

rule of specific entry, 94–95, 97

Salton, Gerard, 125, 137, 164, 166

Sandore, Beth, 202, 213

satisficing, 255–56

saved searches, 190, 231–37, 249–53, 278. *See also* search alerts

Saxton, Matthew L., 33, 39, 45, 46

scanning. *See* browsing

scholar portals. *See* database hubs

scholarly communication. *See* scholarship

scholarship, 2, 6–9, 11, 51, 167, 255, 278
Schrock, Kathy, 246, 252
Science Citation Index database, 167
ScienceDirect database, 143, 165, 232
scope note, 89, 90, 91, *92*, 97, 104, *105, 106*, 278
Scopus database, 132, 143, 148, 154, *155–57*, 172–73, 176, 177, *178*, 179, 181–82, *222*, 223, 256
scraper sites, 258
search alerts, 233–34, 278. *See also* saved searches
search box, 4, 5, 20, 21, 24, 25, *90, 93*, 95, *97*, 108, *118*, 120, *124*, 129, *130*, 131, *132*, 150, 151, 152, 218, *219*, 220, *221*, 243, 244, 261, 262, 278
search engine optimization (SEO), 203, 278
search engines. *See* Web search engines
search history, 93, 95, 97, 106, 120, 184, *189, 207*, 209, 215, 218, 224, 278
search statements, xxi, *42*, 44, 85–86, 113, 125, 136, 184, 202, *208*, 218, 229, 243, 259, 278. *See also* searching languages
    changes to, 31, *96*, 209, 228, 229, 245
    examples of known-item, *131, 144, 148*, 163, 165–66
    examples of subject, *93*, 95, 96, 109–112, 115–18, 120, 123, *124*, 128, 138–140, *155, 225–26*, 263
    first-entered, 185, 189, 196
    formulated using the online thesaurus, 90–94, 224
    misspellings, variants, acronyms, etc., in 96, 147, 153, 164
    retrievals and, 186, 201
    user queries and, 29, 260, 262
    what document representation they search, 51, 62, 71, 72, 73, 85, 220, 228
search strategies, xx, 98–99, 127–28, 183–200, 207, 212, 245, 278. *See also* names of search strategies
search strategy process model, 29
search systems, 278. *See also* names of individual search systems
    becoming familiar with, 217–228
    changes to, 256–58
    conceptualizing queries prior to entering, 75–83
    deceiving, 201–203, 258–259
    defaults in, 85–86, 113–14, 118, *135, 226*
    handling controlled vocabulary in, 85–112
    handling free text in, 113–40, 144, 148–49
    handling known-items in, 141–64
    improving, 262–66
    in the library's database hub, 15–24, 49–73
    mastering, 217–28, 230
    origins of, 1–11
    strategies for, 183–200

search tactics, xx, 201, 206–210, 211–12, 214–15, 279. *See also* displaying retrievals and responding tactically; retrievals; sources
Search Tools, 16–19, 158–59. *See also* database hubs
searching for a journal, 161–63
searching languages, xx, 3, 44, 75, 260, 279. *See also* search statements
    for controlled vocabulary, 85–112, 224
    for free text, 113–40, 144, 148–49, 155, 225
Sebastian, Michael, 203, 213
see from references. *See* use from (UF) references
see references. *See* use references
Seglen, Per O., 176, 180
select-a-field pull-down menu, 96, *97, 118*, 143, 144, 148, 150, 151, *162*, 218, 220, *221*, 247, 279
selecting a relevant database. *See* databases: selecting
sets, 89, 93–94, 95–96, 97, 98, 99, 106, 120, 122, 218, 224, 262, 279
Shannon, Claude E., 28, 46
Shiri, Ali, 109
Shot in the Dark Search Strategy, 190–93, 196, *197*, 199, 200
SIC codes. *See* standard industrial codes
Sidecar Publications, 257, 266
SimplyMap database, 54, *55*
Sittler, Ryan, 252
SMART search system, 125
SmartText searching (via EBSCOhost), 129, 218, 220, 260
Smith, Linda C., 27, 40, 45, 46, 65, 70, 71, 73, 267, 272, 275, 281
social media and networking services, 15, 67, 177, 178, 179
Sociological Abstracts database, 104, 166
source titles, *87*, 151, 152–53, 156, 157, 158–63, 165–66, 172, 174, *222, 227*, 228
source types. *See* sources: genre
sources, *52*, 59, *63–67, 69–72, 74*, 82, 108, 205, 206, 257–58, 279. *See also* displaying retrievals and responding tactically; retrievals; search tactics
    actual, 5, 22, 25, 49, 51, *52*, 62, 64, 73, 95, 114, 217
    cost of, 6, 9, 11, 18, 20, 24
    evaluating, 5, 11, 20, 174–76, 180, 203, 204–206, 246–47, 258, 263–64
    genre, 2, 22, 29, *36, 41*, 56, 57, 58, 62, *64, 71–72, 74, 87*, 100, 101, 142, *156–57*, 204, 206, 224, 228, 246, 272
    in citation management systems, 234–237
    perfect, 247
    reading, 78, 124, 205
    scholarly, 20, 179, 204, 241
    teaching end users about, 246–47

source databases. *See* databases: source
spatial data, 50, 54, *55*, 279
specificity, 94-95, 279
spelling correction, 10, 147, *207*, 215, 247
Spink, Amanda, xx, xxii, 202, 213
SpringerLink database, 143, 165, 248
standard industrial codes, 279
Stanford Encyclopedia of Philosophy database, 71
Statistical Insight database, *54*
Startpage, 259
stemming, *135, 226*, 244, 264, 279
style sheets, 151, 206, 235, 237
subject headings, 58, *59*, 279
   subdivided forms of, *105, 106*, 111, 200, *208, 209*
subject searches, 2, 57, 82, 141, 147, 279
   using controlled vocabulary, 85-112
   using free text, 113-40
subject terms. *See* index terms
Successive Fractions Search Strategy, 184
summaries. *See* abstracts
Summit, Roger, 2, 13
Summon web-scale discovery system, 20, 261
surrogate databases. *See* databases: surrogate
surrogates, xix, 2, 3, 5, 6, 22, 25, 49, 51, 57-58, *63, 64, 72, 74*, 85, *86-87*, 95, 103, 104, 113, 114, 187, 188, 217, 220, *223*, 280
   controlled vocabulary searching of, 90-102
   examples of, *52, 53, 54, 59-62, 94, 131, 132, 223*
   free text searching of, 118-20
   teaching end users about, 238, 247
syndetic structure, 88-91, *92, 106*, 107, 146, 166, *221*, 224, 280
synonyms, *65, 71*, 146, 280
   automatic vocabulary assistance's handling of, 126
   automatic facet recognition's handling of, 127, 128, 262-63
   in facets, 98, 108, 185
   in search statements, 118, 122, 128, 136, 262
   in the thesaurus, 88, 90, 103, 146, 245
   search tactics and, *207*, 215
System Development Corporation, 2-3
systematic reviews, 120, 133, 256, 280. *See also* comprehensive searches; literature reviews

Tananbaum, Greg, 177, 180
Taylor, Robert S., 27, 29, *30*, 46
technical reading of a database, xx, 217-30, 280
technical reading of a source, 205, 247, 264, 280
Tennant, Roy, xx, xxii
Tenopir, Carol, 137

text interviews, 40
texts, xix, 49, *50*, 51, *52*, 56, 73, 217, 280
thesaurus. *See* controlled vocabularies (CVs);
   controlled vocabulary (CV) searching; index
   terms; online thesaurus
Thesaurus of Psychological Index Terms, 89-94
Thomson Reuters, *130, 131*, 167, *168-71, 175*, 180
Thurman, Robert A.F., 58, *66*
title searches, 83, *130*, 141-44, 145, 164, 165, *221, 222*
titles, 2, 51, 57, 58, *59, 60*, 61, *62, 63, 86*, 101, 129, 141-144, 145, 152, 155, 188, 189, 202, 280
truncation, 117-18, 122, *135*, 138-40, *208*, 210, 215, 223, *226*, 264, 280
typecasting, xx, 33, 42, 82-84, 141, 145, 220, 241, 280

Ulrichsweb database, 151, 153, 165
uniform resource locator (URL), 4, 232, 280
Union List of Artist Names, (ULAN) 147
University of Texas keyword-generator, 243, 252
unused synonyms. *See* use references
URL. *See* uniform resource locator (URL)
U.S. Board on Geographic Names database, *72, 74*
use from (UF) references, 88-89, *92, 105, 106*, 136, 280
use references, 88, *115*, 281
user query. *See* queries

Vakkari, Pertti, xx, xxii
Valentine, Barbara, 256, 266
variant forms, 117, 118, *208*, 210, 215, *226*, 227
   of index terms, 103
   of names, 146-47, 150, 168, 172, 174, 215
   of source titles, 152-53
Vaughan, Jason, 5, 10, 13
Venn diagrams, 77, *79, 81*, 83, 281
videos, xxi, 51, 52, *53*, 142, 145

Walraven, Amber, 5, 13
Way, Doug, 262, 266
Web browsers, 4, 5, 6, 10, 234, 235, 258, 260
Web directories, 4, 194-95, 196
Web of Science database, 130-32, 143, 148, 167, 168-72, 173, 174, 178-79, 181, 223, 256
web-scale discovery (WSD) systems, 5, 6, 9, 10, 11, 20-25, 83, 127, 130, 136, 143, 148, 165, 204, 211, 212, 214, 247, 259, 261-62, 263, 264, 281. *See also* names of WSD systems
Web search engines, xix, 1, 4-5, 11, 20, 125-27, 136, 147, 148, 164, 183, 201-203, 211, 214, 258, 259, 260, 281. *See also* names of Web search engines

Weir, Ryan O., 16, 24
white hat, 203, 281
White Pages database, 68
wildcard. *See* truncation
Wikipedia, xx, 5, 6, 9, 10, 13, 69, *71*, 240, *261*
Wildemuth, Barbara M., 145, 165
Willinsky, John, 8, 13
Women's Studies International database, 118–21
word order, 115–17, *134–35, 225*
WordReference database, *72*
working knowledge, xix, 9, 68, 69
workshops. *See* information literacy training
World Wide Web. *See* Open Web
WorldCat database, *64*, 143, 148, 247

WorldImages database, *72, 74*
WSD system. *See* web-scale discovery system

Xia, Jingfeng, 9, 13

Yahoo!, 147, 195, 259
year. *See* dates
yearbooks, *50, 65, 70*, 281
Yellow Pages database, 68
YouTube database, 61, *64*, 229
Yu, Holly, 5, 13

Zhang, Shenglan, 246, 252
Zotero citation management system, 235–37, 249, 252, 253

About the Author

Karen Markey is a professor in the School of Information at the University of Michigan. Her experience with online searching includes the earliest commercial systems, Dialog, Orbit, and BRS; the first end-user systems, CD-ROMs, and online catalogs; and today's open web search engines and proprietary systems for accessing databases of bibliographic records, abstracting and indexing entries, full texts, numeric data, and multimedia. Since joining the faculty at Michigan in 1987, she has taught online searching to thousands of students in her school's library and information science (LIS) program. Her research has been supported by the Council on Library Resources, Delmas Foundation (DF), Department of Education (DoED), Institute of Museum and Library Services (IMLS), National Science Foundation (NSF), and OCLC. She is the author of six books, more than a dozen major research reports, and more than one hundred journal articles and conference proceedings papers.